EXTRA INNINGS

EXTRA INNINGS

More
Baseball Between the Numbers
from the Team at
Baseball Prospectus

BY THE EXPERTS AT
BASEBALL PROSPECTUS

DEREK CARTY ◆ COREY DAWKINS ◆ MIKE FAST
REBECCA GLASS ◆ STEVEN GOLDMAN
KEVIN GOLDSTEIN ◆ JAY JAFFE
RANY JAZAYERLI ◆ CHRISTINA KAHRL
BEN LINDBERGH ◆ JASON PARKS
DAN TURKENKOPF ◆ COLIN WYERS

EDITED BY
STEVEN GOLDMAN

BASIC BOOKS
A Member of the Perseus Books Group
New York

Copyright © 2012 by Prospectus Entertainment Ventures LLC

Published by Basic Books,
A Member of the Perseus Books Group

Books published by Basic Books are available at special discounts for bulk purchases in the United States by corporations, institutions, and other organizations. For more information, please contact the Special Markets Department at the Perseus Books Group, 2300 Chestnut Street, Suite 200, Philadelphia, PA 19103, or call (800) 810-4145, ext. 5000, or e-mail special.markets@perseusbooks.com.

Editorial production by *Marra*thon Production Services. www.marrathon.net

Design by Jane Raese
Text set in 10-point New Aster

A CIP catalog record for this book is available from the Library of Congress.
ISBN 978-0-465-02403-2 (Hardcover)
ISBN 978-0-465-02918-1 (e-Book)

10 9 8 7 6 5 4 3 2 1

As every past generation has had to disenthrall itself from an inheritance of truisms and stereotypes, so in our own time we must move on from the reassuring repetition of stale phrases to a new, difficult, but essential confrontation with reality.

For the great enemy of truth is very often not the lie—deliberate, contrived and dishonest—but the myth—persistent, persuasive, and unrealistic. Too often we hold fast to the clichés of our forebears. We subject all facts to a prefabricated set of interpretations. We enjoy the comfort of opinion without the discomfort of thought.

—PRESIDENT JOHN F. KENNEDY, JUNE 11, 1962

Contents

PART VI: WRAPPING UP

Foreword

So, I know this scout; and yes, that's a sentence I start many a story with. Anyway, this guy is old school. He signed his first professional contract as a teenager before there was such a thing as a major league draft, back when Lyndon Johnson was president. And since signing that deal in 1964, he's been in baseball, be it as a player, college coach, professional instructor, minor league manager, or talent evaluator. There are few people in this business I enjoy talking to more. Five minutes with him and your knowledge of the game goes up considerably.

I've never met him in person. The first time we talked, he reached out to me with a question about True Average, one of the many statistical tools we use at Baseball Prospectus. He's 66 years old, has seen more than 5,000 games, and when he packs his scout bag, he puts the usual items in: radar gun, notebooks, pens, lots of sunscreen, water, and, believe it or not, a yearly copy of the annual *Baseball Prospectus*.

It's that kind of thing I'm most proud of when I think about working here. We have some of the most intelligent baseball minds in the business at Baseball Prospectus, and within these pages, but what we do is nothing without acceptance, and that acceptance comes through communication. We can't just come up with new theories and new ideas and new findings on the how and why of winning baseball games; we need to be able to communicate them properly, and not just to the younger generation who already grew up with an understanding of the statistical side of the game, but also to people like my friend, the old-school baseball guy.

That's where *Baseball Between the Numbers* comes in. Not only was it wildly successful, but it also served as a gateway drug to who we are, and what we do, and let everyone know that they were welcome on our wild ride. It's also where *Extra Innings* comes in. If you follow me on Twitter, you know I love extra-innings baseball. It's where exciting and sometimes strange things happen, and that's what we've brought you here, with more research, more information, more fun, and, we hope, more people coming on board to share with us their interest in a game that contains depths far beyond what one might get from a highlights package.

The landscape of baseball research is changing dramatically. When we published *Baseball Between the Numbers*, concepts like PITCHf/x were in their nascent form. Now we are on the verge of getting f/x data that goes beyond pitching to pinpoint the location, trajectory, and velocity of each batted ball, as well as how the fielders react to it. We've come a long way toward hunting down the great white whale that is defensive statistics, but it's still important to be self-critical and make sure we are doing that right, a point that is addressed by Colin Wyers in this edition. I can't think of a better person than Colin to question what we as an industry are doing with these numbers, because it was his criticism of published data that was being taken for granted as true that inspired us to hire him in the first place.

When *Baseball Between the Numbers* was published, we were still outsiders, looking for acceptance, certainly, but on our terms. Now, three full-time members of the company are part of the Baseball Writers Association of America (BBWAA), led by Jay Jaffe, who has gone from somebody who blogged about the Hall of Fame to the most influential voice in the industry on the subject. If you've been happier about some of the voters' selections of late, thank Jay; many voters have cited him for playing a role in their decisions. The Hall of Fame is an argument that never diminishes in interest and intensity, for it speaks to something basic about the way we value accomplishments both inside baseball and out. Jay goes further than ever before in this edition, trying to figure out how the voters and the Hall should respond to the era of performance-enhancing drugs, if at all, while also explaining both sides of the Jack Morris debate.

Over time, the breadth of subject matter has changed at Baseball Prospectus, to reflect the interest of our readers. At the time of *Baseball Between the Numbers*, we didn't even have a prospect beat per se, but now we have two people focusing on the scouting and player development beat: Jason Parks and myself. Jason, who also does the Up and In podcast with me, is not only a great baseball mind, but also the most unique writer we've ever published, with a voice as much suited for post-modern fiction in the mold of DeLillo or Coover as baseball. You ask him for a slice and he'll give you the whole pizza, as he does in this book, with a focus on where players come from and how they are turned into big leaguers.

Then there is our base. The people who were there from the start, who bought the first book back in 1996 and are reading this now know that at its core Baseball Prospectus is still an argument about how to win baseball games. While baseball teams have clearly become much smarter in the years since we started, one area in which they continue to hurt themselves is in bullpen management. In the pages that follow, Colin and Ben Lindbergh explain not only how to build a bullpen, but how to use one properly.

Steven Goldman's name appears on just two chapters in the book, but his effect on its quality is a constant. As the editor in chief of baseballprospectus.com and the captain of this book, every word you see passes his eye. Everything receives his finishing touch, his feng shui if you will. He's also a fantastic writer who recently received his BBWAA credential, and hopefully he'll get more of the spotlight for it, as too often his brilliance occurs in the shadows, with few witnesses to it.

When I first came to Baseball Prospectus, there was still a kind of battle taking place, at least in the minds of some. Call it stats versus scouts or old thinking versus new thinking, lines were drawn among fans and commentators, but never were for the teams themselves. There is no battle for them; there never was one actually. The sole battle is for information—for more of it, and of better quality. Our team at Baseball Prospectus has provided another big weapon in the war of intelligence, which is the only one that matters.

Kevin Goldstein
DeKalb, Illinois
December 10, 2011

Preface and Note on Statistics

Once Aroused to Anger, a Sacred Cow
Is a Frightening Thing to Behold

STEVEN GOLDMAN

During my aimless teenage years, I spent a great many hours either working in comic book stores or, when I couldn't get paid, simply hanging around them for free. In retrospect, I probably would have been a happier adolescent had I invested the time chasing (and catching) girls, but the experience was highly rewarding in that I acquired many back issues that have since appreciated in worth; spent countless days eavesdropping, Joseph Mitchell style, on a large cast of eccentrics, "down among the cranks and the misfits and the one-lungers and the has-beens and the might've beens and the would-bes and the never-wills and the God-knows-whats," an invaluable opportunity for a future writer; and, thoroughly immersed in the milieu of the comic book collector, I was well prepared for the clubbish and insular world of high-stakes, big-money baseball analysis.

Then, as now, a comic book store was not the most sof enterprises, so by necessity my venue would often change as businesses rose up out of the foam and just as quickly subsided, my pull list and I migrating to a new dealer where I could work off my tab or at the very least find genre-specific conversation. One such shop, which I discovered when I was about 14, was actually an over-large booth in a now defunct flea market. The store was owned by two brothers whose names I no longer recall, but I can still see their odd-couple physiognomies and mismatched bodies. One was tall, thin, clean shaven, ferret faced, and abstemious in his habits, the other short, stout, bearded, with dull features that came to life only when his rat's eyes spotted some head cheese (an obscure and unpleasant cold cut I once watched him devour as part of a regrettably encyclopedic Dagwood).

It was impossible to believe the two had even a single parent in common, but they certainly bickered as much as true siblings or long-warring countries whose mutual enmity has simmered down to an armed border standoff. Just as their names have slipped from memory, I cannot precisely remember the subject of any of their many arguments, but I cannot forget the putdown that ended one of their biggest battles, which very well may have begun over how to cope with a potentially fatal cash-flow crisis precipitated by misjudging the potential sales of Marvel's *Marc Hazzard: Merc* #1. The insults flew fast for about an hour, there in that confined space, but at one point, Ferret-Face, having gone too far, said something too personal, made a weak attempt to be conciliatory, saying, "Look, I didn't meant to touch any sacred cows, but—"

Head-Cheese Guy, too enraged to accept any ratcheting down of tensions, shouted, "I'll murder your sacred cow!"

"Talk about your self-inflicted wounds," Ferret-Face retorted. The rest of us exploded in laughter at this obvious coup de grâce. Head-Cheese Guy slunk away in search of a solacing sandwich, and the argument was over (though the copies of *Merc* would remain unsold despite some desperate exertions).

At Baseball Prospectus, we often do battle with sacred cows, those cherished and comforting notions about baseball that when challenged tend to moo and bleat distractingly before finally bursting into strips of worn leather and droplets of rancid milk. However, despite Head-Cheese Guy's assumption of an easy kill, sacred cows fight back. They are not scrupulous about how they do so, dissembling to protect their proffered illusions. An innocuous example: at the 2011 Winter Meetings in Dallas, I asked Yankees manager Joe Girardi what he would do if struggling pitchers A.J. Burnett and Phil Hughes continued to disappoint in 2012. How quickly would he be willing to call on prospects Manny Banuelos or Dellin Betances? His response:

> I'm not afraid to make a move. If a guy is pitching well and you believe he can help you we'll call him up. We called up a number of guys to our bullpen last year, signed a number of guys that really panned out. If you have a feeling about a guy that he can really help you, and if the guy's in Triple-A, it's not someone that I'm going to see every day. If you have a feeling about calling up a young player, I'm not afraid to do that. We got great contributions out of young players last year.

We got great contributions out of young players last year. It must be comforting to think of Ivan Nova as twins, because that's the only way Girardi's plural "players" makes sense. Here are the teams that got the fewest plate appearances out of young players (here generously de-

TABLE P-1

Team	Pct. Young
PHI	4.2
BOS	5.8
NYA	10.3
LAN	12.6
MIL	14.3
SLN	15.4
OAK	17.1
TBA	19.2
CHA	20.3
SFN	20.3
HOU	21.0
TEX	21.9
CIN	22.5
SDN	23.3
TOR	23.8

TABLE P-2

Team	Pct. Young
PIT	3.4
BOS	6.2
CHA	10.5
CHN	12.1
MIL	15.6
SFN	16.2
MIN	16.8
CLE	17.4
SLN	20.0
ANA	20.7
PHI	22.3
NYA	22.7
HOU	23.3
TOR	23.3
FLO	25.3

fined as 25 years of age or younger) in 2011 (see Table P-1). Now, young pitchers as a percentage of innings pitched (see Table P-2).

Girardi may like to think of his Yankees as being open to youngsters, but in 2011 this was hardly the case, something made powerfully clear by the 34-year-old, replacement-level Burnett's persisting in the rotation despite younger alternatives.

Girardi's dishonesty or self-deception is hardly important except as it pertains to the Yankees' perception of their own roster (which is rapidly aging), but it demonstrates how baseball insiders and fans alike are often reluctant to consult the facts before making an argument that conflicts with their preferred narrative.

When it comes to baseball analysis, one of the arguments against making recourse to the facts is that the information is too abstruse, too often couched in the language of mathematics to be easily understandable. In this book's predecessor, *Baseball Between the Numbers*, it was my task to write a brief introduction for the math-averse titled "Pay No Attention to the Glowing, Orange-Eyed Satan-Dog Behind the Closet Door." In it, I explained that this was hardly the case:

> *Baseball Between the Numbers* comes with its own red herring, and it's right there in the title. Our monster in the closet is Numbers: those squiggly symbols that you seriously contemplate only when trying to guess the correct tip

at the end of a meal. Otherwise you may not have thought about math since you last faced that spinster algebra teacher with the misaligned teeth who sewed her own clothing and glared balefully whenever you dropped your pencil. Government surveys suggest that nine out of ten Americans don't like numbers, don't understand them, and would be favorably inclined toward replacing channel designations for television stations with a system of pictographs.

Fortunately, you need be only mildly conversant with numbers to enjoy this book. The operative word here is "Between" rather than "Numbers." In this book we're *around* the numbers, *beyond* the numbers, and quietly tiptoeing *past* the numbers but not necessarily *through* the numbers. Imagine Druids cavorting at Stonehenge, and you'll get the idea. They danced in the spaces where the big blocks were not. They didn't run right at them (or, if they did, it's no surprise that their religion died out).

Little has changed in the intervening years. The numbers are, we hope, not any more obscure, but in fact, the opposite; the purpose of this volume, as with its companion, is to explore the issues that concern baseball and its fans here in the second decade of the 21st century. The numbers invoked in this book (many of which I go to great length to explain in the pages immediately following this one) are, as I wrote in "Satan-Dog," "a path to understanding, a door to a room, not the room itself. In fact, we only put the word 'Numbers' in the title because we wanted to limit our audience to a crowd of intrepid, enlightened risk-takers who would not be dissuaded by a word that would send the majority of their contemporaries screaming for the exits." Statistics are part of our cow-fighting arsenal, but they are not themselves the point.

In the chapters to come, you will see us take up our swords and do battle with some well-armed bovines, from the effects of performance-enhancing drugs on ballplayers to the cult of the closer. I do not know if our arguments will convert the stubbornly unconverted; I believe the cows succumb in the end, but like slasher-film villains, these undead calfskin calumnies have a stubborn way of climbing out of their graves just when you think they've been dispatched. At the very least, let it nevermore be said that the arguments against them have not been clearly, cogently presented. Ignorance can no longer be a defense.

Read on, then, without fear of retribution from hoofed hoplites equipped with attractive but incorrect notions of how baseball works. We've got your back. And with that out of the way, it's time to moooove on to the rest of the book

And if anyone wants a few copies of *Merc* #1, drop us a line.

Introduction

Beyond the Back of
the Baseball Card
Baseball 101

STEVEN GOLDMAN

In September of 2011, Fox's Ken Rosenthal published a column on the candidates for the American League MVP award in which he chose to pick a fight with "some sabermetricians."

> I understand why some sabermetricians freak out over the MVP voting every year, howling for the mainstream media to get a clue. But you know what? Those analysts need to get over it.
>
> Ignoramuses in the [mainstream media], including yours truly, continue to make greater use of sabermetrics; heck, we even elected 13-game winner Felix Hernandez the American League Cy Young Award winner in a landslide last season.
>
> The MVP, though, is different. Always will be different. And heaven help us if the voting ever disintegrates into a reflexive regurgitation of the Wins Above Replacement (WAR) rankings.
>
> Sabermetrics is the analysis of baseball through objective data. An MVP vote is subjective by design. Voters are instructed—yes, instructed—to vote any way they darn please.
>
> "There is no clear-cut definition of what Most Valuable means," the ballot says. "It is up to the individual voter to decide who was the Most Valuable Player in each league to his team."

TABLE I-1 MVP Award Winners and RBI, 1922–2010

RBI	# Winners
Led League	59 (34%)
Finished Second	19 (11%)
Finished Third	14 (8%)
Finished 4–10	27 (16%)
Position Player Not in Top 10	33 (19%)
Pitcher	22 (13%)

It's not like we're debating how to fix the economy here. We're debating an award that has a flexible definition, and anyone who pronounces his or her own definition superior to any other misses the point.

Putting aside the shot across the bow of those unidentified saber-metricians who need to stop freaking out (some Xanax for the man with the pocket protector, please) and calling for reflexive regurgitation (and some anti-emetics), this is the prelude, not a reasoned argument about who the best player in the AL is, but its antithesis: if an opinion is wholly subjective, then you are relieved of having to make an argument in its support or even the responsibility of making a reasoned choice. You can pick whoever you damn well please, and if that choice doesn't hold up to scrutiny, you can say, "Hey, don't blame me—the award was designed to be subjective."

This isn't so much an attack on sabermetrics as a preemptive weaseling out of making a difficult decision in a year in which there wasn't an obvious choice; if a player isn't standing under a neon sign that says MVP, then "subjective" becomes a cloak under which one can simply throw a dart at the list and then slink out the back door. In attacking the hypothetical sabermetrician who "pronounces his or her definition superior," Rosenthal misses the point: it's not the *definition* that needs to be superior—the award is vaguely defined, so that is a dead end—but the *argument* in favor of one's choice.

Here intellectual rigor is cast as the villain in the ages-old battle between faith ("it's okay for me to believe what I believe, regardless of facts to the contrary") and skepticism, but blind belief and arbitrary conclusions aren't any more ennobling than the dogmatism that Rosenthal rails against—at least that dogmatism is exercised in the pursuit of accuracy and understanding rather than their evasion. As Daniel Patrick Moynihan said, we are all entitled to our own opinions, but not our own facts. Sabermetrics is concerned with the pursuit of fact, and the mainstream media, here exemplified by Rosenthal, is often hostile to sabermetrics because facts impinge upon their ability to pass off myth as knowledge and claim it as fact.

Yet, the facts are never limiting, restricting one's prerogative to be slothful in one's thinking, as Rosenthal implies. As it says in the New Testament, the truth shall make you free—once you have discovered the truth, you are no longer restrained by the cage of your own ignorance, but are free to see the world as it truly is, as vividly colorful as mythology, but more sharply drawn for being without the taint of those tempting, reassuring homilies that comfort us at the cost of dulling our wits.

Herewith, the keys to the cage: the facts, the basics.

When I was a boy in the 1970s, my friends and I collected and swapped baseball cards. The focus was on the front of the cards, the player pictures and the teams; I don't recall ever talking about what was on the back. The backs were less colorful and didn't say a great deal, which was too bad, because they could have taught us not just what the players looked like, but what they actually did. Before the advent of Bill James, the Internet, and websites like Baseball Prospectus's, the scanty statistics printed on the back were the extent of available baseball information for generations of fans. For hitters, they contained just nine columns: games, at-bats, runs, hits, doubles, triples, home runs, runs batted in, and batting average. For pitchers, it was games, innings pitched, wins, losses, runs, earned runs, strikeouts, walks, and earned run average. That was all.

Actually, the reverse of the card contained a relatively generous report for the time, albeit a belated one given that a new set didn't appear until the following spring. In those days, with cable television in its nascency and the Internet still an early-stage military project, season statistics were usually presented only in the Sunday paper, given in the form of a long column containing qualifying batters only (which meant only a fraction of the league was represented), and listing only the "triple crown" stats of batting average, home runs, and RBI. This must have been terribly depressing for a player like Eddie Stanky of the Brooklyn Dodgers: in 1946, he drew 137 walks, thereby leading the National League in the all-important category of on-base percentage. When he looked in the paper, all he saw in the Sunday sports section was—

Stanky: .273–0–36

—which didn't nearly suffice to convey his value to the Dodgers that season, when he was, in fact, the most valuable position player on a team that went 96–60. You could do something similar today with players like Andrew McCutchen of the Pirates or Ben Zobrist of the Rays, who were among the best players on their respective teams. Their triple crown numbers seem unimpressive:

McCutchen: .259–23–89

Zobrist: .269–20–91

Their batting averages are unimpressive, their home run totals are less than spectacular by the standards of the day, and each failed to drive in 100 runs. Yet, there is a lot missing here: qualities of patience, power, speed, and defense, which all need to be accounted for in order to truly convey a player's value. The unassuming McCutchen was the 21st-best player in the majors last year, while Zobrist was the 30th.

Both the Sunday stats dump, which is still duplicated in the presentation of many baseball broadcasts, and the traditional baseball card were almost perfect in the way they presented numbers that actually told us very little about how a player was actually doing. (The cards also had the additional negative of not being available until the following spring.) For many, the bare-boned presentation of the triple crown statistics still says all they need to know, but given the sheer amount of descriptive information now available, limiting oneself to these numbers is a lot like saying you don't need to see a highfalutin' movie because we have hieroglyphics.

It's time to stop being afraid and step into a wider world, one where information adds clarity, not confusion. None of what we've learned since the old days is difficult, nor should much (if any) of it be controversial.

Hitting

Even baseball cards have evolved a bit; the ones above have nine columns, while modern cards have 14. Unfortunately, they're not the *right* columns. If, in the bad old disco days of my youth, the reverse of the baseball card functioned as a portable snapshot of the basics, the acceptable minimum you needed to know to be educated about a player, what would we need to have a modern-day equivalent, something small enough to fit comfortably on the screen of a standard smartphone if you don't have your tablet or cybernetic implant handy? Just like a card, we can do it in 14 statistical columns in a 3" x 5" space. Table I-2 provides all you need for Derek Jeter.

That's 15 columns; to paraphrase *Jaws*, we're going to need a bigger baseball card. Let's take a look at what's here. The most important aspect of the player's basic vital statistics is his age, which can be computed from his **Birth Date.** Potential in baseball derives from a combination of age and talent. The average major leaguer makes his debut at the age of 26. This is a problem in that the average player peaks at 27, and helps explain why the typical major league career lasts roughly seven years—these perishable items are already near their expiration date the very first time you see them. A star like Jeter is by definition an exception to the rule, coming up earlier and sustaining his peak abilities longer than is typical, but even for the greats who seem capable of rolling on forever, there is a cliff in their future, and every day they come closer to dropping over the edge. When teams aggregate too many regular players in their 30s, they run the risk of several taking the plunge at once. When that happens, the team's fortunes follow the players' downward trajectory.

Once a player is in the majors, his **Draft Information** may seem like dispensable trivia, but it remains an important biographical marker, for it suggests what scouting-based expectations were for the player at the time he was selected. When the Yankees took Jeter in the first round, they were expecting him to develop into a player who could solve a shortstop problem that had lasted decades. When they took Don Mattingly in the 19th round of the 1979 draft, they might not even have had a very good idea of who he was, because at that late stage of the proceedings teams are simply trying to gather enough players to fill out their minor league rosters. That Mattingly developed into a star was a surprise to the industry as a whole; the scouting directors running that draft had valued 492 players as more valuable at the point the first baseman's name was called.

There are exceptions to the value of draft information, as teams have sometimes intentionally tanked their pick or selected a talent they knew to be inferior because they wanted to avoid paying the hefty bonuses due first-round talents. For example, in 2001, the Cincinnati Reds selected high school left-hander Jeremy Sowers with the 20th-overall pick of the first round, a pitcher they knew to be committed to Vanderbilt University, with no intention whatsoever of signing him. Any evaluation of Sowers's pitching ability was purely incidental. Similarly, during the years the Pirates were both cheaply run and showed

TABLE I-2 The Back of the New Baseball Card, Hitters

Derek Jeter—SS

Bats: R   THR: R   Birth Date: 6-26-1974   HT: 6'3"   Weight: 175 lbs   Drafted: NYY, 1st Round (6th Pick), 1992 Draft

Yr	Tm	G	PA	BA/OBP/SLG	H	2B	3B	HR	SB/CS	BRR	BB	SO	FRAA	TAv	TAV+	WARP
95	NYY	15	51	.250/.294/.375	12	4	1	0	0/0	0.6	3	11	-1.0	.227	0.0	0.0
96	NYY	157	654	.314/.370/.430	183	25	6	10	14/7	1.0	48	102	-2.2	.283	120	4.3
97	NYY	159	748	.291/.370/.405	190	31	7	10	23/12	7.4	74	125	-8.0	.281	118	4.8
98	NYY	149	694	.324/.384/.481	203	25	8	19	30/6	4.3	57	119	-12.6	.312	146	6.1
99	NYY	158	739	.349/.438/.552	219	37	9	24	19/8	3.4	91	116	-23.1	.333	165	7.3
00	NYY	148	679	.339/.416/.481	201	31	4	15	22/4	7.6	68	99	-24.4	.298	134	4.3
01	NYY	150	686	.311/.377/.480	191	35	3	21	27/3	5.5	56	99	-21.6	.302	137	4.5
02	NYY	157	730	.297/.373/.421	191	26	0	18	32/3	6.5	73	114	-24.3	.281	118	2.9
03	NYY	119	542	.324/.393/.450	156	25	3	10	11/5	2.5	43	88	-22.0	.292	128	2.3
04	NYY	154	721	.292/.352/.471	188	44	1	23	23/4	1.8	46	99	-12.4	.283	120	3.8
05	NYY	159	752	.309/.389/.450	202	25	5	19	14/5	4.3	77	117	-0.3	.296	132	6.5
06	NYY	154	715	.343/.417/.483	214	39	3	14	34/5	3.0	69	102	-19.1	.310	144	5.3
07	NYY	156	714	.322/.388/.452	206	39	4	12	15/8	2.0	56	100	-19.3	.295	131	4.1
08	NYY	150	668	.300/.363/.408	179	25	3	11	11/5	1.7	52	85	-17.9	.270	109	1.9
09	NYY	153	716	.334/.406/.465	212	27	1	18	30/5	-2.3	72	90	-15.4	.300	136	4.3
10	NYY	157	739	.270/.340/.370	179	30	3	10	18/5	2.8	63	106	-13.6	.248	89	1.0
11	NYY	131	607	.297/.355/.388	162	24	4	6	16/6	-2.7	46	81	-10.2	.275	113	1.8
		2426	11155	.313/.383/.449	3088	492	65	240	339/91	49.8	994	1653	-247.3	.291	127	62.9

slavish devotion to the commissioner's bonus slotting system, they often chose a player in the first round who was, according to the scouting consensus, not the best player available but rather the best player available who might be relatively inexpensive. In 2007, the Pirates bypassed catcher Matt Wieters with the fourth-overall pick, in favor of pitcher Danny Moskos. The Orioles took Wieters with the next pick and later signed him for $6 million, whereas Moskos cost the Pirates only $2.475 million.

Games is here as an expression of how a player's team utilized him as well as his own durability. We eschew at-bats in favor of **Plate Appearances**; the former is a subset of the latter, and is a reactionary statistic in that it excludes those trips to the plate that result in a walk. The important question to be asked of any batter is how often he reached base as a percentage of all trips to the plate (on-base percentage), not how often he reached as the result of an at-bat (batting average).

Next up are **Batting Average (AVG), On-Base Percentage (OBP),** and **Slugging Percentage (SLG)**, often called the "triple-slash stats" for the way they are presented. This is the most basic and best presentation of a player's offensive production, but this troika of rates are not quite sufficient unto themselves, for they lack context. Still, this is where to start. As above, the middle leg, on-base percentage, is the most important, followed by slugging percentage, the fraction of a player's hits that go for extra bases. If in possession of these two percentages, you know the most essential information about a player's offensive abilities, how often he reaches base and how well he can move runners around the bases. Next to OBP and SLG, batting average is almost trivial, being more of a "how" than a "what"; when standing next to a player's OBP, his average suggests what proportion of his ability to reach base was provided by hitting safely and what proportion was achieved through patience and selectivity.

On-base percentage, which existed in various forms for years before being promoted by Branch Rickey and Dodgers statistician Allan Roth in a widely read 1954 article in *Life*, was slow to find acceptance in baseball. Even today you can't find it on the back of the Topps baseball cards that inspired this chapter. One wonders if OBP's mirror-image opposite, out percentage, would make more of an impression on the public. Baseball is often celebrated as being alone among the major team sports in not having a clock, but this is really not true: each team's 27 outs are the clock, and each one spent brings the game closer to termination. The equating of outs with time becomes more vivid if you think of them as minutes: "The Mariners, trailing 4-3 in the bottom of the eighth, have just six minutes left in which to tie."

Players who spend outs in a profligate way are simply speeding up the clock and hastening their team on to the outcome, whether it be a win or a loss. OBP and, to an even greater extent, batting average, credit a player for his successes while letting his failures go unremarked. Out percentage might be much more telling (see Table I-3, Highest and Lowest Out Percentages, 2010–2011).

Several of the players on these lists are considered defensive specialists, which provokes this question: Can a player who makes an out nearly 80 percent of the time at bat contribute so many outs on defense that he makes up for his out-eating at the plate? You can find the answer to that question in Chapter 5-2 of this book.

TABLE I-3 Highest and Lowest Out Percentages, 2010–2011 (400 PA mins.)

			Highest Out Percentages		
2010	*Name*	*Outs*	*PA*	*Out%*	
1.	Pedro Feliz	340	429	79.3	
2.	Ivan Rodriguez	326	421	77.4	
3.	Jose Lopez	476	622	76.5	
4.	Cesar Izturis	389	513	75.8	
5.	Casey Kotchman	344	457	75.3	
6.	Kevin Kouzmanoff	441	586	75.3	
7.	Brendan Ryan	363	486	74.7	
8.	Aaron Hill	433	580	74.7	
9.	A.J. Pierzynski	375	503	74.6	
10.	Carlos Lee	483	649	74.4	
2011	*Name*	*PA*	*Outs*	*Out%*	
1.	Miguel Olivo	507	363	71.6%	
2.	Adam Kennedy	409	290	70.9%	
3.	Vernon Wells	529	371	70.1%	
4.	Alex Rios	570	399	70.0%	
5.	Adam Dunn	496	345	69.6%	
6.	J.P. Arencibia	486	336	69.1%	
7.	Alex Gonzalez	593	406	68.5%	
8.	Adam Lind	542	371	68.5%	
9.	Yuniesky Betancourt	584	399	68.3%	
10.	Rick Ankiel	415	283	68.2%	

The triple-slash stats can be misleading without league context. In 1930, Cardinals shortstop Charlie Gelbert hit .304/.360/.441 in 139 games. This looks impressive, but that year the average National Leaguer hit .303/.360/.448. In addition, Gelbert played in Sportsman's Park, a generous environment for hitters. Gelbert's hitting wasn't even overly impressive for a shortstop of the day; while it was above average (the typical shortstop hit .283/.342/.395), five regular shortstops in the 16-team majors out-hit Gelbert that year.

Conversely, if we look at a pitching-rich season like 1906 or 1968, we see the opposite contextual effect at work, good seasons that look like bad ones. In the former season, the average major league hitter averaged only .247/.306/.314, so while the A's Harry Davis's .292/.355/ .459 looks like a mediocre season for a first baseman by modern

TABLE I-3 Highest and Lowest Out Percentages, continued

			Lowest Out Percentages	
2010	*Name*	*PA*	*Outs*	*Out%*
1.	Kevin Youkilis	435	261	60.0%
2.	Joey Votto	648	389	60.0%
3.	Miguel Cabrera	648	396	61.1%
4.	Josh Hamilton	571	349	61.1%
5.	Prince Fielder	714	440	61.6%
6.	Carlos Ruiz	433	269	62.1%
7.	Paul Konerko	631	393	62.3%
8.	Jack Cust	425	265	62.4%
9.	Chase Utley	511	319	62.4%
10.	Albert Pujols	700	437	62.4%
2011	*Name*	*PA*	*Outs*	*Out%*
1.	Jose Bautista	655	339	51.8%
2.	Miguel Cabrera	688	359	52.2%
3.	Mike Napoli	432	237	54.9%
4.	Prince Fielder	692	386	55.8%
5.	Ryan Braun	629	353	56.1%
6.	Joey Votto	719	407	56.6%
7.	Matt Kemp	689	392	56.9%
8.	Adrian Gonzalez	715	408	57.1%
9.	Lance Berkman	587	336	57.2%
10.	Dustin Pedroia	731	420	57.5%

standards, he actually had a year that would be deemed worthy of MVP award consideration today, with production of roughly the same merit as, say, Paul Konerko's or Curtis Granderson's of 2011. Similarly, when outfielder Wildfire Schulte of the Cubs hit .281/.324/.396, he had a season that in its time and place was roughly at the same level as Nick Swisher or Adam Jones in 2011.

The next four columns, **Hits, Doubles, Triples,** and **Home Runs**, are more descriptive than necessary if we're really trying to drill down to the basics, but nowhere is it written that we have to sacrifice detail and color in the pursuit of accuracy. **Stolen Bases** and **Caught Stealing** are also descriptive of a player's speed and propensity to attempt steals, as well as his efficiency. Since 2004, the major league average success rate has hovered between 70 and 74 percent, the best base-stealers succeeding on over 80 or even 90 percent of their attempts. It has long been accepted that stealing at less than a 70 percent success rate is counterproductive given the loss of baserunners that might have scored anyway and outs taken away from batters.

It is interesting to note that stolen bases and stolen base percentage are not necessarily indicators of speed. From 1987 to 1988, Kevin McReynolds, a left fielder with a panda physique, stole 35 bases in 36 attempts for the Mets, including going a perfect 21-0 in the latter season. Jayson Werth of the Nationals isn't going to be mistaken for Brett Gardner, but in his career he's stolen 96 bases against only 14 caught stealing. At the other extreme, Alfredo Griffin was actually fast, but he had no idea how to steal a base, with the result that he had seasons like 1979, when he succeeded only 21 times in 37 attempts, or 1980, when he was successful in 18 attempts and caught in 23 of them.

Fortunately, our next stat, **Baserunning Runs (BR)**, can help clarify just what a player contributes on the bases regardless of his speed. This statistic is the creation of former Baseball Prospectus contributor Dan Fox, who has gone on to become the director of baseball systems development for the Pittsburgh Pirates. Every possible baserunning event (stolen base attempts, advancing on a hit, on a groundout, on a fly out, on a wild pitch, passed ball, or balk) is assigned a run value based on multi-year run expectancies, and then the rate at which each player advanced is compared to the league average advance in that situation. Dan Rosenheck gave a good example of how the stat works in the *New York Times*:

> Suppose there is a man on first base with one out, and a double is hit to left field. If the runner stops at third, his team would have men on second and

third with one out. Between 2000 and 2005, teams in that situation scored an average of 1.4 runs before the end of the inning. By contrast, if he reached home on the hit, the team would have a run in the bank and a man on second with one out. On average, that situation leads to a further 0.7 runs being scored in the inning, for a total of 1.7. So the value of reaching home from first on a double is 0.3 runs—the difference in the team's expected run scoring resulting from the taking of the extra base.

With all of these measurements, each time a player adds 10 runs above average, it can be considered the equivalent of his banking an extra win for his team. Thus, when Michael Bourn was credited with 10.2 BRR in 2010, he improved the Astros' record by a win (for all the good that did them) above and beyond anything he contributed with his bat or glove. Note that Bourn stole a league-leading 47 bases that year and was rated a positive in all other aspects of baserunning, yet the total result of that was only 10 runs above average. Players whose only offensive attribute is speed are not particularly valuable; adding a handful of bases to the player's total only generates so much scoring— or as I like to put it, Wade Boggs scored over 100 runs a year leading off for the Red Sox and he averaged two stolen bases (and four caught stealing) a season. His ability to reach base more than compensated for his sedentary approach to baserunning.

The all-time leaders in this category further underscore the tertiary nature of baserunning. Only one player, Maury Wills in 1962, has been worth over 17 BR (21.6) in a season, and seasons of 10 or more BR are relatively rare, with just 90 recorded since 1950. Conversely, only four players (Milt May in 1981, George Hendrick in 1983, Bengie Molina in 2008, and Manny Ramirez in 1996) have cost their team as many as one win with poor baserunning. Baseball rewards speed in many ways, and it is certainly better to have it than not, but it cannot be a player's sole skill.

The **Walk (BB)** and **Strikeout (SO)** columns should be self-explanatory, though now is as good a time as any to repeat a beloved mantra of sabermetrics: a strikeout is just another out. The batter who strikes out a lot costs his team something in not putting the ball in play and possibly advancing a runner on an out, but also gives his team something by hitting into relatively few double plays.

Batter strikeout rates have been up and down over the last six decades, but the overall trend has been up. In 1950, batters whiffed in 10 percent of their plate appearances. Sixty-one years later, they're up to 18 percent. It took a long time to get there; strikeout rates dropped

TABLE I-4 Baserunning Runs Leaders and Trailers, 2010–2011

	Leaders 2010				*Leaders 2011*	
RK	*Player*	*BRR*		*RK*	*Name*	*BRR*
1.	Michael Bourn	10.2		1.	Ian Kinsler	11.6
2.	Drew Stubbs	9.3		2.	Juan Pierre	10.0
3.	Angel Pagan	8.7		3.	Ichiro Suzuki	8.9
4.	Juan Pierre	8.1		4.	Ben Revere	8.0
5.	Andres Torres	8.0		5.	Emilio Bonifacio	7.9
6.	Brett Gardner	7.8		6.	Brett Gardner	7.7
7.	Martin Prado	6.7		7.	Cameron Maybin	7.2
8.	Coco Crisp	6.1		8.	Elvis Andrus	7.1
9.	Alexei Ramirez	6.0		9.	Dexter Fowler	7.0
10.	Rickie Weeks	5.8		10.	Michael Bourn	6.7

	Trailers 2010				*Trailers 2011*	
RK	*Player*	*BRR*		*RK*	*Name*	*BRR*
1.	Adam Dunn	-5.3		1.	Ryan Howard	-9.4
2.	Jhonny Peralta	-5.3		2.	Adrian Gonzalez	-8.1
3.	Brandon Inge	-5.4		3.	Adam Dunn	-6.4
4.	Jorge Posada	-5.6		4.	Paul Konerko	-6.0
5.	Victor Martinez	-5.7		5.	Matt LaPorta	-5.6
6.	Carlos Ruiz	-5.7		6.	Aramis Ramirez	-5.3
7.	Kurt Suzuki	-6.2		7.	Casey McGehee	-5.2
8.	Adrian Gonzalez	-6.6		8.	David Ortiz	-5.1
9.	Luke Scott	-6.9		9.	Chipper Jones	-4.9
10.	Ryan Howard	-8.0		10.	Yadier Molina	-4.8

with the lowering of the pitcher's mound in the late 1960s and only gradually regained and surpassed their heights of that pitching-dominated decade, finally crossing past the 15 percent mark, seemingly for good, in 1994. Consider the list of best and worst batter grounded-into double-play (GIDP) rates since that time (see Table I-5). Note that with a few exceptions, the players with the least double plays had higher strikeout rates than those with the most. As Chuck Carr, Brett Butler, Curtis Granderson, et al show, it also helps to be fast, but not every player on the list was a speedster, and it is telling that the catching profession is represented in both the best and worst groups.

TABLE I-5 Least and Most Double Plays Per Opportunity (200 GIDP opportunity min.)

Least Double Plays Per Opportunity

Name	DP OPPS	GIDP	GIDP Rate	SO Rate
Chuck Carr	201	8	4.0%	15.6%
Kazuo Matsui	342	14	4.1%	15.8%
Akinori Iwamura	242	10	4.1%	18.8%
Mark Johnson	227	10	4.4%	23.4%
Brett Butler	202	9	4.5%	10.1%
Tony Gwynn	201	9	4.5%	15.8%
Darren Daulton	267	12	4.5%	14.5%
Curtis Granderson	676	31	4.6%	21.8%
Russell Branyan	669	31	4.6%	32.9%
Rob Mackowiak	485	23	4.7%	22.4%

Most Double Plays Per Opportunity

Name	DP OPPS	GIDP	GIDP Rate	SO Rate
Yadier Molina	656	135	20.6%	8.6%
Ron Coomer	658	132	20.1%	13.3%
Johnny Estrada	418	80	19.1%	10.2%
Jason Phillips	296	56	18.9%	11.1%
Jeff Keppinger	380	71	18.7%	6.1%
Lenny Webster	253	47	18.6%	13.6%
Billy Butler	522	97	18.6%	13.5%
Herbert Perry	343	63	18.4%	15.4%
Wilson Valdez	209	38	18.2%	13.4%
Jose Castillo	408	72	17.7%	18.4%

One meme about strikeouts that came up often during the 2011 season was the way new Arizona Diamondbacks general manager Kevin Towers had changed the nature of the team's offense by cutting strikeouts. In 2010, the Diamondbacks had struck out a record 1,529 times, not only destroying the old record for batter strikeouts, but dancing on its grave; they eclipsed the old mark by the 2001 Milwaukee Brewers by 130 whiffs. In 2011, with players like Adam LaRoche and single-season strikeout king Mark Reynolds out of the organization, the D'backs' strikeout rate declined from 24.7 percent to 20.5, just 1.4 percent above the NL average.

When Arizona leapfrogged San Francisco for the division lead, this change was given as one of the reasons why. It wasn't. In 2010, the D'backs scored 4.4 runs a game in a league that scored 4.3 and has a team True Average of .256, good for eighth in the National League. In short, their offense was roughly average. In 2011, they scored 4.5 runs a game in a league that scored 4.1, which is superficially better but was achieved in part through luck and in part through a slightly greater reliance on the generosity of their hitter-friendly home park. Their True Average was, once again, .256, which ranked eighth in the National League.

That decreasing strikeouts did not fundamentally alter the nature of the offense should not have been surprising; that strikeouts dramatically decrease team scoring is not an idea that is supported by the actual data. The correlation between team strikeouts and team runs scored, from 1993 to 2010 (omitting 1994 and 1995, which were partial seasons) is an insignificant or −0.12. A scatterplot of high-strikeout teams and their runs scored totals shows only a tiny decline as strikeouts increase (see Figure I-1). Among the teams depicted is the 1999 Cleveland Indians, a club that struck out 1,100 times (second in the league that year) but nonetheless became one of only seven clubs in history to score 1,000 runs in a season, the first (and so far, only) since 1950.

It may seem obvious, but not everyone, including some longtime managers, realizes that walks are a great way for batters not to make outs. An impatient hitter confronts a binary set of outcomes at the plate: hit safely or make an out. The patient hitter has three possibilities. He can hit safely, walk, or make an out. Because he has an increased chance of reaching base, his opportunities to make an out are correspondingly diminished.

In late August 2006, then-Cubs manager Dusty Baker was asked if his team needed to improve its on-base percentage. In the 30 seasons between 1980 and 2010, only 10 teams would draw fewer than 400 walks in a non-strike season. The 2006 Cubs were one of them, thereby finishing last in the National League in OBP. Baker didn't think that was a problem. In fact, he seemed to think it could *be* a problem. "On-base percentage is great if you can score runs and do something with that on-base percentage," Baker said. "Clogging up the bases isn't that great to me. The problem we have to address more than anything is the home run problem."

This was a very odd bit of reasoning, as "clogging up the bases" is exactly how teams score runs, with or without the home run. Even

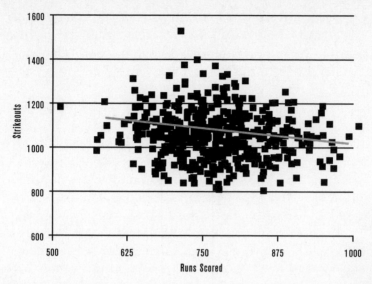

FIGURE I-1 Team Strikeouts and Runs Scored (1993–2004, omitting 1994 and 1995)

with the decline in overall offense observed in 2010 and 2011, baseball is still in an era in which home runs are frequently hit. No team is going to achieve a monopoly on home runs the way the Yankees did in the early 1920s, when Babe Ruth was personally out-homering entire rosters, but a considerable advantage can be gained in having an advantage in walks. If Team A is going to hit a home run in a game, and Team B is almost equally likely to do so, then if Team A wants to win it had better have more runners on base when the ball goes out than Team B does when they hit theirs.

Baker liked the "clogging" idea so much he used it on other occasions, saying in 2008, "The name of the game is scoring runs. Sometimes, you get so caught up in on-base percentage that you're clogging up the bases." The point, he said, was not reaching base, but "driving in runs and scoring runs," both of which require runners to be on base. His confusion was not a new phenomenon. In the 1940s, the American League was graced by a switch-hitting outfielder named Roy Cullenbine. When given a chance to play every day, Cullenbine was good for 100 walks a season, peaking with 137 in 1947. He also hit for good averages and power when he did swing. Overall, he averaged .276/.408/.432, which was highly valuable then and would be equally so now.

Nevertheless, Cullenbine had trouble staying with a team, changing affiliations six times in a 10-season career. In 1941, Cullenbine hit

.317/.452/.465 with 121 walks for a typically weak St. Louis Browns club. The Browns traded him. Said co-owner and general manager Bill DeWitt, "Cullenbine wouldn't swing the bat. [Manager Luke] Sewell would give him the hit sign and he'd take it, trying to get the base on balls. Laziest human being you ever saw."

Players as diverse as Ted Williams and Frank "The Big Hurt" Thomas came in for the same criticism during their careers, but in baseball, what some would characterize as laziness is what generates runs. Consider the expected runs in different base states from 2009 to 2011 (see Table I-6). The "Runners" column indicates how many runners are on base and which bases they are on. The first entry, "000," indicates the bases are empty; the second, "003," shows a man on third; "123" depicts the bases as loaded, and so on. The subsequent three columns show how many runs teams scored, on average, when they achieved these conditions. For example, with a runner on second and no outs, teams averaged a little over a run—a leadoff double is a nice way to start an inning. Putting a runner on second with one out dropped the expected runs by nearly half; teams often scored, but far less frequently. Finally, with a runner on second and two outs, teams quite often did not score at all.

Unsurprisingly, the more runners a team puts on base, the more runs it is likely to score. This would seem to be so obvious as not to need repeating, but from Bill DeWitt to Dusty Baker a great many baseball minds have failed to grasp this elementary aspect of the game.

Fielding Runs Above Average attempts to quantify what a player contributed with his glove. As our Jeter card shows, despite winning multiple Gold Gloves, defense has always been the weakest aspect of Jeter's game.

Unlike many other metrics of this type, like zone rating, Baseball Prospectus's fielding runs are formulated using only play-by-play data rather than the observations of a scorer following the game at the ballpark or on television. In the words of BP's Colin Wyers, who developed this version of the statistic, "Serious discrepancies have been noted between data providers, and research has shown that in larger samples use of that sort of batted-ball data introduces severe distortions in the metrics that impede accuracy. Without evidence that the batted-ball data has redeeming value in the short term, it seems imprudent to use that sort of data in our evaluation of player defense."

The severe distortions referred to above include biases created by observer location. Whether in the ballpark or in front of the television,

TABLE I-6 Run Expectancy, 2009–2011

Runners	Exp. R 0 Out	Exp. R 1 Out	Exp. R 2 Out
000	0.50	0.27	0.10
003	1.33	0.91	0.37
020	1.10	0.66	0.32
023	1.92	1.31	0.59
100	0.87	0.52	0.22
103	1.70	1.16	0.50
120	1.46	0.91	0.44
123	2.29	1.56	0.71

the position of the observer changes the nature of his observations, as does the beginning position of the fielder, something that is never clear from television. A fielder, by dint of canny positioning, may make a hard play look easy, while poor positioning may make an easy play harder. In short, one man's shoe-top catch is another man's can o' corn. As we shall see when we discuss pitchers, any ball put in play is potentially an out—but we're getting ahead of ourselves. The goal of any fielding metric is to answer two questions:

1. How many plays a player has made, and
2. How many plays an average player at the same position would have made given the same chances.

When you frame the issues this way, you can see how difficult the problem is. The first goal is adequately addressed by current statistics or direct observation. The second is very difficult given the impossibility of knowing what one player might have done in the place of another. This is a bit like asking how World War II would have come out if George W. Bush and not Winston Churchill had been prime minister of England, and makes it very clear why students of baseball are eagerly anticipating next-generation metrics that can be built off of unbiased observation systems modeled after PITCHf/x, a camera-based method of measuring the precise speed and trajectory of every pitch. FIELDf/x, now being tested in San Francisco's AT&T Park, promises to record the precise distance and direction traveled by every player, eliminating guesswork in the evaluation of defensive range.

Unfortunately, AT&T Park is just one of 30 stadiums; a full roll-out of FIELDf/x remains in the indeterminate future, as does the actual publication of the data: baseball, having invested the money to create this system, may well decide to keep what it reveals to itself. Thus, we carry on the struggle to define defensive ability with the information that is currently available. In the case of BP's fielding runs, that means eschewing batted-ball and hit-location data for the reasons of bias discussed above, instead utilizing an estimate for expected plays based primarily upon handedness of the batter, the ground-ball and fly-ball rates of the pitcher, and whether or not the fielder is responsible for holding a baserunner.

As with all metrics denominated in runs, a good rule of thumb is that for every 10 runs added above average (or above replacement—more on that in a moment) a player has contributed a win to his team's record. Conversely, for every 10 runs below average, he has subtracted one. Thus in Jeter's worst seasons, he can be seen to have given away as many as two wins with his glove. These were out-weighed by his offensive contributions, but diminished his overall value. As you can see from the 2010 and 2011 leaders and trailers (in Table I-7), in a typical season the range of fielding runs is limited, so this will be the case with most players—their fielding abilities add or take away from their offensive achievements, but do not exceed them.

If we are on the right track with our quantification of fielding runs, it suggests that Casey Stengel only got half the story right when he said, "I don't like them fellahs that drive in two runs and let in three," by which he meant players who were all bat and no glove. He might also have observed the negative consequences of having the opposite, players who save two runs with their gloves but strand three on the bases with their bats (see Table I-8).

Here, at the extremes of the range of defensive success and failure, a player's fielding abilities should be determinative of playing time. If a player can add three wins through run prevention alone, before his hitting is even considered, he is clearly worth playing. Conversely, a player who is costing the team three wins compared to the average player would have to do a great deal of hitting to justify his place in the lineup.

However, such cases are few and far between. If we loosely define regular playing time as being equal to 450 plate appearances on the season, then there have been approximately 8,600 regular players from 1950 until today. In that time there have been only 97 seasons of 20 or more fielding runs above average (roughly equal to one percent) and only 50 seasons of 20 or more fielding runs *below* average (five of them belonging to Jeter). Most major leaguers are neither so good nor

TABLE I-7 Fielding Runs Leaders and Trailers, 2010–2011

Fielding Runs Leaders, 2010			Fielding Runs Leaders, 2011		
Name	Pos.	FRAA	Name	Pos.	FRAA
Jay Bruce	RF	23.4	Omar Infante	2B	21.6
Alexei Ramirez	SS	20.9	Jack Hannahan	3B	16.8
Jose Lopez	3B	20.2	Gerardo Parra	LF	14.9
Alex Gonzalez	SS	16.4	Alberto Callaspo	3B	14.7
Adrian Beltre	3B	15.7	Joey Votto	1B	14.2
Albert Pujols	1B	14.1	Brett Gardner	LF	13.7
Mark Teixeira	1B	14.0	Albert Pujols	1B	13.5
Nelson Cruz	RF	13.8	Placido Polanco	3B	13.3
Cliff Pennington	SS	13.2	Brendan Ryan	SS	13.3
Josh Wilson	IF/OF	12.2	Todd Helton	1B	12.3

Fielding Runs Trailers, 2010			Fielding Runs Trailers, 2011		
Name	Pos.	FRAA	Name	Pos.	FRAA
Colby Rasmus	CF	-18.8	Asdrubal Cabrera	SS	-19.1
Troy Glaus	1B	-17.6	Ichiro Suzuki	RF	-18.2
Chone Figgins	2B	-17.1	Melky Cabrera	CF	-18.0
Raul Ibanez	LF	-17.0	Mark Reynolds	3B	-15.3
Neil Walker	2B	-15.8	Aramis Ramirez	3B	-15.1
Carlos Lee	LF/1B	-14.9	Curtis Granderson	CF	-13.2
Matt LaPorta	1B	-14.0	Kelly Johnson	2B	-13.0
Derek Jeter	SS	-13.6	Chipper Jones	3B	-12.6
Jose Bautista	RF/3B	-12.4	Miguel Cabrera	1B	-11.9
Andrew McCutchen	CF	-12.3	Cliff Pennington	SS	-11.9

so poor at fielding that a bad glove would dramatically negate the effect of a good bat or vice versa. Sometimes fans, broadcasters, and managers like to indulge in the unthinking hyperbole of saying, "I bet our shortstop saved us 100 runs this year." The accurate response is that in any given season there aren't enough difficult defensive opportunities that *only* a great shortstop at his peak would convert to save as many as 100 runs, but perhaps he could have saved, on the extreme high side, 25 runs more than the average player. If in doing so, he hit so poorly that he was 25 runs below average with the bat, then what have you gained?

TABLE I-8 Fielding Runs Leaders and Trailers, 1950–2011

	Leaders		
Name	Pos.	Year	FRAA
Andruw Jones	CF	1999	37.8
Graig Nettles	3B	1971	33.6
Willie Wilson	LF/CF	1980	32.5
Brooks Robinson	3B	1967	32.4
Clete Boyer	3B	1962	32.1
Ivan DeJesus	SS	1977	31.3
Chet Lemon	CF	1977	30.4
Willie Wilson	LF/CF	1982	30.2
Buddy Bell	3B/SS	1979	29.8
Richie Ashburn	CF	1956	28.9

	Trailers		
Name	Pos.	Year	FRAA
Dale Murphy	CF	1986	-32.4
Fred McGriff	1B	2000	-32.3
Gus Bell	CF	1956	-28.2
Toby Harrah	3B/SS	1979	-27.7
Bobby Richardson	2B	1961	-27.5
Chipper Jones	3B	1999	-24.8
Johnny Groth	CF	1950	-27.3
Joe Torre	3B	1971	-27.0
Brad Hawpe	RF	2008	-25.8
Greg Luzinski	LF	1979	-24.9

As we discussed when we encountered the triple-slash stats, understanding offense requires context. This is true both if you want to compare players in the same season who play in different environments—say one hits in Fenway Park, the other in Petco—or if you want to compare players across time, say Ty Cobb and Ichiro Suzuki. One way to do that is with **True Average (TAv)**, a Baseball Prospectus statistic that sums up a player's total offensive output (hits, walks, home runs, stolen bases, and so on) and adjusts for park and league environments so that every hitter has a—pardon the expression—level playing field. TAv is scaled to look and function just like batting average, so .260 is about average, .300 is very good, and .190 very poor. Using TAv, we can see that when you look at them relative to context, several players widely separated by space and time had seasons that were similarly productive (see Table I-9).

Similarly, we can reconcile such diverse seasons as 1968, in which the major leagues averaged 3.4 runs a game, and 2001, in which they averaged 4.78. Consider these Houston outfielders separated by 33 years (see Table I-10). Or consider this comparison of an underrated Tigers catchers and overrated Rangers slugger (see Table I-11)

These comparisons may seem counterintuitive, but that's the whole point: diverse environments camouflage a player's actual abilities. These only become apparent when considered in relationship to that environment. Erasmus wrote that in the country of the blind the one-eyed man is king; similarly, in a league in which the average player posts on-base and slugging percentages of .297 and .339, the man at .366 and .454 starts to look like he should be fitted for purple trimmed with ermine (see Table I-12).

The penultimate statistic is **Adjusted True Average (TAv+)**. We need a sense of how the player performed in relation to his league, so we've taken our all-in-one offensive statistic, True Average, and divided it by the league average to create an index centered around 100, which is league average. If a player has a 120 TAv+, as Jeter did in 2004, he was 20 percent more productive than the average hitter. If the hitter has an 89 TAv+, Jeter's mark in 2010, it means he was 11 percent *below* average. Again, this statistic takes park and league environments into account.

We've come to the final column, the one that sums up everything we've seen so far: **Wins Above Replacement Player (WARP)**. The ultimate goal for all players is to contribute to the winning effort. WARP takes everything a player has done to create or save runs, be at the plate, on the bases, and in the field, totals up the runs, and converts them to wins at the 10:1 ratio mentioned earlier.

The concept to grapple with here, and one that in my experience the uninitiated are likely to struggle with, is the idea of replacement level. In this case "the uninitiated" includes a certain Hall of Fame sportswriter. Two examples from the oeuvre of professional baseball luddite Murray Chass:

September 5, 2010: Integral to those numbers is something called WAR, which stands for wins above replacement. What replacement? A replacement player, of course, but he's mythical. Statistics zealots apparently love

TABLE I-9 True Average Across the Years

Name	Year	G	PA	R	H	2B	3B	HR	RBI	BB	SO	SB	CS	AVG	OBP	SLG	TAv
Mickey Mantle	1964	143	567	91	141	25	2	35	111	99	102	6	3	.303	.423	.591	.368
Reggie Jackson	1969	152	678	123	151	36	3	47	118	115	142	13	5	.275	.411	.608	.368
Willie Stargell	1971	141	606	104	151	26	0	48	125	83	154	0	0	.296	.398	.628	.368
Albert Pujols	2008	147	641	100	187	44	0	37	116	104	54	7	3	.357	.462	.653	.368

TABLE I-10 A Pair of Astros, 1968 and 2001

Name	Year	G	PA	R	H	2B	3B	HR	RBI	BB	SO	SB	CS	AVG	OBP	SLG	TAv
Jimmy Wynn	1968	156	646	85	146	23	5	26	67	90	131	11	17	.269	.376	.474	.348
Lance Berkman	2001	156	688	110	191	55	5	34	126	92	121	7	9	.331	.430	.620	.348

TABLE I-11 And Yet, Only One of Them Won a Major Award . . . Twice

Name	Year	G	PA	R	H	2B	3B	HR	RBI	BB	SO	SB	CS	AVG	OBP	SLG	TAv
Bill Freehan	1968	155	635	73	142	24	2	25	84	65	64	0	1	.263	.366	.454	.323
Juan Gonzalez	2001	140	595	97	173	34	1	35	140	41	94	1	0	.325	.370	.590	.323

to deal with mythical or hypothetical players. The problem for those of us who prefer dealing with reality and actual human beings is we can't buy into the idea of using mathematical formulas instead of real players.

March 6, 2011: I have considered WAR and VORP ("value over replacement player"; yes there's that replacement guy again), and I have a basic problem with them. The replacement player isn't real; he's a myth, and I've never seen a myth play baseball. It's like fantasy baseball. That stuff isn't real either.

(Note that WAR, as referred to here, and WARP can be understood as different abbreviations of the same statistic for purposes of this discussion.)

If you can understand the concepts at work in the nursery tale Goldilocks and the Three Bears, then replacement level should be a piece of cake. Just as Goldilocks had to sample porridge that was too hot and too cold to know which was "just right," we require a point of comparison to correctly perceive a player's value. Sabermetrics has chosen the replacement player as its measuring stick, and despite Chass's cavils, a ruler does not alter the truth of the object it is being used to measure.

In *Baseball Between the Numbers* we defined "replacement level" this way:

> The expected level of performance a major league team will receive from one or more of the best available players who substitute for a suddenly unavailable starting player at the same position, who can be obtained with minimal expenditure of team resources.

Translation: What kind of production do we expect from the typical 25th man, the kind of player who goes through waivers a lot in his career, and/or the quintessential Triple-A veteran? When teams suffer injuries to players for whom they have no promising replacement, or if they simply didn't plan very well in terms of staffing a position, that is often the quality of player they end up having to accommodate in their lineup. The answer is somewhere between 75 and 80 percent of the average regular, depending on the position. We call that level of production, roughly 20 percent off the pace, "replacement level," and the player who performs that way a "replacement-level player."

There is nothing hypothetical or arbitrary about the replacement level; while the exact gap between the average regular and the replacement level varies slightly from season to season (something accounted

TABLE I-12 True Average Leaders and Trailers, 2010–2011 (450 PA min.)

		Leaders, 2010		
Name	*AVG*	*OBP*	*SLG*	*TAv*
Miguel Cabrera	.329	.420	.622	.357
Josh Hamilton	.359	.411	.633	.353
Joey Votto	.324	.424	.600	.350
Jose Bautista	.260	.378	.617	.339
Paul Konerko	.312	.393	.584	.336
Albert Pujols	.312	.414	.596	.336
Adrian Gonzalez	.298	.393	.511	.321
Jayson Werth	.296	.388	.533	.321
Matt Holliday	.312	.390	.532	.319
Luke Scott	.284	.368	.535	.318

		Trailers, 2010		
Name	*AVG*	*OBP*	*SLG*	*TAv*
Cesar Izturis	.230	.277	.269	.203
Brendan Ryan	.223	.279	.294	.216
Alcides Escobar	.235	.288	.326	.217
Jose Lopez	.240	.270	.339	.222
Jason Kendall	.256	.318	.297	.222
Casey Kotchman	.217	.280	.336	.225
A.J. Pierzynski	.270	.300	.388	.228
Trevor Crowe	.251	.302	.333	.229
Ryan Theriot	.270	.321	.312	.234
Julio Borbon	.276	.309	.340	.234

for in our calculations), the relationship between the average regular and his backups has largely remained in the 75–80 percent range for over 100 years. Replacement level, as both concept and reality, allows us to measure a player's value against the worst-case scenario: his total absence. In 1952, the Pittsburgh Pirates endured a 42–112 season. The next spring, General Manager Branch Rickey slammed holdout slugger Ralph Kiner with one of baseball's classic putdowns: "We finished last with you and we can finish last without you." With replacement level, we know that Kiner, who hit a strong .253/.400/.509 in 100 games but with poor defense and baserunning, was worth about three wins above replacement to the 1952 Pirates. On a prorated basis, this

TABLE I-12 True Average Leaders and Trailers, continued

		Leaders, 2011		
Name	*AVG*	*OBP*	*SLG*	*TAv*
Jose Bautista	.302	.447	.608	.373
Miguel Cabrera	.344	.448	.586	.359
Matt Kemp	.324	.399	.586	.350
Lance Berkman	.301	.412	.547	.340
Ryan Braun	.332	.397	.597	.340
Jacoby Ellsbury	.321	.376	.552	.329
Adrian Gonzalez	.338	.410	.548	.327
Prince Fielder	.299	.415	.566	.326
Joey Votto	.309	.416	.531	.323
David Ortiz	.309	.398	.554	.322

		Trailers, 2011		
Name	*AVG*	*OBP*	*SLG*	*TAv*
Orlando Cabrera	.238	.267	.307	.212
Alex Rios	.227	.265	.348	.217
Adam Dunn	.159	.292	.277	.219
Casey McGehee	.223	.280	.346	.221
Jason Bartlett	.245	.308	.307	.225
Alex Gonzalez	.241	.270	.372	.226
Yuniesky Betancourt	.252	.271	.381	.227
Mark Ellis	.248	.288	.346	.227
Ronny Cedeno	.249	.297	.339	.228
Ben Revere	.267	.310	.309	.231

would have been third-best among left fielders in the eight-team National League. More poignantly for Rickey, even playing just two-thirds of the schedule, Kiner was the best position player on a club that even today ranks among the worst of all time. Rickey was right that they could have finished last without him, but wrong in that without him they had no hope of finishing anywhere else. Forget *"Après moi, le déluge"*—after Kiner, *le* Catfish Metkovich.

Instead of judging players against the replacement level, which tends to cause compulsive reactionary fits in some observers, we could measure them against the league averages, the existence of which I trust they would not deny. Doing so would actually give us a distorted picture that would be unfair to most players. As Woolner wrote, "Since all the players who secure jobs are at or above replacement level, then their average performance must be higher than replacement level. A player with average performance is actually playing at a level few others can match players who are average are quite rare." In other words, the population of ballplayers is large enough, and being average so difficult, that players can be below average and still have value. Setting a lower bar, a replacement-level bar, is a measure that better conveys the ability of some players simply to show up regularly and subsist in the major leagues.

This chapter has had as its theme the search for context. As I have written elsewhere:

> Considering a player in a vacuum is no different than asking, "How far is Hong Kong?" without supplying any other point of reference. Do you mean, "How far is Hong Kong from Beijing?" "From Hoboken?" "From Mars?" Or more accurately, it's like asking how far Hong Kong is from "here" when you don't know where you are. When it comes to baseball, we frequently, incorrectly, assume that we don't require a point of reference because our basic knowledge of the game has taught us to distinguish good from bad. Given a line like .295/.360/.500, we may feel that our almost *a priori* knowledge of the game is sufficient to tell us that this is a very good season, but that is not necessarily true, because the ground keeps shifting beneath us. The definition of "good" changes with each season, and it is only by knowing how far we are from some fixed point of reference that we can judge quality.

Or to put it another way, you don't know which bowl of porridge is the hottest or the coldest until you've sampled them all and understood their temperatures relative to each other. You can't know what something's quality is, and perhaps not even one's own identity, until you understand where it exists within a larger continuum.

This is a very handy thing to know; moving beyond wins above replacement player, you can have friends above (or below) replacement level, spouses above replacement level, sportswriters above replacement level, and even politicians above replacement level (we're still searching for the first living example). The guy who sits next to you every day at breakfast and repeatedly thrusts a fork into your thighs seems like a great friend until you understand that there is a world of people out there who won't abuse you; utter gibberish seems like wisdom until contrasted with real knowledge; Willie Bloomquist seems like an MVP candidate until you realize that Albert Pujols exists. In some of these cases, the replacement level is necessarily hypothetical, since we don't have an absolute value for spouses, sportswriters, or politicians, but the baseball form is absolutely *not* hypothetical but instead a literal interpretation of relationships between levels of production in baseball players.

What does vary is the exact formulation of wins above replacement and the weighting of its individual components, depending on which source you are looking at. The 10:1 ratio is also a generalization that may have specific exceptions. In this sense, wins above replacement is an approximation, but as long as it is internally consistent, the relative value of players is accurate. In practice, what this means is that when WARP say that a player was worth 6.2 wins, you can regard those .2 wins with some skepticism. These minor variations in wins above replacement among competing formulae are often grasped at by skeptics as a reason to doubt the utility of the statistic as a whole. As Joe Posanski wrote:

> Bret Saberhagen is .2 WAR better than Sandy Koufax. Would anyone— including Bret and his family—make the argument that Sabes was a better pitcher than Koufax or had a better career? No. Of course not . . . this is a major argument that people want to make against WAR in its various forms, that it is not flawless, that it is not accurate to the 10th or 100th of the decimal point, that its components (particularly the defensive components) are desperately flawed, and thus it allows people to regurgitate the garbage-in, garbage-out argument that helped make O.J. Simpson a free man (for at least a little while).

As Posnanski suggests, focusing on the fractions involved with wins above replacement causes many to miss the forest for the decimal-sized trees. The correlation of runs to wins is well understood, as is the correlation between specific player actions and the generation or prevention of runs. The fractions are an artifact of that correlation, nothing more. They are the numerical embodiment of Emerson's hobgoblin.

One brief example of skepticism that misunderstands the utility of WARP: in September 2011, in a piece titled "Is WAR the New RBI?" a writer calling him- or herself "Hippeaux" argued that wins above replacement does not work and embodies prejudices that we intuitively know to be untrue:

One can't help but notice that a cross-section of the most intimidating hitters in the game are treated with relative disdain by the metric. It doesn't like them because they play first base or left field (or DH), which aren't scarcity positions. It doesn't like that they are fat and slow.

. . . While I applaud WAR (and other metrics) for aiding in our appreciation of defense and baserunning, it's beyond asinine to conclude that [Jacoby] Ellsbury is twice as valuable as [Prince] Fielder. Too often WAR is used as a means of comparing oranges to apples.

Comparing oranges to apples is exactly what wins above replacement was created to do, and the ability to compare disparate talents like Ellsbury and Fielder is one of its chief assets. In 2011, Baseball Prospectus–formulated WARP did not see Ellsbury as contributing twice as many wins as Fielder, but close—Ellsbury was credited with 8.9 WARP; Fielder was well down the list with 5.2, a valuation that is entirely accurate, logical, and defensible, even if some may find it counterintuitive.

Fielder had higher on-base and slugging percentages than Ellsbury did, and did so in a tougher home park. However, we are comparing the players to the replacement level, and the replacement level is higher at Fielder's position of first base than it is at Ellsbury's position of center field because the defensive expectations are less than at any other position. Guy has a bat? Put him in there. The same isn't true of center field, one of the game's most demanding positions. As we have seen with Melky Cabrera, when a team plays a center fielder without the range to play the position it can suffer badly.

This is clearly depicted in the company that Fielder and Ellsbury keep at their position. Fielder hit well, but so did many other first basemen, whereas the competition was much thinner for Ellsbury. When you take into account the additional gap in baserunning and defensive contributions, where Fielder is a net negative, and the distance between the two widens, you don't even need to go that far to understand this simple proposition: two-way (that is both offensively and defensively valuable) players at up-the-middle positions (catcher, second base, shortstop, center field) are relatively rare. If a team has to replace an Ellsbury-level talent, it's doomed to a huge drop-off in all areas of the game. If a team has to replace a Fielder, it might not necessarily be able to duplicate his bat on a one-to-one basis, but it can get 80 percent of the way there. If that replacement is a bit more agile on the bases and in the field, even more of the shortfall will be closed.

This was the lesson of the Yankees' championship teams of the late 1990s through 2001, which got very average production from Tino Martinez at first base, inconsistent hitting from Scott Brosius at third, had no regular left fielder, and endured the declining years of Paul O'Neill. They maintained a productive offense in spite of these problems because catcher Jorge Posada, second basemen Chuck Knoblauch and Alfonso Soriano, shortstop Derek Jeter, and center fielder Bernie Williams provided production at positions where the replacement level is very low—a lesson of WARP confirmed by actual events (see Tables I-13 and I-14).

Things Not Here: Hitters

With WARP, we have completed the back of the hitter's new baseball card, but before moving on to pitchers, let's quickly discuss what is *not* here. Our new baseball card lacks **Runs and RBI**. These are largely the result of a player's lineup placement and number of opportunities he has with runners on base—you can't drive in runners that aren't there—and are a predictable outgrowth of what a player does at the plate. They really tell us little about the player himself, and as such are both inessential and a distraction from the information we really need to know.

Unlike runs and RBI, two columns I would gladly have included in a world of baseball cards the size of beach towels are **Batting Average on Balls in Play (BABIP)** and **Line-Drive Percentage**. These statistics go hand in hand. When batters put a ball in play, the results are fairly consistent; in this century, the major league BABIP has floated between .294 and .303. When a hitter dramatically exceeds or underperforms the league average, it is likely that luck played a part and he's due for a turnaround, since batters don't show year-to-year consistency in BABIP, except as it is correlated to his line-drive rate.

It is only a slight exaggeration to say that most successful hitting takes place as the result of line drives. Over the last five years, hitters have averaged .238 on ground balls, .141 on non-home-run fly balls, and .729 on line drives. If a batter's BABIP is low and his line-drive rate is low as well, it can be inferred that his results were "earned." Conversely, if a batter is low despite hitting his share of line drives, it may be that he has hit in bad luck.

One caution with line-drive rate: due to the same problems of bias that have caused us to discard stringer-reported data in our fielding runs, reported line drives (the only kind there is) should be taken with a grain of salt given the difficulty in classifying batted-ball types.

TABLE I-13 Batter WARP Leaders and Trailers (non-pitchers), 2010

		Leaders		
Name	*AVG*	*OBP*	*SLG*	*BWARP*
Albert Pujols	.312	.414	.596	8.2
Adrian Beltre	.321	.365	.554	7.5
Evan Longoria	.294	.372	.507	7.4
Josh Hamilton	.359	.411	.633	7.2
Joey Votto	.324	.424	.600	6.8
Carl Crawford	.307	.356	.495	6.8
Miguel Cabrera	.329	.420	.622	6.7
Robinson Cano	.320	.381	.534	5.9
Alexei Ramirez	.282	.313	.431	5.8
Jose Bautista	.260	.378	.617	5.8

		Trailers (non-pitchers)		
Name	*AVG*	*OBP*	*SLG*	*BWARP*
Matt LaPorta	.221	.306	.362	-2.1
Brandon Wood	.146	.174	.208	-1.9
Casey Kotchman	.217	.280	.336	-1.9
Pedro Feliz	.218	.240	.293	-1.8
Cesar Izturis	.230	.277	.269	-1.6
Alex Cora	.210	.266	.278	-1.3
Carlos Lee	.246	.291	.417	-1.3
Garret Anderson	.181	.204	.271	-1.2
Akinori Iwamura	.173	.285	.250	-1.1
Garrett Atkins	.214	.276	.286	-1.0

Finally, a word on **on-base plus slugging**, or **OPS**. OPS is, to be blunt, *stupid*. From the *Los Angeles Times*:

Dodgers General Manager Ned Colletti endorsed OPS as a worthy tool for gauging offense because it takes into consideration power as well as the ability to reach base.

Don Mattingly, the Dodgers' manager and a former American League batting champion, said he preferred runs scored.

"Think about it," Mattingly said. "You have to be on base to do it; you have to be getting yourself in position [to score]. If you're scoring 100 runs,

TABLE I-14 2011 WARP Leaders and Trailers

		Leaders		
Name	*AVG*	*OBP*	*SLG*	*BWARP*
Jose Bautista	.302	.447	.608	10.5
Matt Kemp	.324	.399	.586	8.9
Jacoby Ellsbury	.321	.376	.552	8.9
Alex Gordon	.303	.376	.502	7.5
Ian Kinsler	.255	.355	.477	7.1
Joey Votto	.309	.416	.531	7.0
Miguel Cabrera	.344	.448	.586	6.8
Alex Avila	.295	.389	.506	6.7
Evan Longoria	.244	.355	.495	6.5
Ryan Braun	.332	.397	.597	6.4

		Trailers		
Name	*AVG*	*OBP*	*SLG*	*BWARP*
Adam Dunn	.159	.292	.277	-2.6
Casey McGehee	.223	.280	.346	-1.0
Orlando Cabrera	.238	.267	.307	-1.0
Ryan Ludwick	.237	.310	.363	-0.7
Alex Rios	.227	.265	.348	-0.7
Ichiro Suzuki	.272	.310	.335	-0.5
Derrek Lee	.267	.325	.446	-0.4
Aaron Hill	.246	.299	.356	-0.3
Kelly Johnson	.222	.304	.413	-0.3
Juan Pierre	.279	.329	.327	-0.2

you're out there a lot, so it means your on-base [percentage] is up there, it probably means you have some extra-base hits or been a guy that can steal a bag."

Colletti's rebuttal: Runs scored are influenced by other hitters in the lineup, so they're not the most valuable measurement.

The addition of on-base percentage to slugging percentage to create an imaginary number doesn't tell you very much because you don't know what is going into the sauce. Let's look at three of the top second basemen in baseball in 2011:

Robinson Cano	882
Dustin Pedroia	861
Ben Zobrist	822

Note that I didn't include a decimal point—OPS usually has one, but it's not a fraction of anything, so its inclusion is nothing but an affectation. The three players are roughly identical, right?

Wrong. Although OPS gives the illusion of similar kinds of production, each player got there in a different way:

Cano	.349	.533
Pedroia	.387	.474
Zobrist	.353	.469

Here is what TAv says about them:

Cano:	.313
Pedroia	.306
Zobrist:	.305

To use an even more extreme example, here are two great player seasons from 1951 by OPS:

Eddie Yost:	847
Yogi Berra:	842

The problem is that there is nothing identical about these seasons. Yost, a right-handed hitter nicknamed "The Walking Man," was a stickler for the strike zone who took 126 free passes that year but hit only 12 home runs. His rates were .283/.423/.424. Berra, who won the MVP award, was almost a left-handed Vladimir Guerrero, a famous bad-ball hitter who could make contact with anything in the same area code as the plate. He walked only 44 times but socked 27 home runs. His rates were .294/.350/.492. There is nothing similar about these players or their production, and when you take all the factors into account, Yost's OBP gave him a slight edge on Berra's power in terms of overall production. OPS reflects this, but not the how and the why.

The key here is that OBP is slighted. OPS gives it equal weight to slugging percentage, but (again) at the end of the day, the main thing in baseball is *not to make outs*. OBP reflects just how well a player did at this essential task. OPS pretends that slugging is just as important.

◆

Our improved pitcher's card is similar to the hitter's card in that we eschew a number of crutches from days gone by, props that have long since been rendered superfluous by our improved understanding of the game (see Table I-15). The first two-thirds of the pitcher's card is basic, so we will deal with them quickly. **Games** and **Games Started** provide information as to how often a pitcher was used, and whether as a starter or a reliever. **Innings Pitched, Hits, Runs, Walks, Strikeouts,** and **Home Runs** provide a basic picture of what the pitcher did. The key here is to compare what the pitcher allowed to how many innings he pitched to get a sense of his performance on a rate basis.

Were we not restricting ourselves to a baseball-card-sized patch of real estate, we would do the math for you and include the information. From the perspective of learning to think about the interactions inherent in pitcher performance, it is better that we did not, as it can be more instructive to think through these things rather than just glance at a number. This is particularly true when it comes to comparing starter and reliever performance. Almost every pitcher is going to see cosmetic statistical changes when pitching in relief, especially in the area of strikeout rate, because a starter must pace himself in order to maintain his stuff for 100 or more pitches, whereas relievers go all out for a shorter period of time. This has always been true; witness Christy Mathewson in his 1912 book, *Pitching in a Pinch*:

I have always been against a twirler pitching himself out, when there is no necessity for it, as so many youngsters do. They burn them through for eight innings and then, when the pinch comes, something is lacking. A pitcher must remember that there are eight other men in the game, drawing more or less salary to stop balls hit at them, and he must have confidence in them. Some pitchers will put all that they have on each ball. This is foolish for two reasons.

In the first place, it exhausts the man physically and, when the pinch comes, he has not the strength to last it out. But second and more important, it shows the batters everything that he has, which is senseless. A man should always hold something in reserve, a surprise to spring when things get tight. If a pitcher has displayed his whole assortment to the batters in

TABLE I-15 The Back of the New Baseball Card, Pitchers

Roy Halladay—RHP

Bats: R THR: R Birth Date: 5-14-1977 HT: 6'6" Weight: 230 lbs Drafted: TOR 1st Round (17th Pick) 1995 Draft

Year	Tm	G	GS	IP	H	R	BB	SO	HR	BABIP	FIP	GB/FB	TAvA	FRA	FRA+	WARP
1998	TOR	2	2	14	9	4	2	13	2	.194	3.65	1.00	.188	4.04	113	0.2
1999	TOR	36	18	149.1	156	76	79	82	19	.285	5.43	1.90	.265	5.88	90	1.1
2000	TOR	19	13	67.2	107	87	42	44	14	.380	6.56	1.55	.329	6.49	78	0.3
2001	TOR	17	16	105.1	97	41	25	96	3	.309	2.39	3.10	.219	3.17	135	3.6
2002	TOR	34	34	239.1	223	93	62	168	10	.289	3.06	3.29	.223	3.98	120	5.4
2003	TOR	36	36	266	253	111	32	204	26	.285	3.29	3.25	.224	4.60	110	5.0
2004	TOR	21	21	133	140	66	39	95	13	.311	3.90	2.93	.240	5.09	103	2.1
2005	TOR	19	19	141.2	118	39	18	108	11	.264	3.07	3.27	.199	4.07	117	3.0
2006	TOR	32	32	220	208	82	34	132	19	.277	3.64	3.62	.221	4.67	104	3.0
2007	TOR	31	31	225.1	232	101	48	139	15	.201	3.62	2.89	.236	4.65	102	2.9
2008	TOR	34	33	246	220	88	39	206	18	.286	3.06	2.64	.218	3.76	118	4.8
2009	TOR	32	32	239	234	82	35	208	22	.306	3.10	2.25	.233	3.65	123	5.7
2010	PHI	33	33	250.2	231	74	30	219	24	.294	3.03	2.40	.224	3.62	119	3.9
2011	PHI	31	31	227.2	204	65	34	217	10	.307	2.15	2.70	.212	3.23	124	5.1
		377	351	2525	2432	1009	519	1931	206	.295	3.36	2.73	.229	4.23	113	46.1

the early part of the game and has used all his speed and his fastest break-ing curve, then, when the crisis comes he "hasn't anything" to fall back on.

Despite this being common knowledge at least as long ago as the reign of Woodrow Wilson, teams will still see a promising starter's stuff jump when he is used out of the bullpen and decide that the pitcher would be best utilized in relief work—for example, see Jonathan Papelbon with the Red Sox, Joba Chamberlain with the Yan-kees, or Neftali Feliz with the Rangers. Despite being groomed as starters, these pitchers did not fail as starters in the majors but were routed to the pen do to transient need and then not allowed to leave once their stuff played up in a relief role.

This is a shortsighted way to do business given that teams almost always face a shortage of quality starting pitching, whereas in some ways the whole purpose of the minor leagues is to create failed starters for relief usage. A starter will have a higher strikeout rate as a reliever; a reliever will have a lower strikeout rate as a starter. Even with unique specimens like Randy Johnson, Pedro Martinez, and Nolan Ryan dominating the list of top strikeout rates by starting pitch-ers, the relievers pick up where the starters leave off (see Tables I-16 and I-17). Note the presence of 2011 pitchers Jansen and Kimbrel on the all-time list. The top strikeout rate by a starting pitcher in 2011 was Zack Greinke's 10.5.

Batting Average on Balls in Play (BABIP) is one of the most re-cent additions to our arsenal and also one of the most important. Back in the 1980s, Bill James wrote that much of what we perceive to be pitching is actually defense. In 2001, a statistician named Voros

TABLE I-16 Top Single-Season Pitcher Strikeout Rates, 50-Inning Min.

	Pitcher	Year	IP	SO/9 IP
1.	Kenley Jansen	2011	53.2	16.09
2.	Carlos Marmol	2010	77.2	15.99
3.	Eric Gagne	2003	82.1	14.98
4.	Billy Wagner	1999	74.2	14.95
5.	Brad Lidge	2004	94.2	14.93
6.	Craig Kimbrel	2011	77.0	14.84
7.	Armando Benitez	1999	78.0	14.77
8.	Billy Wagner	1998	60.0	14.55
9.	Billy Wagner	1997	66.1	14.38
10.	Byung-Hyun Kim	2000	70.2	14.14

TABLE I-17 Top Single-Season Pitcher Strikeout Rates, 150-Inning Min.

	Pitcher	Year	IP	SO/9 IP
1.	Randy Johnson	2001	249.2	13.41
2.	Pedro Martinez	1999	213.1	13.20
3.	Kerry Wood	1998	166.2	12.58
4.	Randy Johnson	2000	248.2	12.56
5.	Randy Johnson	1995	214.1	12.35
6.	Randy Johnson	1997	213.0	12.30
7.	Randy Johnson	1998	244.1	12.12
8.	Randy Johnson	1999	271.2	12.06
9.	Pedro Martinez	2000	217.0	11.78
10.	Randy Johnson	2002	260.0	11.56
11.	Nolan Ryan	1987	211.2	11.48
12.	Dwight Gooden	1984	218.0	11.39
13.	Pedro Martinez	1997	241.1	11.37
14.	Kerry Wood	2003	211.0	11.35
15.	Nolan Ryan	1989	239.1	11.32

McCracken wrote an article for Baseball Prospectus that took the first steps toward proving the truth of James's words. In a finding that was simultaneously surprising and painfully obvious, McCracken showed that pitchers had little direct control on the outcome of balls in play.

If you think about it, this makes perfect sense. Imagine three identical fly balls hit to identical locations in center field on identical pitches in three different games. In the first, the speedy Jacoby Ellsbury jogs lightly to the spot and makes an easy catch. In the second, Willie Mays—not the youthful 12-time Gold Glover Mays of the Giants, but the 42-year-old Mays playing for one year too long with the 1973 Mets—runs as hard as he can but just misses the catch, the ball falling in for a single. In the third instance, it doesn't matter who the center fielder is—whether by virtue of good scouting or blind luck, he happens to be standing in the exact spot to which the ball is hit; Ellsbury, Mays, a spot-start by the lumbering Pete Incaviglia, peak-form Andruw Jones, it doesn't matter—the catch gets made.

In all three preceding examples, the pitcher's actions were identical. It was the fielders who determined the outcome. You can see this same process at work at every position on the diamond. The pitcher makes an offering, and the batter hits it to some point on the compass. Almost everything that happens after that is dependent on the abilities and positioning of the fielders. The pitcher has some small impact on where the ball is hit, and some pitchers, such as heavy ground-ball or fly-ball types, have more influence than others, but for the most part, James was right: with the exception of walks, strikeouts, and home runs, pitching *is* defense.

Knowing this lets us infer certain things about a pitcher's record. League-average BABIP tends to hover in the vicinity of .300 (over the last three years, the majors have averaged .297), so if a pitcher is vastly above or below that mark, we can guess that a few things have happened. If the BABIP is high, the pitcher might have performed in front of an abysmal defense, had very bad luck or simply been pounded on his own merits. Conversely, if the BABIP is very low, he might have pitched in front of a stellar defense, had very good luck, or simply been really tough to hit. It requires more investigation to discern exactly what has happened, but we know two things for sure: something is not "normal" and it is going to change. A year down the line, that high BABIP is very likely to sink and that low BABIP is going to rise.

Consider the case of Chris Bosio of the 1987 Brewers. Bosio, a rookie, swung between the rotation and the bullpen, pitching 170 innings, walking 50, and striking out 150 batters. His rates of walks, strikeouts, and home runs allowed—he gave up 18, or roughly one per nine innings—were all above average in a year in which pitchers were generally battered. Despite this, Bosio gave up 187 hits and allowed 5.40 runs per nine innings, well above the league average of 4.95. How does a pitcher who pitched so well get such bad results? What did he do wrong?

If anyone had been thinking about BABIP at the time, they would have known that Bosio was an innocent man. The average American League pitcher of that season allowed a .288 average on balls in play. Brewers pitchers had a BABIP of .303 as a group. Bosio's BABIP was .330. Further, as measured by their ability to turn balls in play into outs, the Brewers had one of the worst defenses in baseball that season. Bosio's only sin was to let batters hit the ball between the lines, where his fielders, either due to their own limitations or an unlikely chain of batters hitting 'em where they ain't, were not prepared to help him. Had we been aware of this in 1987, we would have been able to predict great improvement for Bosio the following year, when presumably he would receive better defensive support or his luck would return to normal. Indeed, Bosio's RA dropped to 3.96 (versus a league average of 4.40) in 1988.

The same phenomenon of luck regressing can be seen with unusually good BABIPs as well. Consider Steve Trachsel, the notoriously methodical starting pitcher, with the 1996 Cubs. After a rough 1995 in which he allowed an average of 5.82 runs per nine innings, Trachsel appeared to right himself with a 3.03 ERA/3.60 RA the following year. League average RA was 4.71. Trachsel made the All-Star team, and at 25 could have been viewed as a dependable part of the Cubs' rotation for years to come. However, there were signs that Trachsel's improvement should have been taken with a grain of salt: while his walk rate was good, his rate of strikeouts and home runs allowed was poor—given just how many balls Trachsel allowed into play, rather than the 181 hits in 205 innings actually totaled against him, we would have expected him to give up about 205. The Cubs had the second-best defense in the league. The league average pitcher allowed a .299 average on balls in play, the average Cubs pitcher .288, and Trachsel .248.

Today, we would forecast that Trachsel was in line for a severe correction, and indeed that is what happened; in 1997 his RA jumped to 4.92. It would be six years before he posted another ERA lower than 4.46. In that second year, Trachsel actually increased his strikeout rate while raising his walk rate by an insignificant amount. The real difference was that the Cubs' defense was less effective—among other changes, they ditched shortstop Rey Sanchez, one of the best gloves ever at his position (too bad he couldn't hit), in favor of 34-year-old Shawon Dunston—and Trachsel's luck just wasn't as good; his BABIP jumped to .320.

A caution: just as Freud is supposed to have said that sometimes a cigar isn't a symbol, sometimes it's just a cigar, BABIP isn't an excuse to stop thinking. A pitcher's BABIP can also be a legitimate expression of how well or poorly he pitched—as the relief great Sparky Lyle said to teammate Jim Kern in 1980, "I've seen guys pitch bad and I've seen guys pitch in bad luck, but you've done an outstanding job of putting it all together." Quite often, BABIP is a clue that will lead us in the right direction—note that even an excellent pitcher like Halladay, above, has BABIPs that tend to coalesce around the league average—but no single piece of information provides us with the full picture of a pitcher's performance.

Fielding-Independent Pitching (FIP) does some of the thinking involving balls in play for us by estimating what a pitcher's ERA woulda-shoulda-coulda been without the intervention of his defense. Developed independently by sabermetricians Tom Tango and Clay Dreslough, FIP deals only with a pitcher's "three true outcomes": walks, strikeouts, and home runs. Several variations of the formula exist, but in its most basic form, FIP is (13*HR + 3*BB−2*K)/IP, plus a constant (usually around 3.2) to put it on the same scale as ERA. The result is far more predictive of a pitcher's future ERA than his *actual* ERA, because it takes out the noise, such as the Cub's substitution of the superannuated Dunston for the smooth Sanchez in the example above. That's not the pitcher's fault, and he shouldn't be penalized for it.

In the hitting section of the baseball card, we focused on the search for context. With pitchers, we can't even begin to place them in context until we've isolated their performance from that of their teammates, and BABIP and FIP assist in that pursuit.

Ground Ball/Fly Ball Ratio (GB/FB) is a straightforward recounting of how many ground balls were hit off of a pitcher compared to the number of fly balls. This statistic suggests a pitcher's style and repertoire. From 2009 to 2011, the major league average pitcher allowed slightly more flies than grounders, resulting in an average of 0.81. Pitchers who emphasize a sinking fastball in their repertoire can more than double this ratio, and in an era when home runs are plentiful, this can be quite a competitive advantage. "How often," the Hall of Fame pitcher Jim Bunning once asked rhetorically, "have you seen a 420-foot ground ball?" Despite this commonsense wisdom, the correlation between this statistic and how many home runs a pitcher gives up is not as strong as you might think, as Table I-18 demonstrates.

As you can see, ground-ball pitchers don't always allow as few home runs as we might expect given their tendency to keep the ball down, and some fly-ball pitchers don't give up as many as we might expect even though their approach is geared toward getting batters to send the ball toward the fences. It seems that the ability to prevent home runs may be a discernible skill as opposed to a function of luck, though this is not yet well understood.

Our next statistic, **True Average Against (TAvA)**, is simply a representation of how batters did against this pitcher as depicted by our all-in-one offensive statistic, true average. Once again, true average is scaled like batting average and includes all aspects of a player's offensive performance. In 2011, the major league leader in TAvA among pitchers with 150 innings or more pitched was Justin Verlander, who held hitters to .205. The hardest hit was beer-guzzling John Lackey, who was tagged for a .305 TAv, as shown in Table I-19.

We now reach the section of our baseball card that replaces—improves, really—on **Earned Run Average**. ERA has problems, among them letting the pitcher completely off the hook for unearned runs, pinging him for how his bullpen does with men on base (and

TABLE I-18 Ground Ball/Fly Ball Leaders and Trailers, 1950–2011 (1000 IP min.)

		Leaders	
Pitcher	*IP*	*GB/FB*	*HR/9*
Brandon Webb	1319.2	4.02	0.6
Roger McDowell	1050.0	3.93	0.4
Bill Swift	1599.2	3.68	0.7
Derek Lowe	2515.2	3.53	0.7
Kevin Brown	3256.1	3.52	0.6
Aaron Cook	1312.1	3.20	0.8
Scott Erickson	2360.2	3.18	0.9
Jake Westbrook	1456.1	3.12	0.8
Bob Wickman	1059.0	3.10	0.7
Greg Maddux	5008.1	3.02	0.6
		Trailers	
Pitcher	*IP*	*GB/FB*	*HR/9*
Sid Fernandez	1866.2	0.71	0.9
Jeff Reardon	1132.1	0.72	0.9
Dick Hall	1259.2	0.79	0.9
Steve McCatty	1188.1	0.79	0.9
Catfish Hunter	3449.1	0.80	1.0
Juan Berenguer	1205.1	0.80	0.9
Dave LaRoche	1049.1	0.82	0.8
Bobby Bolin	1576.0	0.83	0.9
Luis Tiant	3486.1	0.83	0.9
Eric Milton	1582.1	0.84	0.8

ignoring how he does when inheriting someone else's runners), and crediting him for the action or inaction of his defense. **Fair Run Average (FRA)** adjusts for these things, and most important, the pitcher's sequencing. Sequencing is important because, for example, the damage inflicted by walking a batter with the bases empty is different than that of walking a batter with the bases full. The former may or may not eventually result in a run, but the latter automatically does. By going through every possible situation in a year or a period of years, we can see what the run potential of each event is, and adjust the pitcher's RA accordingly.

Unlike a fielder, who only impacts the game when the ball is hit or thrown to him, or a hitter who only gets to the plate once each time

TABLE I-19 TAv Career Leaders and Trailers, 1950–2011 (1000 IP min.)

Leaders			Trailers		
Pitcher	IP	TAvA	Pitcher	IP	TAvA
Mariano Rivera	1211.1	.200	Jesse Jefferson	1085.2	.283
Trevor Hoffman	1089.1	.215	Randy Lerch	1099.1	.282
Pedro Martinez	2827.1	.215	Jimmy Haynes	1200.2	.279
Tim Lincecum	1028.0	.225	Ramon Ortiz	1423.0	.277
Sandy Koufax	2324.1	.225	George Stone	1020.2	.277
Hoyt Wilhelm	2254.1	.226	Bill Krueger	1194.1	.277
Roger Clemens	4916.2	.226	Curt Young	1107.0	.277
Greg Maddux	5008.2	.228	Tom Griffin	1494.2	.276
Curt Schilling	3261.0	.229	Nate Robertson	1152.1	.276
Johan Santana	1908.2	.229	Dan Spillner	1492.2	.276
Roy Halladay	2531.0	.229	Johnny Klippstein	1967.2	.276
Brandon Webb	1319.2	.229			

through the order, we credit the pitcher with agency, the ability to influence almost every event directly. Thus, we treat those occasions on which he gives up a walk followed by a home run differently from when he gives up a home run followed by a walk. This makes for some significant differences from ERA. Consider Roy Halladay, our baseball-card guinea pig, and his differing ERAs and FRAs as depicted in Table I-20.

Halladay's 4.23 FRA, a run higher than his 3.23 career ERA, suggests the impact of fielders and relief pitchers on his performances, but this is in no way unique to him. Since 1950, ERA has averaged about .65 lower than FRA in both major leagues.

TABLE I-20 Roy Halladay ERA vs. FRA

Year	ERA	FRA	Year	ERA	FRA
1998	1.93	4.04	2006	3.19	4.67
1999	3.92	5.88	2007	3.71	4.65
2000	10.64	6.49	2008	2.78	3.76
2001	3.16	3.17	2009	2.79	3.65
2002	2.93	3.98	2010	2.44	3.62
2003	3.25	4.60	2011	2.35	3.23
2004	4.20	5.09			
2005	2.41	4.07	Career	3.23	4.23

To further our search for understanding through context, we also present **FRA+**. It simply takes a player's FRA, adds a park and league adjustment, divides it by the league FRA, and then multiplies by 100 so you get a number in which 100 is average, 90 is 10 percent below league average, 110 is 10 percent above league average, and so on. Halladay, at 113, has been 13 percent above league average in his career. Indexed numbers like FRA+ can be very handy for getting a sense of a pitcher's performance at a glance.

WARP: As with hitters, wins above replacement seeks to capture a player's total contribution to the winning effort. This number includes pitcher hitting and defense and is compatible with the WARP used for hitters, so we can compare hitters and pitchers. For example, in the fall of 2011, the American League MVP award debate centered around a few position players and pitcher Justin Verlander. With WARP, we can place them in the same context (see Table I-21). Verlander's placement in the midst of the MVP race is unusual. Normally, we're more concerned with ranking pitchers against pitchers, and WARP will serve there as well, as indicated in Table I-22.

TABLE I-21 2011 AL WARP Leaders, Hitters, and Pitchers Combined

Name	WARP
Jose Bautista	10.5
Jacoby Ellsbury	8.9
Alex Gordon	7.5
Ian Kinsler	7.1
Miguel Cabrera	6.8
Alex Avila	6.7
Justin Verlander	6.7
Evan Longoria	6.5
Robinson Cano	6.4
Mike Napoli	6.0

TABLE I-22 2011 Pitchers Ranked by WARP

AL		NL	
Name	WARP	Name	WARP
Justin Verlander	6.7	Clayton Kershaw	7.3
Jered Weaver	5.5	Cliff Lee	6.2
Dan Haren	4.5	Roy Halladay	5.5
C.C. Sabathia	4.4	Yovani Gallardo	4.5
C.J. Wilson	4.2	Madison Bumgarner	4.4
Daniel Hudson	4.2	Ian Kennedy	4.4
Cole Hamels	4.1	Matt Cain	4.3
David Price	4.0	Zack Greinke	4.2
Justin Masterson	3.9	Chris Carpenter	4.2
Doug Fister	3.9	Daniel Hudson	4.2

Things Not Here, Pitchers

Won-Lost Record: At the team level, wins and losses are what the game is all about. On the individual level, they don't tell us anything usefully descriptive about a pitcher. We can, very, *very* broadly guess that a starting pitcher with a high win total or positive won-lost record has pitched well (and vice versa), but it's not always true. At times, a pitcher gets a disproportionate amount of offensive, defensive, and bullpen support and lucks into a good record. Conversely, a pitcher may receive none of these things, pitch well, and still post a losing record.

A classic example: in 1985, Los Angeles Dodgers pitching great Fernando Valenzuela opened the season with a terrific run of games. On Opening Day, he pitched seven innings against the Astros and allowed just two runs, both unearned. Five days later, he started against the Giants and shut them out on five hits. Five days after that, he toed the rubber against the Padres and pitched another shutout, this time limiting the opposition to *two* hits. He followed with a return match against the Giants, and while he failed to pitch a third consecutive shutout, the two runs he allowed were both unearned. Finally, in his last start of April, he took on the Padres again and allowed only a solo home run.

See Table I-23 for how Valenzuela's overall line looked at the end of April.

TABLE I-23 Valenzuela's Start

GS	CG	IP	H	R	ER	BB	SO	HR	ERA
5	4	42.0	22	5	1	9	35	1	0.21

At that moment, Valenzuela's won-lost record was 2-3. The home run he allowed to future Hall of Famer Tony Gwynn came in the ninth inning of his fifth game and 33rd inning of the season. He lost that game 1-0 and had dropped two other decisions 2-1. Valenzuela had done nothing wrong in those three games except fail to pitch a shutout. Even if you count Valenzuela's unearned runs against him, his RA was only 1.07—in a fair world, Valenzuela would have been 5-0 and on his way to a second Cy Young Award.

A pitcher can wander through this kind of desert for an entire season. In 1987, future Hall of Famer Nolan Ryan led the National League in ERA and strikeouts but had a record of 8-16 because his offense-starved Astros supported him with an average of three runs a game; in Ryan's 34 games, the Astros scored one or no runs 11 times. At the opposite extreme we have Ramon Ortiz of the 2003 Los Angeles Angels, who won 16 games despite an ERA of 5.20 (against a league average of 4.86) and absolutely no positive aspects to his overall performance—the Angels gave him nearly six runs a game of offensive support and their bullpen was the best in the American League.

The most famous and controversial example of a pitcher's record not aligning with his performance came in 2010, when Felix Hernandez, pitching in front of an exceedingly poor Mariners lineup, led the American League in ERA and innings pitched. Hernandez wasn't necessarily the best pitcher in the league that year, but he clearly deserved consideration for the Cy Young Award. However, his 13–12 record would traditionally have disqualified him. No starter had ever won the award with fewer than 15 wins in a non-strike year (Rick Sutcliffe, 1984 NL Cy Young winner, had only 16 wins in the senior circuit, but 20 between the two leagues). Of 100 Cy Young Award winners through 2010, 68 have won 20 or more games.

The Mariners scored an average of three runs a game when Hernandez was pitching, and scored one or no runs in 10 of his 33 starts. Hernandez won the award easily, taking 21 of 28 first-place votes. The hopeful interpretation of this vote is that the Baseball Writers' Association of America, if not the public in general, has begun to understand that individual pitcher won-lost records are often as descriptive of team performance as of an individual pitcher. Yet, the old guard still caviled, with Bob Elliott of the *Toronto Sun* saying, "If a general manager has been out of touch for a weekend and comes home . . . he says did we win. He doesn't ask did the starter have a quality start or strike out 10."

This is correct, but Elliott misunderstood the point he was making. The general manager asks, "Did *we* win?" not "*Who* won?" He may ask that question eventually, perhaps even immediately following on his initial interrogative, but it is not his paramount consideration. If the answer is, "We won Friday, Saturday, and Sunday. In each game, the starting pitcher gave us seven solid innings but got a no-decision," the GM is not going to pout, except perhaps about an offense that could not capitalize on a series of good starts.

A last note on won-lost records. Look back at Table I-19 above. These are the pitchers who were most consistently punished by opposing batters. Of the 10 pitchers listed, four (Ramon Ortiz, George Stone, Bill Krueger, and Curt Young) had winning records.

Saves: Not all saves are created equal. Since the saves rule was instituted, managers have operated under a spell cast by the conditions it stipulates for the awarding of a save.

The official scorer shall credit a pitcher with a save when such pitcher meets all four of the following conditions:

1. He is the finishing pitcher in a game won by his team;
2. He is not the winning pitcher;
3. He is credited with at least 1/3 of an inning pitched; and
4. He satisfies one of the following conditions:
   (a) He enters the game with a lead of no more than three runs and pitches for at least one inning;
   (b) He enters the game, regardless of the count, with the potential tying run either on base, or at bat, or on deck (that is, the potential tying run is either already on base or is one of the first two batters he faces); or
   (c) He pitches for at least three innings.

Note that these are instructions for the *official scorer,* not the manager, but managers utilize relievers as if Moses not only received these rules from on high at Mount Sinai, but he was acting on behalf of the managers' lobby when he did so. Managers use their best relievers as if the rules for awarding a save correctly identified the moments when that reliever might be most needed. This is hardly the case, and as a result, some very good pitchers are reserved for situations where they are not truly needed. A simple illustration will suffice: from 1991 to 2011, relievers handed a three-run lead converted 96 percent of their opportunities. "Relievers" includes not only Mariano Rivera, Trevor Hoffman, and the game's most reliable relievers, but any number of hurlers who at one point or another were entrusted with protecting a lead.

TABLE I-24 Save Conversion Rates, 1991–2011

Run Diff	Saves	Blown Saves	Pct	Pct of all Save Opps
1	5234	1690	76	41
2	5077	617	89	33
3	4269	187	96	26
Total	14580	2494	85	

In the manner of Onan spilling his seed on the ground, managers have thrown away more than a quarter of their best relievers' innings on game situations that were unworthy of them. Because saves tell us little about a pitcher's actual performance, it is far preferable to look at the pitcher's actual performance, including overall statistics like WARP, before consulting saves. A large saves total may tell us how the pitcher was used, but never how well he performed.

Last, **WHIP**, or **Walks and Hits per Innings Pitched**, is a favorite of fantasy players, but because hits allowed is so closely intertwined with defense, the information is not valuable in evaluating a hurler. It goes without saying that the lower a pitcher's WHIP the better, but our intention here is to credit the pitcher only with what is his.

Beyond the Back of the Baseball Card

Baseball Between the Numbers was a book-length exegesis of 21st-century thinking as it applies to baseball, which is another way of saying that we spent roughly 400 pages explaining a rationalist approach to the game through what is often referred to dismissively as "sabermetrics." The image of sabermetrics, largely shaped by its detractors, has come to be a tendentious, holier-than-thou, statistics-driven method of argumentation about player value, current or historic, all wrapped up in a pocket protector and some fresh-baked cookies delivered by Mom to the room in the basement.

As in any area of endeavor that attracts passionate enthusiasts, sabermetrics can be all of those things, but this depiction represents just one facet of what is at its heart a classically American field of inquiry: find a subject, then take it apart and put it back together until you know its workings intimately, improving it if you can. Along the way, debunk received wisdom—the bromides and clichés that have been mistaken for knowledge—throwing off the pretensions, dogmas, and strictured thinking of the intellectually bigoted, luddites, and reactionaries. In short, question whether we think of that subject in the way we do because it truly is that way, or simply because no one has thought to question ancient doctrines that are no less inaccurate for their long veneration. As the evolutionary biologist Thomas Huxley wrote, "skepticism is the highest of duties; blind faith the one unpardonable sin."

The Hall of Fame manager Earl Weaver titled his autobiography *It's What You Learn After You Know It All that Counts*. That is a philosophy we share. Taking a thought from Benjamin Franklin, the moment when we doubt a little of our own infallibility is inevitably concurrent with the moment we are able to learn: "Having lived long, I have experienced many instances of being obliged by better information, or fuller consideration, to change opinions even on important subjects, which I once thought right, but found to be otherwise."

Baseball Between the Numbers was widely read—hence this sequel—and yet there are still some recalcitrant types who remain convinced of their own infallibility, who fiercely cling to their RBI and pitcher wins. Forget them, though, because there are more important matters at stake. In the pages that follow, there is much to learn, analyze, debate, and grapple with, with the goal of emerging wiser fans, with a better understanding of the game of baseball. We may or may not convert the unconverted, but in this case the journey is as important as the destination, for if we really do the thinking and truly question our hard-won beliefs, we will inevitably discover that our game is a much larger, complex, and beautiful world than can be adequately depicted on a 3.5" × 2.5" piece of cardboard.

TABLE I-25 The Baseball Prospectus Top 100, 1900–2011

Rank	Name	Pos.	First	Last	Seasons	ADJ WARP
1	Babe Ruth	RF	1914	1935	22	173.8
2	Barry Bonds	LF	1986	2007	22	162.3
3	Willie Mays	CF	1951	1973	22	160.8
4	Ty Cobb	CF	1905	1928	24	148.6
5	Hank Aaron	RF	1954	1976	23	145.7
6	Tris Speaker	CF	1907	1928	22	136.5
7	Honus Wagner	SS	1897	1917	21	131.1
8	Ted Williams	LF	1939	1960	19	128.1
9	Walter Johnson	SP	1907	1927	21	125.3
10	Rickey Henderson	LF	1979	2003	25	123.6
11	Rogers Hornsby	2B	1915	1937	23	121.4
12	Stan Musial	LF	1941	1963	22	121.1
13	Mickey Mantle	CF	1951	1968	18	117.7
14	Frank Robinson	RF	1956	1976	21	116.7
15	Mike Schmidt	3B	1972	1989	18	115.4
16	Cy Young	SP	1890	1911	22	112.9
17	Roger Clemens	SP	1984	2007	24	110.3
18	Alex Rodriguez	SS	1994	2011	18	107.2
19	Joe Morgan	2B	1963	1984	22	100.5
20	Mel Ott	RF	1926	1946	21	100.3
T21	Eddie Collins	2B	1906	1928	23	99.4
T21	Grover Alexander	SP	1911	1930	20	99.4

continues

TABLE I-25 The Baseball Prospectus Top 100, continued

Rank	Name	Pos.	First	Last	Seasons	ADJ WARP
23	Nap Lajoie	2B	1896	1916	21	98.9
24	Carl Yastrzemski	LF	1961	1983	23	98.0
25	Lou Gehrig	1B	1923	1939	17	97.2
26	Jimmie Foxx	1B	1925	1945	20	96.4
27	Randy Johnson	SP	1988	2009	22	95.8
28	Al Kaline	RF	1953	1974	22	94.8
29	Cap Anson	1B	1871	1897	27	93.1
T30	Albert Pujols	1B	2001	2011	11	91.8
T30	George Brett	3B	1973	1993	21	91.8
32	Christy Mathewson	SP	1900	1916	17	91.5
33	Eddie Mathews	3B	1952	1968	17	90.1
34	Greg Maddux	SP	1986	2008	23	86.9
35	Roberto Clemente	RF	1955	1972	18	84.8
36	Pete Rose	1B	1963	1986	24	84.7
T37	Lefty Grove	SP	1925	1941	17	84.3
T37	Luke Appling	SS	1930	1950	20	84.3
39	Joe DiMaggio	CF	1936	1951	13	81.9
40	Charlie Gehringer	2B	1924	1942	19	81.3
41	Ken Griffey	CF	1989	2010	22	79.4
42	Wade Boggs	3B	1982	1999	18	79.2
43	Reggie Jackson	RF	1967	1987	21	78.8
44	Paul Molitor	3B	1978	1998	21	77.8
45	Richie Ashburn	CF	1948	1962	15	77.6
46	Frankie Frisch	2B	1919	1937	19	77.3
47	Jeff Bagwell	1B	1991	2005	15	76.6
48	Robin Yount	SS	1974	1993	20	76.0
49	Gary Sheffield	RF	1988	2009	22	75.8
50	Manny Ramirez	LF	1993	2011	19	75.5
51	Kid Nichols	SP	1890	1906	15	74.4
52	Bill Dahlen	SS	1891	1911	20	74.3
53	Roger Connor	1B	1880	1897	18	73.9
54	Eddie Plank	SP	1901	1917	17	73.3
55	Johnny Bench	C	1967	1983	17	73.0
56	Cal Ripken Jr.	SS	1981	2001	21	72.9
T57	Brooks Robinson	3B	1955	1977	23	72.7
T57	Frank Thomas	DH	1990	2008	19	72.7
59	Pedro Martinez	SP	1992	2009	18	72.3
60	Rod Carew	2B	1967	1985	19	72.2
61	Darrell Evans	3B	1969	1989	21	71.6
62	Johnny Mize	1B	1936	1953	15	71.3
T63	Jim Thome	1B	1991	2011	21	71.0
T63	Duke Snider	CF	1947	1964	18	71.0

TABLE I-25 The Baseball Prospectus Top 100, continued

Rank	Name	Pos.	First	Last	Seasons	ADJ WARP
T63	Reggie Smith	RF	1966	1982	17	71.0
66	Arky Vaughan	SS	1932	1948	14	70.8
67	Billy Hamilton	CF	1888	1901	14	70.6
68	Dave Winfield	RF	1973	1995	22	70.5
69	Chipper Jones	3B	1993	2011	18	69.7
T70	Carlton Fisk	C	1969	1993	24	69.1
T70	Billy Williams	LF	1959	1976	18	69.1
T70	Tim Raines	LF	1979	2002	23	69.1
73	Jimmy Wynn	CF	1963	1977	15	68.9
74	Curt Schilling	SP	1988	2007	20	68.5
75	Yogi Berra	C	1946	1965	19	68.1
76	Dan Brouthers	1B	1879	1904	19	68.0
77	John Smoltz	SP	1988	2009	21	67.7
T78	Mike Piazza	C	1992	2007	16	67.6
T78	Bob Gibson	SP	1959	1975	17	67.6
T80	Jim Edmonds	CF	1993	2010	17	67.1
T80	Al Simmons	LF	1924	1944	20	67.1
82	Dwight Evans	RF	1972	1991	20	67.0
T83	Scott Rolen	3B	1996	2011	16	66.6
T83	Steve Carlton	SP	1965	1988	24	66.6
85	Bert Blyleven	SP	1970	1992	22	66.5
86	Joe Cronin	SS	1926	1945	20	66.4
87	Ron Santo	3B	1960	1974	15	66.1
88	Bobby Bonds	RF	1968	1981	14	66.1
89	Graig Nettles	3B	1967	1988	22	66.0
90	Bobby Wallace	SS	1894	1918	25	65.9
91	Tom Glavine	SP	1987	2008	22	65.8
T92	Harmon Killebrew	1B	1954	1975	22	65.7
T92	Ed Delahanty	LF	1888	1903	16	65.7
T92	Mike Mussina	SP	1991	2008	18	65.7
95	Barry Larkin	SS	1986	2004	19	65.5
T96	Tom Seaver	SP	1967	1986	20	65.4
T96	George Davis	SS	1890	1909	20	65.4
98	Willie McCovey	1B	1959	1980	22	64.8
99	Sam Crawford	RF	1899	1917	19	64.7
100	Edgar Martinez	DH	1987	2004	18	64.5

PART 1

The Elephant in the Room

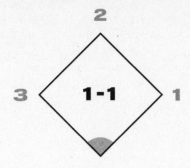

What *Really* Happened
in the Juiced Era?

JAY JAFFE

No one can pinpoint exactly when baseball's so-called steroid era began. According to former Braves relief pitcher Tom House, who was
drafted in 1967 and spent 1971–1978 in the majors, players were "doing steroids they wouldn't give to horses" even in the sixties. In 2005,
he estimated that during his time in the majors, six or seven pitchers
on every staff were "fiddling" with steroids or human growth hormone. However, it wasn't until the late eighties that the mainstream
media began to recognize the influx of the drugs into the national pastime, and not until the early nineties that it began to be perceived as a
problem. Despite the advent of mandatory drug testing in 2005, nobody can be entirely sure that the steroid era has ended. Even without
exact dates to bracket the era, the decreasing incidence of steroid-
related allegations provides enough distance that we can attempt to
put the period in perspective.

While both spitting on the sidewalk and murder are crimes that
should always be condemned, we reserve a special degree of disap-
proval for the latter, a far more serious violation of society's rules.
When it comes to steroids, we don't know if what occurred should be
categorized as a misdemeanor or a felony. Specifically, when it comes
to baseball's great records, we don't know if the numbers have been
slightly distorted or badly defaced.

When *Baseball Between the Numbers*, this book's predecessor, was written in 2005, the dimensions of the scandal were still being established. Much in the way of evidence was still being discussed, and the Mitchell Report, which galvanized the condemn-the-sinners phase, was not released until more than a year later, in mid-December 2007.

As such, we treated the issue only briefly in a chapter called "What Do Statistics Tell Us About Steroids?" within which Nate Silver, acknowledging that we were just scratching the surface, pointed out these four facts:

- In baseball, unexplained changes in performance are the norm, not the exception: once you control for park and league effects, "power spikes" in which established veterans have increased their home run rates by at least 10 homers per 650 plate appearances have been fairly consistent across eras.
- Relatively few players are steroid users: while players such as Jose Canseco and Ken Caminiti suggested that more than half of major leaguers were using, the 2003 anonymous survey found just seven percent of players using, and subsequent punitive testing has found even lower rates. Even if such testing is catching only a fraction of users, it seems such high estimates are inaccurate.
- Marginal players are more inclined than star performers to use steroids: for players on the fringe of making even the major league minimum, the financial incentives are much greater than for a star making millions of dollars.
- The average performance improvement from steroid use is detectable, but small: Silver estimated an effect of an average gain of 10 points of AVG (average), OBP (on-base percentage), and SLG (slugging) for a position player, and statistically insignificant gains for a pitcher.

Seven years later, Silver's findings remain true but unsatisfactory given curiosity about the true benefit that these players reaped and ongoing litigation involving Barry Bonds and Roger Clemens, as well as the exclusion (so far) from the Hall of Fame of Mark McGwire, Rafael Palmeiro, and, perhaps tragically, Jeff Bagwell, who has never been implicated in any substantial way but seems to have been tarred due to his career having been contemporaneous with the period in which most of the juicing took place. As such, it is necessary to revisit steroids, this time with seven years' more evidence in front of us and with a special focus on that baseball feat that was seemingly most affected by the era's abuses, the home run.

Big Mac Attack

On August 21, 1998, an award-winning Associated Press reporter named Steve Wilstein broke a story that raised questions about Mark McGwire's pursuit of Roger Maris's single-season home run record. During the previous month, while gathered with other reporters in front of McGwire's locker following a Cardinals game, Wilstein had spotted a brown bottle of pills labeled androstenedione. Sold over the counter as a dietary supplement, "andro" had been banned by the National Football League, the National College Athletic Association, and the Olympics because it was, in effect, an anabolic steroid precursor. Once ingested, it was converted by the body into the male hormone testosterone, able to accelerate the pace of muscle growth and recovery. McGwire admitted to Wilstein that he had used andro for more than a year, and said he wasn't the only one: "Everything I've done is natural. Everybody I know in the game of baseball uses the same stuff I use."

Less than a week after Wilstein's article ran, the *New York Times* ran an editorial that both expressed concern over "uncertainties about androstenedione's impact on the body" and any view of McGwire's potential record as tainted: "Some have even suggested, not entirely in jest, that if McGwire beats the record he should have an asterisk next to his name denoting that he did so under questionable circumstances. Our view is that this is an unproductive line of argument, not so much because androstenedione is legal in baseball but because even the experts who believe the substance could build muscle strength also say there is no evidence that it improves the eye-hand coordination required of every successful hitter."

While that position may not have represented any kind of consensus with regard to the baseball industry, the media, and fans, it does stand as a milepost. In the coming years, nearly all interested parties would find themselves far removed from that position with regard to performance-enhancing drugs. Steroids, human growth hormone, and amphetamines would be banned, and players caught using—or simply alleged to have done so—would be branded as cheaters, publicly shamed by media, fans, and government officials, blamed for compromising the integrity of the game, for corrupting the nation's youth, and for threatening the moral fabric of America. "Steroids did to baseball what Watergate did to the presidency," wrote *Sports Illustrated*'s Tom Verducci on the occasion of Barry Bonds's passage of

Babe Ruth's career total of 714 home runs in 2006. Once-revered icons' legacies would be tarnished, their places in the pantheon denied. The entire era—the steroid era, to some—would be held under suspicion, its statistical record regarded as tainted.

The influx of steroids into baseball did not happen overnight. It took willful ignorance on the part of the powers that be—the owners, the Players Association, the commissioner—to avoid action on the issue as the interested parties immersed themselves in furthering decades-old animosities centered around player salaries. Without action to prevent their spread, competitive athletes searched for any edge they could get given their desire to win and to make their millions in an increasingly lucrative sport. All of this happened under the nose of a media that was largely complicit, and a fan base that fell in love with the era's chief by-product, the home run, all over again. It was a complete institutional failure for which all of the aforementioned parties bear some responsibility.

Baseball reveres its statistical records like no other sport. As we look back over the landscape of the past two decades, how should we regard this era? Can we detach ourselves from the moralizing and the propaganda long enough to sort out what happened, or must we dismiss as meaningless the accomplishments of those who were implicated as users? This chapter will attempt to piece together what we know, and how we can better understand the era's history.

A Brief History of Steroids

Steroids were not the only drugs that baseball eventually banned, but they remain at the center of the controversy surrounding performance-enhancing drugs, and they will be the focus of this inquiry. Before delving further into the effect they may have had upon baseball, it's worth revisiting some basic biology as well as some history as to how these supposedly nefarious substances came to prominence.

In the human body, steroids generally function as hormones: chemicals released by a cell or a gland in one part of the body that signal cells in another part of the body to act. There are five main classes of steroid hormones, all of which are derivatives of the steroid cholesterol, which is also an essential structural component of cell membranes. Androgens and estrogens, produced in the gonads and the adrenal cortex, are the primary sex hormones, which regulate sexual differentiation and secondary sex characteristics; androgens such as testosterone and androsterone produce masculinizing effects (facial hair growth, deepening of the voice, heavier bone structure and muscle mass than in females, and so forth), while estrogens produce feminizing effects (enlarged breasts, widened hips, smaller features than males, and so on). Both androgens and estrogens are present in the bodies of each gender, but at different levels. Progestins are another class of sex hormone produced by females in the ovaries; they mediate the menstrual cycle and maintain pregnancy. Mineralocorticoids and glucocorticoids, which are produced in the adrenal cortex, are corticosteroids that help to regulate metabolism, immune function, renal function, inflammatory reactions, and the capacity to cope with stress.

Anabolic steroids, more accurately called anabolic-androgenic steroids (AAS), are synthetic derivatives of testosterone that can mimic its function in the body. Delivered via a variety of means—injections, pills, creams, sprays, patches—they interact with the androgen receptors found in muscle cells, stimulating those cells to increase protein synthesis (anabolism), which results in the building of muscles and bones as well as the maintenance of secondary sexual characteristics. The binding of the steroid to the receptor also inhibits the breakdown (catabolism) of old proteins; it is believed that this happens because androgens interfere with glucocorticoid functioning, shifting the balance of muscle protein turnover in favor of protein accrual, resulting in additional muscle mass.

Testosterone was first isolated in 1935, four years after a less potent gonadal steroid called androstenone (not to be confused with androstenedione) was isolated. Three research teams, subsidized by competing pharmaceutical companies, raced to do so and publish their results, and soon after it was isolated, it became the first hormone ever synthesized. By 1937, scientists were conducting clinical trials, using synthetic testosterone as a replacement therapy to treat hypogonadism, allowing men to develop fully and maintain secondary sexual characteristics. They also used testosterone to address a variety of problems in women, including estrogen-driven breast cancers, on the grounds that testosterone neutralized estrogen; by altering the hormonal balance, they could cause the metastatic breast tumors in certain women to regress. The ability of testosterone to counteract estrogen led to its being used as a treatment for male homosexuality—via court order or parental injunction, in some cases.

During the early 1940s, scientists discovered that testosterone could enable the growth of muscle tissue. Speculation about the hormone's potential to affect athletic performance began almost immediately. Also in that decade, testosterone began to be used to treat traumatic injuries and burns as well as the wasting suffered by victims of Nazi concentration camps, a sad irony given that one of the three teams involved in the hormone's initial isolation was led by Nazi party member Adolf Butenandt.

By the late 1940s and early 1950s, West Coast bodybuilders were experimenting with testosterone. At the 1954 world weightlifting championships, US Team physician Dr. John B. Ziegler learned from his Soviet counterpart that the Soviet lifters were using testosterone. Upon his return to the states, Ziegler experimented with testosterone on himself and some competitive bodybuilders. Concerned with its androgenic side effects (aggressiveness, increased libido, facial hair, deepened voice, enlarged prostate), he manipulated the molecular structure of testosterone to decrease those effects, thus developing an anabolic steroid called methandrostenolone (trade name Dianabol), which he began using in his experiments. After several of its users won championships, word of mouth spread the use of the drug to other strength-based sports, including track and field and football.

In 1963, strength coach Alvin Roy served unwitting San Diego Chargers players Dianabol at breakfast every day, helping to turn what had been a 4–10 team the previous year into American Football League champions. In the 1970s and 1980s, the East German government secretly mandated that its elite athletes—as many as 10,000—be administered doping regimens using Oral Turinabol, some of them as young as 10 years old; the drugs were presented as vitamins. Although the athletes won Olympic medals and so forth, the consequences were horrific, leading to health and psychological problems as well as infertility, and even pushing masculinized female athletes down the road to gender reassignment surgery.

Since the introduction of Dianabol, the ongoing challenge for drug manufacturers—legitimate pharmaceutical companies with medical applications for their drugs as well as illicit underground labs—has been to balance the anabolic effects (those that build muscle and tissue) with the androgenic ones (the "side effects"). The ratio of anabolic to androgenic effects is called the therapeutic index, with testosterone serving as the reference point, with the value of 1. Dianabol's therapeutic index is in the 2–7 range. Deca-Durabolin (nandrolone decanoate), one of the steroids that Barry Bonds, Roger Clemens, and others are alleged to have used, is in the 11–12 range. Winstrol (stanzolol), for which both Rafael Palmeiro and sprinter Ben Johnson tested positive, and which both Bonds and Clemens are also alleged to have used, is in the 5–20 range.

In 1969, Bill Gilbert of *Sports Illustrated* devoted a three-part series to the growing presence of drugs in sports—amphetamines, barbiturates, painkillers, and anabolic steroids among them. In the third article of the series, he noted that not a single major US sporting organization, either amateur or professional, had anti-doping regulations or means of enforcement. He quoted National League president Warren Giles as saying, "Nothing has ever come to my attention that would require a special ruling. It never has come up, and I don't think it ever will."

The issue of performance-enhancing drugs bubbled just under the surface for the next three decades, not coming to a full boil until the beginning of the next millennium. In October 2000, the *New York Times* published a special report by James C. McKinley Jr., in which he wrote, "No one knows for certain how many professional ballplayers are using testosterone-based drugs, but there is a growing suspicion among many people in baseball that the national pastime has become tainted with steroid abuse . . . suspicions abound, especially in recent years, as more and more players have put on muscle during off-season training and hitters have begun slugging home runs at a record pace." Strength coaches and former and current players offered estimates of 30 to 40 percent of players using steroids, not only to add muscle mass to but to recover from injuries more quickly.

McKinley's report highlighted the clash between Major League Baseball (MLB) and the Players Association as to the effect of steroids on the game. Said Rob Manfred, baseball's top labor relations official, "We are clearly interested in getting some sort of steroid testing program in place . . . We would rather have it for steroids and performance-enhancing drugs. At the end of the day, the guy who's smoking marijuana at home has less impact on the integrity of the game." Countered Gene Orza, the number-two official in the union, "The players reserve the right to distinguish between the random testing of baseball players for drugs that are not performance enhancing and those that are performance enhancing. The question of whether they are performance enhancing is debatable." McKinley reported that the union wanted a scientific study to determine whether steroids actually improved baseball performance.

No such study materialized. In 2001, Bud Selig, commissioner of MLB, unilaterally implemented random testing in the minor leagues, taking advantage of the fact that those players were not protected under the Collective Bargaining Agreement. At the major league level, 36-year-old Barry Bonds, noticeably bulkier than the player who had combined tremendous power with electrifying speed and won three

MVP awards in four years during his twenties, surpassed McGwire's single-season home run record by hitting 73 home runs, 24 more than in any other season of his career. Even as he closed in on McGwire's total, the connection between his showing and steroids was rarely made; though he noted Bonds's "barrel-chested and thick-necked" physique, *Sports Illustrated*'s Tom Verducci made no mention of steroids in his October 8, 2001, article about the chase.

On the other hand, an April 2002 *New York Times* article by Murray Chass noted Bonds's conditioning regimen, compact swing, maple bat—a relatively new innovation in the annals—and the generalized discussion that steroids could have something to do with the rise in home runs:

> When Bonds was zeroing in on McGwire's record last season, two major league officials expressed concern about the possible use of steroids to build greater muscle mass, which in turn could produce more home runs.
>
> The officials, speaking on condition of anonymity, did not single out any player, but one said: "Look at all these guys. Look at their arms, their upper bodies, their thighs. All of a sudden they're huge. They talk about players being bigger and stronger. Where are they getting bigger and stronger? Not in a gym. You can't do it in the gym."
>
> But the Giants' trainer, Stan Conte, said: "They all take vitamin supplements; Barry does that, uses protein drinks, over-the-counter, G.N.C.-type stuff. He uses a personal trainer who provides him with that stuff. He could come to us, but he uses a trainer. Ultimately, it's impossible to know about anyone. You're not with someone 24 hours a day. No athlete is ever going to admit doing anything. From an organizational standpoint, there's no way to accuse anyone."

Thanks to pitchers' fear of his surgically precise swing, Bonds would never again hit more than 46 home runs; instead they would walk him an absurd number of times, both intentionally and unintentionally, such that he would own the top three single-season records in both categories, with totals that stood as even greater outliers than his home run mark.

Bonds would become the new face of baseball's battle against steroids, beginning with a 2003 investigation into the Bay Area Laboratory Co-Operative in which the aforementioned personal trainer, Greg Anderson, was indicted by a federal grand jury. Testifying before the grand jury in December 2003, Bonds admitted to using two substances, "the clear" and "the cream," that contained previously undetectable steroids; he claimed that Anderson had told them they were flaxseed oil (a nutritional supplement) and a balm for arthritis. Several other players, including Jason Giambi, Jeremy Giambi, and Gary Sheffield, were also called to testify, as were athletes from other sports.

Where the McGwire-Wilstein incident had begun turning the baseball media and fans on to the idea that steroids might be affecting the legitimacy of on-field results, the BALCO scandal, which would drag on beyond the end of the decade as Bonds was indicted for perjury and obstruction of justice, turned the public tide against the alleged users and cast suspicion on their accomplishments to a much greater extent. "Is Baseball in the Asterisk Era?" asked Verducci in a March 15, 2004, feature in *Sports Illustrated*. So greatly was the tide turned, in fact, that it became clear that a desire to see users identified, punished, and publicly shamed trumped legal principles such as due process and the right to privacy, even among the media. After all, the grand jury testimony detailing the case and the allegations against Bonds had been illegally leaked, and some of the evidence presented by investigators—including the supposedly anonymous results of MLB's 2003 survey testing—had been obtained illegally.

The ongoing BALCO case would overshadow Bonds's climb up the all-time home run list. His passage of the career home run records of Babe Ruth (2006) and Hank Aaron (2007) turned into a joyless affair. Of the former, Verducci would write:

> Steroids did to baseball what Watergate did to the presidency. They ended what had been an organic trust in the institution, and there is no going back. Bonds is H.R. Haldeman, the guy who bragged, "Every president needs an s.o.b., and I'm Nixon's." Bonds has lasted longer and slugged more prodigiously than any of his notorious Steroid Era contemporaries. Mc-Gwire, Sosa, Palmeiro, Canseco . . . all of them long gone since the March 17, 2005, congressional hearings on steroid use in the national pastime. . . .
>
> So it is left to Bonds, however chemically enhanced he may be, to remind us of what has been breached, which he did last weekend in Philadelphia. His pursuit of Ruth and Aaron is a recalibration of statistical values done in real time, not the revisionism of the hocus-pocus seasons of 1998 and 2001. That process is, as evidenced last weekend, difficult and ugly and profane. And maybe that's because it is more about us than it is about Bonds. He only hits the home runs. We must decide what to make of them.

Before Bonds could get to those marks, baseball finally toughened up its drug policy, though it took a push from the federal government.

In early June 2002, *Sports Illustrated* ran a Verducci cover story in which 1996 National League MVP Ken Caminiti not only admitted to his own usage but contributed a graphic account of the drug's side effects: "It took four months to get my nuts to drop on their own," he said of the period after he stopped taking the drugs, and estimated that 50 percent of major league players were using. In the same article, Jose Canseco estimated that 85 percent of major leaguers were using. Within three weeks, the Senate Commerce Committee—the committee with the legislative jurisdiction to oversee US professional and amateur sports—called the Players Association to the carpet. In a two-hour subcommittee hearing, Senators Byron Dorgan and John McCain pressured union executive director Don Fehr to come to an agreement that would institute a mandatory testing program. Weeks later, in the negotiations for the collective bargaining agreement, the players agreed to anonymous survey testing the following spring. If more than five percent of players on teams' 40-man rosters tested positive in 2003 or 2004, players would be randomly tested, though no punitive action would be taken.

Sure enough, in November 2003, MLB announced that more than five percent of players tested positive, 96 of them for substances that were banned by MLB at that point, and 104 in all. Selig took the relatively small number of positives as evidence "that there is not widespread steroid use in baseball." Orza agreed, saying, "Plainly, many of the widely publicized claims regarding steroid use in the sport turn out to have been grossly uninformed, as do the suggestions that the agreement with the clubs was designed to avoid a penalty-based testing regimen."

The ensuing program called for players to be tested twice during the 2004 season without prior notice. A player testing positive would be placed on the "clinical track" to be treated for steroid usage. If he failed another test, was convicted or plead guilty to the sale and/or use of a prohibited substance, he would be moved to the "administrative track" and subject to discipline; only then would he be identified publicly. With the BALCO story having broken in the ensuing months, the Senate Commerce Committee was not satisfied that the policy went far enough; at a hearing in which Selig and Fehr testified, McCain warned, "We will have to act in some way unless the MLB players association acts in an affirmative and rapid fashion. The integrity of the sport and the American people demand a certain level of adherence to standards that frankly are not being met."

Given that the program produced no announcement of positive

tests in 2004—and thus no public shaming—McCain and company had a point, though it would not be until January 2005 that the league and the union would agree to a new policy that included random testing, offseason testing, and unpaid suspensions of 10, 30, and 60 days for first, second, and third offenses, and a one-year ban for the fourth. Players testing positive would be publicly identified for even one positive test.

In February, Canseco's salacious tell-all memoir, *Juiced*, rocked the sport; in the book, Canseco claimed to have helped inject teammates McGwire, Jason Giambi, Juan Gonzalez, Rafael Palmeiro, and Ivan Rodriguez with steroids. When baseball officials refused to investigate the allegations, Congress's interest was again piqued. On March 17, 2005, the House Government Reform Committee held 11 hours' worth of hearings in which Canseco, McGwire, Sammy Sosa, Palmeiro, Curt Schilling, and Frank Thomas were questioned, as were Selig, Fehr, Sandy Alderson, and Padres general manager Kevin Towers. Sosa, Thomas, and Palmeiro testified under oath that they had never used performance-enhancing drugs, the latter punctuating his statement with an indignant wag of his finger. Fearful of further prosecution for any admission, a tearful McGwire stated, "I'm not here to talk about the past. I'm here to be positive and talk about the present and the future." Congressman Henry Waxman urged Selig and Fehr to strengthen their program "or we'll do it for you. And you don't want that."

That season, 12 major leaguers, mostly lesser-known players, received 10-day suspensions. Palmeiro was the exception; to baseball's great embarrassment, he tested positive just weeks after surpassing the 3,000-hit milestone. Blaming the positive on a vitamin B-12 shot he received from teammate Miguel Tejada, he was soon hounded from the game. After returning from his suspension, he was booed so intensely that he wore earplugs to the plate, and left the team after collecting just two hits over a 16-day period. Congress opted not to pursue perjury charges against him.

In November 2005, baseball unveiled a new policy with increased penalties of 50- and 100-game suspensions for first and second timers, and a lifetime banishment for a third offense. The policy also banned amphetamines for the first time. The following March, with *Game of Shadows* on bestseller lists, Selig appointed former Senate majority leader George Mitchell to head an independent investigation into the game's steroid usage. Finally unveiled in December 2007, the 409-page report outlined the game's history of performance-enhancing drug use and the steps that were (and weren't) taken to curb it. Though far from comprehensive, it implicated 89 former and current players, including not only the BALCO bunch but also stars such as Roger Clemens and Andy Pettitte—yes, pitchers—as well as scrubs, the majority of whom were identified as clients of former Mets clubhouse employee Kirk Radomski.

At the major league level, the number of suspensions tailed off in the years following the Mitchell Report. From 12 suspensions in 2005, three in 2006, and seven in 2007 (including three for amphetamines), just one player was suspended in 2008, two apiece in 2009 and 2010, and one in 2011. The 2009 suspension of slugger Manny Ramirez, who had ranked among the game's elite hitters for over a decade, revealed the growing sophistication of baseball's drug program, as Ramirez didn't test positive for a steroid but was found to have an elevated testosterone level. This gave MLB license to examine his medical records, whereupon they found documented proof that he was taking human chorionic gonadotropin, a women's fertility drug often used to restart natural testosterone production following a steroid cycle.

Ramirez would soon number among the players implicated as users via another route. The identities of the 104 players who tested positive during the 2003 survey tests were supposed to remain anonymous, but the key to match up players to test results was never destroyed. Overzealous federal agents seized the information during the BALCO investigation, and while it was supposed to be kept under seal, the identities of several players who tested positive were leaked to the media. Ramirez, Sosa, David Ortiz, and Alex Rodriguez were all implicated in this manner, and while Rodriguez confessed, the incidents underscored the extralegal extent to which government officials were willing to go to reveal the identities of users. Both Bonds and Clemens would be indicted and tried not on charges that they used steroids, but that they committed perjury when they lied under oath about not using. At this writing, Bonds has been convicted of one count of obstruction of justice, but the jury deadlocked on three charges of making false statements, and those charges were ultimately dismissed. Clemens's first trial ended in a mistrial when on the second day of testimony, the prosecution presented barred evidence to the jury; he will be tried again.

The Effects of Steroids and How They Might Relate to Baseball

Since the 1960s, researchers have attempted to investigate the effects of anabolic steroids in athletes, but their studies have been fraught with pitfalls, with many of them producing contradictory findings.

Most notably, many of the studies failed to blind, randomize, or control for nutrition or exercise, thereby introducing any number of ways of skewing the results. One common problem was the inclusion of competitive athletes more geared toward winning than compliance with standardized regimens of dosage, diet, and exercise for clinical purposes. Another was inadequate dosages; most studies have used amounts of testosterone equivalent to or less than the replacement dose used to treat hypogonadism, much less than the amounts used by athletes, sometimes by an order of magnitude. The bottom line is that it's very difficult to design a scientific study that approximates the steroid habits of athletes, and that's without considering the confounding factors of using multiple drugs ("stacking"), a common practice among athletes.

A 2004 paper by two Dutch doctors in *Sports Med* illustrates the bewildering and often conflicting results produced by the studies. Authors Fred Hartgens and Hart Kuipers cite 24 studies—most dating between the mid-1960s and the early 2000s—on the effect of strength training with anabolic-androgenic steroids that produced an increase in body weight, but another eight that found no effect on body weight. They found 15 studies that observed increases in muscle circumference, but another seven that found no increase. For increases in lean body mass, the split was 12 to 5; for increases in strength, the split was 21 to 8. From a chronological standpoint, the more recent studies tended to find effects relating to increased strength and muscle growth with far more consistency, likely because the scientists learned from the mistakes of their predecessors, but what a mess! In the absence of straight answers from the scientific community, it's hardly a wonder that baseball dragged its feet in battling the problem.

Summarizing the literature in search of consensus, Hartgens and Kuipers found that for strength athletes, both short- and long-term steroid use will increase lean body mass (i.e., everything but fat), while fat mass is not altered. In the upper body, type II (fast-twitch, those used for short bursts of power) muscle fibers are more affected by short-term steroid use—a finding that may have some relevance with regard to improved reaction times—though type I (slow-twitch, those used for long durations) are more affected by persistent long-term use. The effects on lean body mass are dose dependent, meaning that they change with the amount taken, though it is unclear which drug regimens lead to the most pronounced results. At therapeutic (i.e., lower) levels for short-term regimens, the effects on strength don't appear to be measurable, although body changes are observable.

After drug withdrawal, the effects fade away but may persist for longer than 6–12 weeks. "However, we should emphasize again that laboratory studies may not adequately mimic the actual AAS-induced improvements of strength since the drugs and doses investigated in most studies are not in agreement with current steroid administration regimens by AAS abusers." As to the effects of improved recovery times from strenuous exercise due to AAS use—a common topic of public discussion, particularly as it pertains to baseball—the research "is too limited to draw definite conclusions yet." Nowhere in their work did the authors cite any studies pertaining to the effect of AAS on eyesight, another common topic.

In their survey, the authors found no shortage of potentially undesirable physical side effects linked to steroid use, including testicular atrophy, infertility, breast enlargement, acne, increased cardiovascular risk, and liver diseases and disturbances. Furthermore, they also found profound effects on mental state and behavior, including mood disturbances and increased aggression and hostility, though they noted that such problems tend to become serious in only a small number of users. Case reports also revealed other dramatic side effects, including tendon pathology, alterations of the prostate and bladder, and renal carcinoma: "Although a large number of reports associated AAS abuse in healthy young athletes with the occurrence of a broad spectrum of (sometimes dramatic) side effects, this may not always reflect a causal relationship with AAS and, therefore, such reports must be interpreted with caution."

It's nearly impossible to find any clinical studies that pertain directly to the impact of steroids on baseball performance, but the topic does pop up tangentially from time to time. In a 2002 review for *Recent Progress in Hormone Research* ("Anabolic Steroids"), Dr. Cynthia M. Kuhn noted that the androstenedione supplements Mark McGwire had taken were not a particularly efficient delivery mechanism. The first scientific study of the anabolic efficacy of andro did not appear until 1999, and the studies done since then showed that subjects who received andro did not show greater increases in strength than those who received a placebo. As a 2002 review of research put it, "Since, at most, 10–15% of a dose is converted to testosterone, it is unlikely that regimens used by athletes will prove anabolic but the research has not been conducted. No published studies report effective anabolic activity of suprapharmacologic doses of androstenedione."

One study that crops up frequently throughout the literature on steroids and strength is a 1996 study ("The Effects of Supraphysiologic Doses of Testosterone on Muscle Size and Strength in Normal Men") published in the *New England Journal of Medicine* by Dr. Shalender Bhasin and his co-workers. Noting the aforementioned pitfalls of steroid studies, they created a carefully designed, controlled double-blind experiment involving 43 adult male weightlifters. Double-blind experiments are those in which neither the subjects nor the researchers know if a given individual is in the control group or experimental group, which lessens the effect of the various biases that can affect the results; they are considered the gold standard of clinical research studies. The lifters, who were between the ages of 19 and 40, and within 15 percent of their ideal body weight, were randomly divided into four groups: placebo with no exercise, testosterone with no exercise, placebo with exercise, and testosterone with exercise.

The testosterone group was given 600 milligrams a week of testosterone enanthate—a dosage more comparable to that used by athletes and six times that used in replacement therapy—for 10 weeks. Nutrition and exercise regimens were subject to the experiment's control. Over the course of the program, the testosterone-with-exercise group's muscle mass increased by 9.3 percent, their maximum bench press increased by 23 percent, and their maximum squat by 37 percent. The placebo-with-exercise group saw their muscle mass increase by 2.7 percent and their maximum lifts and squats increase by 9 and 20 percent, respectively. Meanwhile, the testosterone-with-no-exercise group reported larger gains in muscle mass than the placebo with exercise group. Their maximum bench press increased by 9 percent and their maximum squat by 13 percent.

Additionally, no differences were found between the groups with regard to anger (as assessed by the Multidimensional Anger Inventory). No significant changes in mood or behavior (as assessed by the Mood Inventory) were reported by the men or their spouses, live-in partners, or parents. The authors did include a caveat: "Our results, however, do not preclude the possibility that still higher doses of multiple steroids may provoke angry behavior in men with preexisting psychiatric or behavioral problems."

Back onto the Field and over the Wall

Bhasin's results sparked a foray into the physics of home run hitting via a 2008 paper for the *American Journal of Physics* by Roger G. Tobin ("On the potential of a chemical bonds: Possible effects of steroids on home run production in baseball"). Drawing from the well-established principle that the maximum force a muscle can exert is proportional to its cross-sectional area, Tobin estimated that a 10 percent increase in an athlete's muscle mass—a plausible gain from steroids given the findings of Bhasin—would correspond with a 10 percent increase in the force exerted by those muscles. That in turn would correspond to a 10 percent increase in the kinetic energy of the bat, assuming a batter's swing and technique remained the same, and a 5 percent increase in bat speed upon contact with a pitched ball.

From there, Tobin drew from physicist Alan Nathan's model of the collision between the ball and the sweet spot of the bat; accounting for the additional energy needed to move the player's additional mass, that would correspond to a 3 percent increase in batted ball speed of the ball leaving the bat. Using two different models of post-contact trajectory that involved different drag coefficients, normal (Gaussian) distributions of angles and ball speeds, and the assumption that any ball at least nine feet off the ground at a distance of 380 feet from home plate is a home run, Tobin concluded that the 3 percent increase would result in a 30 to 70 percent increase in home runs per batted ball (at-bats minus strikeouts).

Those numbers are worthy of a double take, but consider that home runs are fly balls at the far right edge of a distribution curve. If the center of the distribution shifts to the right slightly, so does the tail, and a significantly larger fraction of fly balls will become home runs. As Tobin put it, "This disproportionate effect arises because home runs are relatively rare events that occur on the tail of the range distribution of batted balls. Because the distribution's tail is particularly sensitive to small changes in the peak and or width, home run records can be more strongly affected by steroid use than other athletic accomplishments."

For a 30-homer power hitter, that 30 to 70 percent increase corresponds to a jump somewhere between 39 and 51. More colloquially, that's 30-homer sluggers becoming 40- or 50-homer sluggers thanks to a very small change, one that could plausibly have come from the documented strength gains produced by steroids.

Using that 3 percent increase in batted ball speed, Nathan himself arrived at a similar range of increases in home runs via a different route, drawing upon 2007 data on actual home run distances supplied by Greg Rybarczyk of Hit Tracker, which collects data on every dinger. By inspecting the distance of the landing point from the nearest fence, Nathan estimated that each additional foot of fly ball distance increases the probability of a home run by 4 percent. Combining that with an aerodynamics rule of thumb that each additional mile per hour of batted ball speed increases the fly ball distance by 5.5 feet, he estimated that a 3 percent increase in batted ball speed could result in a 66 percent increase in home run probability. Nathan also cited the work of Robert Adair, who in *The Physics of Baseball* estimated that each additional percent increase in fly ball distance increases the probability of a home run by 7 percent: "Using 380 ft as the baseline home run distance, a 3 mph increase in batted ball speed leads to a 4.3% increase in batted ball distance and therefore a 30% increase in home run probability." This is in the same ballpark as Tobin.

Tobin and Nathan were addressing the gains that might be possible in individual sluggers via steroids. The rub is that the range of increase in home runs per batted ball that they project as resulting from a 10 percent gain in muscle mass is on the order of *what actually occurred throughout the entire majors from 1993 onward*, steroids or no. Consider that from 1988 to 1992, a very stable period of time for home run hitting, 2.7 percent of batted balls were home runs. In 1993, that number jumped to 3.1 percent, and then to 3.6 percent (36 percent above that five-year baseline) the following year. It peaked at 4.2 percent (56 percent above the baseline) in 2000, and even in 2010 it was at 3.52 percent (31 percent above the baseline); in 2011, it fell to 3.47 percent, 29 percent above the baseline. In every year between 1994 and 2010, the rate of homers per batted ball ranged from 31 to 56 percent above that five-year baseline, a range that fits neatly in the estimates of steroid-related gain provided by Tobin and Nathan.

It's plausible that *some* of that increase could be attributed to steroids via the mechanism outlined above. Nathan has suggested that within a reasonable range (say, a 5 percent increase in mass, or 20 percent), the effect is linear, with respective increases ranging from 15 to 35 percent or 60 to 140 percent in terms of home runs per batted ball. Even with some individual players toward the higher end of those estimates contributing extra home runs to compensate for those whose outputs didn't increase, the suggestion that *all* of the increase came courtesy of steroids is a stretch, particularly if the rates of use were close to that of the survey test levels rather than the extreme Canseco-level estimate. So it's worth examining what other conditions may have contributed to the rise in home runs.

A Brief Word about Human Growth Hormone and Amphetamines

After steroid testing was introduced, much of the concern about MLB's ability to eradicate performance-enhancing drugs from the game centered around human growth hormone (HGH), a naturally occurring peptide hormone that stimulates cell growth, reproduction, and regeneration. Banned by baseball in January 2005—it had already been banned by the International Olympic Committee (IOC) and by the National College Athletic Association (NCAA)—HGH is legal only via prescription, but many players, including Bonds, Giambi, Clemens, and Pettitte are alleged to have used it, either alone or in conjunction with steroids. Exogenous HGH cannot be detected via the urinalysis protocol approved under the Collective Bargaining Agreement. A blood test to detect it was introduced in the minor leagues in July 2010; Mike Jacobs was the first player suspended due to a positive test.

While exogenous HGH has approved therapeutic uses, very little work (if any) has been done in the way of clinical testing related to athletic performance, and what experimental work has been done suggests that it does not increase muscle strength. It has been theorized that HGH can help athletes recover faster from injuries, and certain segments of the medical community have promoted it as an anti-aging agent, but its efficacy in both areas is far from proven. In the absence of any mechanism via which we can apply some quantifiable link to performance, we have confined our focus in this chapter to the possible effects of steroids.

Long banned by the IOC and the NCAA, amphetamines were added to baseball's list of banned substances in 2006. They are central nervous stimulants that became popular during World War II, when they were used to increase alertness and delay the onset of fatigue among soldiers. Soon afterward, they were introduced to baseball, where "greenies" (as they were commonly called) were used to help players withstand the long grind of the season—cross-country flights, day games after night games, weeks without a day off. Jim Bouton made several references to them in his landmark 1970 book, *Ball Four*, and stars such as Ted Williams, Mickey Mantle, Hank Aaron, and Willie Mays are alleged to have used them at some point during their careers. Prior to being banned, players' estimates of use ranged as high as 80 percent. "Players use amphetamines to be the player they can't be when they're tired," explained one anonymous veteran player around the time of the ban. Nonetheless, in the absence of any mechanism by which we can apply a quantifiable link to performance, we have confined our focus to steroids.

A Brief Word about Pitchers
To date, 13 of the 23 major league players suspended for the use of steroids or HGH have been pitchers, as have 46 of the 129 players im-

plicated via all means through the end of the 2011 season—not only through testing but also BALCO, the Mitchell Report, the leaked 2003 survey test results, Canseco's book, self-admission, or myriad other routes (Chuck Finley's divorce trial, the seizure of Manny Alexander's car, and so on). Perhaps because they were not setting records in the manner of McGwire, Sosa, and Bonds, much less attention has been paid to the effects that steroids may have had on their performance. Tobin's paper makes a brief foray into the topic: "By the same mechanical analysis, a 10% increase in muscle mass should increase the speed of a thrown ball by about 5%, or 4–5 mph for a pitcher with a 90 mph fastball." He cites "a significant correlation" between fastball speed and earned run average (ERA), with a 4–5 mph increase corresponding to a decrease in ERA of 0.50. That conclusion derives from Baseball Info Solutions data from the 2002–2005 postseasons—a limited enough data set to cause some concerns about sample size, not only with regard to the limited population of pitchers and post-season innings but also the extent to which ERA itself is a metric that can be clouded by fluctuations in defensive support.

The reduction in ERA, according to Tobin, is "enough to have a meaningful effect on the success of a pitcher, but it is not nearly as dramatic as the effects on home run production. The unusual sensitivity of home run production to bat speed results in much more dramatic effects, and focuses attention disproportionately on the hitters."

The widespread availability of PITCHf/x velocity data may make this topic worth revisiting in the future using a metric such as fielding independent pitching (FIP) that can better isolate the effects of pitcher skill. Without discounting the possibility that steroid usage may have benefited pitchers—perhaps the era's rising strikeout rate may owe something to that—we have confined our focus to hitters. It is worth noting, however, that the prospect of pitchers using steroids as well as hitters does subvert the claim that the latter were the only ones gaining unfair advantages. If a steroid-using pitcher faces a steroid-using hitter, where does the advantage lie? At this stage, the question is unanswerable.

Alternate Explanations
Historical Scoring and Home Run Rates
The parallel rises of scoring and home run rates over the course of the 1990s and 2000s are often taken as evidence of the effect steroids and other performance-enhancing drugs (PEDs) had on the game. How-

ever, it's a mistake to simply attribute all of that offense—and particularly the toppling of the long-standing home run records of Maris and Aaron—solely to the effects of players using PEDs. The game was in the midst of an era of rapid change, one that brought new franchises, new ballparks, geographical realignment, the wild card, interleague play, and new equipment into the sport over a span of two decades. To find a similar parallel for the rapidity of major changes, one has to go back to 1945–1962, a period that included the return of ballplayers serving in World War II, the breaking of the color barrier, the handful of franchise relocations that redrew the map of the major leagues, the fall of the Pacific Coast League as a rival for talent, and the first addition of new teams to the two leagues since 1901.

What is certain is that baseball from 1993—the year that the National League (NL) introduced expansion franchises in Denver and Miami—through 2010 produced scoring levels largely unseen since the 1920s and 1930s; not until 2011, when teams scored 4.28 runs per game, did they recede to a level that wouldn't have been out of place in the 1970s or 1980s. Scoring for the two leagues combined shot up 11.7 percent from 1992 to 1993, from 4.12 runs per team per game to 4.60. Only once since 1953 had scoring levels increased by such a large increment. That was in 1987, an isolated year whose characteristics bore some resemblance to the post-1993 era in more ways than one; the two leagues averaged 4.72 runs per game, increasing from 4.41 in 1986 and then falling to 4.14 in 1988. Scoring rates would creep even higher during the period, reaching 5.04 runs per game in 1996 and peaking at 5.14 in 2000, both levels last reached in 1936.

On a percentage basis, only a small handful of times since the end of the deadball era (from 1919 to 1920, and then from 1920 to 1921) had scoring increased as sharply from year to year as it did from 1992 to 1993. In 1969, expansion and rule changes in direct reaction to the "Year of the Pitcher" led to a 19.1 percent increase in scoring. In 1973, the introduction of the designated hitter in the American League (AL) coincided with a 14.3 percent rise in scoring. In 1977, another round of expansion and a change in ball manufacturers led to an 11.9 percent rise.

On a decade basis, neither the 1990s nor the 2000s could unseat the 1920s and 1930s as the highest-scoring decades. Decades are admittedly arbitrary constructs, but even if you were to shift the endpoints, the general pattern is the same; scoring during the 1993–2010 era rivaled but did not surpass the level seen from 1921 to 1940. But while

TABLE 1-1.1 Scoring by Decade

Decade	R/G
1901–1910	3.92
1911–1920	3.97
1921–1930	4.93
1931–1940	4.85
1941–1950	4.32
1951–1960	4.39
1961–1970	4.06
1971–1980	4.15
1981–1990	4.30
1991–2000	4.77
2001–2010	4.70

TABLE 1-1.2 Home Runs per Game by Decade

Decade	HR/G
1901–1910	0.134
1911–1920	0.176
1921–1930	0.439
1931–1940	0.546
1941–1950	0.544
1951–1960	0.845
1961–1970	0.824
1971–1980	0.731
1981–1990	0.816
1991–2000	0.997
2001–2010	1.056

the scoring level was not particularly unique in the annals, the rise in home runs was. Aside from the anomalous 1987 season, the strike-torn 1994 season marked the first time in the game's history that teams crossed the 1.0 home run per game threshold. The rate of homers would stay above 1.0 in every season through 2009, rising as high as 1.17 per game in 2000. (See Tables 1-1.1 and 1-1.2).

Of the 20 highest per-game home run rates in history, only three hailed from seasons prior to 1993, one of them an expansion season and one the 1987 anomaly. As you might expect given those high rates, the number of players per team reaching various home run plateaus in a given season rose dramatically. In 1999, a record 103 players hit at least 20 homers, an average of 3.43 per team; a year later, 102 would reach the level. The 2000 season featured the highest number of 30-homer players, 47 (1.57 per team), while the 1996 season featured the highest number of 40-homer players, 17 (0.61 per team). (See Tables 1-1.3 and 1-1.4.)

Both statistically and symbolically, home runs were the signature of the era. Despite high levels of offense, the game didn't suddenly produce a glut of .400 hitters, or even one; Tony Gwynn's .394 mark, the era's high, came in the strike-shortened 1994 season. Thirty-seven players hit .350 or higher between 1993 and 2010, an average of two per year; while just 24 had done so between 1961 and 1992, 174 did so between 1920 and 1960—roughly twice as many per year at a time when just 16 teams existed.

TABLE 1-1.3 Highest Single-Season Home Run Rates

Year	HR/G	Year	HR/G	Year	HR/G
2000	1.172	1987	1.059	2007	1.020
1999	1.138	2002	1.043	1995	1.012
2001	1.124	1998	1.041	2008	1.005
2004	1.123	2009	1.037	1961	0.955
2006	1.109	1994	1.033	2010	0.949
1996	1.094	2005	1.032	2011	0.937
2003	1.071	1997	1.024	1956	0.926

TABLE 1-1.4 Home Run Plateaus by Decade

Decade	20 HR	30 HR	40 HR
1901–1910	0.00	0.00	0.00
1911–1920	0.03	0.01	0.01
1921–1930	0.53	0.24	0.10
1931–1940	0.89	0.37	0.10
1941–1950	0.88	0.27	0.05
1951–1960	1.79	0.61	0.23
1961–1970	1.68	0.53	0.15
1971–1980	1.50	0.35	0.07
1981–1990	1.82	0.46	0.05
1991–2000	2.32	0.91	0.29
2001–2010	2.87	1.00	0.24

Expansion

From 1901 through 1960, the major leagues consisted of 16 teams, eight per league. Prior to the 1961 season, the AL added the Los Angeles Angels and the second Washington Senators franchise, with the NL adding the New York Mets and Houston Colt .45s the following year. Two more teams were added to each league for 1969 (the Montreal Expos, San Diego Padres, Kansas City Royals, and Seattle Pilots), bringing the total to 24. The Seattle Mariners and Toronto Blue Jays were added to the AL for 1977.

Having added 10 teams in a 17-season span, the majors rested, the size of the leagues remaining stable until the NL added the Colorado Rockies and Florida Marlins in 1993. Two more teams were added in 1998, one per league (the Arizona Diamondbacks and Tampa Bay

Devil Rays), with one team (the Milwaukee Brewers, née the Pilots) switching from AL to NL.

The successive waves of expansion have tended to trigger complaints regarding the lack of quality pitching to support more teams. Indeed, as pitching staffs have swelled due to specialization, each new expansion team has added another 10 or 12 pitchers who might otherwise be in Triple-A to the major league ranks. However, it's important to remember that the talent pool from which baseball draws has enlarged considerably over the years. In 1960, when the US census counted over 179 million people, just 9.6 percent of players on major league rosters were foreign born. By 2010, when the census count was above 308 million, 27.7 percent of players on opening day rosters were foreign born, down from the 2005 high of 29.2 percent but still about triple the rate a half-century earlier. The addition of Latin America to the talent pool—particularly Venezuela (29 million) and the Dominican Republic (nine million), which together combined to produce 17.3 percent of those 2010 Opening Day rosters—has easily compensated for expansion, to say nothing of the additions of Japan (128 million) and Canada (34 million) to the talent pool.

In terms of home run rates, expansion does appear to have had an effect in that home run rates have increased in all but one such season. In all, expansion years showed a 15.7 percent increase in home runs over the previous season, but a few caveats apply. The 1968–1969 data is skewed by the so-called Year of the Pitcher, which produced the majors' lowest scoring rate (3.42 runs per game) since 1908, and its lowest home run rate (0.61 per game) since 1946. Major rule changes were put into effect in 1969, including the lowering of the mound and the redefinition of the strike zone, and both scoring and home run rates rebounded significantly (see Table 1-1.5).

TABLE 1-1.5 Expansion's Effect on Home Runs

Years	Pre HR/G	Exp Yr HR/G	Pct Chg
1960–1961	0.86	0.96	10.9%
1961–1962	0.96	0.93	-3.0%
1968–1969	0.61	0.80	30.5%
1976–1977	0.58	0.87	50.3%
1992–1993	0.72	0.89	23.2%
1997–1998	1.02	1.04	1.7%
Average	**0.79**	**0.91**	**15.7%**

The 1977 expansion coincided with a shift in the supplier of baseballs. From 1878 through 1976, Spalding had been the exclusive manufacturer. Rawlings took over the following year. Though no change in the manufacturing process was announced, the power spike was undeniable. Homer rates jumped 53.4 percent in the expanded AL, and 46.5 percent in the NL, which contained the same twelve teams and ballparks as the year before. It's also worth noting that in the year prior to expansion, the two leagues' combined rate of homers per game had, for no apparent reason, dipped to 0.58—even lower than in 1968—after averaging 0.75 per game from 1969 through 1975. Home run rates fell back to 0.70 in 1978, and didn't top 1977 levels again until 1986, at 0.91 per game. The role of changing baseballs in this power explosion will be explored further below.

The 1993 expansion introduced major league baseball to high altitude in the form of the Rockies. Playing in the accurately named Mile High Stadium, they and their opponents combined to average 1.14 homers per team per game. In all other games, homers were hit at a rate of 0.88 per team per game. The Rockies and their opponents, playing in Coors Field since 1995, have continued to outpace the league's home run rate by a considerable margin.

It's tempting to credit expansion for at least some of the increase in home runs, but with the exception of the 1993 round, homers have receded to previous levels within a year or two after introducing the new teams, suggesting that any "expansion effect" is either the result of randomness or merely short-lived.

Ballparks

The Rockies' role in the 1993 surge raises the question of how much impact new ballparks made on this power surge. In June 1989, the Toronto Blue Jays moved out of Exhibition Stadium, the ballpark they had called home since their 1977 inception, and into the Skydome. Though it wasn't heralded as such at the time, the new ballpark was the advance guard of a building boom that would last more than 20 years, putting 20 of the 26 existing teams into new venues, while adding four new teams as well; at this writing, the expansion Florida Marlins are set to move into their new ballpark in 2012. Two temporary facilities came and went during this time as well, Mile High Stadium and Washington's RFK Stadium, the latter featuring the former Montreal Expos, the only team to relocate during this era.

Before MLB began testing for steroids, the unprecedented turnover in stadiums made for a convenient culprit to explain the rising home

TABLE 1-1.6 Changing Ballpark Dimensions

Section	1990	1995	2000	2005	2010	1990–2000	2000–2010	1990–2010
LF	329.4	331.4	330.7	331.5	331.4	+1.3	+0.7	+2.0
LCF	377.2	377.4	379.3	381.1	381.5	+2.1	+2.2	+4.3
CF	404.8	404.3	404.5	404.4	404.1	-0.3	-0.4	-0.7
RCF	376.5	376.3	379.2	381.5	381.3	+2.7	+2.1	+4.8
RF	327.7	328.6	328.5	328.9	328.8	+0.9	+0.3	+1.1
Height*	10.3	9.9	10.1	9.9	10.2	-0.2	+0.1	+0.1
Altitude**	374.5	528.5	527.2	512.4	511.6	+152.7	-15.6	+137.1
HR/G	0.79	1.01	1.17	1.03	0.95	+48.7%	-19.0%	+20.5%

* average measurement (in feet) of LF, CF, and RF points
** feet above sea level

run rates, in part because the move away from large, multipurpose stadiums toward more intimate single-purpose venues planted the "smaller ballparks" meme in the minds of the public and the media. For example, the Cleveland Indians moved out of Municipal Stadium (capacity 74,483) and into Jacobs Field (43,345), the Houston Astros moved from the Astrodome (54,816) to Minute Maid Park (40,950), the Philadelphia Phillies moved from Veterans Stadium (62,382) to Citizens Field (43,000), and the San Diego Padres moved from Qualcomm Stadium (67,544) to Petco Park (46,000).

Smaller though they may have been, the new parks were hardly bandboxes. In fact, the average fence distances at the five points common to all parks (left field, left center, center field, right center, and right field) generally increased during this time, if only by slight amounts, while home run rates increased much more sharply (see Table 1-1.6).

The left- and right-field foul poles moved back by about a foot from 1990 to 2000, even while home-run rates increased by nearly 49 percent to their all-time high. The slight decrease in center field was more than offset by the increases in left center and right center. Even when the dust settled and home run rates finally fell back below 1.0 per game in 2010, the fences were at least two feet farther at three out of five points, and more than a foot farther in the fourth.

Those figures do include Coors Field, which features some of the game's most distant fences in an attempt to offset its 5,197-foot altitude. The park measures 347 and 350 feet down the left- and right-field lines, 390 and 375 feet to the gaps, and 415 feet to center. None of

TABLE 1-1.7 Changing Ballpark Dimensions sans Coors

Section	1990–2000	2000–2010	1990–2010
LF	+0.7	+0.7	+1.4
LCF	+1.7	+2.3	+4.0
CF	-0.6	-0.4	-1.0
RCF	+2.8	+2.2	+5.0
RF	+0.1	+0.3	+0.4

those measurements lead the majors, but no other park has a center-field distance greater than 400 feet and foul pole distances of at least 340 feet. Take Coors out of the equation and the decade intervals still show the fences backing away from home plate; absent Coors Field, the fence distances still increased everywhere but center field, but just not by as large a magnitude. "Ballpark size" does not explain the change (see Table 1-1.7).

That doesn't mean that ballpark changes haven't had an impact. If we examine home run production (home runs per batted ball) since 1988, the year before the Skydome opened, we find that 23 of the 27 new or changed parks featured higher rates than their predecessors. Furthermore, when we compare the park home run factors of the new and changed parks to their predecessors (with 1.0 the norm), we find that the magnitude of those that increased is much greater than those that decreased, and that some of the largest increases date back to the period's earliest changes. Toronto's Exhibition Stadium had a park home run factor of 0.89 in 1988, while the Skydome was at 1.06 from 1989 through 2010, a 20 percent increase. The White Sox' Comiskey Park was at 0.76 from 1988 to 1990, while US Cellular has been at 1.11 since, a 46 percent rise. The Rockies' two parks, considered together, combined to be 25 percent above average over an 18-year period. Even a park where only the fences changed, Kansas City's Kauffman Field, rose from 0.68 from 1988 to 1994, to 0.95 since, a 39 percent rise. Meanwhile, no new or changed park decreased home run rates by more than 21 percent relative to its predecessor (see Table 1-1.8).

We can get a better sense of the cumulative impact of these parks by breaking the data down into five-year samples. From 1988 to 1992, the Skydome, US Cellular, and Baltimore's Camden Yards replaced older parks, while Seattle's Kingdome, Oakland's Coliseum, and St. Louis's Busch Stadium II saw fence adjustments. During that five-year period, home run rates were 11.8 percent higher for those new and

TABLE 1-1.8 The Ballpark Building Boom and Home Runs

Team	Type	Year Change	PHRF Before	PHRF After	Change	Years
White Sox	Park	1991	0.76	1.11	46%	21
Royals	Fences	1995	0.68	0.95	39%	17
Brewers	Park	2001	0.90	1.13	25%	11
Rockies	Exp	1993	n/a	1.25	25%	19
Astros	Park	2000	0.87	1.07	23%	12
Blue Jays	Park	1989	0.89	1.06	20%	23
Yankees	Park	2009	1.02	1.18	16%	3
A's	Fences	1991	0.84	0.96	14%	21
Indians	Park	1994	0.86	0.97	14%	18
Cubs	Unch.	n/a	n/a	1.12	12%	23
Phillies	Park	2004	1.03	1.13	10%	8
Rangers	Park	1994	1.02	1.10	8%	18
Diamondbacks	Exp	1998	n/a	1.07	7%	14
Reds	Park	2003	1.12	1.19	6%	9
Orioles	Park	1992	1.02	1.07	5%	20
Rays	Exp	1998	n/a	0.98	-2%	14
Dodgers	Unch.	n/a	n/a	0.96	-4%	23
Cardinals	Park	2006	0.94	0.89	-5%	6
Marlins	Exp	1993	n/a	0.95	-5%	19
Red Sox	Unch.	n/a	n/a	0.94	-6%	23
Nationals	Park	2005	0.96	0.89	-6%	7
Mets	Park	2009	0.99	0.93	-7%	3
Angels	Fences	1998	1.04	0.96	-8%	14
Mariners	Park	1999	1.05	0.95	-10%	13
Braves	Park	1997	1.09	0.97	-11%	15
Twins	Park	2010	0.95	0.84	-12%	2
Pirates	Park	2001	1.01	0.87	-14%	11
Tigers	Park	2000	1.14	0.97	-15%	12
Padres	Park	2004	1.02	0.86	-16%	8
Giants	Park	2000	1.09	0.87	-21%	12

changed parks than for the rest of the majors. From 1993 to 1997, when Florida, Colorado, Cleveland, Texas, and Atlanta got new parks, Kansas City renovated, and both the Giants and the Padres moved fences, the new and changed parks (including the 1988–1992 batch) produced home run rates 13.4 percent higher. The parks that arrived or changed after that have kept home run rates more or less at equilibrium, balancing increases and decreases; the 1998–2002 period saw the new and/or changed parks rise just 5.2 percent, while the 2003–2007 period saw them fall 2.2 percent. The shortened 2008–2010 period has seen them rise by just 0.1 percent. The 1998–2010 cumulative sample has risen by just 0.3 percent. It appears that most of the upward pressure on home run rates came via the parks that changed from 1988 to 1997, with rates stabilizing since.

It is important to note that the foregoing doesn't *prove* that the parks were responsible for the rise in rates. We can say that their arrivals and changes coincided with the rise and may have been a contributing factor even with the increased fence distances. Home run rates vary from park to park for more reasons than just fence distances; in the short term, personnel can distort the numbers, which is why multiple years of data are always preferable. Beyond that, fence heights are a factor (though they didn't change much over the years), as are wind patterns (a product of both geography and architecture), weather and climate (scoring and home run levels rise with the temperature, and the average surface temperature in the US increased at a rate of 0.56 degrees per decade from 1979 to 2005 according to the Environmental Protection Agency), and altitude (note that besides Coors Field, expansion brought Arizona's Chase Field, at 1,086 feet, the majors' second-highest park). A comprehensive analysis of all these individual factors is beyond the scope of this book, but taken as a whole, the data support the view that the first waves of new and changed parks contributed more substantially to the rise in home runs than later changes and revisions.

Interleague Play

In 1997, for the first time in major league history, teams from the two leagues began playing each other in season, much to the horror of purists. While intrastate "natural rivalries" (Yankees/Mets, Cubs/White Sox, Dodgers/Angels, Giants/A's, etc.) drew a great deal of the initial interest, over time, the allure of the games has worn off due to the lack of spark produced by pairings like the Pirates and Indians or the Mariners and Nationals.

Interleague play, which has constituted 10.2 percent of the overall major league schedule since 1997, hasn't had a drastic effect on either scoring or home runs. Interleague games averaged 4.75 runs per game from 1997 through 2010, while intraleague games averaged 4.76. Interleague games during that span did produce a slightly higher home run rate, 1.08 per game to 1.06, a difference of 2.1 percent. While that may seem noteworthy, the small footprint of those games means an increase of just 10.4 homers per year; we can attribute just a 0.2 percent rise to the impact of interleague play, an exceedingly minor effect that may be a random artifact of smaller sample size.

The Strike Zone

Over the years, MLB has tinkered with the strike zone as a means of maintaining the delicate balance between pitchers and hitters. That tinkering has taken place with increasing frequency since expansion began.

As of 1887, a strike was defined by the rule book as a pitch that passed over home plate "not lower than the batsman's knee, nor higher than his shoulders." Additional definitions of strikes caused by foul balls and foul tips were added within the next few years, but that basic definition remained in place until 1950, when it became the space over home plate "between the batter's armpits and the top of his knees when he assumes his natural stance."

In 1963, the zone was expanded to include the top of the shoulders, but after several lean years of scoring climaxing in 1968, it reverted to the previous definition (the space between the armpits and the top of the knees) for 1969. However, from this point to the start of the power boom, the zone got progressively smaller in practice. "Today's strike zone basically runs vertically from the belt buckle to the bottom of the knees and horizontally maybe a shade or two outside of the plate," wrote Peter Gammons in *Sports Illustrated*'s 1987 baseball preview.

That 1987 season featured home run and scoring rates more in line with the post-1993 era than with its own surrounding seasons. Homers rose above 1.0 per team per game for the first time in history, from 0.91 in 1986 to 1.06 in 1987, an increase of 16.8 percent. In part due to that barrage, the zone was redefined in 1988 as "that area over home plate the upper limit of which is a horizontal line at the mid-point between the top of the shoulders and the top of the uniform pants, and the lower level is a line at the top of the knees."

In 1996, well into the boom years, the lower end of the zone was moved to the bottom of the knees, but the fireworks continued. In 2001, Major League Baseball decided that the umpires were taking too much liberty with their individual interpretations of the strike zone, which generally remained shorter and wider than the rule book definition. As a means of enforcing a more rigid interpretation of the rule book, MLB introduced the QuesTec Umpire Information System, a network of computers and cameras used to evaluate each umpire's pitch-calling accuracy. Umpires and pitchers complained vehemently;

hurler Curt Schilling infamously smashed a QuesTec camera in 2003. The system, which was installed in only about one-third of major league parks, was replaced in 2009 by the Zone Evaluation system in all 30 parks. Made by Sportvision, the same company that created PITCHf/x, the system increased the ability of MLB to monitor umpires, though the official definition of the strike zone remained unchanged.

Of the five post-expansion strike zone redefinitions, three explicitly increased the size of the zone, which is to say they were designed to decrease scoring, while one decreased the size of the zone to increase scoring. As for the fifth change, which was designed to enforce what was already on the books, one would assume that the exchange of tough pitches on the outside corners of the plate for more hittable ones over it would favor hitters. The volume of squawking from pitchers over being squeezed certainly made it seem that way, but the changes were instituted when both scoring and home run rates were at their recent peaks (5.14 runs and 1.17 homers per game, respectively). Even in an era where the powers that be were glorifying the longball, it's difficult to imagine them wanting to push those rates even higher.

If that assumption is true, then it appears as though all but one of the changes, the 1996 one, had their desired effect, at least in terms of direction, if not magnitude. In all, the years in which the strike zone has changed have cumulatively combined to decrease both scoring and home runs. Nonetheless, the two changes during the post-1993 era include one opposite effect and one in which the intent was ambiguous, making it difficult to credit the changed strike zone with any direct effect on home run rate (see Table 1.1-9).

TABLE 1-1.9 Effect of Strike Zone Changes

Year	R/G	HR/G	Year	R/G	HR/G	Zone	Scoring Change	HR Change
1962	4.46	0.93	1963	3.95	0.84	Increase	-11.5%	-9.8%
1968	3.42	0.61	1969	4.07	0.80	Decrease	+19.1%	+30.6%
1987	4.72	1.06	1988	4.14	0.76	Increase	-12.4%	-28.5%
1995	4.85	1.01	1996	5.04	1.09	Increase	+3.9%	+8.2%
2000	5.14	1.17	2001	4.78	1.12	Enforce	-7.1%	-4.1%
AVG	4.59	0.98		4.44	0.94		-3.3%	-4.5%

Juiced Balls

We come to the next major possibility and the one most shrouded in secrecy, the baseball itself. Perhaps more than any other culprit, "juiced" baseballs could explain the rise in home runs. Unfortunately, much of the evidence for changes in the ball is indirect, accompanied by a generous helping of anecdotes, and cloaked in perennial denials from manufacturers and other officials.

Recall that the switch from Spalding to Rawlings as the supplier of major league balls in 1977 coincided with a 50 percent jump in home runs across the two leagues. The 1977 rates weren't unprecedented; both leagues had been at similar heights as recently as 1970, itself a spike year for homers. The 1976 rate of 0.58 homers per game was the lowest since 1946, even lower than 1968. Prior to the switch in manufacturer, the last major change to the ball had come in 1974, when the outer coating switched from horsehide to cowhide because of a shortage of the former. Homer production fell from 0.80 per game to 0.68, a 14.7 percent drop. It increased 2.4 percent in 1975, but then fell off another 17.4 percent in 1976.

Given those ups and downs, it's possible that Spalding didn't perfect the process of using the new covering before surrendering the manufacturing process to Rawlings, or that the balls used at the end of their run were leftovers that were slightly substandard in resilience, leading to the dip in home runs. It would take a "Deep Throat" to provide insight into the matter, but unlike in the Watergate scandal of that decade, none has ever come forward. In any event, aside from 1976, the rises and falls around that time fit right in with the garden-variety season-to-season variation in the expansion era.

Here it's worth reviewing the composition and construction process of a major league baseball. The ball starts as a pill of cushion cork (a mixture of cork and ground rubber) of prescribed weight (0.50 ounce) and diameter (2.86 to 2.94 inches). The pill is then wrapped in two layers of rubber, one black and one red, bringing the diameter to 0.85 (+/-0.05) ounce and 1.375 (+/-0.01) inches. After that, the sphere is tightly wrapped with three layers (166 yards) of wool yarn and one layer (150 yards) of cotton-polyester yarn. The materials are important. Wool's natural resiliency and "memory" allows it to rapidly return to its original shape after being struck, while the cotton-poly blend reduces the risk of tears when the cowhide is applied. The balls are measured for size, weight, and tension after each layer to ensure that they fall within similarly tight tolerances.

The wound ball is trimmed of excess tailings, coated with a layer of latex adhesive, and then surrounded by the familiar two pieces of leather, which are hand-sewn together with 88 inches and 108 stitches worth of waxed red thread. After stitching, the balls are machine-rolled to compress the seams, dried in a dehumidifier, and rolled again before being cosmetically graded to check for abrasions and blemishes. They are then measured and weighed again. To meet official specifications, balls must measure 9 to 9.25 inches in circumference across two seams, and weigh from 5 to 5.25 ounces. From there they are stamped, weighed, inspected again, and then hand-packed for shipping.

After they arrive at a central warehouse, approximately 28 out of every 10,000 balls are run through tests. The balls are shot out of a pitching machine at 85 feet per second into a board of northern white ash (the same as used in the majority of bats), with its speed coming off the board measured to determine its coefficient of restitution. Balls must have a coefficient of restitution between .514 and .578, meaning that they must rebound at between 43.69 and 49.13 feet per second to meet standards.

Note that at every stage, some amount of tolerance is allowed, an amount that is hardly trivial. In 2000, as balls were flying out of the park at record rates, Major League Baseball and Rawlings funded a study at the University of Massachusetts-Lowell Baseball Research Center; there a team of mechanical engineers led by Professor Jim Sherwood put 192 unused 1999- and 2000-vintage balls through a battery of tests and accompanied MLB personnel on tours of the plants where various components were manufactured, issuing a 28-page report on their findings. The tests "revealed no significant performance differences and verified that the baseballs used in Major League games meet performance specifications." Yet they also found that "some of the internal components of the dissected samples were slightly out of tolerance on baseballs from each year . . . despite the thorough inspection process in place at the assembly plant in Costa Rica." Thirteen out of the 192 baseballs supplied (6.8 percent) were underweight as well.

The most glaring finding was the effect of the tolerances. According to the study, "two baseballs could meet MLB specifications for construction but one ball could be theoretically hit 49.1 feet further," which breaks down to 8.4 feet attributable to being on the light side of the tolerance for weight (5.0 ounces, as opposed to 5.25 ounces) and another 40.4 feet attributable to being on the high end for the coefficient of restitution (.578). Given that finding, it's not difficult to imagine how the slightest differences in the balls from batch to batch or year to year could lead to a plethora of towering 425-foot home runs instead of 375-foot warning track fly balls. The researchers also noted that minor league balls, with pure cork centers (as opposed to cushion cork, which contains ground rubber), didn't fly quite as far, a shortfall of about eight feet, illustrating how minor changes in the core can manifest themselves on one side of the warning track or the other.

That same year, several independent researchers also tested year-2000 balls against older stock, but some of those tests are of questionable validity since the older balls had not been stored in climate-controlled environments. A test sponsored by the *Cleveland Plain Dealer* that didn't use aged baseballs drew some interesting results. Using baseballs from 1999 and 2000, engineers at the Lansmont Corporation in Silicon Valley replicated National Bureau of Standards liveliness tests that had been done in 1945, and found that the big-league balls sampled could fly up to 48 feet farther than their counterparts, which hailed from 1942.

At the time of this wave of testing, the common refrain from Rawlings was that since 1931 there had been no changes in specifications for the balls outside of humidity and temperature controls, improved quality control, and testing. That 1931 date corresponds to the introduction of the cushion cork pill, following the two highest-scoring seasons in the history of post-1900 baseball (5.19 and 5.55 runs per game in 1929 and 1930, respectively); prior to that, the ball had had a pure cork center.

Even so, a close look at the UMass-Lowell report—which in addition to detailing the official specifications of the ball, covered the sourcing and construction of the cork and rubber used in the pill, the wool used in the winding, and cowhide used in the cover—reveals gaps, discrepancies, and hints of change over the years. Perhaps the most notable omission from discussion is the presence of a red ring used in the assembly of the pill, unaccounted for in the specs. The ring sits between the hemispheres of black rubber that encase the cushion cork sphere; in the report, it is referred to as a hard red-rubber washer sliced from a hard red-rubber tube, made at the same Mississippi facility as the rest of the ball's rubber components, but whereas those pieces are meticulously documented as to their content, the washer, though photographed as a separate item and as part of a partially assembled pill prior to being encased in the red layer, is not otherwise mentioned anywhere in the report.

Fast-forward to January 2007, when a diagnostic imaging company called Universal Medical Systems (UMS), with assistance from scientists from the Center for Quantitative Imaging at Penn State, examined the ball hit by Mark McGwire for his 70th home run in 1998 via computerized tomography (CT) scans. The scans clearly showed the presence of the ring, leading the scientists to conclude that the ball was juiced. Said UMS president David Zavagno, "The synthetic rubber ring of the modern-day baseball, in this case that of Mark McGwire's prized 70th home run ball, acts as both a spring and a "stop" . . . Much like a sling shot pulled back 10 or 20 degrees farther than normal, the subsequent restitution or rebound allows an object to fly faster and farther. The changes to the center directly affect the restitution and energy distribution within the ball."

MLB spokesman Rich Levin claimed that the ring was more like "a cardboard washer." He did not elaborate on that absurd explanation, but Bob Dupuy, MLB's chief operating officer, carefully refuted the imagers' claims. "All of our balls are subject to rigorous quality control standards and testing conducted by Rawlings," he said. "No changes have been made to the core of the ball through the entire time they have manufactured it. We are satisfied that the ball comports with all major league specifications." Dupuy noted that annual tests were still being conducted at UMass-Lowell under Sherwood's direction.

The UMass-Lowell report was somewhat evasive in discussing the yarn as well. In the specifications, the first three winds are to consist of different-sized yarns that are "approximately 85% wool and 15% other fibers," with the fourth consisting of "a white 20/2 poly-cotton 50/50 blend yarn," meaning that it's a 2-ply yarn weighing 8,400 yards per pound, with half the fibers made of polyester and half of cotton. In the sourcing section, the report notes that the wool yarn comes solely from the D&T Spinning plant in Ludlow, Vermont—a plant founded in 1984 by Paul Dubin, a Rawlings consultant since 1962—where it recovers wool fibers via scraps from a nearby carpet mill. The methodology for processing and determining the wool-versus-nonwool content for the first three yarns is detailed ("A sample size of 110g is put in bleach. The bleach literally eats the wool. Assuming that 10g of the 110g is water due to moisture absorption, the remaining dried material should be 15±3g—denoting the percentage of nonwool"), as is the spinning and twisting of those yarns, but that information for the fourth yarn is not, and in fact at one point in the section, the report refers to "all three of the yarns used to make the baseball."

Shortly after the report came out, a team of University of Rhode Island (URI) forensic scientists led by Dennis Hilliard solicited the donation of foul balls via a radio station for the purposes of testing. They obtained only a handful, one apiece from 1963, 1970, 1989, 1995, and 2000, which limited any claims as to statistical significance produced by their coefficient of restitution tests (reportedly, the two newest pills rebounded about 30 percent higher), but their examinations of the balls contrasted with the report as well as Rawlings's claim.

Using infrared spectroscopy and digital photography, the URI team determined that the 2000 pill was similar in color to the 1985 and 1999 pills. However, they also noted that "the design is unique among all years with a larger space between the two black rubber hemispheres." Furthermore, the team's findings with regard to the yarn were at odds with the UMass-Lowell report, particularly when they performed their own bleaching. "As expected, the yarn from the 1963 ball dissolved completely, as the bleach ate away the protein in the wool. But when the 1970 sample was tested, trace amounts of synthetic fibers remained, and with the 1989, 1995, and 2000 balls, 'the fibers were pretty much still intact,' [textile scientist Linda] Welters says." Preliminary tests found as much as 21.6 percent synthetic fiber in the yarns from the 2000 ball, thus falling outside the 15±3 percent tolerance detailed in the UMass-Lowell report. The URI scientists were at odds with the manufacturer over such matters:

> "My guess would be that they're somehow getting a lot of polyester mulched into the mix, since it's very hard to find all-wool carpets being made these days," Welters says. Paul Dubin strenuously disagrees. He says his company tests the yarn every day to ensure that it is within Major League guidelines.

Back to Zavagno, who made headlines again in 2007 when he alleged that contemporary (Bonds-era) baseballs differed materially from "traditional" (Aaron-era) balls from earlier decades:

> In 1999, one year after Mark McGwire broke the single-season home run record, the League decided to remove the timeless imprint "cushioned cork center" from official baseballs, according to David Zavagno, president of UMS, a worldwide innovator of diagnostic imaging technology for various industries.
>
> "The League decided to juice itself so they pumped the new ball into their system . . . By examining the CT images of Bonds-era baseballs, you can see the ball has been upgraded to include a rubberized pill, the addition of polyester in the windings and a very hard synthetic ring or spring.

> As the CT images demonstrate, the League apparently allowed the composition of the baseball to further change from 1998 to 2001 destroying the integrity of the game's statistics, including home run records."

Zavagno was mistaken in claiming that the pill was suddenly "rubberized," since rubber had been part of the cushion cork mix since 1931. Nonetheless, a side-by-side comparison of the CT scans he presented did illustrate density differences between the otherwise undated Aaron- and Bonds-era balls, both with regard to the pill and the yarn. Beyond the knowledge that the former is a Spalding-made ball (Aaron retired in 1976, Spalding's final year as supplier) and that the yarn may have been hand-wound instead of machine-wound (it's unclear exactly when the switch was made), the significance of this is unclear, as there's no way to know under what conditions—particularly with regard to heat and moisture—the older ball was stored. The scan of the older ball does show an analogous rubber ring, smaller and less dense than its modern-day counterpart.

Physicist Alan Nathan is among those who believe that the ball has changed. Nathan, whose credentials include chairing the Society for Baseball Research's Baseball & Science Committee and serving on a scientific panel advising the NCAA on issues related to bat performance, is quite familiar with Sherwood's study and his laboratory, having served as part of a scientific advisory committee for a 2002 study of bats (more about which below) that was done at the Lowell lab.

Of the Zavagno scans, Nathan says, "What he shows is that the *construction* of baseballs has changed. There's no question that the construction has changed, the pill has changed, the percentage of wool in the windings has changed, some of it's synthetic now. There are structural differences between the baseballs." In Nathan's eye, showing that isn't enough. "Structural changes do not necessarily imply performance changes. If you think you have two baseballs that differ from each other, the right way to do it is send them to one of these labs and have them test it properly by doing impacts, measure the coefficient of restitution. I tend not to give much thought to those [CT scan] studies because they don't prove that the balls *perform* differently."

Coefficient of restitution (COR) testing on baseballs is generally done in two ways. For purposes of compliance with the official specifications, there's a "wall test" in which the ball is fired from an air cannon at a speed of 85 feet per second (58 mph) into a flat panel of northern white ash. That speed is well below game conditions; that's a velocity reversal characteristic of a bunt, suitable for checking the consistency of the manufacturing process but not for establishing performance with regard to long fly balls. The UMass-Lowell lab also has facilities to do a bat test using a ball fired at 70 mph to a hitting machine whose bat tip is moving at 90 mph and whose sweet spot (6 inches from the barrel) is at 70 mph—still below game conditions, but closer. Because the ball has a nonlinear COR, it decreases given collisions at higher velocities. In the 2000 tests, both the 1999 and the 2000 balls were around .550 for the wall test, and around .500 for the bat test.

The challenge in proving that a ball is "juiced" is in obtaining unused balls from previous eras for comparative testing. As it happened, Nathan and fellow physicist Lloyd Smith, an associate professor of mechanical and materials engineering at Washington State University whose Sports Science Laboratory performs the official bat testing for the NCAA, were provided a box of unopened late-1970s baseballs by the niece of former A's owner Charlie Finley, which they compared against a sample of 2004 balls purchased directly from Rawlings—a pairing not far off from Zavagno's "Aaron" and "Bonds" scan pairing. Both sets of balls were placed in a humidor for a month at 70 degrees and 50 percent relative humidity, then subjected to wall tests at 60, 90, and 120 mph, and a bat test at 125 mph. The tests found no significant difference in the COR of the balls from the two eras; in fact, they were alarmingly close at the various speeds given the likely structural differences. Alas, the small sample of balls used in the study limits its power to settle the issue:

> Although our principal finding is the lack of evidence that today's baseball is not more lively than that of an earlier time, we caution readers that this result applies only to the very small sample of balls that we tested. It is not possible to extrapolate this result to more general statements about the relative liveliness of baseballs without more extensive testing. Given the difficulty of obtaining older unused baseballs, we will likely never be able to make such statements.

Nathan notes that the UMass-Lowell team continues to test balls, but that Major League Baseball doesn't publicize the results, or allow Sherwood or anyone else involved to discuss them in great detail. From the standpoint of ball composition, one further area of interest is the aforementioned ring, about which Nathan says, "The ring has a certain orientation associated with it. It's in a certain plane. You can imagine hitting the baseball perpendicular to that ring versus in the plane of that ring, and try to see whether they're any differences. That would be a very interesting experiment. There are unknown answers to those questions, at least that we don't know about. I suspect that these have been thoroughly studied by Rawlings."

To the extent that COR tests for balls of different vintages have been made public via means like the UMass-Lowell, *Plain Dealer*, or Nathan-Smith studies, they have shown relatively little difference among small batches of balls obtained via a minimal number of sources. Even so, it's important to remember just how wide MLB's tolerances are. Says Nathan, "The specs on major league baseballs, they almost don't deserve to be called specs, they're so loose that the range of performance from the top end to the bottom end is so different."

Indeed. The 49.1-foot discrepancy in flight for two balls at the extremes of tolerance is roughly three times the distance produced by a three percent increase in batted ball speed according to the rule of thumb cited by Nathan, where each additional mile per hour of batted ball speed increases the fly ball distance by 5.5 feet. That's a lot of extra homers added to the ledger without anyone violating the rules.

The Bat

Having considered the ball, we turn to the other crucial piece of equipment when it comes to home runs, the bat. Once upon a time, the game's big sluggers swung the biggest sticks. Babe Ruth wielded war clubs as heavy as 54 ounces in his early years, though by the mid- to late 1920s, he had gravitated to the 38–42 ounce range. According to Hillerich & Bradsby Company, makers of the Louisville Slugger, Ruth used a 38.5 ounce model in 1927, when he hit 60 homers. Teammate Lou Gehrig hefted bats in the 38–40 ounce range. Rogers Hornsby is said to have gone as high as 50 ounces. Joe DiMaggio used a 42-ounce bat.

As time marched onward, even the big sluggers gravitated toward lighter sticks with which they could generate more bat speed. Willie Mays preferred a 34-ounce bat, while Hank Aaron generally used a 33-ouncer, as did Roger Maris when he hit 61 homers in 1961. Mickey Mantle swung a 36-ounce stick from the right side, a 32-ouncer from the left. Mark McGwire's 35-ounce bats have ranked among the heaviest in recent years, while Alex Rodriguez, Barry Bonds, and Ken Griffey Jr. used bats in the 32–33 ounce range.

The trend toward lighter bats owes to the woods predominantly used to make them. In the early days, hickory was favored for its strength and durability; such bats were thick handled, stiff, and resistant to breakage. Because of its heavy weight, hickory gave way to white ash, which is lighter and has more elastic properties, producing a springboard effect and a larger sweet spot.

In 1998, the first maple bat, the Sam Bat made by the Original Maple Bat Company of Ottawa, was approved for major league play. Roland Hernandez, a former wood scientist who founded a bat-manufacturing company called RockBats, explained maple's appeal: "According to the USDA Forest Products Laboratory Wood Handbook, Hard Maple is approximately a 5% to 10% stronger, stiffer, harder, and tougher wood than White Ash." Maple bats quickly gained high visibility thanks to Barry Bonds, who switched to Sam Bats in time for his 73-homer 2001 season. That season's NL Rookie of the Year, Albert Pujols, sported a Sam Bat as well.

As maple bats have made significant inroads, so have smaller manufacturers. Hillerich & Bradsby, which began making bats in 1884, once held a virtual monopoly on the majors, but as of 2010, they were just the largest of 32 manufacturers supplying bats, a figure down from 48 in 2002. The makers of the Louisville Slugger still hold 55 to 60 percent of the major league market, but by 2006, their maple bats were outselling their ash ones; in recent years, the company has said the split is about 50–50 between the two woods.

Maple's greater density and durability relative to ash allow for thinner barrels and hence lighter and faster-swinging bats while maintaining the size of the bat's sweet spot. Such lighter bats help batters generate more speed and more control while allowing them to wait a fraction of a second longer—choosing a more desirable pitch—before deciding whether to swing. But a lighter bat doesn't translate into hitting the ball farther (corked-bat controversies to the contrary). As Adair wrote in *The Physics of Baseball:*

> From elementary principles of mechanics, we can say with complete reliability that for a given bat speed, a heavy bat will drive a ball farther than a light bat. Conversely, for a given kinetic energy of the bat, a light bat will drive the ball farther than a heavy bat (for bat weights greater than 20 ounces). To this we add the (very plausible) condition that no player can swing a heavy bat faster than he could a light bat. And we hold that no player can put more energy into a light bat than into a heavy bat. The energy transmitted to the bat is simply the product (better, *integral*) of the force of the bat that the hands apply along the direction of motion times the distance through which the hands move. If we assume that the arc of the hands—and bat—is the same for a light or heavy bat, the larger force

that it is possible to apply to the more slowly moving heavy bat will result in a larger energy transfer to that bat.

Adair employed several theoretical models in his chapter on bat properties, each time coming to the same conclusion: with everything else constant, heavier bats drive the ball farther, but for some players, the additional reaction time allowed by swinging a lighter bat may well outweigh the slight gain in distance produced by adding a few ounces.

Adair's book was written before the rise in popularity of maple bats, but Nathan, who advises the NCAA on issues related to bat perform-ance, is convinced there's little difference. In a 2007 interview with Baseball Prospectus's Dan Fox, he said, "I am skeptical that there are any significant performance differences between ash and maple, de-spite the claims of Sam Holman [maker of the Sam Bat, used by Bonds]. Laboratory testing has shown similar performance character-istics."

MLB has shied from publicizing its studies since the controversy caused by the 2000 ball study, but they have continued to conduct re-search into balls and bats. In a more recent interview, Nathan ex-plained that he served on the scientific advisory committee for an MLB-commissioned 2002 study at Sherwood's UMass-Lowell lab. "Af-ter Bonds broke the single season record for home runs with a maple bat, and everyone started switching to maple bats, Major League Baseball rightly asked the question, 'Is there something to this? Is a maple bat a better hitting instrument than an ash bat?'

"The conclusion was that in terms of hitting performance, there was no reason to believe that a maple bat hit the ball any better or any worse than an ash bat," says Nathan. "Pretty much to the extent that the bats can withstand the impact, all wood bats that have roughly the same length and weight and shape are going to hit the ball more or less the same. Certainly, that's true near the sweet spot of the bat. Once you get away from the sweet spot, then the vibrational proper-ties might be a little different, some woods are stiffer than others. For batted balls near the sweet spot there wasn't anything that you could really choose from between maple and ash."

Nathan cites studies done independently of MLB, particularly at Washington State University, under the guidance of the aforemen-tioned Lloyd Smith of the Sports Science Laboratory. "Again they show that maple and ash perform the same," said Nathan. "There was absolutely no reason from a theoretical physics point of view to expect that the bats would perform differently from each other, and they didn't. That's based on very good science both from a theoretical point of view as well as from an experimental point of view."

"There is really no advantage in switching wood species," said Smith in November 2010. Daniel Halem, MLB's senior vice president for labor relations, agreed. "All we know is what we're told by our experts, and the studies we've seen show no difference in performance."

In a 2010 article for the Baseball Analysts website, "Comparing the Performance of Baseball Bats," Nathan reiterated the tradeoff between the two woods:

> Careful studies have shown that there is no difference in BBCOR [the ball-bat coefficient of restitution, or the "bounciness," as he termed it] between ash and maple. . . . A maple bat of the same dimensions as an ash bat (same length and radius profile) would have a larger MOI [moment of inertia] since maple is a bit more dense than ash. So, switching from ash to maple would be sort of like "anti-corking," the opposite of corking. Since corking results in a slightly lower BBS [batted ball speed], then anti-corking results in a slightly higher BBS, at the cost of less quickness.

Having explored a variety of alternate explanations for the rise in home runs over the 1993–2010 era, it is clear that by far the strongest candidates for increasing home runs are changes in ballparks and the ball. It is difficult if not impossible to quantify exactly to what extent those two factors have contributed to the boom, but we cannot discount the likelihood that both have played substantial parts.

The Players

Let us return to the increase in the rate of home runs per fly ball that Tobin and Nathan discuss as a plausible range of outcomes for the strength gains produced by steroids, a 30–70 percent increase in home runs per batted ball. Recall that the period following the odd 1987 spike year was one of relative stability for home run rates; balls flew out at an average of 2.7 percent over the next five seasons before increasing sharply beyond that baseline, until they were 31 to 56 percent higher over the next 18 seasons. The 2011 season was the first since 1993 in which the rate was less than 30 percent above that five-year baseline, and even then, it only dipped to 29 percent above.

 Suppose we make a list of the top 25 home run hitters from the years 1988 to 2007, the latter date chosen because it was the final year of the careers of Bonds and Sosa as well as the last before the Mitchell

Report was released. Seven of the top 10 sluggers on that list, and 12 of the 25, have been implicated as steroid users via one means or another—the BALCO scandal (Bonds, Giambi, Sheffield), self-admissions (McGwire, Canseco, Rodriguez, Mike Piazza), positive tests (Ramirez, Palmeiro), leaks of the 2003 survey test results (Sosa, Rodriguez, Ramirez again), appearances in the Mitchell Report (Gonzalez)—which gets to the sordid heart of the scandal.

Because we have imperfect information about when those individuals may have used steroids and how long the effects may have lingered, suppose we consider the entire careers of those 12 "dirty" players in one pile, and the other 13 "clean" sluggers in another pile. The latter group contains at least one player about whom there have been rumors of PED usage, but instead of dwelling upon hearsay, we will rely upon the facts as we have them.

If we compare the two groups of hitters in that 1988–2007 range, we find that the "dirty" group hit a combined .290/.384/.551 in a total of 103,175 plate appearances. The "clean" group closely approximated that, hitting .293/.384/.541 in 109,361 plate appearances (about 6 percent more). We're not controlling for park or league levels, but it's clear that we have two very similarly talented groups of hitters here. The biggest difference between the two is their home run rates; the "dirty" group produced homers on 8.3 percent of their batted balls, about 11 percent more often than the "clean" group, which produced homers on 7.4 percent of their batted balls.

If we isolate to the 1988–1992 time period—which includes only 17 of those players, a few of whom had relatively little playing time—we find that the "clean" group outhit the "dirty" group in terms of rate stats, .281/.365/.484 versus .268/.347/.475. That's a difference of 27 points' worth of OPS (on-base percentage plus slugging percentage), enough to produce a bit of separation, but not a lot, and it's mitigated by the fact that the "clean" group had 31 percent fewer plate appearances. Whatever the differences in performance, the two groups were extremely close in terms of home runs per batted ball, with the "dirty" group at 6.0 percent and the "clean" group at 5.8 percent.

Turning to the 1993–2007 segments of their careers, the "dirty" group hit .296/.392/.569 in 83,864 plate appearances (PA), while the "clean" group hit .296/.388/.550 in 94,395 PA, about 13 percent more playing time. The "dirty" group homered in 8.8 percent of its batted balls, a 47 percent gain over their collective 1988–1992 baseline, while the "clean" group homered in 7.7 percent of its batted balls, a 33 percent gain over their collective 1988–1992 baseline. Note that the 33 and 47 percent figures jibe with the estimates from Tobin and Nathan, and are in the same range as the overall MLB increase of 41.7 percent from the 1988–1992 period to 1993–2007.

For the 1993–2007 span, that's a 14 percent advantage for the "dirty" group. Over the course of 650 plate appearances, that's a difference of 4.8 homers. Knock off the 2.0 homer advantage per 650 PA for the "dirty" group in the 1988–1992 era (presumably a gap that derived naturally as the result of differences in inborn talent), and we're down to an average increase of 2.8 homers per year for the "dirty" group versus the "clean" among elite sluggers (see Table 1-1.10).

Three (or, more accurately, 2.8) homers per year is not an insignificant amount, even for an elite slugger; it might represent 5–10 percent of his total in an average season even in those boom years. When you consider that the sluggers in our group accumulated an average of 11 650-plate-appearance "seasons" in the 1993–2007 period, it's about 31 extra homers in a career. Note the wide variance of home run rates increases from the pre-to post-1993 era; excluding the small-sample-based increases of Thome and Piazza and the players who had no playing time in the earlier span, five of the top seven with the largest gains are among the implicated, but so are three of the bottom four.

We've made no guess as to the distribution of those extra homers, which might be concentrated in a small number of players at higher levels over a shorter time period. If we follow the commonly reported narrative that Bonds didn't start using until after the 1998 season and apply his 1993–1998 HR/Con rate of 9.1 percent to his 1999–2007 numbers, we can estimate that he gained an extra 101 homers. This is a dangerous habit to get into, however, because we have far less information about the timing of PED usage among the other implicated players. Making arbitrary endpoint decisions based upon eyeballing stat lines is not good sabermetric practice. We've computed a group average, and in Bonds we have an example of the margin by which a player can exceed it. We'll leave the guesswork about other players' gains for someone else to calculate.

Beyond this group, the vast majority of hitters who used PEDs likely gained less than 31 homers overall. Of the 81 non-pitchers implicated, 30 of them hit 31 homers or fewer *total* during the 1993–2007 period. Twelve hitters (Bonds, Sosa, Rodriguez, Ramirez, Palmeiro, Sheffield, Piazza, Giambi, McGwire, Gonzalez, Mo Vaughn, and Troy Glaus) accounted for 49 percent of the homers hit by this particular pool of players in that span, hitting 8.9 percent of their batted balls out of the park. The other 69 homered on 4.1 percent of their batted

TABLE 1-1.10 Elite Sluggers in the Steroids Era

Player	Implicated	HR	HR/Con	88–92 HR	HR/Con	93–07 HR	HR/Con	Gain
Barry Bonds	yes	721	9.6%	135	6.1%	586	11.0%	81.3%
Sammy Sosa	yes	609	9.4%	37	4.0%	572	10.3%	159.4%
Ken Griffey	no	593	8.2%	87	4.7%	506	9.4%	100.2%
Rafael Palmeiro	yes	552	6.2%	78	2.9%	474	7.7%	163.4%
Mark McGwire	yes	531	12.9%	168	8.5%	363	16.8%	96.1%
Alex Rodriguez	yes	518	8.9%	518	8.9%			
Frank Thomas	no	513	7.8%	63	5.9%	450	8.1%	37.7%
Jim Thome	no	507	10.6%	3	1.8%	504	10.9%	498.3%
Manny Ramirez	yes	490	8.9%			490	8.9%	
Gary Sheffield	yes	480	6.4%	54	3.5%	426	7.2%	102.7%
Fred McGriff	no	473	7.1%	171	8.3%	302	6.6%	-20.7%
Jeff Bagwell	no	449	7.2%	33	3.6%	416	7.8%	120.0%
Juan Gonzalez	yes	434	8.2%	75	7.6%	359	8.3%	9.4%
Carlos Delgado	no	431	8.6%			431	8.6%	
Mike Piazza	yes	427	7.4%	1	1.8%	426	7.4%	323.0%
Jose Canseco	yes	393	9.5%	166	9.8%	227	9.2%	-5.8%
Chipper Jones	no	386	6.6%			386	6.6%	
Larry Walker	no	383	6.7%	58	5.0%	325	7.2%	43.5%
Albert Belle	no	381	7.8%	70	7.0%	311	8.0%	14.0%
Andres Galarraga	no	374	7.0%	91	5.0%	283	8.0%	60.1%
Matt Williams	yes	370	6.8%	113	6.7%	257	6.8%	2.4%
Andruw Jones	no	368	7.3%			368	7.3%	
Jeff Kent	no	365	5.5%	11	4.8%	354	5.6%	15.9%
Vladimir Guerrero	no	365	6.8%			365	6.8%	
Jason Giambi	yes	364	7.8%			364	7.8%	

balls, a hair above the MLB-wide rate of 3.8 percent for the period—which is to say that whatever positive effect they may have gained over a short period was minor relative to the rest of their careers.

Are three homers per year at the top end enough to compromise the moral fabric of America? More important, is that even what we can really attribute to steroid usage—knowing that ballparks and balls may represent substantial portions of those increases, that we have almost certainly overestimated the fraction of those elite sluggers' careers in which they actually used, or that pitchers may have been using steroids in equal numbers during that time period, suggesting that the playing field was closer to level than has been suggested by the mainstream media?

We don't have all of the answers from the era. We almost certainly never will. This is not to exonerate the players who may have used, to excuse the risks they have taken with their own health, or the ways in which their use had an impact upon others. But to suggest that the numbers of the era have been entirely distorted by the use of steroids would appear to be a stretch given the number of other factors in play. How we should regard the elite of this era in terms of the Cooperstown question is a topic we will turn to in the next chapter.

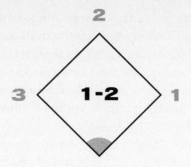

How Should the Hall of Fame Respond to the Steroids Era?

JAY JAFFE

The thorny question of how to place the principals of the so-called steroid era into the context of baseball history arose before the sport's official day of reckoning arrived. Mark McGwire first appeared on the Baseball Writers' Association of America (BBWAA) Hall of Fame ballot in November 2006, just over a year before the release of the Mitchell Report. On the occasion of receiving his ballot, ESPN's Jayson Stark summed up the dread that many of his colleagues felt:

> I used to look forward to the day the Hall of Fame ballot arrived every November. Not this year. It isn't just because the already-ugly Mark McGwire Debate is going to crash what is supposed to be Tony Gwynn and Cal Ripken's party, either. It's because this is only the beginning . . . With every new name that appears on these ballots now, we're not just going to have to ask ourselves, "Was this guy a Hall of Famer?" We're going to have to ask ourselves, "What are the chances that this guy used steroids?" . . . How many years will this debate hover over what used to be the only Hall of Fame debate? Ten years? Fifteen? Twenty? Thirty?

Thirty years may not be an outlandish guess as far as worst-case scenarios go. Figure that Alex Rodriguez retires after his 10-year contract runs out in 2017. After the mandatory five-year waiting period, he'll reach the 2023 ballot, which will be released in November 2022. Assuming he receives less than the 75 percent of the vote necessary for enshrinement in Cooperstown but more than the five percent needed to remain on the ballot, his eligibility will run 15 seasons, through the 2037 ballot, which will be 31 years after Stark's article was written. That's without considering how a Veterans Committee to be named later might regard him.

When McGwire's name came up for a vote, the judgment was quite harsh. Despite finishing with a career total of 583 home runs (seventh all-time at that juncture), leading his league in that category four times, making 12 All-Star teams, and serving as a key component of three pennant winners, he received just 23.5 percent of the vote, less than one-third of what's needed for enshrinement. His not-so-near miss did give him one distinction: his home run total easily surpassed that of seventies and eighties slugger Dave Kingman, whose 442 homers—"The Kingman Line"—stood for two decades as the high-water mark for anybody eligible for the Hall but not enshrined. McGwire could have fared worse; former teammate and alleged partner in juicing Jose Canseco, whose 462 homers also surpassed Kingman, received just 1.1 percent of the vote, banishing him from the ballot.

The ensuing years have hardly been kinder to McGwire's candidacy. He topped out at 23.7 percent in 2010, but shortly after the voting results were announced, acknowledged what had long been suspected, that he had used steroids and human growth hormone during his career. "There's not a pill or an injection that's going to give me, going to give any player the hand-eye coordination to hit a baseball," McGwire told Bob Costas on the MLB Network. "The only reason I took steroids was for health purposes." His version of the truth did not set him free; in the next year's voting, he fell to 19.8 percent. Since 1967, when the Hall reverted to annual balloting (it had been biennial for a stretch), no player who received that low a percentage in his fifth year of eligibility has gone on to gain entry via the BBWAA ballot; Bert Blyleven (26.3 percent) and Jim Rice (29.4 percent) made the greatest comebacks from that juncture, topping 75 percent in their 14th and 15th years of eligibility, respectively.

Big Mac will have to wait, as will Rafael Palmeiro, who reached the ballot in 2011. The fourth player ever to amass both 3,000 hits and 500 homers—Hank Aaron, Willie Mays, and Eddie Murray are the others—he appears to have two virtually automatic qualifiers for Cooperstown. No other eligible player besides McGwire had topped 500 homers without gaining entry, and none but the banned Pete Rose has been kept outside despite 3,000 hits. In fact, every player who reached 3,000 hits since the end of World War II gained first-ballot entry. Alas, Palmeiro has other baggage that sets him apart from McGwire: a positive test for steroids, one that effectively ended his career in 2005. He received just 11.0 percent of the vote in his initial go-round, lower than Blyleven's 14.1 percent debut, the lowliest of any player who has rallied to gain election via the writers.

The question is how much company those two will have among the elite players whose statistics appear Hall-worthy but who have been linked to PEDs, particularly from among the ballot class of 2013: Barry Bonds, Roger Clemens, Sammy Sosa, and Mike Piazza. Three of those players have cases as the best ever at their positions, while the fourth is the only man ever to hit 60 or more homers three times. None ever tested positive during the punitive phase of MLB's Joint Drug Prevention and Treatment Program, which began in 2004 (Sosa is alleged to have done so during the supposedly anonymous survey of 2003). Two of them wound up at the centers of federal cases that appear to have been prosecuted more for their public relations value than their legal merits, while one admitted to using what was then a legal substance. Will the writers keep all of them out? Should they?

The Rules of Engagement

In exploring the question of whether PED users should be enshrined in Cooperstown, it's important to remember that the Hall of Fame is a private institution that acts as both a museum of record and a means of honoring the game's best players. It is not subject to the direct control of Major League Baseball. When commissioner Bart Giamatti placed Rose on baseball's permanently ineligible list in 1989 for gambling, the BBWAA maintained that the decision on whether he would be allowed into the Hall was still theirs to make. However, in early 1991, the Hall's board of directors voted to exclude any person banned from baseball. Rose nonetheless got a smattering of write-in votes from 1992 to 1994, topping out at 9.5 percent in what would have been his first year of eligibility.

Those implicated as PED users have not been similarly banned, and aren't likely to be, particularly after the Mitchell Report's recommendation that no players named in the report be punished, because such proceedings "will keep everyone mired in the past." In an interview with Stark, commissioner Bud Selig stressed that the decision on admitting users was up to the BBWAA:

I'm not going to make a judgment on what the writers decide. If they decide Mark McGwire shouldn't be in the Hall of Fame . . . then that's a judgment they'll have to make . . . It's their commentary on the sport, and I'm not being critical. They're entitled to feel whatever they want to feel.

In bypassing McGwire and other users, many writers have cited the Hall of Fame's rules for election, which include the following statement: "Voting shall be based upon the player's record, playing ability, integrity, sportsmanship, character, and contributions to the team(s) on which the player played." Even before McGwire had reached the ballot, *New York Daily News* columnist Bill Madden, a member of the Hall's Historical Overview Committee (responsible for vetting Veterans Committee ballot candidates) and future recipient of the Hall of Fame's Spink Award, proclaimed, "I'm not voting for any of those guys—Bonds, McGwire, Sosa, Palmeiro, any of them. I draw the line at eyeball evidence and what I personally believe . . . If the Hall of Fame doesn't want me or any other writers to take a stand, then take that clause out of the ballot. I plan to invoke that clause."

Some voters echoed that sentiment. ESPN's Pedro Gomez, a voter since 2002, said, "If these traits didn't matter or shouldn't be considered, they shouldn't and wouldn't be part of the process. Voters cannot and should not start to overlook certain aspects of a player's integrity, sportsmanship and character just because many players from the same time span were equally morally bankrupt and were doing the same." Other writers have gone further than simply citing the clause. *Chicago Sun-Times* columnist Rick Telander refused to turn in his 2008 ballot, arguing that he couldn't trust that *anyone* on it was clean, and therefore couldn't vote for any of them. In the 2010 balloting, five writers turned in completely blank ballots as protest votes; three others did the same in 2011.

Voter Jeff Pearlman, who has written unauthorized biographies of Bonds and Clemens, went even further than most who wouldn't vote for the likes of McGwire and Palmeiro. On the 2011 ballot, he announced his refusal to vote for Jeff Bagwell, a player never implicated by a positive test, an appearance in the Mitchell Report, a legal process, or any of the other routes by which more than 100 players have been linked to PEDs. In justifying his non-vote, Pearlman settled for Madden's flimsy, subjective standard of eyeball evidence and personal belief. He compared the photographic evidence of the differing physiques of a young Bagwell and an older one to the similar contrasts of Bonds, Sosa, Jason Giambi, and Bret Boone, all implicated as PED users by various means. Furthermore, he held Bagwell's silence on the matter against him:

> No two teams in baseball had more PED connections than the Texas Rangers and the Houston Astros . . . Where was Jeff Bagwell, one of the best players in baseball, when someone inside the game needed to speak out and demand accountability? Answer: Like nearly all of his peers, he was nowhere. He never uttered a word, never lifted a finger.
>
> This, to me, is why we are allowed to suspect Jeff Bagwell and, if we so choose, not vote for him. The baseball players have cast this curse upon themselves—A. By cheating . . . B. By not standing up against cheating and doing everything to assure a clean product.
>
> If he did use, Jeff Bagwell deliberately sought an advantage over other players—an illegal advantage.
>
> If he didn't use, Jeff Bagwell stood by and watched his sport morph into WWE nonsense.

Never mind that few other players spoke out while their peers were using, or that Pearlman didn't hold a silent Roberto Alomar to the same standard in justifying his vote. Bagwell, despite statistical qualifications that suggest Hall-worthiness, received 41.7 percent of the vote in the 2011 election. Though not an insurmountable shortfall (nine players have been voted in by the writers after making lower debuts), that does suggest a long wait ahead.

Hall of Fame president Jeff Idelson believes that the language of the rules exists to serve such an exclusionary purpose. "The character clause exists as it relates to the game on the field. The character clause isn't there to evaluate and judge players socially," he told Joe Posnanski in a 2010 interview. "The voters should have the freedom to measure that however they see fit."

Idelson's words appear to suggest that steroid users should be distinguished from the various other categories of social miscreants enshrined in the Hall, including (but not limited to) the following:

- Nineteenth-century star Cap Anson, whose overt racism led him to refuse to take the field against black players such as Moses Fleetwood Walker and George Stovey in exhibition games back in the 1880s, and to use his influence to help draw the color line that stood until 1947.
- Commissioner Judge Kenesaw Mountain Landis, who is believed

to have written the aforementioned clause circa the Hall's inception in 1936, and who upheld the color line during his 24-year tenure as commissioner.

- Red Sox owner Tom Yawkey, whose franchise was the last to integrate in 1959, 12 years after Jackie Robinson's arrival. Yawkey's racism led the team to bypass Robinson and Willie Mays, both pursued by his scouts. He also hired racist managers such as Pinky Higgins and Joe Cronin.

- George Weiss, who as general manager saw to it that the Yankees did not integrate until 1955, after 12 of the other 16 teams had done so. In *The Boys of Summer*, Roger Kahn recounts a high-ranking Yankee executive—Weiss, according to a wide consensus of historians—declaring circa 1952 that he would never allow a black man to wear a Yankee uniform, saying, "We don't want that sort of crowd. It would offend boxholders from Westchester to have to sit with niggers."

- Tris Speaker and Rogers Hornsby, both members of the Ku Klux Klan.

- Ty Cobb, who not only was alleged to have been a KKK member but who once climbed into the stands to assault a handicapped heckler.

- Babe Ruth, not only the most notorious of many inveterate drinkers and womanizers in the Hall, but one who got a good share of his kicks during Prohibition, when alcohol was illegal.

- Grover Cleveland Alexander, another Prohibition-era alcoholic who is believed to have been drunk when he closed out Game Seven of the 1926 World Series for the Cardinals.

- Hack Wilson, who drank his way through Prohibition to the point that he passed out on the field and in the dugout.

- Orlando Cepeda, who was arrested in 1976 for smuggling 150 pounds of marijuana into Puerto Rico, and who served 10 months in a Florida prison.

- Ferguson Jenkins, who was arrested in 1980 when customs agents found cocaine in his suitcase.

- Paul Molitor, who used cocaine and marijuana early in his career.

- Dennis Eckersley, who battled alcoholism and who was identified as a cocaine user via a convicted drug dealer's testimony.

- Gaylord Perry, who confessed to using saliva, mud, sweat, Vaseline, and K-Y jelly to doctor baseballs in his autobiography, *Me and the Spitter*.

- Don Sutton, who acquired the nickname "Black and Decker" due to his use of sandpaper and other means to deface balls.
- Whitey Ford, who defaced balls using his wedding ring, mud pies he planted on the mound, and a "gunk" mixture of baby oil, turpentine, and resin.
- Leo Durocher, who managed the 1951 Giants (which also included Mays and Monte Irvin), a team whose miraculous pennant race comeback was aided by an elaborate system of illegal sign-stealing.
- Kirby Puckett, who was accused of multiple incidents of violence against women. In 2001, he was charged with false imprisonment, criminal sexual conduct, and assault by one; in 2003, his wife, Tonya, told *Sports Illustrated* that he tried to strangle her with an electric cord and held a gun to her head.
- Alomar, who was accused of domestic violence by his wife.
- Mays, Aaron, Mickey Mantle, Ted Williams, and many other stars who used amphetamines at some point in their careers to give them enough energy to play.

And so on. Not all of those people were voted into Cooperstown by the writers, and not all of the allegations were public knowledge at the time they were elected. Some of them committed crimes, while some exercised bad moral judgment, and some broke baseball's rules by cheating. They weren't all beyond redemption; some of them owned up to their wrongdoings, or cleaned up their acts.

Whether they did or not, it seems a double standard to suggest that those players, managers, and executives are somehow more fit to occupy the Hall of Fame than otherwise-qualified candidates who used PEDs, or that the latter constitute some special brand of wrongdoers worthy of being singled out for exclusion. If racists like Anson, Speaker, and Yawkey were reflections of the attitudes that prevailed and the shortcomings of their surrounding institutions, then the same could be said about McGwire, Bonds, and other PED users. Ruth and Alexander broke the laws of the land in a time of lax enforcement; so too the PED users. If Ford and Perry were looking for that extra edge, or Mantle and Mays just trying to stay in the lineup more often, is that really so different from those cast as the villains of the steroid era?

That said, most of the PED users under discussion have arguably committed crimes, exercised bad moral judgment, and broken baseball's rules by cheating. The sale of steroids for non-medical purposes was outlawed via the Anti-Drug Abuse Act of 1988, which created criminal penalties for anyone who "distributes or possesses with the intent to distribute any anabolic steroid for any use in humans other than the treatment of disease pursuant to the order of a physician." The 1990 Anabolic Steroids Control Act added anabolic steroids to Schedule III of the Controlled Substances Act, placing them in the same legal class as amphetamines, opium, and morphine, and creating more stringent regulations and harsher penalties for use and distribution.

Steroids were banned by baseball in June 1991, when commissioner Fay Vincent sent a memo to teams and the players' union explicitly prohibiting "the possession, sale or use of any illegal drug or controlled substance by Major League players or personnel . . . This prohibition applies to all illegal drugs . . . including steroids or prescription drugs for which the individual in possession of the drug does not have a prescription." While it outlined treatment and penalties, the prohibition did not include random testing, which had to be bargained with the union. Vincent was ousted in September 1992, replaced by Selig in the role of acting commissioner. Though Selig would reissue Vincent's memo in May 1997, it was not until 2005 that the first players were suspended for testing positive for steroids.

It seems rather clear that players who used PEDs were violating both federal laws and baseball's rules, in addition to taking advantage of lax enforcement of those rules in an attempt—not always successful—to gain an edge on their competitors. At the same time, they were able to do so in large part due to the reluctance of owners and the commissioner to enforce the rules, or to prioritize pushing for more stringent rules. Having been found liable for $280 million in damages related to their 1985–1987 collusion to suppress salary growth, the owners were busy trying to break the players' union, eliminate salary arbitration, restrict free agency, and institute revenue sharing tied to a salary cap—the matters that led to the 1994–1995 strike. After the strike, they were more interested in winning back fans by any means necessary, including turning a blind eye to the origins of the offensive surge of the post-strike years. To reiterate, this was an institutional failure.

The writers who failed to report the story as it unfolded were part of that failure as well, a fact that some of them acknowledged while backing off from roles as moral arbiters. In a 2006 *New York Times* op-ed piece, Buster Olney, who as a beat reporter covered the Padres, Orioles, Mets, and Yankees from 1993 to 2001 and thus was exposed to many a PED user, bemoaned his own complicity:

I could have done a better job of reporting how people in baseball thought the game was being changed by performance-enhancing drugs . . . I had a role in baseball's institutional failure during what will be forever known as the Steroid Era. But I was only part of the problem, because just about everyone in baseball is to blame.

Discussing his Hall of Fame ballot four years later, Olney explained:

I have a hard time applying retroactive morality. Even in the case of Palmeiro, the way baseball dealt with it was so incredibly weak; he got roughly the same suspension you get for scuffing a baseball . . . The use was so widespread, more than 50 percent, you can do one of two things. You can vote for no one from the era, or you can put the issue aside and vote for the best players, and that's what I did.

The chilly receptions of McGwire and Palmeiro suggest that not all of the voters agree with Olney. Some believe that lifting the character clause would ease the voters' burden. As Posnanski wrote in 2009:

The clause is now causing real problems for the Hall of Fame. Because, the majority of voters have decided, at least for the moment, that steroid use disqualifies a player from the Hall of Fame. And the fact that McGwire got fewer votes this year than he did last year suggests that the opinion is hardening . . . The clause demands integrity. The clause demands sportsmanship. The clause demands moral judgments by the Baseball Writers Association of America.

I would ask the Hall of Fame to change the clause. I think the clause should have been changed a long time ago; it makes me queasy to think about sportswriters (or anyone else) trying to judge a man's character.

The logical extension of the electorate's hardline stance on steroids is a Hall of Fame without the all-time home run leader (Bonds), the man who may surpass him (Alex Rodriguez, with 629 homers through the 2011 season), and four other players among the all-time list's current top 15 (Sosa, McGwire, Palmeiro, and Manny Ramirez). Such a policy would leave the number-three pitcher in terms of wins since World War II on the outside looking in as well.

It would also leave a void in the Hall, particularly if the trust-no-one attitude prevails. The game's checkered history includes tales of institutionalized racism, the use of other illegal substances, and no small amount of gambling and other chicanery. Setting aside a broad swatch of its recent history on the grounds that it is somehow worse than what came before it, so that only a sanitized version of the national pastime should be presented and preserved, will cost the Hall of Fame its relevance.

Bringing Order to Chaos

Hall of Fame arguments, whether by fans or voters, tend to be passionate ones where logical consistency often takes a backseat to emotion. Add PEDs to the mix, and the arguments can get downright combustible, or at the very least unruly. The elevated scoring levels of the steroid era have many writers feeling as though the statistics from the period are artificial, lacking in authenticity, and the difference between, say, Ruth's lawbreaking and Bonds's is a question of on-field impact. However, as shown in the previous chapter, scoring levels have fluctuated widely throughout baseball history. The steroid era's high scores and soaring home run rates cannot be entirely attributed to PEDs; changes in ballparks and balls played substantial parts as well, though the exact degree of either is unclear. Even among top sluggers, the gains in home runs appear to have been relatively marginal. With that knowledge in mind, the impact of PED use on a player's Hall of Fame case should be a marginal one relative to the totality of a player's career.

Even without the impact of PEDs remaining a muddy question, those inflated offensive totals make a difficult task of determining those who are truly worthy of the Hall of Fame. Fortunately, Baseball Prospectus came into being armed with a toolkit built to grasp this new era, and an understanding that familiar numbers like a .300 batting average, 30 home runs, 100 RBI, and 20 wins aren't always created equal; their values vary from one period to another, and are often distorted by the work of players' teammates and the influences of their environment. Stats such as wins above replacement player and True Average—both explained elsewhere in this book—are built to level the playing field, making it easier to compare players across eras because they adjust for park and league context, particularly the wide fluctuations in scoring levels over time. They can bring order and consistency to an often disorderly and inconsistent debate.

Since 2004, I've used a tool called the Jaffe WARP Score (JAWS) to evaluate Hall of Fame ballots at the Baseball Prospectus website. The stated goal of JAWS is to raise the standards of the Hall of Fame by identifying and endorsing candidates who are as good or better than the average enshrined player at their position, a bar set so as to avoid further diluting the quality of the institution's membership, a danger to which the Hall was particularly vulnerable during the heyday of the Veterans Committee. The system is built to compare players according to their career values and their peak values, both denominated in WARP so as to incorporate hitting, fielding, and pitching contributions. Career value speaks for itself, while peak value is defined as a player's best seven years at large; JAWS is the average of those two, an attempt to recognize that longevity is not the sole determinant of Hall-worthiness. In essence, a player's best seasons are double-counted, an appropriate strategy given the research regarding the premium value of star talent. Individual greatness can have a non-linear effect on a team's results both in the standings and on the bottom line. Table 1-2.1 shows the positional standards at this writing, in fall 2011.

TABLE 1-2.1 JAWS Standards by Position

Position	Career	Peak	JAWS
C	54.9	35.7	45.3
1B	63.4	42.0	52.7
2B	66.7	44.4	55.6
3B	73.0	46.4	59.7
SS	62.2	41.0	51.6
LF	67.3	43.1	55.2
CF	75.5	48.2	61.8
RF	68.5	41.7	55.1
SP	53.0	37.1	45.1
RP	29.1	17.5	23.3

For all that goes into JAWS, the system does not cover every aspect of a player's Hall of Fame case. It makes no attempt to account for postseason performance, awards won, leagues led in important categories, milestone plateaus, or historical importance. A useful (if imperfect) tool for dealing with those aspects of a player's case is the Bill James Hall of Fame Monitor (HOFM), which uses a point system to provide a decent approximation of the aforementioned types of things that Hall voters tend to recognize but that JAWS doesn't cover. The HOFM is calibrated so that an average Hall of Famer accumulates 100 points.

Nor does JAWS itself measure the factors that go into the infamous character clause; no metric can do that. That doesn't mean such considerations shouldn't be weighed when discussing cases, but as you can probably guess if you've read this far, the position I've staked out for this evaluation is a nuanced one that goes beyond simple did-he-or-didn't-he, accounting for the route of implication, weight of evidence, and timing of the infractions. Bearing those factors in mind, as well as each candidate's statistics, some historical perspective, and logical consistency, one can avoid applying the ill-fitting retroactive morality to which Olney referred. If you're of the mind that any PED

TABLE 1-2.2 Upcoming Hall of Fame Candidates Implicated as PED Users

Player	Position	Eligible	TAv	Career	Peak	JAWS	JAWS +/-
Barry Bonds	LF	2013	.350	162.3	73.2	117.7	+62.5
Roger Clemens	SP	2013	.226	110.3	46.3	78.3	+33.2
Gary Sheffield	RF	2015	.314	75.8	43.6	59.7	+4.6
Mike Piazza	C	2013	.313	67.6	47.6	57.6	+12.3
Manny Ramirez	LF	2017	.326	75.5	39.5	57.5	+2.3
Sammy Sosa	RF	2013	.292	59.2	45.5	52.4	-2.7
Mark McGwire	1B	2007	.332	55.1	39.5	47.3	-5.4
Rafael Palmeiro	1B	2011	.299	59.7	32.1	45.9	-6.8
Andy Pettitte	SP	2016	.250	55.2	32.1	43.7	-1.4

use should automatically disqualify a player from Hall consideration, you'll get little satisfaction from reading what follows.

Turning to the cream of the crop among retired players who have been implicated as PED users, Table 1-2.2 shows their JAWS components and how far above or below the JAWS standards they finished. For pitchers, the entry in the TAv column is for true average against.

Mark McGwire

Beyond the steroid allegations, one of the main justifications writers have used for not voting for McGwire is that he was a one-dimensional player whose value was largely confined to home runs. It's true that he didn't have much to offer as a defender; first base is the easiest position to play, and according to our fielding runs above average metric, he was 64 runs below average for his career; by comparison, the average Hall of Fame first baseman was seven runs above average. McGwire wasn't much of a baserunner either; our equivalent baserunning runs stat, which accounts not only for stolen bases but for advancement on hits and outs, values his work on the bases at 41 runs below average; between those two categories, he knocked off at least 11 wins from the value he created in the batter's box.

Still, he created a ton of value with the stick alone. McGwire's True Average ranks 20th among batters with at least 7,500 plate appearances, just below Frank Robinson and above the aforementioned Anson. He's 38th all-time in batting runs above average at 595, nestled between no-doubt Hall of Famers Eddie Mathews and Mike Schmidt. Once you start adjusting for position and accounting for the aforementioned below-average figures, he's less special. His career WARP ranks 22nd among all first basemen, and is 8.3 shy of the standard set by the average Hall of Fame first sacker; the injuries that shortened his career—he had the equivalent of less than 12 full seasons of 650 plate appearances—work against him. His peak WARP is tied for 18th among all first basemen, 2.5 wins shy of the standard; those extra runs around the margins add up. His JAWS is 20th among first basemen, and 5.4 shy of the standard. Eleven of the Hall's 18 first basemen have higher JAWS, as do three players who share space with McGwire on the ballot, one who will be eligible in 2014, and three still active (see Table 1-2.3).

McGwire's Hall of Fame Monitor score is 170; if given a reckoning consistent with past elections, he'd be a slam-dunk candidate, one whose fame and historic importance to his time—the man who brought baseball back from the strike—would carry the day over his shortcomings. Of course, McGwire's chance at a traditional reckoning is long gone, and even from a sabermetric standpoint, his candidacy has significant faults, though it's worth noting that past versions of WARP, which featured a lower replacement level, a different fielding system, and didn't include baserunning, have shown him to be marginally above the standard. In light of JAWS, one needn't delve headlong into the PED issue to justify not voting for him. He simply wasn't as valuable as the lofty (and inflated) home run totals made it appear.

Rafael Palmeiro

In a career that featured 57 percent more plate appearances than McGwire, Palmeiro was "only" 511 runs above average at the plate, 65 runs shy of the average Hall first basemen. He was 2 runs above average in the field, but 28 below on the bases. Relative to the Hall's first basemen, he's closer than McGwire to the career standard, but still 3.7 WARP shy; more problematically, he is 9.9 shy of the peak standard, more than a full win per year over his best seven years.

Remember those complaints when Palmeiro reached the 3,000-hit plateau that he didn't "feel" like a Hall of Famer? His critics may have been on to something, namely that he piled up his hits and homers in some of the game's most favorable hitting environments during a time when runs were plentiful. Historically speaking, each run he created in Texas and Baltimore must be discounted more steeply than those created by some of the game's other great hitters in other places and times. Largely because of that, Palmeiro falls short of the standard for first basemen by 6.8 JAWS, and again, it's not even necessary to invoke a PED-based argument against his candidacy; he may have been aided

TABLE 1-2.3 First Basemen Ranked by JAWS

Rank	NAME	Status	TAv	Career	Peak	JAWS
1	Lou Gehrig	HOF	.374	97.2	60.8	79.0
2	Albert Pujols	Active	.342	91.8	65.6	78.7
3	Jimmie Foxx	HOF	.351	96.4	59.4	77.9
4	Cap Anson	HOF	.331	93.1	40.4	66.7
5	Pete Rose	Banned	.290	84.7	47.4	66.1
6	Jeff Bagwell	Ballot 2011	.321	76.6	48.5	62.6
7	Johnny Mize	HOF	.339	71.3	49.4	60.4
8	Roger Connor	HOF	.339	73.9	39.7	56.8
9	Jim Thome	Active	.320	70.9	39.5	55.2
10	Dick Allen	Retired	.328	61.9	48.2	55.0
11	George Sisler	HOF	.300	59.8	49.5	54.7
12	Willie McCovey	HOF	.324	64.8	43.9	54.4
13	Dan Brouthers	HOF	.356	68.0	40.2	54.1
14	Harmon Killebrew	HOF	.318	65.7	41.8	53.7
15	Hank Greenberg	HOF	.344	58.8	47.9	53.4
	Average HOF	1B	63.4	42.0	52.7
16	Todd Helton	Active	.306	58.1	44.8	51.5
17	Eddie Murray	HOF	.297	61.1	38.5	49.8
18	Jason Giambi	Active	.318	54.3	41.4	47.9
19	Keith Hernandez	Retired	.299	56.6	38.7	47.6
20	Mark McGwire	Ballot 2007	.332	55.1	39.5	47.3
21	Orlando Cepeda	HOF	.310	56.4	37.3	46.9
22	Rafael Palmeiro	Ballot 2011	.299	59.7	32.1	45.9
23	Norm Cash	Retired	.312	55.2	35.7	45.5
24	Tony Perez	HOF	.292	53.2	37.1	45.1
25	John Olerud	Retired	.301	52.0	37.0	44.5

by the drugs, but to a far greater extent, he was aided by favorable surroundings. The presence of a positive test could hardly help him with the voters, and would seem to be among the most solid reasons to withhold a vote—he broke the rules after the rules were made explicitly clear—even in light of otherwise full qualifications.

Note that Bagwell, who spent nine of his 15 seasons calling the offensively barren Astrodome home, scores quite well by this measure despite having lower career totals (2,314 hits and 449 homers) than Palmeiro. He was an outstanding defender (+70 FRAA) as well as run producer (.322 TAv, 639 BRAA), putting up better slash stats than Palmeiro (.297/.408/.540 versus .288/.371/.515) under less favorable conditions for offense, and he's well above the Hall's standards for first baseman via career, peak, and JAWS. Given the lack of credible evidence connecting him to PEDs, the BBWAA voters *should* have little hesitation in voting for him.

Barry Bonds

Bonds ranks second only to Babe Ruth in terms of career WARP and JAWS, and sixth in terms of peak score behind Ruth (92.9), Cobb (75.6), Mays (73.8), Hornsby (73.8), and Ted Williams (73.6)—in other words, among the greatest players ever. While his transgressions with regard to the steroid saga certainly aren't flattering, by the time he began using after the 1998 season, he had already accumulated three MVP awards, made eight All-Star teams, and won eight Gold Gloves while hitting 411 home runs in his first 13 seasons—the trajectory of a Cooperstown-bound career. On a per-batted-ball basis, had Bonds simply hit home runs at the same rate from 1999 to 2007 as he had from 1993 to 1998 (9.1 percent of the time he made contact, instead of 12.8 percent), he would have ended his career with 101 fewer homers, leaving him at 661, one more than his godfather, Mays, who incidentally ranks third all-time in career WARP (160.8) and JAWS (117.3). Bonds may owe his title as the all-time home run leader to his ill-gotten gains, but he was also clearly a Hall of Famer without those homers or that title.

The intense scrutiny under which Bonds fell, both in the courts given BALCO and on the field of play given his home run records, should be kept in perspective, as should the timing. Other than being a prickly personality, none of the major allegations against him occurred during the testing era. Furthermore, it bears repeating that the BALCO investigation featured wrongdoings far more grave than gaining advantage in a sport; evidence was illegally seized, grand jury information was illegally leaked, and the principles of due process and the right to privacy were violated. More than $50 million in taxpayer money was wasted in an attempt to put Bonds behind bars not for using steroids, but for perjury and obstruction of justice, important principles worth defending, but ones whose application was misdirected. It's time to set that circus aside. One need not celebrate Bonds as the equal of Ruth, Aaron, and Mays to recognize that he belongs in the Hall.

Roger Clemens

Clemens, whose career WARP ranks third among pitchers behind Walter Johnson and Cy Young, and whose JAWS ranks fourth behind those two and Alexander, was almost as clearly Hall bound as Bonds when he left Boston for Toronto following the 1996 season. At 33 years old, he had a won-loss record of 192–111, a career 3.06 ERA, 2,590 strikeouts, and an MVP and three Cy Young awards under his belt. To that point, every retired three- or four-time Cy winner (Sandy Koufax, Tom Seaver, Jim Palmer, and Steve Carlton) was in Cooperstown, with four-time winner Greg Maddux contemporaneously building his own case, Randy Johnson having secured the first of his record seven awards, and Pedro Martinez about to go on his own three-Cy spree. Clemens's final four years with the Red Sox had yielded just 40 wins, but he led the AL in strikeouts in his swan song, underscoring the strength of his remaining skills with a 20-strikeout game on September 18, 1996, a performance that tied his own 10-year-old major league record.

In Toronto, Clemens began working with strength and conditioning coach Brian McNamee, who is alleged to have injected him with various PEDs, both with the Blue Jays and later with the Yankees. Not only did Clemens win back-to-back Cy Young Awards in 1997 and 1998, he won the rare pitching "triple crown" (league leads in ERA, wins, and strikeouts) in both years. He would go on to win two more Cy Young Awards, one with the Yankees in 2001, and one with the Astros in 2004, when he was 41 years old. We can theorize that none of the hardware from that latter stage of his career might have been earned without steroids, but without any mechanism to help quantify his potential gains in a manner paralleling what we did for sluggers in the previous chapter, we're in the realm of pure speculation. Even without steroids, it's likely he would have finished with over 3,000 strikeouts, another Hall bona fide (nine out of 10 pitchers to reach that plateau were already enshrined) while pushing his win total well into the 200s. The circus that came after Clemens was named in the Mitchell Report was largely of his own doing; even so, the timeline still suggests his major transgressions date to the pre-testing era. Vote him in and move along.

Gary Sheffield

On paper, Sheffield looks like a Hall of Famer, with 509 career homers, 2,689 hits, a lifetime .292/.393/.514 line, nine All-Star appearances, three top-three showings in the MVP voting, and a 156 on the Hall of Fame Monitor. His advanced metrics support his cause; he ranks eighth among all right fielders in career WARP, 10th in peak WARP, and eighth in JAWS. He cleared the right-field standard by a solid margin even though he was an estimated 101 runs below average in the field for his career, some of that from his early days in the infield, when he was something of an enfant terrible.

Like Bonds, Sheffield was named in the BALCO case. According to his grand jury testimony, he obtained "the clear," "the cream," and steroid pills directly from Bonds, with whom he had trained in the Bay Area during the 2001–2002 offseason as he was recuperating from knee surgery. Sheffield said he was unaware that what he received was steroids; he recounted rubbing testosterone cream directly on his knee after his stitches popped out, believing it to be "no different from the Neosporin you buy at Rite Aid." If there was an effect on Sheffield's performance after that, it's virtually impossible to see, because his statistics took a mild dip in 2002, likely due to a torn thumb ligament suffered midway through the season. After hitting a monstrous .311/.417/.583 with an 8.0 percent rate of homers per batted ball with the Dodgers in 2001, he fell off to .307/.404/.512 with a 5.7 percent rate with the Braves in 2002 despite playing in a much more hitter-friendly ballpark. His rate of homers per batted ball from 1993 through 2001 with the Marlins and Dodgers was a fairly unremarkable 7.6 percent, vacillating as his myriad injuries came and went; he peaked at 10 percent in 2000, the year when homers were at their most plentiful. From 2002 through the end of his career in 2009, his rate fell to 6.3 percent.

As can be said of many sluggers of the period, it's not outside the realm of possibility that Sheffield's 1990s numbers were aided by PEDs, but absent any evidence or specific, credible allegations, the impact of PEDs upon his career appears to be almost negligible. His route to the Hall of Fame shouldn't be impeded, though it remains to be seen whether the BBWAA will see it that way.

Manny Ramirez

Ramirez certainly has Hall-worthy numbers: 555 home runs, 2,574 hits, a .312/.411/.585 career line, 12 All-Star appearances, four top-five finishes in the MVP vote, a whopping 29 postseason home runs, two World Series rings, and so on. His advanced metrics are strong as well. His True Average ranks 24th among hitters with 7,500 PA. His career WARP ranks sixth among left fielders behind Bonds, Ted Williams, Rickey Henderson, Stan Musial, and Carl Yastrzemski; it's far enough beyond the Hall standard for left fielders (67.4) that it overcomes a peak score 3.6 WARP lower than the standard. His notoriously poor defense (-76 FRAA) chips away at his peak value, though he's still 2.3 JAWS ahead of the standard.

Alas, Ramirez has more evidence of post-testing-era wrongdoing than any other player. Not only is he alleged to have failed the 2003 survey test, he was suspended twice for positive tests once MLB's full program was in place, first in 2009 and again in 2011. He failed in 2009 due to the presence of artificial testosterone, and was found to have an unauthorized prescription for human chorionic go-nadotropin, a female fertility drug often employed by steroid users to restart natural testosterone production after a steroid cycle. The cause of his 2011 positive was never publicly identified due to his immediate retirement after the positive test was revealed. Despite being one of the era's great hitters, such flaunting of baseball's post-reform drug policy will likely be enough to prevent him from being voted into the Hall, and it probably should be.

Sammy Sosa

Sosa finished with 2,408 hits and 609 homers; he was the fifth player to reach the 600-homer milestone after Ruth, Mays, Aaron, and Bonds. At this writing he ranks seventh on the all-time list, likely to be surpassed by Jim Thome (604) in the 2012 season. Yet despite those totals and seven All-Star appearances, an MVP award, and an off-the-charts Hall of Fame Monitor score of 201 (higher even than Mc-Gwire), his admittance into the Hall of Fame is in jeopardy. Sosa was long presumed by many to be a steroid user due to his broad, bulky physique and his proximity to McGwire in the breaking of Roger Maris's single-season record. *Sports Illustrated*'s Rick Reilly infa-mously went to the Cubs locker room and dared him to subvert the MLB Players Association by submitting a urine sample to an indepen-dent lab in the summer of 2002, while in 2005, Sosa joined McGwire, Palmeiro, and Canseco at the congressional hearing, where he denied ever having used PEDs. He escaped mention in the Mitchell Report, and had never been linked via any specific allegation until June 2009, when his name was leaked to the *New York Times* as one of the players on the 2003 survey list.

Sosa falls considerably shy of the career standard for right fielders. Despite all the home runs, he spent the first half of his career (1989–1997) as an impatient hacker; he only learned to take a walk once pitchers found pitching around him desirable. As a result, he was just 363 runs above average at the plate, a full 193 runs below the av-erage enshrined right fielder, and while he closed the gap considerably in the field—his 82 FRAA are 91 more than the average Hall right fielder, he winds up 9.3 WARP shy of the career standard at his posi-tion. He's 3.8 WARP ahead of the peak standard, but his career shortfall leaves him 2.7 JAWS shy, much closer than McGwire or Palmeiro, yet still on the wrong side of the line.

Nonetheless, Sosa's positive survey test makes it difficult to counter the suspicion that his otherwise-impressive heyday was fueled by PEDs. Even without specific dates to attach to his use, the unprecedented nature of his 243-homer spree from 1998 through 2001, during which he topped 60 homers three times, raises more than one eyebrow. Given where he falls relative to the standard, and to what is known about his usage, it's difficult to justify granting him enough leeway to merit a vote for the Hall of Fame.

Mike Piazza

Piazza clears the JAWS standard at his position by the widest margin among those above besides Bonds and Clemens. He is the best-hitting catcher of all time; in a 16-year career, the 12-time All Star hit 427 homers (a record 396 while serving as catcher) and compiled a .308/.377/.545 line despite playing in a succession of pitcher-friendly parks. His 457 runs above average is tops among catchers, 113 runs ahead of the second-ranked Mickey Cochrane, and his true average is tops as well. Despite being 40 runs below average on defense, he's tops in peak WARP among catchers, and fourth in career WARP, winding up second in JAWS behind Johnny Bench (60.1).

In part because he was drafted by the Dodgers in the 62nd round of the 1988 draft and subsequently went on to excel at the major league level, Piazza had often been suspected as a steroid user. He never tested positive, and did not turn up in the Mitchell Report despite spending seven years with the Mets, whose clubhouse employee Kirk Radomski was at the epicenter of the report's allegations. Even so, when the *New York Times* article published an article on steroids in the wake of *Sports Illustrated*'s Ken Caminiti cover story in the spring of 2002, the catcher admitted his record wasn't spotless: "Piazza has said he briefly used androstenedione early in his career, stopping when he did not see a drastic change in his muscle mass. He said he had never used steroids because 'I hit the ball as far in high school as I do now.'"

At the time Piazza spoke to the *Times* reporters, andro was still legal. Not until 2004 was it added to the Controlled Substances Act, banned for sale by the FDA, or banned by MLB. He is surely not the only star player besides McGwire who used andro before it was banned; as such, it seems excessive to hold that against him in the context of a Hall of Fame argument.

The subject of Piazza and steroids resurfaced in Jeff Pearlman's 2009 biography of Clemens, *The Rocket Who Fell to Earth*, in which he wrote:

> According to several sources, when the subject of performance enhancing was broached with reporters he especially trusted, Piazza fessed up. "Sure, I use," he told one. "But in limited doses, and not all that often." (Piazza has denied using performance-enhancing drugs, but there has always been speculation.) Whether or not it was Piazza's intent, the tactic was brilliant: By letting the media know, off the record, Piazza made the information that much harder to report.

Even given Piazza's previous andro admission, it's difficult to accord such a secondhand report weight on par with a positive test, actual or leaked, or even an appearance in the Mitchell Report. The public outcry with regard to Piazza's andro admission came nowhere close to the level that greeted any of the players in the aforementioned categories, and likewise with regard to the media; on the contrary, both slipped under most radars. Given that, and the absence of more incriminating evidence, the BBWAA should have little hesitation voting for Piazza for the Hall of Fame.

Andy Pettitte

By a traditional reckoning, Pettitte doesn't look much like a Hall of Famer; his credentials are a mixed bag. His 240–138 (.635) won-loss record is gaudy, but as is discussed elsewhere in this book, any modern-day starting pitcher's record owes plenty to the offenses, defenses, and bullpens that supported him. Pettitte's 3.88 ERA is higher than any pitcher's in Cooperstown, just edging Red Ruffing's 3.80. Once you adjust for his ballpark and the high scoring levels of the era, that ERA doesn't look so outrageous; he was 17 percent better than the park-adjusted league average according to ERA+, equal to or better than 23 pitchers, including eight 300-game winners; then again, those in that latter group threw about 60 percent more innings in their careers. Though Pettitte finished in the top five in the Cy Young voting four times, he never won the award, and pitched in just three All-Star games; at the same time, he was a key component of five world champions and eight pennant winners in his 16-year career, such a staple of October that he holds career records for wins (19, against 10 losses), starts (42), and innings (263), and is tied for second in strikeouts (173).

Pettitte clears the career standard by 2.2 WARP, but falls 5.0 WARP short on peak, leaving him 1.4 shy of the JAWS standard. The weight of his postseason contributions enhances his case—he's got more than a full season of replicating his performance under circumstances of the highest stakes—but on the other hand, he was named in the Mitchell Report for having used injections of human growth hormone (HGH) in 2002 and 2004.

Pettitte claimed that he used the HGH in an attempt to heal faster from elbow injuries, not to gain a competitive advantage, and that he never used steroids. In the latter instance, he obtained the HGH via a prescription for his seriously ill father, and subsequently underwent surgery for a torn flexor tendon. While MLB has no test for HGH, and while there is no scientific evidence to connect its benefits to any meaningful improvement in baseball performance, it is nonetheless troubling that his second instance occurred after the implementation of the punitive phase of the Joint Drug Prevention and Treatment Program; at that point, he had to be aware he was violating baseball's rules. Perhaps that is why Pettitte is the only one of the players under discussion here besides McGwire who felt the need to offer public apology. Pettitte's fans certainly seemed inclined to forgive him, and the media never came down particularly hard upon him. In the balance, the weight of his transgression doesn't seem to be enough to prevent a vote for him, though his merits as a candidate are borderline enough that one could be excused for voting either way.

Performance-enhancing drugs were a significant, if unfortunate, reality of baseball for nearly two decades, their presence in the game prolonged by a lack of will on the part of players, owners, the commissioner, and the media to honestly reckon with what was happening and to take responsibility for their elimination. Inevitably, many of the game's brightest stars used them, often taking advantage of gray areas, such as the legal status of androstenedione or the lack of a test for HGH. To sweep all of that under the rug in an attempt to present a sanitized version of history by keeping all PED users outside the Hall of Fame is ultimately a dissatisfying endeavor that will cost the institution its relevance.

As the foregoing exercise has illustrated, advanced statistics can help tackle the thorny question of how to handle the cases of PED-implicated candidates. Better than simply applying a blanket zero-tolerance policy when it comes to PED use, we can see through the era's distorted stats to realize that the sudden plenitude of home runs means that not all 500-homer sluggers are equally worthy of enshrinement; we needn't strain ourselves trying to figure out how Coopers-town can survive the omission of a few. We can see which players still rise far enough above their contemporaries and compare favorably to their predecessors to merit inclusion despite their transgressions; the Hall's rolls were never a boys choir anyway. Armed with tools like JAWS and the Hall of Fame Monitor as well as a historical perspective on the myriad ways in which the steroid problem manifested itself, and of the steps taken to curb their use, we can address each candidate's case on its own merits using consistent, logical standards. Ultimately, we can only hope that the voters will be able to do so as well.

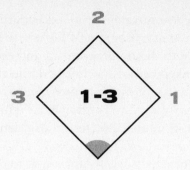

What Is the Next Stage in Athlete Enhancement?

COREY DAWKINS

Imagine we're in a future that isn't all that far off—say, 10 or 20 years from now. There are many similarities between our time and this one; for instance, here sits a 25-year-old up-and-coming pitcher on an examination table in a doctor's office. His name is Johnny, and his professional career is at a crossroads thanks to a notorious pitching injury, the dreaded torn rotator cuff and labrum. Platelet-rich plasma (PRP) injections initially worked their magic, alleviating his symptoms, but ultimately proved unsuccessful at healing him. Now Johnny is willing to try an experimental treatment to get his once-promising career back on track—the kind of treatment that wasn't available back when he was just a child, watching his heroes play the game he loves.

For Johnny, attempting to overcome his reduced abilities by recourse to performance-enhancing drugs (PEDs) is out of the question, as it was in our time. But there are other ways of achieving the same goals—and even more effectively—without nasty side effects like an early death or unspeakable horrors like backne. To us, reading this in the present day, robots and robotics are still largely the province of science fiction. In Johnny's future, robotics are a commonplace tool of the medical profession. Nanotechnology could be just what this pitcher needs to get back on the mound.

Johnny's isn't quite the future envisioned by Super Baseball 2020—a 1993 video game in which players, enhanced with robot technology, utilized jet-packs to help them play defense. Instead, robots too small to be seen with the naked eye will be injected into the pitcher, rebuilding him from the inside and making him capable of performing at a level he would otherwise no longer be able to achieve. With a simple shot in the shoulder, a new age in technology and sports will have dawned.

For centuries, athletes have looked for a way to delay the aging process. While the above scenario hasn't happened yet, it's not far off. In ancient times, gaining an edge could have meant the difference between living or dying, eating or going hungry. While athletes today aren't fighting their food before they put it on the table for their families, it's not surprising, given the economic setting of today's game, where the minimum salary is over $400,000 and the average salary over $3 million, that players continue to look for ways to gain an advantage on the competition. PEDs have been around baseball for decades, even if they have only seemed relevant as of late. There is a new age of athlete athletic enhancement just around the bend: one where new technologies, gene doping, and nanotechnology will create pathways for getting the same—if not better—results than are currently achieved with PEDS, and in ways that are currently undetectable. Baseball may think it has licked the PED problem with testing and stiff penalties, but there is no holding back the future.

Back to the Future with PEDs

Performance-enhancing drugs have been around for centuries. They are not an invention of baseball or the 1990s, despite what Hall of Fame voters might try to tell you. Opium derivatives were used in the ancient Olympics. When most people discuss PEDs, the conversation is generalized, only considering known anabolic steroids and human growth hormone, whereas the Bay Area Laboratory Co-operative (BALCO) case showed that newly created drugs are the cutting edge of pharmaceutical-based enhancement. Their effectiveness, however, is not set in stone: no scientific studies have been able to correlate improved performance in baseball with anabolic steroids (for more on this, see Chapter 1-1).

The abuse of anabolic steroids in the modern age of sports began with power lifting and then spread to other sports, including the infamous East German women's swimming team of the 1960s and 1970s. Baseball players initially rejected the notion that anabolic steroids could help their performance, slowing steroids' entry into the game. In the early years of abuse, players used substances produced by legitimate pharmaceutical companies that were intended for use in medical or veterinary care. As time wore on, some of same substances, such as boldenone and stanozolol, began to be abused by players.

Anabolic steroids are substances that improve protein synthesis and increase cell growth. When used properly, they are dispensed and administered in conjunction with the monitoring of various hormone levels through blood tests at regular intervals, to ensure there have been no deleterious side effects such as hypertension, cholesterol issues, cardiovascular disease, or liver damage. Despite these risks, anabolic steroids have legitimate medical purposes: treatment of pituitary dysfunction in young males, testicular cancer, or muscle wasting diseases are just a few of these.

Another substance that flies under the radar in terms of PEDs is insulin-like growth factor (IGF-1). It too has legitimate medical uses, but in sports it is almost always used in conjunction with other substances to create a "stack" of drugs. While its anabolic-related effects on performance are unknown, IGF-1 does help decrease cell death and can lead to faster recovery times.

Once it was clear that anabolic steroids could improve performance in sports such as swimming and weight lifting, the race was on to find other substances that could make athletes bigger, faster, and stronger than before. Human growth hormone (HGH) was first abused in sports in the 1970s, and has since been banned by most governing bodies in sports. HGH is a naturally occurring hormone used to treat growth disorders, but is only available legally through a doctor's prescription. Until recently, there was no test that could detect the difference between the naturally occurring version of growth hormone created in the pituitary gland and the manufactured version, the one most associated with PEDs.

Due to the cost involved, it can be difficult for entry-level minor league players to consistently take manufactured HGH, but once players reach the majors it is not prohibitively expensive. Unlike many readily available anabolic steroids, HGH is costly and difficult to store and transport, and therefore not as likely to be abused.

Building a Better Athlete

It became apparent that the readily available anabolic agents would not remain undetected forever. As a result, "designer drugs" are being created to be undetectable, but with the same, if not better, performance-enhancing effects. The most famous of these was at the heart of the BALCO case: tetrahydrogestrinone (THG). THG was manipulated to be undetectable to all of the testing methods of the time; its success has inevitably led to the creation of many more that are still undetectable.

There are a few different ways for a drug to remain undetectable in drug tests. The most difficult and expensive method is to create a new chemical that, when broken down during analysis, is in structures not already on the banned list. This method has become more difficult with the ever-increasing list of banned substances and their metabolites. Another method involves tricking the system into believing that the body's ratio of testosterone to epitestosterone is within a normal range. By carefully monitoring these substances, a player can continuously train while having an elevated ratio to the baseline, but still be within the "normal" range.

Chemical compounds are not the only ways to create performance enhancement; body modification techniques are becoming commonplace and more accepted. LASIK eye surgery, for one, uses a laser to reshape the cornea of the eye to correct a person's vision. Normal vision is considered 20/20. This means a person can see an object 20 feet away as if it were exactly 20 feet away. Many of the corrections performed on baseball players now bring that level to 20/15 or better. Being able to recognize a pitch a split second quicker has obvious benefits, and a few studies have noted a positive effect.

The wave-front-guided LASIK procedure maps out the eye and then creates a custom profile to shape the cornea to the exact needed dimensions. Theoretically, eyesight can be improved past 20/15 to even 20/10, creating even more of an advantage. LASIK does come with risks. Potential complications include irregular astigmatism, dry eyes, infection, night vision difficulties, or blurry vision. Atlanta Braves catcher Brian McCann, who underwent LASIK correction in 2007, started to experience visual changes that affected him in the 2009 season. After a trip to the disabled list and the use of customized glasses, he was able to return and finish out the year, before having repeat LASIK surgery in the offseason.

Players can get the same corrective benefit of LASIK surgery with customized contact lenses. Lenses can be crafted to create vision better than 20/20, and only require minimal adjustment on the player's part without as much risk of serious side effects. Contact lenses can also filter out background colors and make the baseball stand out. They can also be created to improve low-light visibility.

There are also legal, though experimental, surgeries that don't involve a player's eyes, but can resurrect his career or improve performance in much the same way. In the not too distant future discussed at the start of this chapter, Bartolo Colon may be remembered as the first player since Tommy John to have a procedure named after him.

Colon had missed 428 days—well over two seasons' worth—from 2006 through 2010 due to various injuries, many of them to his throwing shoulder. His arm, in a word, was junk. Like our intrepid hypothetical man of the future, he was in a position where he had nothing to lose.

The idea of separating out the body's own tissue and injecting it into a specific area it is not new. Platelet-rich plasma injections have been around for decades and are being used increasingly in treatment of orthopedic injuries. Blood is drawn and spun down to separate its components. The drawn-out plasma is then injected into the area of damaged or necrotic tissue, where it releases growth factors to accelerate healing by signaling the body to release mesenchymal stem cells (MSCs).

Colon's stem cell therapy took PRP to an entirely new level. It involved those same MSCs found in the body's bone marrow, adipose tissue, synovial tissue, and muscle tissue that are released in response to the growth factors in PRP injections. MSCs are not the same as embryonic or fetal stem cells, the controversial version that the media has spent most of its time focusing on. MSCs are present in everyone throughout their life, and have been shown to be able to differentiate into different bone, cartilage, and tendon cells in addition to releasing other growth factors that assist in tissue repair.

Colon's procedure, performed outside the United States in his native Dominican Republic, took advantage of the wide-ranging properties of MSCs to return the body to normal function. In this five-hour procedure, the first step is to draw fat tissue out of the patient. Bone marrow is then drawn through a soft spot in the back of the pelvic bone into a syringe. Two ounces of specimen containing MSCs, platelets, and other types of stem cells are drawn and then placed in a container.

The container is put in a centrifuge where it is spun down, similar to PRP, to separate the different components of the specimen. Bone marrow, platelets, and fat are then drawn, and placed underneath an LED light to activate the healing properties inside them. Once activated, the MSCs, like other cells, know what to do and what to become. MSCs are bossy, telling the damaged cells to repair themselves.

Two PRP injections spaced four to six weeks apart follow, in order to keep the MSCs active.

According to PITCHf/x, in 2009 Colon averaged 89 mph on his four-seam fastball, down from 92 in 2008. On April 3, 2011, nearly a year to the day after getting the MSC injections in his shoulder, Colon was back to averaging 92 mph on his four-seamer, and even maxed out at over 94 mph. A hamstring injury suffered in June slowed down his season, hampering his mechanics and velocity, but his arm remained healthy. That's a significant step forward for a pitcher who had missed as much as Colon in recent years and an encouraging sign for use of MSC therapy in the future.

MSC therapy has the greatest benefit over traditional methods in areas of low blood supply such as around the shoulder rotator cuff tendons and areas of the labrum. As Dr. Joseph Purita of the Institute of Regenerative and Molecular Orthopaedics and one of Colon's surgeons describes it, to heal properly, injuries need good blood flow that acts as a supply line, and these two structures have been extremely difficult to return to baseline function even with traditional surgical methods. Stem cell and PRP therapy can act as that supply line and greatly increase the chances of a positive outcome in these areas.

The prognosis for those patients receiving MSC therapy depends in large part on the quality of the physician and the quality of the injectable stem cells. Stem cell therapy would be more beneficial and likely result in a better outcome if performed earlier in the injury process, such as when only fraying or a minimal partial tear is present. There are no set limits as to how often MSC therapy can be performed, which raises the possibility of MSC interventions on a semi-prophylactic basis where there is some damage, but not enough to cause significant symptoms.

MSC therapy without pharmacologic supplementation does not have the same effect as anabolic steroids or HGH. In injured or damaged tissues, MSC therapy can restore function to pre-injury levels, but it does not enhance it further, even in healthy tissue. However, MSC therapy with pharmacologic supplementation on healthy tissue can have an anabolic effect past baseline. Since PEDs are banned in baseball, Dr. Purita does not supplement MSC with HGH for any baseball player, even at the high school or collegiate level.

MSC therapy will likely find quick acceptance in baseball as stem cells are already being used in microfracture surgery. In that procedure, bone is drilled into the marrow, causing bleeding, after which a clot forms. The bone marrow cells released during the microfracture procedure are in fact MSCs, and could theoretically be used to form a concentrate for injection back into the body during MSC therapy. Microfracture simply releases far fewer of these cells at once compared to MSC therapy and cannot be performed on soft tissue. Microfracture surgery has become an accepted treatment for various injuries, so despite MSC's still-experimental nature, it's a short leap from there to widespread usage. However, the FDA is attempting to categorize MSC therapy as a drug, possibly delaying its impact on sports medicine in the United States. It is already frequently used in other countries, initially only for Achilles and patellar tendon injuries, and now for hamstring, ligamentous, and oblique injuries. Despite the FDA's tactics, MSC therapy will likely become as commonplace as PRP injections are now.

Where No One Has Gone Before

The next frontier in performance enhancement will be genetic modification techniques, otherwise known as gene doping. The idea of using genes to treat illnesses isn't new, having been around for many years in the treatment of autoimmune diseases and certain blood disorders.

Gene doping involves changing the DNA structure of biological regulation processes to improve speed, power, or endurance. Tens of thousands of genes are in the human body, meaning there are too many to systematically check to see if gene doping has a performance-enhancing affect. There are a multitude of genes that can be used in gene doping, and they can be administered through different pathways. One possible pathway involves altering a virus's genetic sequence to insert the new gene variant, and allow the gene to gradually become replicated in the target cells. The virus itself is almost always inactivated in order to allow stability of the delivery system. Other methods include using microsyringes, or other biochemical injection vehicles, to insert the genes into the body.

Initially most gene doping in baseball will be limited to increasing the size and strength of the skeletal muscles. Angiotensin-converting enzyme (ACE) is a gene that plays a part in the capabilities of the skeletal muscles throughout the body. The ACE-I variation improves endurance capacities, while the ACE-D variation is associated with explosiveness of fast-twitch muscles. By altering these variations, a pitcher may be able to throw more pitches without fear of fatigue.

Actinin-binding proteins control the mechanics of skeletal muscle contractions. ACTN3 is associated with improved explosiveness in fast-twitch muscle fibers, while ACTN2 improves endurance. The previously mentioned IGF-1 can also be introduced through gene doping to local skeletal muscle tissue. This can increase muscle size and power, and improve recovery without as much risk of systemic side effects. Additionally, since it stays in the local muscle tissue and does not travel through the body, it can be very hard to detect during any sort of drug testing.

Another important gene that could be altered is myostatin. Unlike the others noted above, an increased amount of myostatin will actually *decrease* muscle size and power, and increase the amount of time needed for recovery. By inhibiting myostatin, the affected skeletal muscle will become bigger and stronger, and require less time to recover.

Genes available for doping are not limited in their improvements to just increasing the size of muscle tissue. Interleukin-1RA has shown positive trial results in the lubrication of joints, and has been used to treat osteoarthritis. Introducing this gene before osteoarthritis sets in might help to fend off the disease for some time, leading to longer careers. Mechano-growth factor (MGF) can help skeletal muscle tissue heal, and is activated by muscle stretching or overload, an obvious benefit to those with muscle strains. Studies have shown that there has been a 15 percent increase in muscle size with MGF usage.

It is going to be extremely difficult to catch baseball players who are gene doping. With many of the genes acting on skeletal muscle, they will not be readily seen in the urine or even in the blood. Muscle biopsies will have to be required at first, at least until there is a reliable urine or blood test (if that ever occurs). In the biopsy, testers will search for evidence of the viral vehicles that brought the genes into the system in the first place.

Other methods of gene doping detection, such as a partial genetic map, could be utilized. Rather than one or two genes being monitored, hundreds would be tracked. Certain pattern changes would be analyzed further to determine if there had been any untoward changes. Microchip arrays that monitor the expressions of DNA and RNA could observe thousands of genes simultaneously to detect gene doping.

Nanotechnology

A younger technology than gene doping, nanotechnology involves altering matter on an atomic and molecular level. Nanotechnology is already in use at the amateur levels with many composite bats. These bats have nanotubes that are interlaced with carbon fibers to give them ten times the strength of steel at a fraction of the weight. Kim B. Blair, Ph.D., vice president of Cooper Perkins, Inc. and founding director of Sports Innovation @ MIT agrees that nanotechnology would have its greatest impact in Major League Baseball if composite bats were allowed to be used without the exit speed restrictions in place at the amateur levels. He acknowledges, however, that MLB would be extremely unlikely to consider using such materials in bats. Other applications in equipment, such as in cleats or uniforms, are unlikely to produce any game-changing performance.

Material nanotechnology could also eventually be used for performance enhancement outside the rules of baseball. Eventually, baseball players could use liquid nanotech that coats on clear to a wooden bat, hardening it more than the current lacquers and adding less weight. Pitchers may use a substance to coat their hands and increase their grip while decreasing the risk of blisters or other injuries. Miniature fibers, called nanowhiskers, would project out from this substance, allowing the resulting spin of a breaking ball to be greater, thanks to the enhanced grip.

According to Dr. Blair, the most advantageous aspect of nanotechnology over traditional methods of cheating would be the difficulty of detecting it on the field of play; opposing managers or umpires aren't going to see nanowhiskers on a pitcher's hand the same way they can see pine tar. Had this technology existed in 1988, Los Angeles Dodgers closer Jay Howell wouldn't have been ejected from the National League Championship Series against the New York Mets; and if it had been around in 2006, no one would have ever seen a substance on Kenny Rogers's left hand that led to questions about how legitimate his performance was.

Nanotechnology will also play a role in improving performance following injuries. With most of the attention placed on PEDs, players will turn to nanotechnology as a way to get back to their baseline or better. Back in 2006, researchers created artificial muscles that were over 100 times stronger than natural muscles. In 2009, different researchers improved upon this by creating artificial muscles that could stretch over 10 times the length of natural muscles, while also able to produce 30 times more force. While prophylactic surgery involving artificial muscles using this technology isn't the best idea, if the player is already going to have surgery to repair a muscle or tendon, he might request the new muscle and dramatically increase his baseline levels.

In cases where direct repair of damaged muscle tissue is needed, nanotechnology also holds promise. Researchers believe that nanotechnology will be extremely useful in cardiac muscle repair, and it would only be a matter of time before the same concepts are applied to skeletal muscle tissue.

Baseball players will always look for ways to improve their performance. Some will choose to stick to the rules, while others will decide to jump over the line and use performance-enhancing substances ranging from medication to, eventually, nanotechnology. To start off with, gene doping and nanotechnology will remain expensive, meaning that cheap pharmaceutical PEDs will not be going away anytime soon, even if the rich can replace them. Gene doping is already being used in other sports—it is only a matter of time before the first baseball player is caught and we have a new set of regulations.

PART 2
Questions of Team-Building

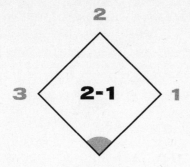

How Are Players Scouted, Acquired, and Developed?

JASON PARKS

When scouts are sent out into the world to discover the next great hero, they carry with them the burden of hope. The future is always bright when it lives in an abstract reality, and we baseball fans have a tendency to tailor that reality to provide comfort when faced with the disappointments and discomforts of the present. Scouts are tasked with fulfilling these dreams, bringing in the raw materials necessary to construct the parameters of what is possible. The process of dream construction begins in the eyes of the talent evaluators. This is what they look for.

Talent Evaluation: Scouting 101
When evaluating talent, one has to make multiple determinations based on small sample sizes, unbalanced competitive landscapes, and a plethora of unknown eventualities. Not to get overly existential, but scouting is a profound philosophical pursuit: Is it possible to separate our own deficiencies and insecurities from the process? Does the fact that I used to be quite fast influence my ability to appreciate speed in a lower-level prospect? If I once had dreams of being a ballplayer, does that heighten my ability to recognize those who are athletically superior to me, or does my failure create a form of subjective justice that I wield upon those that get to play out my fantasy for a paycheck?

133

Scouting is about asking questions—"What is this player all about? What can he do now and what will he be able to do in the future?"— but it's also important to ask, "Why am I forming these conclusions. Why do I value certain physical characteristics and discount others?"

On the Mound

With pitchers, the first thing to look for is the body. While it's true that size doesn't always matter, it's also true that size *often* matters, and a pitcher's physical attributes form the skeleton of any report. Ideally, when scouting a younger player, you look for signs of physical projection. Can the frame hold weight/mass? How mature is the present body? How athletic is the body? Projection gives scouts the freedom to dream. Given a young six-foot-three, 175-pound body, one can envision arsenal projection before actually seeing the arsenal. It's the starting point.

I am an admitted velocity junkie, but my fancy is even more susceptible to the tickle of fastball command, especially with lower-level arms. Fastball command is the perfect building block for the rest of the arsenal. It creates the opportunity for a more effective secondary arsenal before the secondary arsenal is even deployed. Fastball command is the product of repeatability and comfort. When I look for command projection in a pitcher, I start with the mechanics. How fluid is his overall motion? Does his arm take a smooth and easy journey from hand break to extension? Can he repeat the delivery? Is his arm slot and release point consistent on every pitch? How is his overall tempo and pace of the process? Does the pitcher speed up or slow down when runners reach base? How does this affect his delivery and mechanics?

Fastball velocity is the meat in a pitcher's cheeseburger. Without it, you'd better bring a 70-grade bun with several above-average accoutrements to make up for the missing protein. Raw velocity is easy to identify and grade, which makes it one of the more tangible aspects of scouting (see Table 2-1.1).

Radar gun readings can be sexy, but if velocity isn't accompanied by command and movement, velocity is exploitable by hitters at the highest levels of the game. While it certainly affords pitchers more room for error, it is only one variable to the overall fastball equation, and very rarely is it strong enough to survive on its own. Straight fastballs often find barrels, and hard contact isn't a desired end result of any at-bat. Some pitchers are fortunate when it comes to fastball movement; it occurs naturally for many left-handed pitchers, with their fastballs

TABLE 2-1.1 The Hierarchy of Fastballs

Velocity	Grade
97+ mph	80: Elite; bacon
94–96 mph	70: Well above average, plus-plus; chicken-fried steak with cream gravy and Texas toast
92–94 mph	60: Above average, plus; wine and cheese
89–91 mph	50: Average; standard cheeseburger, no frills
87–89 mph	40: Below average; salad, no cheese or bacon
85–87 mph	30: Well below average; boiled broccoli
82–84 mph	20: Poor; tofu

showing some arm-side movement, meaning the pitch has a little boring action into lefties and running action away from righties.

Different pitch grips will create different fastballs, each offering unique movement and velocity. Most pitchers feature either a two-seam or four-seam fastball in the arsenal, and it is quite common for a pitcher to offer both. The four-seam fastball, gripped across the seams, allows for maximum velocity. Of course, the faster the pitch the straighter it becomes, so most four-seam fastballs lack aggressive movement. Two-seam fastballs are often called "sinkers," and sometimes this is accurate and sometimes not; some pitchers throw traditional sinkers, which are a little slower than the average two-seamer and feature more extreme vertical movement. Two-seam fastballs aren't thrown with the same velocity as four-seamers, but they often provide more movement, normally featuring some horizontal movement (run) and some natural weight to the pitch (sink). Keep this in mind: every pitcher is unique, so every hand will form a different relationship with the ball and therefore produce a different result. You have to look at the pitcher as an individual.

Scouting movement in person can be very challenging, as your eyes can play tricks on you, convincing you of movement that isn't there. Because of this phenomenon, pay close attention to the hitters. Watch their reactions to each pitch, judging movement not only from the ball, but also from where the bat starts versus where it ends up in the zone; a hitter's swing can tell you a great deal about what a pitch is doing, especially if the pitch starts on one plane and finishes on another.

One often hears tales of late movement on a fastball. This is often the product of visual subterfuge. Some pitchers help create the environment for this illusion with their arm action and extension. When a pitcher has a fast arm, the ball appears to explode out of his hand, with a little hop or jump as it nears the plate. The same is true of a pitcher with excellent extension; the ball is released closer to the plate, and therefore has less distance to cover. It appears to have more velocity than it actually does and seems to "jump on the hitters." Again, if you doubt your eyes and don't want to fall victim to the trompe l'oeil, just watch the hitter.

Secondary Pitches, Presence, Poise, and Pitchability

While a good fastball can carry the majority of the load, the secondary and tertiary components of the arsenal (curve, slider, change, and so on) will ultimately define the possible range of success. Outliers always exist, so you might run across arsenals that aren't built on the fastball, or arsenals that consist of one super-wizard pitch (say, Mariano Rivera's cutter), but generally speaking, we are scouting human beings and not knuckleballers or Panamanian relief wizards.

Much like the fastball, secondary pitches come in different shapes and sizes, some classified as balls that break, others identified as "changes of pace." Let's start with the breaking stuff. People seem to like breaking balls for the same reason they like fastball velocity: you can clearly identify the degree of nastiness involved ("nasty," like "wicked," is a word that has associated itself with a particularly sharp curve ball). The average set of eyes might not be able to distinguish a slider from a curve, but they know when a hitter is made to look foolish. People like watching other people look foolish.

It's said that a pitcher either has a curve or he doesn't; this speaks specifically to the wrist, which can either snap a breaking ball, creating a tight forward rotation and subsequent break, or it can't. Scouting the minutiae of the pitch can be quite difficult, but making the initial observation of break or no break is very easy. Depending on the arm slot and relationship the fingers form with the ball, the curveball will offer different shapes (that is, the horizontal and vertical break as it relates to the face of a clock). Pitchers who have high arm slots (straight overhand, overhand, high three-quarters) are more likely to throw curves that feature the traditional 12–6 shape, which, as you can probably interpret, means the pitch has sharp vertical movement, starting on one plane (12) and dropping straight down (6).

When watching a curve, it's important to note the shape it shows, but also when the disguise comes off the pitch. Good secondary offerings are thrown off the fastball, meaning the pitcher establishes the fastball and then throws his complementary pitches from the same arm slot with the same arm speed, thus creating deception. Curves that break late will bring a hitter into the zone on fastball timing only to see the pitch arrive on a different plane; obviously, the longer a pitch takes to show its true intentions the better. After observing the presence of the pitch, the shape, and when the great reveal occurs, it's important to make note of the command component. Secondary command is paramount to effectiveness. The pitcher must have the confidence to throw the pitch in any count, to any hitter, at any point in the game, as well as be able both to throw the pitch for strikes and to drop it in the dirt as a chase pitch.

Sliders share a bloodline with the curve, but it's a pitch that was raised by a different parent. The slider is normally thrown with more velocity than a traditional curve, ranging from the upper 70s to the upper 80s, depending on the arm in question. Sliders feature more two-plane movement than the curve, with the increased velocity limiting the depth of a vertical break but allowing for more horizontal movement.

The changeup comes in different forms as a result of different grips and different means of delivery, but the purpose of the pitch remains the same: keep hitters off the fastball. Changeups are feel pitches, so they are usually slow to develop and take time to refine. Deception is the key is to secondary-pitch efficiency, and this is especially true of changeups, which play directly off the fastball; a pitcher who can disguise the changeup as a fastball can add a dimension to his overall arsenal. A good changeup will look identical to a fastball from a hitter's perspective except that it will be thrown eight to 12 mph slower and hopefully feature some movement as a result.

The action of a changeup can be the difference between a good "show me" pitch used to keep hitters honest and a knockout pitch that can send them back to the dugout shaking their heads.

When scouting a changeup, the first thing to notice is the arm speed and slot consistency of the pitch; movement will vary based on grips and releases. It's important to pay attention to how the ball is moving: whether it drops like a curveball or fades and sinks like a slower two-seam fastball. Be patient when evaluating an immature changeup, as the pitch requires a great deal of feel to properly execute, and feel isn't something that can be forced. Pitching is about comfort, and if a pitcher shows signs of repeatability and offers up signs of touch with his other pitches, it's much easier to project a quality changeup, even in the face of a poor present pitch.

"Pitchability" is a vague term often used to describe a pitcher's overall feel for pitching. While I agree with the broad-stroke definition, I tend to view pitchability as a more complicated and thought-provoking pursuit, an often intangible and somewhat spiritual connection between a pitcher and the act of pitching. To focus on the reductive definition, feel is as important to pitching as the raw stuff coming out of the hand. The ability to change speeds, set up hitters, establish command, and create a pace that is under the complete control of the pitcher are examples of how "feel" manifests on the mound—call it a certain ownership of the trade. Pitchers who can combine the plus raw stuff with the feel for the mound can exceed the ceilings suggested by their tool-based grades.

Hitting

The process of evaluating hitters begins in the cage, where you can start to piece together the swing mechanics and the way the body works in connection to hitting. Initially, I look at the way the hips work and the overall coordination being displayed, for the simple reason that well-coordinated athletes are better equipped to make adjustments, both at the plate and in the field. The ability to make adjustments is the key to finding sustainable success at the highest level.

Hitting is a combination of several factors, the most important of which is strength. Without strength, you could possess the hand-eye coordination of a Korean StarCraft champion, but your contact ability would be rendered obsolete when velocity was able to knock the bat out of your hands. As to swing mechanics, the better the hands, the better the hitter. Hands establish the physical connection with the bat, but they also control the navigational system that takes the bat into the load, into the zone, into the path of the baseball, and through the secondary extension. Hands are the mothers of hitting. Everything starts with the hands.

The act of making contact with a baseball has everything to do with timing, and the load—during which the hands move back into hitting position and the weight shifts to the back foot—is the first phase in the mechanical process before triggering: pulling the bow back before firing the arrow. Watching the load, I look for fluid, tranquil movements. The hands should slowly drift back, not forward. There should be a balanced weight shift. The front shoulder and hips should be aligned (not already open), and it should all be fluid. When a hitter rushes or drops his hands, such mechanical hitches either get ironed out or the hitter gets exposed in a graphic manner.

As the ball approaches the plate, the single most difficult act in any sport is put into motion: triggering the bat into the zone for the purpose of making contact with an object being thrown with exceptional velocity. It's at this point when the hips should fire, meaning the core begins its rotation and the hands get ready for business. As the weight starts to shift and the hands begin the journey to contact, you want to see them remain close to the body in order to create a quick and efficient path into the zone. Long swings usually don't translate into long careers.

At this point, the hitter's weight has shifted and his front leg has planted, creating the leverage necessary to send the bat through the zone with authority. The hands control the bat in the zone to the point of impact, where the first extension takes place and a hitter drives through the ball. Finally, the second extension takes place as the hitter rolls his hands, continues the process of driving through the ball and, as Bret Easton Ellis might have written, climaxes in a euphoric wave; the follow through should leave the hitter balanced and in a good position to explode out of the box on his way toward first base.

In addition to balance, a hitter must possess mechanics conducive for a clean, compact stroke. You want to see skill in the hands, which allows for bat control. You want to see hand-eye coordination, which will allow for contact ability. You want to see a hitter drive the ball with authority and then show the ability to do it again. You want to see fluidity in all the movements. Finally, and most important, you want to see comfort. A hitter has to be comfortable at the plate in order to allow the muscle memory involved to execute a series of movements in the blink of an eye.

The Hit Tool
The hit tool sits atop the great pyramid of tools, trumping its own offspring—power—as well as the three remaining tools in a position prospect's physical cache: speed, glove, and arm. The hit tool is the simple measure of how often a ball is properly squared up, driven with authority, and deposited into the field of play. The better the hit tool, the more likely a player will hit for a high batting average. Hit-tool grades correlate to major league results like those seen in Table 2-1.2. When scouting a hitter against live pitching, you want to see not only all the academic components you focused on in the cage, but also the practical application of those components in an unpredictable environment. When the object of the game demands that a pitcher defeat you lest you defeat him, the intensity of the battle not only accelerates reactions but also introduces important variables outside of the raw mechanical components of the swing.

TABLE 2-1.2 Hit-Tool Grades and Major League Expectations

Grade	Batting Average at the Major League Level
80: Elite; The Beatles	.320-plus; perennial batting title contender
70: Well above average, plus-plus: The Beach Boys	.300-.320
60: Above average, plus; Pixies	.285-.300
50: Average; Oasis	.270-.285
40: Below average; WHAM	.250-.270
30: Well below average; New Kids on the Block	.225-.250
20: Poor; Backstreet Boys	Up to .225

One cliché of prospecting is "[Player Name]'s approach at the plate limits the effectiveness of his hit tool." The ability to recognize pitches, make adjustments to those pitches, work the count for favorable hitting conditions, and execute when presented with those conditions are what take the physical tool from its raw state to its ultimate ceiling. A hitter can possess a plus (60 grade) hit tool, but if he can't influence the hitting environment in his favor, he will struggle to find sustained success. That does not necessarily mean drawing walks, although walks are an important aspect of the overall offensive package. The ability to draw walks is not part of the hit tool. For our purposes, it is a skill, not a physical tool. The perceptivity to pick up the ball out of the pitcher's hand, diagnose its ultimate agenda, decide how to proceed ("Should I swing or should I abstain?"), and then execute that decision is essential to fully exploiting the hitter's physical gifts.

Every hitter in professional baseball is capable of putting good wood on a ball. The grade given to a hit tool is a measure of the frequency and overall execution of that capability.

Power
The power tool is derivative of the hit tool, but requires specific swing characteristics to manifest in game action. First, a hitter won't show power in the present or project to hit for power without quality bat speed. Strength and fluidity in the swing create bat speed, but plus raw strength does not automatically equal plus power potential. If strength were the only component to power, "Sweet" Lou Ferrigno would be in the Baseball Hall of Fame.

Power hitters are able to create leverage in their swings. It stems from the firing of the hips in association with the movement of the upper body, which creates torque. Without a certain fluidity and ease, this violent movement will fail to produce a swing conducive to power. Fundamentally speaking, the hit tool has to be present in order for the power to flow through it. You can't just power up a swing and let 'er rip and expect consistent results.

For example, up-and-coming young power hitter Eric Hosmer uses his fluid swing to produce power without selling out or loading up for power. His swing mechanics remain consistent, free from the length often created when a swing is leveraged for moon shots. Hosmer stays short to the ball and balanced, showing some natural loft in the swing plane, but it is not so exaggerated that holes emerge. Like all great hitters, Hosmer builds his power from the hit tool, showing light-tower pop without sacrificing the ability to make contact.

Power hitters possess a slight uppercut to their swing, but it's not as extreme as you might think. Good hitters send their bat into the zone on the same plane as the pitch, but with a slightly elevated path. Backspin and loft, key components for distance and carry, are created when hitters make contact slightly below the center of the ball as they power through their extension.

When evaluating the future power tool of a young hitter, you want to see signs of these characteristics in the swing, however underdeveloped he might be. As is often the case, the missing ingredient is strength, which arrives as the body matures, assuming it arrives at all. Not every hitter will have a swing conducive for power; just because there's a blueprint doesn't mean execution is possible. You have to look at each hitter as an individual, assess his strengths, and project accordingly. Putting a grade on the present power is difficult in its own right, but power projection can be so conceptual that scouts often find themselves several grades off the mark when the music stops (see Table 2-1.3).

TABLE 2-1.3 Batting Grades and Home Run Expectations

Grade	Home Runs at the Major League Level
80: Elite; New York–style pizza	39-plus; perennial home run champ
70: Well above average, plus-plus; Chicago-style pizza	32–38
60: Above average, plus; New Haven–style pizza	25–32
50: Average; Midwest pizza	17–25
40: Below average; California pizza	11–17
30: Well below average; frozen pizza	5–11
20: Poor; no pizza	Up to 5

In the Field

It's not easy to evaluate defensive tools, especially in the amateur ranks or the lower levels of professional baseball. It takes time to put the total defensive package together. Good defense is a product of sound fundamentals established through raw physical ability, instruction, and refinement through repetition.

First Base This is an offensive position in the modern game. The conventional wisdom is that if the bat is above average, the value provided by the glove is gravy. This belief does an equal disservice both to the value of defense at first base and gravy.

You don't need speed or a plus arm to excel at first base, but you do need good hand-eye coordination, *some* reaction ability, and an instinctive connection to the glove that lives on your hand. It sounds obvious, but when your ability to catch a ball is directly tied to the proper execution of a play, you can't have stone hands. The best first-basemen inspire confidence.

Second Base The first question to ask when scouting a second baseman is, "Can he play shortstop?" The most skilled athletes start up the middle and move to the corners when their skills diminish or get exposed by the level of competition. If a lower-level talent is already playing second base, the burden of success has shifted to the bat—and that's a heavy burden.

A second baseman has to have first-step quickness and a good glove, but the arm doesn't have to be plus to play to the position. Negotiating the double play requires good footwork, body control, and coordination, so the body needs to be athletic and project to remain that way throughout the player's development. Second base requires more athleticism than a corner spot, but it doesn't require a shortstop's fast-twitch skills, so if the bat plays, the glove stays. To put it another way, take a shortstop, subtract the soft hands, strong arm, and range, and you have a second baseman.

Shortstop We have exited the age of the slugging shortstops; shortstops are once again cultivated for their defensive chops rather than their middle-of-the-order potential. The leather wizards of the 1970s and '80s have returned, and with the Latin American academies pumping out slick fielding shortstops at an accelerated pace, the future of the position looks like it will be with the glove men for a long time to come.

Shortstops require the deepest physical skill-set on the diamond. The first thing to look for when evaluating defense is the feet. The quality of the footwork (first step, coordination, balance, and so on) can tell you more about the future of the player than the glove or the arm. You want to see grace in the steps. Footwork as it pertains to fundamentals can be sculpted, but athleticism can't be taught. If the feet are heavy and clumsy in the present, projecting elegance in the future is an exercise in futility.

Shortstops need to be slick. You want to see fluid actions at the position, with the ability to control the body and the leather. You want to see how the glove functions when presented with balls from varying angles, meaning you want to see how the backhand looks, if the glove can stick to the dirt on balls that force the fielder to the left, and so on. As with all good fielders, the glove needs to form a relationship with the hand that goes beyond the basic corporeal bond to metaphysical Velcro.

Good range requires a quick first step, but instinct is just as important. Instincts are to a shortstop what the Force is to a Jedi. It can't be taught. It can be harnessed, but like athleticism, you either have the Force or you don't. Instinctual players appear to have the ability to slow the game down, and to find themselves in locations on the diamond where the ball happens to be. At times this is nothing more than pure athletic ability and luck, but the most gifted defensive players appear to have more luck than others, and the reason is their natural connection to the position and the game itself. You know it when you see it.

Elvis Andrus seems to move toward the ball before the ball announces its path. A preternatural wizard of the infield can often make physically complicated plays appear routine. You expect Yoda to be able to levitate; after a while, it's just not all that remarkable, but, unlike Elvis, the average player can neither levitate nor instinctually drift to his glove side to snag a line drive headed to center field.

A shortstop also needs to have a strong, accurate arm, capable of making all the throws from their wide pocket of the field. Sound throwing mechanics (which confers accuracy) and a quick release are important aspects of the overall evaluation of the arm. Glove first shortstops that don't have the arm strength to excel at the position or the bat to survive elsewhere often die a slow death in the minors.

Third Base This is a middle-of-the-order offensive position, but one that requires a specific skill-set. A good third baseman is a shortstop with plus reactions rather than range. He needs to possess the same qualities as a good shortstop: good footwork, good glove, strong, accurate arm, and instincts. Whereas shortstops also require coast-to-coast range, a third baseman requires split-second reactions in order to survive on the frontline of the infield.

When evaluating a young third baseman, you want to make sure the body and feet will survive the physical maturation process; you don't have to be fast to play the position, but you can't stand in cement. Hot corner defense can be the most exciting to watch on the diamond. Third basemen are tasked with handling lasers off the bat, charging in to field bunts or slow rollers (which often require the coordination and balance of a gymnast to convert into outs), cutting off balls to their left, and snagging balls that are touching the chalk all the way to their right. It's a challenging position to play and an incredibly difficult position to play well.

Outfield The first question I ask when evaluating an outfielder is, "Can this guy play center field?" Center fielders are the shortstops of the outfield. They need to possess speed (straight-line speed and quickness) and athleticism. The ability to read the ball off the bat and take a proper angle or route is also extremely important; though some players have enough speed to recover from poor routes and angles, athleticism can't always save the day. Center fielders aren't required to have plus arms, although if given a choice, you always want to see a strong arm on a position player. It's important to focus on the body, especially when evaluating a young player, because the position is very physically demanding and most athletes (even above-average athletes) lack the overall ability to handle the demands of center.

Basic glove skills are very important, as the nature of the position is to track down balls and secure them in the mitt. Like other middle-of-the diamond players, you want to see instincts for the position, whether you define that as a quick first step, a relationship with the coverage area, or a natural gift to make plays.

The corner spots often suffer defensively due to their offensive requirements, and those who play there are often best known for what they can't do. When evaluating corner outfielders, you want to see enough athleticism to handle the lateral movements required by the position; slow feet and poor body control aren't positive attributes at any position, and when your job requires that you run around catching balls, it helps to be able to move a bit (even if corner outfielders do not have to have above-average range to play). The strongest arms tend to end up in right field; left fielders need quality gloves, but can get away with having weaker arms.

Catchers Just as with the other positions, evaluating low-level talent behind the plate begins with the body and movement. Players don't always arrived wrapped in prototypical packages, and this is especially true when it comes to catchers. When evaluating a catcher, I care more about the athleticism, coordination, and strength involved than inherent physical characteristics like height and weight. Not every player carries weight well, or projects to carry weight well, while others inhabit bad bodies that somehow allow the requisite quickness and agility for the position to shine through. You can't judge the body in isolation; you need to see the body walk the runway in order to see how it moves.

The most important component of body evaluation is how well the feet work. Again, just because the body isn't a chiseled work of art doesn't preclude the possibility of athleticism and/or agility. When watching footwork, you want to see the same sort of fluidity and coordination you would expect to see from a middle infielder. Slow, clumsy feet limit the range of success a catcher can have, and the chain of physical events starts at the base of the body. When evaluating a catcher's body, ask yourself, "Do those feet look heavy and slow? From the balls of the feet, does the catcher have spring, or are the feet cemented in the ground?"

Good defense behind the plate is a recipe made up of several ingredients, including the ability to block balls in the dirt, position oneself to make throws, and field the position. Catchers need not have average speed, but what they lack in straight-line speed they need to make up in quickness and agility. This is where my evaluation tends to get monochromatic, as the basics of the defensive skill-set are either present (or projectable) or they aren't. If the athleticism is there, the *basic* fundamentals—how to block balls, how to block the plate, how to field a bunt—can be taught.

The premium physical weapon of a catcher is his arm or, more specifically, the ability to combine the raw physical strength of the arm with the necessary fundamentals (throwing mechanics, footwork) to assist in the process of controlling the running game. I use the word "assist" with clear intent, as a catcher can't control the running game on his own. With a runner on first base, a pitcher needs to deliver the ball to the plate in a timely manner, preferably under 1.5 seconds. The clock on this process starts when he makes his first movement to the plate (front-leg lift) and stops when the ball reaches the leather of the catcher. A catcher might possess an 80-grade arm with an ultra-fast release, but this elite skill-set will be rendered obsolete if a pitcher is leisurely to the plate. The running game is actually controlled by the men on the mound, not the men behind it. Catchers are the executioners, but pitchers have to create the environment for the execution.

Determining the raw strength of an arm shouldn't require many viewings; in many cases, you can grade the arm from watching pre-game infield drills. It gets more complicated when you attempt to grade the overall functionality of that arm, which is an amalgam of raw strength, the body movements leading up to the throw, the actual release of the ball from the hand, and the overall accuracy of the arm. From the balls of the feet, a catcher is required to quickly reach a throwing position, which requires not only spring in the legs but also the footwork to form a solid base from which to throw. Again, having a strong arm is only one part of the equation. Sloppy footwork, a slow release, and a lack of overall fluidity will negate raw strength.

You have no doubt heard the term "pop time," which is the time (in seconds) applied to the action of receiving the ball, transferring the ball from the glove to the hand, and delivering the ball to second base. The stopwatch starts upon contact with the catcher's glove and stops when the ball reaches the glove covering second. An average major league time (pop time) is in the 1.9–2.00 range, with plus times coming in under 1.85 seconds. In order to achieve above-average pop times, not only does a catcher need to possess a strong arm with a quick release, but his footwork and glove-to-hand transfer need to be fluid and smooth.

The emotional relationship between a pitcher and the catcher he is pitching to is arguably the most important and fragile in the game of baseball. It is one of the aspects of the game most likely to be underestimated by outside observers because it lives in the abstract, free from the boundaries and definitions of value. It's emotional, specific, and at the core of what makes baseball beautiful and unique.

A good game-caller acts as a proxy for the brain trust in the dugout, not only relaying the pitch selection (if the manager or pitching coach is calling the game), but also setting up the environment to properly execute said selection. A good game-caller can help define the parameters of the day's strike zone for both pitcher and umpire, access the pitcher's present arsenal, and assist in the adjustment process in order to maximize effectiveness, as well as observe the tendencies of the hitters in the box and relay this intelligence back to the pitcher. It's a cerebral quality, and one we can't quantify. Beyond the observational intelligence involved with game calling, a catcher must also take on a more personal role with a pitcher, one that could best be described as part coach, part best friend, and part psychologist.

Observation of the pitcher's comfort is vital. Do the pitcher and catcher seem to be on the same page? Does the catcher appear to be an active participant in the process, or merely a receiver of the ball? Good catchers are more than just catchers, managing the emotions on the field. That management can be scouted, and forms an important component in the overall assessment of the catcher's ability behind the plate. It takes more than just a glove and an arm to play the position. However, when you find a backstop who marries the physical gifts with the intellectual and emotional requirements of the position, you might just have a player who can reach the highest level of baseball without making reference to the bat. Good catchers take time to develop, as their skills need refinement through repetition and situational experience.

The Need for Speed

Speed is the preferred tool of the baseball pest, a player who uses a specific physical attribute to affect the chemistry of the action on the field. Speed can propel a player into professional baseball, and can disguise the overall effectiveness of that player during the developmental process. Speed is a tool with psychotropic properties.

A measure of the tool is collected by timing the journey a hitter takes from the batter's box to the bag at first. Upon contact with the ball, as the batter starts his transformation from hitter to runner, the stopwatch button is plunged. The second plunge occurs when the runner's foot makes contact with the first-base bag. Context is very important. Ground balls with double-play implications create an ideal environment, but any ball that encourages "hustle" should do the trick. Caveat: Jailbreak bunts (that is, bunts that occur when the batter is already leaving the batter's box on his way to first base) make for exaggerated times.

One final note on speed: at its best, it's a catalytic tool, one that can enhance offensive and defensive capabilities, but a player can lack what scouts consider good speed and still possess the necessary athleticism (coordination, quickness, agility) to achieve at the highest professional level. Rangers second baseman Ian Kinsler is hardly fast; he reaches first base in the 4.3–4.4 range, on a good ball. That's average speed (at best) if you grade the tool according to Table 2-1.4, but

TABLE 2-1.4 Speed and Grade Correlation

Speed (Left/Right)	Grade
3.9 (L)/ 4.0 (R)	80: Elite; *The Wire*
4.0 (L)/ 4.1 (R)	70: Well above average, plus-plus; *Breaking Bad*
4.1 (L)/ 4.2 (R)	60: Above average, plus; the first ten seasons of *The Simpsons*
4.2 (L)/ 4.3 (R)	50: Average; the last ten seasons of *The Simpsons*
4.3 (L)/ 4.4 (R)	40: Below average; *The Real Housewives of New Jersey*
4.4 (L)/ 4.5 (R)	30: Well below average; *The Jersey Shore*
4.5 (L)/ 4.6 (R)	20: Poor; *Jerseylicious*

what he lacks in flat-line speed he makes up with quickness and acceleration; he can reach his top speed in only a few strides. Also intelligent on the base paths, Kinsler is one of the best base runners in the game, despite not possessing what scouts would classify as game-changing speed. It's not only about the watch, it's about watching the player.

Makeup: When Is It an Issue?

I define "makeup" as the personal responsibility a player accepts to take the steps that will translate his innate physical abilities into on-the-field production. Makeup is the hidden hand of the developmental process pushing a player to the heights suggested by his physical tools or, in its absence, pulling him away from them.

It doesn't matter if a player is a sinner or a saint, or if an adolescent male displays the emotional maturity of an adolescent male, as long as it doesn't affect business on the field. It's foolish to assume that an underdeveloped human can transition to a professional environment without displaying the behavior of an underdeveloped human. I'm not expecting flash-boiled maturity, and from a moral perspective, I don't care what floats your bloat as long as your waves don't affect the buoyancy of others, but I do want to see a player take ownership of his trajectory.

In short, I do not care if you are of questionable moral fiber, but I do care if you don't care. Work ethic is the biggest part of the developmental process. The majority of players who fail to develop to the level suggested by their physical qualities do so because of the emotional components involved. You can't develop someone who isn't willing to participate in the process of development.

Rule 4 (Amateur Draft) Talent Acquisition

High School vs. College: The Pros and the Cons

When it comes to drafting amateur talent (via the Rule 4 amateur draft), the paradigms for future success are in flux as often as is adolescent emotion. While it's true that every team in baseball will reach into both high school and college baskets for talent, some are more reluctant than others to use feature picks and feature money on one specific basket over another. This stems from a combination of personal preference and the management of risk versus reward; basically, some teams would rather place the safer bet on the safer product than gamble higher stakes for the higher score.

The name of the game is talent, whether it arrives from the ranks of high school or college, but it's not the only aspect in the process; it would be nice if superior raw talent had a direct correlation to superior professional results, but the further away from maturity the player is, the more responsibility is placed on the developmental process to grow and refine that talent. Growing talent requires excessive amounts of money, patience, and personnel, not to mention the pressure to produce fruit; so the longer you are tasked with refining a player the larger the all-around investment. This is why teams don't throw every dollar they have in their budget on lottery-ticket talent, even if the possible payouts exceed other options. The converse is also true: teams that don't spend a dime on a lottery ticket don't give themselves an opportunity to win the lottery.

What's the big difference between high school and college talent, anyway? One could make a case that high school talent is more similar to the talent found in the international free-agent markets than the talent found in college. Let's examine some of the pros and cons of each of the Rule 4 avenues of talent acquisition, as to which is the most efficient from a standpoint of cost versus reward.

High School: The Good, the Bad, and the Ugly

The Good The younger you can get players into the developmental process the better, so taking quality immature athletes at 18 years old and allowing them to mature under a professional hand will make them more malleable than athletes entering the process at a more physically mature state. Physical immaturity allows room for projection, the tool scouts and team personnel use to forecast the talent of a player at the top of his developmental arc. Projection is what separates the majority of high school athletes from their college counterparts, allowing teams to dream of a future that will find players more advanced than they are at the point of initial acquisition. This is the foundation of the argument in favor of drafting high school talent over college talent.

The Bad Higher risk. As with any human experience that requires stages of development to reach fruition, the likelihood of finding projected promise is rather slim. Just take a look at your own experiences, starting with the life you scripted back in high school. Did you end up going to the college of your choice, graduating with the degree you envisioned, and turning that degree into the career you always dreamed of? Can you look back and say, "Yep, this is exactly how it was supposed to go. I'm so awesome"? For most of us, life's road has many turnings. Now imagine how difficult it is to accurately forecast an amateur baseball player, not only in the physical sense (which is easier), but to accurately peg who that person will become as an adult. This is the real challenge in making an investment in high school talent. Simply put, forecasting the physical characteristics and abilities is hard enough; accurately projecting emotional development as it pertains to the enhancement of the professional role is next to impossible. For some teams, that's too potent a cocktail in which to invest millions of dollars.

The Ugly It seems that in recent years the majority of draftable high school talent has found a spotlight in the showcase circuit, a series of sponsored events that allow the industry to see premium talent in one geographic location. The structure of the showcases can alienate certain pockets of talent. Kids without the money to pay for travel to these events (normally in the Southeast), as well as lodging, ancillary expenses, and the cost of participation itself, are shut out of a spotlight opportunity. Obviously, those who come from families of means are not the only players worth scouting; it is an unfortunate reality that players with fewer financial resources fail to receive the same opportunities as players with means, which can cause talent to fall through the cracks.

College: The Good, the Bad, and the Not Quite So Ugly, but Not Really Pretty, Either

The Good Draft-eligible talent coming from the college ranks gives teams a clearer picture of what they are getting; players are more mature, both physically and mentally, creating a more representative view of who those players will be as professionals. It's never a given that players will transition their present skills to professional ball, but college players give you less to be wrong about, as the conceptual space between present and future isn't nearly as wide and unforgiving as with high school draftees. When you are able to remove some of the guess from the guessing game, you set yourself up to develop more major league talent. Developing cost-effective major league talent is necessary to sustainability within the game; without it you are forced to pay extra for someone else's developed talent, suffocating your budget.

The Bad Because the talent coming out of college is (normally) more physically mature, the opportunity to arbitrage high-ceiling talent (regardless of the risk) isn't as available. Scouts love physical tools, but most of the toolsy players get drafted out of high school, or as is often the case, find glory in other college sports where their tools find more appreciation and more attention (basketball and football). It's not that toolsy college athletes aren't available in the draft; rather, it's just rare to find the same combination of tools, projection, and ceiling that can be offered in other markets. At the college level, you are getting a more refined product, but finding premium talent outside of the first few rounds is unlikely.

The Not Quite So Ugly, but Not Really Pretty, Either It's to be expected that a college coach should focus on winning versus the development of the players he is tasked with coaching. It's hard to fault a coach for riding his ace to wins, even if that means starting him on Friday and bringing him out of the bullpen on Sunday. It seems excessive to fans of the professional game, and of course it is, but the program has to take precedence over the progress of the individual after he leaves said program. However, that doesn't always leave the product coming out of college undamaged.

It's easy to see how a win-at-all-costs mentality could endanger pitchers; their workloads can be excessive and the throwing programs less than ideal. Hitters face their own risks. Because of the nature of the offensive game in college, hitters often adopt bad habits. With inferior pitchers toeing the hill on most days, hitters can alter their swing mechanics to punish those with velocity deficiencies. The mechanical flaws created by either cheating into the zone, taking an upper-cut plane to the ball, or showing an extreme timing kick or load often aren't adjusted at the college level, especially when they meet with good results. Unfortunately, this doesn't always paint a promising picture of the player, as the deficient swing mechanics either turn off professional eyes or prove problematic to adjust once that player reaches professional ball. The college game often creates an environment where fundamentals are either glossed over or misappropriated for the benefit of the program, which is great for the team but not always great for the player.

Player Development

We've looked at the evaluation process and the pros and cons of two forms of amateur talent acquisition, building the skeleton inside baseball's body. It all starts with eyes on the talent, forming observations and a framework for what is possible in the future. This ranges from the physical to the emotional, both necessary in the DNA of player development. Talent is then acquired, with team philosophy, scouting talent, and internal necessity dictating which avenue is better suited for the particular draft slot.

Player development is reducible to talent. One director of player development put it rather bluntly: without talent, the best developmental team in place can't turn shit into a shiny stone. Without quality amateur talent, you can't develop quality professional talent, so the key moment in player development happens not at any point after a prospect puts on his uniform for the first time, but before it, when he is drafted. What happens subsequently is an act of talent refinement, not talent creation.

After the amateur handoff occurs, it falls to coaches and coordinators to begin the process of acclimation. They will be responsible for teaching the basics of the organization, including conveying a sense of expectations and obligations. This task normally takes place at the team complex, which instructional leagues and spring training call home base. The blanket philosophies are usually the same for most organizations, emphasizing a winning attitude along with progress and personal responsibility.

However simple that might sound, getting the organizational tone to ring between the ears of immature players is quite difficult, and the patience of the coaching and coordinating staff is likely to be tested almost immediately. In order for the process to work, a team's development staff, from the front office down to the on-field personnel, have to maintain a united front. Dissention and mixed signals will only be met with confusion and stagnated results. You can't teach a baseball player to play baseball (*your* brand of baseball) with a chorus of voices singing different songs at different times for different reasons. The developmental hierarchy has to communicate in order to develop the best possible plan for the player in question. It's a team effort and when it loses that consensus, the player suffers.

In order to begin the developmental process, several questions have to be answered, including establishing who the player is at present and what you expect him to develop into in the future. Scouts offer this conceptual reality with their initial reports, but as players move into their new professional life, some of their tools will evolve faster than others. Having received the player, it's up to the developmental team to reevaluate their stock, deciding which deficiencies need the most attention. Internal evaluation is ongoing during the developmental process; there is no road map for development until the player provides one based on his own qualities.

When a breakdown in the process occurs, the likelihood of success diminishes. Yes, some players have the raw physical ability to reach the major leagues based only on those characteristics, but the true ceiling is rarely reached if a player lacks the intangible qualities that help push the physical ones to their limit. Just take a look back at all the high-ceiling talent that has fallen short over the years. Was the problem purely a physical one, meaning, was the player not as physically gifted as the evaluation suggested, or was the culprit the inability to take advantage of those qualities on the field?

The push for success requires intense mental focus and fortitude. It's the job of the developmental team not only to help a player refine those physical skills on the field, but also to instill and encourage the work ethic and mental push necessary to maximize the potential offered by the physical. When any one variable in the equation fails, the process itself fails, and the player and the team are left pondering what could have been.

As we watch our heroes on the diamond, their origin often seems secondary, pushed behind the curtain of our present experience. Too rarely do we stop to appreciate the journey taken by that talent from seed to superstar. Players don't magically appear at the highest level without first being discovered, developed, and delivered by a series of events and the intervention of a large contingent of experienced baseball men. They have been given shape by the evaluation, acquisition, and developmental process. The next time you cast eyes upon the splendid geometry of a stadium, watching as your favorite players play your favorite game, remind yourself of the incredible procedure that was necessary in order to bring those players to life. At one point, every jersey on the field was an immature amateur wandering through the wide chasm between the realities of the present and the possibilities of the future. That talent was evaluated, acquired, and developed by the men who stand in the shadows of the game, the ones who make everything you see possible—the backbone of the game.

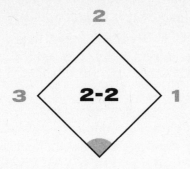

2-2

3 1

2

How Does Age Affect the Amateur Draft?

RANY JAZAYERLI

Everyone missed on Mike Trout. Don't get me wrong: Trout was a well-regarded player headed into the 2009 draft, a certain first-round talent. But he wasn't yet a phenom. Everyone *liked* Trout; it's just that no one *loved* him. *Baseball America* ranked him as the 22nd-best player in the draft. No one doubted his athleticism or his work ethic; a lot of people doubted the level of competition he faced as a high school player from New Jersey. The Angels drafted him with the 25th pick overall, and they'll tell you today that they knew he was destined to be a special player. What they won't tell you is that they had back-to-back picks at #24 and #25, and they announced Randal Grichuk's name first.

It didn't take Trout long to prove that everyone had underestimated him. He hit .360 in rookie ball that summer, which was just an appetizer for his 2010 season, when he hit .341/.428/.490 with 56 steals in A-ball, and was ranked as the #2 prospect in the minor leagues by *Baseball Prospectus*. In 2011 he jumped to Double-A and hit .326/.414/ .544, was named *Baseball America*'s Minor League Player of the Year, and debuted in the major leagues at the age of 19. If you were starting a franchise from scratch today, there aren't 10 players in baseball you'd pick before Trout.

Anytime a team misses on a player the way almost every organization in baseball missed on Trout, there's bound to be some soul searching: What did we miss? Many times, there's no satisfactory answer to that question. Albert Pujols was a 13th-round pick in 1999, and less than two years later was one of the best baseball players in the world. To this day, no one has been able to adequately explain why every team in baseball misjudged him so badly.

In Trout's case, there's one astoundingly obvious reason why he was underrated going into the draft. It's one of the most basic pieces of information we have about a player, a piece of information that precisely because of its ubiquity is easily ignored: his date of birth. Mike Trout was born on August 7, 1991. This is relevant because, unlike most players drafted out of high school, Trout was still just 17 years old when he was picked. His performance as a high school senior came at an age when many of his fellow draftees were still in their junior year; he played as well as he did without the benefit of an extra year of development.

Baseball's aging curve is fairly well known by now. Most hitters peak at or around the age of 27, and their performance usually follows a parabolic curve, rapidly improving in their late teens and early 20s, then a more gradual improvement in their mid 20s, before a gradual decline in their late 20s that accelerates in their 30s.

The implication of the aging curve is that the younger a player is the more improvement he is likely to show over a given period of time. Take two players who are equally valuable today; if one of them is 25 and the other is 26, the difference between their long-term projections is minor. If one of them is 20 and one of them is 21, the differences can be massive, and much greater than you would intuitively expect.

Nearly a quarter-century ago, Bill James addressed this very point in the 1987 edition of his *Baseball Abstract*:

> Suppose that you have a 20-year-old player and a 21-year-old player of the same ability as hitters; let's say that each hits about .265 with ten home runs. How much difference is there in the expected career home run totals for the two players?

As best I can estimate, the 20-year-old player can be expected to hit about 61 percent more home runs in his career. That's right—61 percent.

The list of 20-year-olds who perform well as everyday major league hitters is small, and they almost all go on to have stellar careers. This is what made Jason Heyward's rookie season so promising. His .277/.393/.456 performance isn't particularly noteworthy for a rookie, but for a *20-year-old* rookie it was almost unprecedented. This is why, despite his sophomore struggles, he has almost limitless upside. Incidentally, like Trout, Heyward didn't turn 18 until the August after he was drafted.

If there is such a substantial difference in the expectations between 20-year-old and 21-year-old players, it stands to reason that the difference between 17-year-olds and 18-year-olds would be even more massive. At such a young age, a difference of even eight or nine months—the difference between an 18-year-old born in September and an 18-year-old born in May—might move the needle.

The two best high school hitters ever selected with the first overall pick in the draft, Alex Rodriguez and Ken Griffey Jr., were both 17 on draft day. Griffey was born in November, making him one of the youngest first-round picks ever. Meanwhile, the oldest high school hitter selected first overall, Shawon Dunston, already 19 at the time, spent his entire career leaving people wanting more.

No one would argue that, all else being equal, a 17-year-old player is likely to develop into a better player than an 18-year-old player. Yet, given these and other examples, I wondered if the baseball industry as a whole has underestimated the importance of age. I wondered if, given two players taken at the same slot in the draft, the younger player returned greater value. In other words, *even accounting for the fact that teams took age into consideration*—presumably, a player who is particularly young for his draft class might get picked earlier—I wondered if those players were *still* undervalued.

I compiled a list of every high school hitter selected in the first 100 picks of every draft from 1965 through 1996. I stopped the data set at 1996 because I wanted to look at how these players performed over the course of their careers—I defined "careers" as the 15 years after they were drafted.

I began with high school players because the impact of age, if there is one, would be much more likely to show up in evaluating players who are 17 or 18 rather than players who are 20 or 21. I started with hitters because the aging curve for pitchers is much less predictable than it is for hitters, as many pitchers never throw as hard again as they did in high school. If there is an effect to be seen, it should be most obvious in high school hitters.

Roughly nine percent of the players in the data set have no date of birth information available—most of these players flamed out of pro ball too quickly to leave an impression. Those players were eliminated from the study, leaving us with a data set of 846 players. In order to determine if players who were younger than average on draft day tended to return more value than expected, the first step was to figure out what "expected value" was for each player.

Wins above replacement player (WARP) is an incredibly handy tool whose express purpose is to estimate a player's value, so I took the WARP generated by each draft pick for the 15 years after he was selected. However, I also applied a discount factor of eight percent— meaning that 1.00 WARP generated the year after a player was selected was worth 0.92 WARP in the year he was selected. By year 15, 1.00 WARP was only as valuable as 0.29 WARP generated in his draft year. Obviously, the team that drafted a player in 1980 was far more likely to benefit from his performance in 1982 than from his performance in 1990, when he was far more likely to have moved on to another team via trade or free agency. Incorporating a discount value accounts for this. I also "zeroed out" any seasons in which a player generated negative WARP. Given that most draft picks don't reach the major leagues at all, it would be misleading to penalize a player who was good enough to reach the majors for having a negative-WARP season relative to a player who might never have gotten out of rookie ball.

Using the data, I tried to determine the best formula to predict a player's expected value in discounted WARP based on when he was picked. The expected value of a draft pick is highly dependent on when he was picked, as we revealed in a series of articles published on the Baseball Prospectus website regarding the draft in 2005. It isn't a linear relationship—the expected value of a draft pick drops quickly from the #1 to the #2 pick in the draft, and gradually levels out so that the difference in expected value between picks #99 and #100 is miniscule.

I looked at a number of different formulas that would best fit the data, and the most accurate correlation I came up with was a linear relationship between "expected value" and 1/SQRT(PK). That is to say, the value of a draft pick correlates with the reciprocal of the square root of the pick number.

An easier way to look at it is this: the square root of the pick number is a measure of how much more valuable the #1 overall pick is relative to that pick. By this formula, the #1 overall pick is three times more valuable than the #9 pick, four times more valuable than the #16 pick, and so on. It also means that the #6 pick is twice as valuable as the #36 pick, and the #25 pick is twice as valuable as the #100 pick.

Performing a linear regression on the data leads to this formula:

$$XP = 11.21/\text{SQRT(PK)} - 0.04$$

The variable *XP* refers to a player's expected value. By this formula, the #1 overall pick is expected to bring back 11.17 discounted WARP (henceforth known as DW). The #10 pick has an expected value of 3.50 DW; the #100 pick would be valued at 1.08 DW. The correlation between DW and 1/SQRT(PK) is highly statistically significant; the p value was essentially zero. And if you've made it to the end of this paragraph, you need to get out more.

Now that we have a simple formula for calculating what a particular draft pick "should" be worth, we can evaluate whether players who were particularly young or old were likely to return more or less value expected on their investment. For example, we can look at the very first draft in 1965, when 25 high school hitters were selected among the top 100 picks. The oldest of them was a shortstop named Carl Richardson. Richardson was born on June 2, 1946. For the sake of standardization, we set "draft day" as occurring on June 1 for every year, so in our system, Richardson is listed as a day shy of 19 years old on his draft day.

Richardson was selected #77 overall by the Cincinnati Reds. The expected return of that draft slot was 1.32 DW. Richardson never made the major leagues, so his actual DW was zero. On the other hand, the youngest high school hitter selected in the 1965 draft was a catcher from Oklahoma who was born on December 7, 1947, making him more than 18 months younger than Spencer. He was also selected by the Reds, with the #36 overall pick, which has an expected value of 1.91 DW. It turns out that hitter, Johnny Bench, was worth considerably more than that. Bench ranks fifth among all high school hitters in our study with 34.05 DW, behind only Alex Rodriguez, Rickey Henderson, George Brett, and Ken Griffey Jr.

Now that you get the idea, here's some data. I took the five youngest players from every draft from 1965 through 1996, and compared them to the five oldest players from the same draft. "Young XP" refers to the expected value of the five youngest high school hitters in that year's draft, based on where they were selected. "Young DW" refers to the total discounted WARP those five players actually earned. "Old XP" and "Old DW" refer to the same for the five oldest high school hitters in that year's draft. "Return" refers to the return on investment above or below expectations; "+100%" would mean that those five players returned, in total, 100 percent more than (i.e., double) what was expected from them (see Table 2-2.1).

Now that the explanations are out of the way: wow. Over the 32 years combined, the youngest players in each year's draft were ex-

TABLE 2-2.1 Young vs. Old Draftees

Year	Young XP	Young DW	Young Return	Old XP	Old DW	Old Return
1965	8.50	34.55	+306.47%	11.00	2.50	-77.27%
1966	17.23	18.47	+7.20%	9.01	22.42	+148.83%
1967	11.45	0.00	-100.00%	19.91	12.18	-38.82%
1968	25.79	16.92	-34.39%	11.95	0.00	-100.00%
1969	9.60	0.00	-100.00%	10.25	11.75	+14.63%
1970	6.71	2.63	-60.80%	10.24	2.56	-75.00%
1971	10.61	8.15	-23.19%	9.88	10.57	+6.98%
1972	9.05	26.22	+189.72%	8.50	0.06	-99.29%
1973	13.00	52.37	+302.85%	8.91	0.00	-100.00%
1974	7.95	2.97	-62.64%	10.77	21.87	+103.06%
1975	8.47	0.77	-90.91%	19.01	0.00	-100.00%
1976	8.27	54.48	+558.77%	10.80	10.47	-3.06%
1977	11.18	10.06	-10.02%	10.28	14.31	+39.20%
1978	10.13	16.43	+62.19%	20.70	16.52	-20.19%
1979	8.01	5.12	-36.08%	12.50	1.13	-90.96%
1980	13.20	18.90	+43.18%	9.59	1.20	-87.49%
1981	7.86	2.69	-65.78%	8.95	0.00	-100.00%
1982	7.73	1.63	-78.91%	20.07	28.63	+42.65%
1983	7.78	2.34	-69.92%	13.29	1.66	-87.51%
1984	20.86	1.26	-93.96%	8.50	0.00	-100.00%
1985	8.04	7.27	-9.58%	8.03	0.00	-100.00%
1986	11.12	36.61	+229.23%	8.04	1.62	-79.85%
1987	17.48	36.55	+109.10%	8.34	2.40	-71.22%
1988	7.12	0.12	-98.31%	14.08	8.92	-36.65%
1989	13.29	3.43	-74.19%	9.20	2.27	-75.33%
1990	12.17	1.16	-90.47%	12.70	13.13	+3.39%
1991	12.64	5.38	-57.44%	6.89	3.52	-48.91%
1992	14.05	56.16	+299.72%	8.62	20.32	+135.73%
1993	8.99	13.65	+51.84%	13.17	13.27	+0.76%
1994	7.41	7.68	+3.64%	16.38	0.16	-99.02%
1995	10.06	0.00	-100.00%	10.84	0.00	-100.00%
1996	7.42	22.30	+200.54%	8.96	1.35	-84.93%
Total	**353.17**	**466.27**	**+32.02%**	**369.36**	**224.79**	**-39.14%**

pected to produce slightly less value than the oldest players, because on average they were taken with slightly later draft selections. *Despite that, the five youngest players in each year returned more than twice as much value as the five oldest players*. If you adjust for the fact that the older group had a slightly higher expected value on Draft Day, the

TABLE 2-2.2 Young vs. Old Draftees by Four-Year Segments

Year	Young XP	Young DW	Young Return	Old XP	Old DW	Old Return
1965–1968	62.97	69.94	+11.07%	51.87	37.10	-28.48%
1969–1972	35.97	37.00	+2.86%	38.87	24.94	-35.84%
1973–1976	37.69	110.59	+193.42%	49.49	32.34	-34.65%
1977–1980	42.52	50.51	+18.79%	53.07	33.16	-37.52%
1981–1984	44.23	7.92	-82.09%	50.81	30.29	-40.39%
1985–1988	43.76	80.55	+84.07%	38.49	12.94	-66.38%
1989–1992	52.15	66.13	+26.81%	37.41	39.24	+4.89%
1993–1996	33.88	43.63	+28.78%	49.35	14.78	-70.05%

younger group had a return that was 117 percent higher than the older group.

Let me repeat that: a team that drafted one of the five youngest high school hitters selected among the top 100 picks could expect *more than twice as much value* from him as a team that selected one of the five oldest high school hitters. And that's not a small-sample-size fluke; that's a result derived from 32 years of the draft, looking at 160 players from both camps.

While the advantage enjoyed by younger players ebbs and flows, it doesn't appear to grow or diminish over time. If we combine the draft years into four year bins (i.e., 1965–1968, 1969–1972, etc.), we can see that with the exception of the four-year span from 1981 to 1984—thank you, Shawn Abner—the young players beat their expected return (and beat the pants off the older players) every time. Hedge funds would kill to beat the market this consistently (see Table 2-2.2).

Young high school hitters are simply much more likely to develop into stars, particularly players who weren't elite picks. I already mentioned Johnny Bench, who went from the second round to the Hall of Fame. In 1972, Chet Lemon was selected with the 22nd overall pick; Lemon was 17 years, 3 months, and went on to a fantastic career. The following year, two of the five youngest high school hitters went on to the Hall of Fame. Maybe it's not a surprise that Robin Yount did, given that he was the third overall pick and was starting at shortstop in the majors the following year—the only 18-year-old to play regularly in the majors in the last 75 years—but it *was* a surprise that Eddie Murray, drafted as a catcher/first baseman with the 63rd overall pick, went on to find the success he had. It shouldn't have been so shocking; Murray was two weeks younger than Lemon had been. Murray and Lemon, in fact, were both among the six youngest hitters in the entire study.

The youngest player in our study from 1976 was taken with the 96th overall pick: Rickey Henderson. He was a month younger than Mike Scioscia, drafted 19th overall that year. In 1980, the 71st overall pick was used on a young high school second baseman named Danny Tartabull. In 1986, the Brewers had the sixth overall pick, and didn't screw it up, using it to select Gary Sheffield. In 1987, the Mariners selected Ken Griffey Jr. first overall. In 1992, Derek Jeter was selected at #6 overall, and Jason Kendall, born on the same day, was selected with the 23rd pick. In the last year of the study, 1996, the youngest player selected in the top 100 was Jimmy Rollins, who was drafted 46th overall.

The best players in the entire study selected from among the five *oldest* high school hitters in their draft class were Willie Wilson, Johnny Damon, and Richie Hebner. The conclusion is clear and dramatic: when it comes to the drafting of high school hitters, even slight differences in age matter. At least when it comes to high school hitters, young draft picks are a massive market inefficiency. The youngest high school hitters in a draft class have had twice the return on investment as the oldest high school hitters, and this advantage does not appear to be diminishing over time.

Let's take a more comprehensive view of the data. I've taken all 846 players in the draft study and separated them by age into five roughly equal bins—very young, young, average, old, and very old. I then calculated the combined expected value of the players in each bin, based on where they were drafted, and the combined discounted WARP that they actually generated.

In Table 2-2.3, "Very Young" players were less than 17 years, 296 days old on draft day; "Young" players were between 17 years, 296 days and 18 years, 38 days; "Average" players were between 18 years, 38 days and 18 years, 120 days; "Old" players were between 18 years, 120 days and 18 years, 200 days; "Very Old" players were more than 18 years, 200 days old.

As you can see, there is an almost shockingly smooth progression in the data. Very young players, as a whole, return 25 percent more value than expected by their draft slots. Young and average players also return positive value, whereas old and very old players return substantially less value than expected. The youngest group returns about 86 percent more value than the oldest group, as opposed to the 117 percent cited above. It's still an enormous difference.

TABLE 2-2.3 Results by Age Bracket

Age	# Players	DW	XP	Return
Very Young	169	482.26	386.31	+24.84%
Young	169	453.05	405.98	+11.59%
Average	170	418.58	390.68	+7.14%
Old	168	282.65	407.65	-30.66%
Very Old	170	249.07	370.42	-32.76%

TABLE 2-2.4 Young vs. Old, 1965–1980

Age	# Players	DW	XP	Return
Very Young	86	261.67	197.87	+32.24%
Young	88	249.44	223.69	+11.51%
Average	86	277.59	224.57	+23.61%
Old	88	179.16	211.91	-15.45%
Very Old	86	135.91	216.94	-37.35%

TABLE 2-2.5 Young vs. Old, 1981–1996

Age	# Players	DW	XP	Return
Very Young	82	218.79	179.42	+21.94%
Young	83	190.93	185.98	+2.66%
Average	81	124.57	167.11	-25.46%
Old	84	146.36	185.16	-20.95%
Very Old	82	101.20	168.39	-39.90%

This difference does not appear to have changed over the years. The same data as above, but limited to players drafted in the first 16 years of our study, from 1965 to 1980, is shown in Table 2-2.4; data from players drafted in the last 16 years of our study, from 1981 to 1996, is in Table 2-2.5.

The data in each half of the study is not quite as smooth, which isn't surprising given that the sample size is half as large. In the first study, average players are a better value than young players, while in the second, average players return less value than old players. But otherwise, both halves of the data show the same thing: the younger the player, the better the return on investment. Additionally, if you compare the very young players with the very old players, you'll notice that the advantage enjoyed by the youngest set of players is greater in *each* half of the data than in the data as a whole. From 1965 to 1980, very young players return 111 percent more value than very old players; from 1981 to 1996 they return 103 percent more value.

It would seem counterintuitive that the advantage enjoyed by young players is greater in each half than in the study as a whole, but there is a reason for this, which is something that isn't very well known: *high school players are getting older over time*. This isn't something limited to baseball; a better way of putting it is that high school *students* are getting older over time. There is a societal trend toward holding back children from starting school early. Whereas 40 years ago, parents frequently tried to get their soon-to-be-five-year-old child, whose birthday might be in October or November, into kindergarten when school opened in the fall, today parents frequently will hold back their 5-year-old, whose birthday might fall in July or August, until the following year. There is a growing, albeit controversial, belief in educational circles that kids who are among the oldest in their class do better academically than those who fall on the youngest end of the spectrum.

As a result, the average high school player drafted in 2010 is roughly three months older than the average high school player drafted in 1965. When I broke the data into two halves above, the age cutoffs for "Very Young," "Young," etc., were about six weeks higher for the draft group from 1981 to 1996 than for the draft group from 1965 to 1980.

This is why the results we get from pooling the data for all players from 1965 to 1996, without regard to the year they were drafted, might actually *underestimate* the advantage younger players have. Derek Jeter and Jason Kendall would not have ranked among the ten youngest high school hitters from 1965, but when teams are drafting, what matters is the draft pool in front of them, and both Jeter and Kendall were among the five youngest high school hitters in 1993. As draft classes get older as a whole, the youngest players in each class get older as well—but so do the oldest players, giving the youngest players the same age advantage they've always had. We can safely say that the youngest 20 percent of high school hitters in any particular year will return, on average, about double what the oldest 20 percent of high school hitters will.

We can sum up all the data above by performing a second linear regression, this time including a player's age along with his pick number as variables. If we do so, here is the formula we get:

$$\text{Expected Return} = 18.61 - (1.03 * \text{Age}) + (11.47/\text{SQRT(PK)})$$

The p-value for the age variable is very low, at just .0139. This means that there is less than a two percent chance that we would get data like this if there weren't an actual correlation between age and expected return. This is a statistically significant result.

Secondly, we can now estimate to what degree teams should be drafting younger players earlier. If Player A is exactly one year younger than Player B, and they were both selected with the same pick in the draft, Player A should be expected to return an additional 1.03 discounted WARP over his career. Because the value of draft picks does not go down in a linear fashion, we can't say that one year of age is worth exactly x number of picks in the draft—x changes depending on where you are in the draft. What we can say, using the above formula, is that 1.03 discounted WARP is roughly the difference between the expected values of picks #28 and #100. In other words, a 17-year-old player drafted #100 overall has as much expected value as an 18-year-old drafted #28. If a player who might look like a third-round pick on talent alone happens to be a full year younger than his draft class, he ought to be considered a late-first-round pick.

That is a massive, massive impact. One year of age is the difference in the expected value of pick #25 and pick #12. It's the difference between pick #5 and pick #8. Remember, this is even *after* adjusting for the fact that teams—at least some teams—may already be taking age into consideration, and drafting younger players earlier than they would otherwise. They clearly don't take age into account enough. Even a six-month difference is meaningful. The difference in value between a player born in, say, October and in April is the difference in value between the #100 pick and the #48 pick, or the difference between the #30 pick and the #19 pick.

It's hard to overstate the importance of this. I can't say that major league teams have ignored age *completely* when drafting players, but age has clearly been subordinate to present talent, and this study argues strongly that this has been a mistake. If Player A grades out slightly better than Player B, but Player B is six or 12 months younger than Player A, teams have been drafting Player A first, and they should have been drafting Player B.

As this data set ends with the 1996 draft, it is quite possible that the edge toward younger players has diminished if some teams have privately done their own research and realized the bonanza to be had in younger high school hitters. In order to study whether this was true or not, I performed an abbreviated study of high school hitters drafted from 1997 to 2003.

For this eight-year span, I calculated discounted WARP in the same way as above, with the exception that I only looked at the first eight years after the draft. (This way, even players drafted in 2003 had a full eight years of data through 2011.) This is an incomplete measure of a player's value—we're cutting off every player's contribution after the age of about 27—but it's the best we can do at this point.

As with the data set from 1965 to 1996, I used linear regression to come up with a formula to estimate a player's DW based on his pick number. That formula was:

$$XP = (6.39/\text{SQRT}(PK)) + .04$$

I then grouped the 176 players in this study into five groups by age—from the youngest 20 percent (those who were younger than 18 years, 15 days old) to the oldest 20 percent (those who were at least 18 years, 263 days old). Table 2-2.6 shows the results.

According to the data, it appears that the importance of a draft pick's age has, in fact, changed over time, but not in the direction you'd expect: the advantage enjoyed by young players increased dramatically from 1997 to 2003. The average return from the youngest 20 percent of draft picks during this span was more than triple the return of the oldest 20 percent.

From 1997 to 2003, 22 high school hitters drafted in the top 100 were at least 18 years, 293 days old. Just two of them reached the majors—Sergio Santos, who only made it after he converted from shortstop to reliever, and Jorge Padilla, who got 25 below-replacement-level at-bats for the Nationals in 2009, when he was 29 years old. None of the other 20 players sniffed the majors, including a #4 overall pick (Corey Myers).

TABLE 2-2.6 High School Hitters Drafted, 1997–2003

Age	# Players	DW	XP	Return
Very Young	35	64.55	49.10	+31.47%
Young	35	69.32	56.48	+22.73%
Average	35	50.22	40.32	+24.55%
Old	36	25.71	41.00	-37.29%
Very Old	35	17.19	40.09	-57.12%

Meanwhile, among the 22 *youngest* high school hitters drafted in that span were Daric Barton, Carl Crawford, Grady Sizemore, Adam Jones, and Brandon Phillips—none of whom were drafted in the top 25 picks. Crawford was taken at #52, Phillips at #57, and Sizemore (who, granted, got $2 million to sign) at #75.

Much as I did with the data from 1965 to 1996, I performed a linear regression for the 1997 to 2003 data that included a player's draft status and his age as variables. The formula I got was:

$$\text{Expected Return} = 19.96 - (1.08 * \text{Age}) + (5.97/\text{SQRT(PK)})$$

What you'll notice is that the coefficient for a player's draft pick number (5.97) is much lower than it was in the study from 1965 to 1996 (11.47). This isn't surprising, because in the more recent data set, we're only looking at how he played in the first eight years after he was drafted instead of the first 15, so his expected return should be lower. However, by comparison, the coefficient for a player's age (1.08) is actually slightly higher than the previous formula (1.03). What that means is that, relative to where the player was drafted, his age had a significantly *greater* impact from 1997 to 2003 than it did from 1965 to 1996.

The data from 1965 to 1996 suggested that a player drafted #100 overall could be expected to perform as well as a player one year older who was drafted 28th overall, but from 1997 to 2003, the impact of age was so great that the 17-year-old player drafted #100 was as valuable as the 18-year-old player drafted #13 overall.

The conclusion is clear: at least as recently as 2003, the baseball industry as a whole *massively* underrated the importance of age in drafting high school hitters, and *massively* undervalued high school hitters who still needed their parents' permission to sign their contract. While we simply don't have enough data to evaluate more recent drafts, Mike Trout and Jason Heyward are two powerful data points in support of the notion that the advantage toward younger high school hitters in the draft is still there, and teams ignore it at their own peril.

Having proven that young high school hitters are an undervalued commodity in baseball, it logically proceeds to ask the question as to whether the same is true of young college hitters, or of pitchers of either type. From 1965 to 1996, 510 hitters were selected from four-year colleges in the first 100 picks of each draft. (For the purposes of these studies, we've eliminated junior college players from consideration.) If we split those 510 hitters into quintiles based on age, we arrive at the returns shown in tables 2-2.7 and 2-2.8. There's definitely a trend

TABLE 2-2.7 College Hitters, 1965–1996

Age	# Players	DW	XP	Return
Very Young	102	361.56	329.41	+9.76%
Young	101	467.74	353.73	+32.23%
Average	104	310.39	322.43	-3.73%
Old	102	192.77	311.21	-38.06%
Very Old	101	263.40	279.07	-5.62%

TABLE 2-2.8 College Hitters Younger and Older Than Average

Age	# Players	DW	XP	Return
Young	254	1018.87	825.79	+23.38%
Old	256	576.98	770.08	-25.08%

there, but it's a lot less smooth than what we observed with high school hitters. The youngest and oldest players show only a modest effect, but the middle quartiles show a dramatic drop in return as the players get older. If we make the data less granular and simply split up the players into two groups—those younger than average and those older than average—the impact is clear.

There are some complicating factors that might explain why the data is not as smooth for college hitters as for their high school counterparts. The first is that while college players are not eligible for the draft today until after their junior year (or unless they're 21 years old), that wasn't always the case.

In the very first draft (1965), Rick Monday was selected #1 overall. Monday had just completed his sophomore year and was still 19 years old. Only 16 college hitters in our data set were still 19 when they were drafted—nine of them were drafted in 1965 or 1966, and just four were drafted after 1972. The average age of college players selected in the early years of the draft was significantly younger than those selected in later years, and as with high school hitters above, that may be making the true impact of age appear less than it really is.

Another factor is that while most high draft picks out of college are selected as juniors, some players do not sign until after their senior year. We were not able to get comprehensive data on how many years of college every draft pick had completed, so we were unable to isolate only those players who were college juniors. This means that some of the oldest players in our draft set were taken as college seniors. If we theorize that the reason why young players are undervalued is that teams mentally categorize all players of a specific draft type to-gether—"high school player," "college junior," and so on—then pre-sumably teams evaluated college seniors differently than players who still had a year of eligibility left, and only the truly elite college seniors were taken with early picks.

The oldest star position player drafted out of college, Ozzie Smith, was halfway to turning 23 when he was taken as a senior—he had been drafted the year before by the Detroit Tigers but chose not to sign. (Don't weep for Detroit, who got Alan Trammell, Dan Petry, and Jack Morris in the same draft.) The Wizard's Hall of Fame career doesn't disprove our theory that older college players tend to under-perform; it just proves that not every great college talent is signed af-ter his junior season.

If we perform a linear regression on the data for college hitters, we arrive at:

$$\text{Expected Return} = 15.39 - (0.72 * \text{Age}) + (15.48/\text{SQRT(PK)})$$

As we saw with high school hitters, the older the player, the lower the expected return. However, the impact is not nearly as large. Rela-tive to the value of the draft pick, the impact of age on a college hitter is roughly 52 percent as great as the impact on a high school hitter. With high school hitters, one year of age was the equivalent of the dif-ference between pick #100 and pick #28. With college hitters, one year is only the difference between pick #100 and pick #47.

The impact is small enough that it is not, in fact, statistically signif-icant. The p-value of the linear regression is 0.1765, which means there's a 17.65 percent chance that the perceived advantage for younger college hitters is simply caused by chance. Now, the fact that a result is not "statistically significant" is not the same as saying the result is not true. It simply means that it is possible the results we are seeing could have been caused by blind luck. We simply don't have enough data to say what is the true cause one way or the other.

One of the reasons why our results are not significant is that the sample size is smaller. While 846 high school hitters were drafted in the top 100 picks from 1965 to 1996, only 510 college hitters were se-lected. If we had the exact same results, but a larger data sample, the results might be statistically significant. Let's say you had a weighted coin that landed heads 70 percent of the time. If you flipped it 10 times and got seven heads, that would not be statistically significant, because a perfectly fair coin could do the same thing. If you flipped it 100 times and got 70 heads, you'd be able to state with confidence that the coin was weighted. Same coin, same results, but a larger sample size makes all the difference.

Given that we have seen a similar, but more dramatic, effect with high school hitters, there is reason to believe that the results we are seeing with college hitters is more likely than not to be real. Even if it is, though, the effect appears to be less than half as large. We can't say with complete certainty that young college hitters are a market inefficiency, but the data is suggestive. We shouldn't be at all surprised that the impact of age on college hitters is less than that for high school hitters; the improvement curve is much flatter at the age of 21 than it is at the age of 18. So far, the data conforms to common sense pretty strongly.

When college pitchers are broken down into quintiles, we see a strong correlation between younger players and a positive return on investment (Table 2-2.9), but as with college hitters, the trend isn't perfect; players in the middle-age range performed worst overall. If we break the data into two halves (Table 2-2.10), the results are in line with our general theory: younger is better.

The youngest 20 percent of college pitchers were those younger than 20 years, 10 months at the time they were drafted. They include Ken Holtzman (#61 overall), Bob Welch (#20), Pete Harnisch (#27),

TABLE 2-2.9 College Pitchers

Age	# Players	DW	XP	Return
Very Young	100	405.91	308.05	+31.77%
Young	97	357.51	318.39	+12.29%
Average	101	263.80	322.49	-18.20%
Old	99	314.49	345.53	-8.98%
Very Old	99	250.42	297.66	-15.87%

TABLE 2-2.10 College Pitchers, Young vs. Old

Age	# Players	DW	XP	Return
Young	248	917.84	792.55	+15.81%
Old	248	674.30	799.57	-15.67%

Denny Neagle (#85), Andy Benes (#1), Mark Langston (#35), Ron Darling (#9), Eric Milton (#20), and the greatest college pitcher of the draft era, Roger Clemens (#19). That's nine pitchers out of 99 who accumulated at least 17 discounted WARP. By comparison, the only college pitchers among the oldest 20 percent—those who were at least 21 years, 7 months on Draft Day—to amass that much value were Kevin Tapani (#40), Jon Lieber (#44), and Randy Johnson (#36).

Once again, the linear regression tells the story. Here's the formula we derive from the data for college pitchers:

$$\text{Expected Return} = 13.66 - (0.61 * \text{Age}) + (13.44/\text{SQRT(PK)})$$

While the coefficient for age is less than that for college hitters, so are the coefficients for the other terms. This isn't surprising, since historically college pitchers have not fared as well as college hitters in general. Relative to the value of the draft pick, the impact of age for college pitchers is almost identical to the impact for college hitters. As with college hitters, the results do not reach the level of statistical significance. The combination of a slightly lower coefficient and a slightly smaller sample size (there were only 496 college pitchers in our study) combine to make the p-value slightly higher at 0.2261. Again, despite the lack of statistical significance, the consistency of the results—younger players have had an advantage with every group we've studied so far—suggests that the results are meaningful.

If there's a surprise here, it's that among collegiate players, age is just as important for pitchers as it is for hitters. Intuitively, you wouldn't suspect that to be the case. While an extra year of development for a 20-year-old hitter is immensely valuable, it's not as clear that the same is true for 20-year-old pitchers. For one thing, pitchers at the age of 20 or 21 are so likely to suffer an arm injury that you might think you'd be better off drafting the slightly older pitcher, figuring that he's already managed to get past his 21st birthday without suffering a catastrophic injury. What the data suggests is that there is still a dramatic difference in projection for a 20-year-old pitcher over a 21-year-old. He might get injured, but he is also far more likely to add velocity or master a breaking ball or something else that lets him take a step forward.

As for high school pitchers (Table 2-2.11), we finally have some data that doesn't appear to show any sort of pattern at all. High school pitchers who are particularly old continue to do poorly, but this time the *youngest* pitchers in the study do worst of all.

TABLE 2-2.11 High School Pitchers

Age	# Players	DW	XP	Return
Very Young	117	197.41	235.98	-16.34%
Young	117	304.91	251.28	+21.34%
Average	118	283.37	277.13	+2.25%
Old	116	261.47	243.31	+7.46%
Very Old	118	232.62	266.77	-12.80%

TABLE 2-2.12 High School Pitchers, Young vs. Old

Age	# Players	DW	XP	Return
Young	293	687.04	623.65	+10.16%
Old	293	592.74	650.82	-8.92%

The youngest quintile of pitchers—those who were less than 17 years, 10 months old—include Dwight Gooden and Jon Matlack (both taken among the first five picks), as well as Dennis Eckersley (#50). The problem is, that's about it. The fourth-best pitcher in that group is probably Ken Brett, who was also a top five pick. If we split the data into two groups (Table 2-2.12), there is still a slight advantage for the younger half over the older, and a linear regression still shows a modest trend in favor of younger pitchers, as seen by the formula

$$\text{Expected Return} = 6.01 - (0.31 * \text{age}) + (9.84/\text{sqrt(pk)})$$

Relative to the value of the draft pick, the impact of age for high school pitchers is about 69 percent of the impact for college pitchers, and about 35 percent of the impact for high school hitters. As you can imagine, the trend is so slight that it's almost meaningless. The p-value of the data is 0.5074. That fails to reach not only statistical significance, but practical significance.

The question is why this is so. Our model suggests that the younger the player, the more rapidly he is improving. Slight differences in age should be more important for high school players than college ones. Indeed, that's exactly what we saw with hitters, but while age is as important for college pitchers as it is for college hitters, high school pitchers show no effect whatsoever.

The most compelling answer resides with that youngest quintile of pitchers, the ones who screw up our perfect slope by underperforming their expectations most of all. For the entire history of our study, pitch counts—even at the lowest levels of the minors—were kept sporadically if at all. Younger pitchers are still developing physically, and still perfecting their mechanics, making them significantly more likely to hurt their arms than older pitchers.

It's not a stretch to suggest, then, that the 17-year-old with a live arm is more trouble than he's worth, because he's going to wind up on an operating table. With pitchers, the gradual improvement in skills as a player ages is being counteracted by the high risk of injury. What our data suggests is that once a pitcher reaches the age of 20, the risk of injury has diminished to the point where it's overwhelmed by the potential for improvement. At the age of 17, however, the injury risk is more formidable than the odds of a breakthrough performance.

If that's the case—and we're deep into the realm of the hypothetical here—then the historical data may only have limited application in today's game. Every team in baseball keeps its pitchers on pitch counts, and teenage pitchers in particular are monitored with a degree of caution that borders on paranoia. It's possible that a 17-year-old pitcher who is not overworked, and who is much less likely to blow out his arm, does in fact have the same potential for dramatic improvement as a hitter of the same age. But if that's the case, it might be 20 years before we have the data to prove it.

To summarize our findings:

1. High school hitters who are particularly young for their draft class produce a dramatically higher rate of return than their older classmates. This effect has persisted throughout the history of the draft, and is large enough that major league teams should adjust their drafting tendencies significantly to accommodate for it.

2. College draft picks, both hitters and pitchers, show a similar tendency for younger players to outperform older ones. However, the effect is barely half that for high school hitters, and does not yet rise to the level of statistical significance. Still, it probably makes sense for major league teams to tweak their draft boards to bump younger players up a few slots.

3. The impact of age on high school pitchers is considerably smaller—on the order of one-third that for high school hitters—if it exists at all. The risk of injury with high school pitchers appears to trump any age considerations. In particular, pitchers

drafted before their 18th birthday have historically not fared well, and need to be handled with extreme caution to prevent injury.

In the post-*Moneyball* era, there are fewer and fewer market inefficiencies left to exploit. Teams are spending millions of dollars on the most sophisticated data analysis possible—proprietary defensive metrics, setting up PITCHf/x systems in their minor league stadiums, sophisticated internal computer systems like the Indians' DiamondView and the Red Sox' Carmine. Yet it turns out one of the biggest market inefficiencies in all of baseball was right under their noses, and they don't need to spend millions of dollars to obtain the information. All they need is a copy of a player's driver's license.

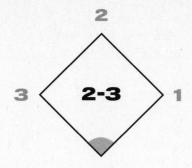

From the Buscone to
the Big Leagues

How Is Latin-American Talent
Acquired and Developed?

JASON PARKS

The place where long odds could turn into large payoffs, the Latin-American market is a vast, corrupt (and often corrupting) wilderness of political and socioeconomic obstacles, but also the most fertile prospect soil in the world. It would take volumes to craft a representational image of all the complexities of the market. Hunting talent in Latin America is 80-grade complicated, and no one authority, no matter how experienced, can supply a definitive perspective, so varied are the possible outcomes.

When researching this chapter, I found the range of thought on the Latin-American market could not have been any more diverse, with superlatives and salivation directly countered with cries of uncertainty and disdain for the process. Given the aforementioned obstacles involved with such a complex form of commerce, divergent opinions were to be expected; however, their intensity was surprising, with respondents dividing themselves into opposing camps. Many love prospecting in Latin America, but some fear it with equal passion.

Reasons to Love It

◆ First and foremost, the talent coming out of the Latin-American market, whether it originates from Venezuela, the Dominican Republic, Colombia, Panama, Curacao, or Brazil, is rich with promise. The region is stacked with natural athletes; it's a market of projection, where the raw physical gifts of the players allow for remarkable ceilings and fantastic outcomes. It's the epicenter of the superstar and a market that some believe represents the future of the game. The talent is superior, from a physical standpoint, to our domestic product: the athletes are bigger, stronger, and faster than talent found in other markets, and available earlier. That head start on the developmental process affords teams more time to sculpt those physical gifts into baseball skills. When you take a superior athlete and get him into a professional developmental program at 16 rather than at 18 or 21, you increase your chances of building a monster.

◆ It's an open system. Not subject to the draft (at least for now), the Latin-American market is one big pot of free agency, allowing teams to scout and sign players at their discretion. The level of investment is without boundaries. Some teams throw millions of dollars into the process, building and maintaining year-round training and developmental academies to evaluate immature talent, paying scouts and *buscones* (agents) to scour the globe in search of quality product, and then buying said product by awarding bonuses predicated on the market-established value of the player. If a team is willing to spend, cash is king. Top dollar buys access to top talent, allowing those willing to gamble an opportunity to win big. If you have the money, honey, players and buscones have the time.

◆ When the signing window opens on July 2 of every year, prospective teams have the opportunity to offer the aforementioned bonuses to the amateur athletes, who become eligible to sign a professional contract when they are 16 years old. This might be the biggest "pro," as the sooner you get the talent into the development/cultural assimilation process, the better.

◆ You can still find value without paying the most money. Although money rules when it comes to the most obviously talented players, spending less doesn't preclude the opportunity of finding value, because the market is so rich with immature talent. Quality prospects often fall through the cracks for a variety of reasons, including poor workouts, limited game action, injury, suspect behavior on the part of the buscone/family, etc. Because of the inherent risk of the investment itself, some teams prefer a "quantity over quality" signing philosophy, as "quality" is more subjective in the Latin-American market than any other—which shouldn't come as a shock given the complexities of the market. The sands of the market are littered with diamonds, and the cost to acquire a bucket of sand is still far less than any other traditional method of diamond excavation. A team can scout and sign 20 players for the cost of one seven-figure international bonus baby, increasing your odds of winning the lottery.

Reasons to Fear It

◆ As more teams look to participate in the market, the demand has further complicated the landscape, giving more power to the often corrupt buscones and inflating player bonuses to the point where the risk-reward ratio has shifted decisively towards the former. Buscones are an amalgam of scout, agent, father figure, and underworld procurer. It should be noted that not every buscone operating in the Latin-American market is a criminal, and not every international deal is loaded with corruption. Corruption exists in every pore of commerce, and the Latin-American market just happens to have really oily skin. For those who are less scrupulous than others, finding financial gain by manipulating the system is easily accomplished. Because of the socioeconomic climate that exists in parts of the market, influencing those without education or general ignorance of the negotiation process doesn't require a Ponzi scheme to operate; often, it takes little more than words: "Sign with me and do what I say or suffer the consequences," be that a physical threat or a professional one. I've heard numerous stories about buscones who operate as figures in organized crime, extorting and controlling through intimidation and force. The flip side of that coin shows ethical buscones that put the future of the player and his family first when it comes to negotiation. Obviously, teams would prefer to deal with buscones who have a positive reputation, but the allure of talent is often too intoxicating to walk away from, even when corruption is attached to the talent via the buscone.

◆ The calculus behind bonuses is often political and counterintuitive. The buscones smell money like reality show celebrities smell fame, which pushes bonus demands up on some players, making them more similar to the high-stakes gambles found in the domestic markets. Simultaneously, the extreme depth of the market and frequent focus on a few expensive talents allow high-ceiling (but not high-dollar) talent to hide in the shadows. Some teams encourage demand on some players in order to price teams out of the market; others encourage demand on some players to dim the light on others they might be targeting.

◆ Culture and language. This is perhaps the most unrecognized con, as the failure of Latin-American talent in professional baseball has more to do with the emotional and psychological components involved than the physical ones. That is not to say that properly adjusted talent can't fail; it can and does. When you sign a 16-year-old child from an underdeveloped region of the world, and then ask him to develop his athletic skills at an accelerated rate while simultaneously adjusting to a foreign culture and learning a second language, you are putting a remarkable amount of strain on the makeup of that player. Often, baseball is the easy part of the equation. Learning on the field requires development off the field as well and, given the financially and educationally impoverished environments from which many Latin-American prospects have been extracted, that is a bigger gamble than the initial financial expenses required to acquire the talent in the first place.

◆ Limited baseball experience. This is especially true in places like the Dominican Republic, where organized youth baseball is not firmly in place. As teams begin working out players in their early teenage years, they find the refinement level is quite often grossly inferior to that of kids of the same age in the United States, despite the physical gifts of the players and the cultural significance of the game itself. There is no record of how successful teams have been at converting unformed teenage talent into viable big-league prospects, so forecasting the development of that talent based on workouts and limited game exposure is another big risk.

◆ Establishing credible player identity in some regions in the market can be problematic. It's not uncommon to have amateur talents falsify their identities in order to draw interest from professional baseball. Projectable 16-year-olds can draw huge bonuses. Nineteen-year-olds encourage the same demand. Such a market creates corruption. Historically, the Dominican Republic has been the most corrupt in this regard, forcing teams to do extensive and often expensive background research before moving forward with a player, where similar measures are not required in more ethically aware (as far as identity is concerned) regions in the market, like Venezuela.

◆ Unstable political environments in countries likes Venezuela can affect teams with permanent interests in the region, i.e., teams that operate year-round training and developmental academies on foreign soil. Governmental interference and corruption has forced some teams out of the region altogether, as the price of the player comes at an even higher price in both time and treasure. It's hard enough to navigate the complex world of amateur talent evaluation, much less to do so with the government taking a ride on your back.

Developing the Potential

Now that we have discussed the avenues of Latin-American amateur talent acquisition, it's time to look at the ways and means of transforming that talent into professional ballplayers. Every organization in baseball takes a slightly different approach to player development, but the general philosophy is universal: every player has value; it's up to the development team to extract maximum value from the asset in question.

Player development is a partnership between the players and their organization, personified by developmental staff and coaches who have a common goal of maximizing potential for maximum value. It all starts with talent; the process of development cannot unlock talent that doesn't exist in the first place. Talent is the lifeblood of the game, but even teams with the most majestic of financial and human capital will not be able to extract physical characteristics from a player in the absence of those characteristics. Think of player development personnel as locksmiths tasked with unlocking the future of the game. Over time, as they work at their task, the individual characteristics of the lock will change, and the environment in which the doors exist won't remain constant.

The first step is evaluation. Scouts build the initial model for the player, in terms of both what he is now and what he might be in the future. The developmental staff then take their turn at the wheel. They begin with a series of questions that will establish the initial program for the professional journey about to take place: Who is the player now? What more can he become? What skills are more deficient than others? How can those deficient skills be refined? What training programs (strength, diet, language, cultural, and so on) would this player benefit from? Which environments would this player struggle or succeed in? This is key: You can have an umbrella developmental philosophy, a blanket construction by which you will build the heroes of tomorrow. But every player is an individual, and if you fail to recognize the developmental idiosyncrasies required for unique growth, you might exclude the one you are trying to embrace.

The developmental staff, comprised of coordinators, coaches, and front office personnel, are the unsung heroes of the process, standing in the shadows while the children turn into men under the bright lights. Quick: name as many directors of player development as you can in 30 seconds.

. . . Thought so. The talent on your favorite team was cultivated by men who devote most of their lives to the game, spending 300-plus days a year focused on bettering the quality of others. They are merely names on the team's web page and bodies standing in the minor league sun, but without their diligence, patience, and experience, the players of tomorrow will never emerge from the process of the present.

In order to take a closer look at some of the specific hurdles that might arise for an individual prospect caught up in that process, and the responses from the men in charge of the process when he trips over those hurdles, let's take a hypothetical but not atypical scenario from the Dominican Republic involving a promising pitching prospect. Prepare yourself for a convoluted experience.

Name: *José Latin America*
Position: RHP
Team: The Greens
Acquired: Free agent; Dominican Republic
Age When Acquired: 16

After a trusted buscone spoke of an intriguing young right-handed pitcher from the outskirts of Santo Domingo, the Greens sent a scout to watch the precocious arm in action. Over the next few years, the Greens kept tabs on the projectable pitcher, eventually bringing José Latin America to the team facility for a private workout and evaluation. During the process, the buscone suggested other teams were set to make offers when the July 2 window opened, but he would steer the young pitcher toward the Greens for certain (wink-wink) considerations. The market dictated that Jose was a seven-figure arm, as his name was now appearing in stateside publications as a top prospect in the region, and no less than five teams had brought the teenager to their facility for an intimate audition.

July 2 arrives and the Greens win the day, offering José $2 million to become part of their organization, a move the team's front office has convinced ownership is a calculated gamble based on several key factors, including projections for his baseball skills and his makeup.

Standing close to six-foot-two and weighing only 160 pounds (wet), the gangly 16-year-old oozed physical projection, with fast-twitch athleticism and coordination that some teams thought could find a home in center field. The present stuff on the mound was good, but the future could be great, as the fastball already touched the low 90s with some semblance of command, and consistently worked in the 86–88 mph range without much effort. The Greens loved the easy action of the arm itself, and despite being only 16 years old, José showed a preternatural feel for secondary offerings, showing both a promising curve and a slider to go along with a changeup that most evaluators graded as his best pitch.

Ironically, as José's professional education began, his education in most other areas was through. Whereas a 16-year-old American prospect would complete high school and perhaps go on to college or junior college, teams require their Latin-American acquisitions to focus on matters related to baseball or assimilating in American culture and take no responsibility for producing a well-rounded citizen-athlete, whether of the United States or another country.

Teams often target kids who come from stable home environments, which usually indicates some element of disciplinary structure and education. Sadly, most kids from the Dominican Republic leave school at an early age and as a result are woefully underdeveloped. It is in a team's best interest to educate a player in order to maximize his ceiling, but if a kid stops the traditional education process around age 12, and the parents come from a similar background (or worse), it's often an exercise in futility to attempt to properly educate the player. For the most part, the kids are prepared to be productive baseball players and not productive humans: developing prospects in Latin America is an agro-business.

More prosperous countries often allow for opportunities beyond futures consisting of manual labor, unemployment, or baseball. With stronger educational systems in place, in terms of both classroom (fundamental) education and more structured baseball environments like Little League, school teams, organized traveling teams, and so on, kids from (say) Venezuela often come to professional baseball with an advantage over kids from underdeveloped regions. It's not uncommon to find prospects in the Dominican Republic that not only have underdeveloped classroom fundamentals, but also have little to no experience playing in any form of organized baseball. It's a major hurdle to overcome.

Because of their lack of education both before and after their joining an organization, players who do not succeed in baseball are sent back to their native land with little to no real-life skills. Considering most don't receive seven-figure bonuses, and families and buscones take so much of the money, the players return home without much to live on. In some cases, even the players that do make it often end up without much money after their playing days are over. Unless they participated in a structured educational system or come from financial means, they will struggle to exist outside the world of baseball. In the Dominican Republic, failed players often end up back in sugar fields or become criminals. The Dominican Republic is a fifth-world country—when a player fails and returns home, it's basically a death sentence.

These were some of the risks José would face, but in the Greens' estimation he had some advantages. When it comes to giving $2 million to a 16-year-old pitcher, feeling confident of the player's makeup is as important as the present stuff shown on the field. The Greens felt that José was a developmental staff's dream, showing emotional maturity beyond his years with a quiet yet intense fire that fueled his overall approach to the game. The Greens felt they had a player who would respond to the challenges ahead: a player who could fail and recover despite the environment he was placed in.

That fall, the team brought José to the United States to participate in the fall instructional league at the team facility. Despite being a fresh 16-year-old, José navigated the foreign world like a seasoned traveler, mixing well with the culturally diverse and more experienced roster, holding his own in the limited game action he saw, and even getting the chance to throw a bullpen session in front of the major league pitching coach. Through it all, he seemed to relish the pressure, affirming the evaluations of his makeup. All the signs were pointing to a stateside assignment to start the upcoming season, as his on-the-field ability suggested aggressive promotion and his off-the-field maturity suggested he could handle it.

Professional season number one: Winning fans with every encounter, José was invited to stateside spring training, where the developmental staff would continue their evaluations before dictating his first professional assignment. José's strengths and weaknesses were documented and discussed, and his ability to assimilate to a new culture and language was going more smoothly than the already confident organization could have anticipated. The 16-year-old found immediate comfort in his surroundings, both on the field and in the clubhouse, and his physical performance on the field was turning the heads of much older players. After a month of standard spring training action that saw José participate in several back-field Low-A games, the developmental staff scripted a plan for year one, keeping José in extended spring training until short-season ball opened up in June, opting to keep him at the team facility for rookie ball rather than push him to short-season Low-A.

The decision wasn't unanimous. José wasn't set to turn 17 until June, but the overall maturity of both the man and his game had some on the developmental team ready to push the pitcher beyond the complex league to start his professional journey. The organization's developmental philosophy is tailored to the individual, so the team will push players with aggressive assignments if the player is ready. The Greens had only one rule when it came to aggressive assignments: the developmental staff had to be unanimous in their support for the plan to move forward. If any one individual, be he a coach or coordinator, had doubts then the conservative plan was to be followed until unanimity was achieved.

Just as every player is unique, every set of eyes that evaluate that player is unique. As a result, finding consensus is often difficult. Because of the investment involved, what's best for the player takes priority over what's best for the team itself, at least in the early stages of development, so despite a rotation spot being open in short-season Low-A, and despite broad agreement that José was both mentally and physically prepared for the aggressive assignment, the conservative approach won out. The now 17-year-old arm would begin his professional career at the lowest level, the complex league (i.e., rookie ball).

The first setback for the rising prospect occurred just a few days before his first scheduled professional start. José confessed he felt some discomfort in his shoulder during a bullpen session at the team facility. To the sweet relief of all parties involved, an examination revealed no structural damage in the shoulder, and treatment would come in the form of rest. As a result, the professional starter pistol was stored away for another two weeks, with José spending more time in the training room than on the field.

For the Greens, this was a run-of-the mill development, but José didn't meet this setback with the same patient understanding. Already disappointed by the complex league assignment, the seemingly mature pitcher showed some emotional immaturity, sulking during treatment, focusing about as much as a student taking a test the day before summer break. This, too, was to be expected, having been seen countless other times with José's many predecessors.

The complex league coaches and coordinators had established a good relationship with the young arm, but a disconnect was growing, with José feeling isolated by his enforced downtime. When the shoulder remained sore despite two weeks of rest and treatment, the timetable for a return to baseball activities became increasingly vague and distant. Despite further examination, the medical reports continued to suggest that the sore shoulder was structurally sound. The confirmation of José's condition was simultaneously reassuring and disturbing in that it allayed fears that his development would be transiently or permanently altered by a serious physical problem, but provoked a scenario just as disturbing: Was the player legitimately injured?

Speculations about the injured shoulder were kept in-house. A decision was made to push José back into light baseball activities despite the sore shoulder. This was met with consternation from the 17-year-old, who was adamant that pain and discomfort attended every pitch. José spent more and more time alone in his hotel room sending email and text messages to his girlfriend back home, expressing increasing bitterness at his situation. Greens staffers were practically omniscient beings at this stage of the process; having been down this road many times before with previous Josés, the situation at hand was not unexpected, but was worrisome, regardless. Pushing José had failed.

With the season over a month old, José had yet to throw his first professional pitch in the complex league; he was still ahead of his peers' development curve, but behind the original timetable crafted during extended spring training. As the heat of the summer intensified and the rest of the rookie league roster gelled with exposure to routine, José was left out, resultantly growing more detached and disinterested in baseball activities. His mouth opened more often for meals than for conversation, his only solace found in romanticizing the memories of home in private conversations with his family and girlfriend back in the Dominican Republic.

After more than four weeks of soreness and setbacks, the coaching staff informed José that he would be scheduled to make his first professional appearance. It had been unanimously accepted among the staff that José's shoulder soreness was psychological; neither the coaches nor the training staff could find anything physically wrong with the shoulder itself. It was time to encourage a step forward in the maturation process, despite the obvious resistance from the teenage prospect.

Hours before the scheduled start, José told his roommate what the coaching staff and most of his teammates already knew: the shoulder problem could more accurately be described as homesickness, and the thought of toeing the rubber in an official minor league game was far too daunting a task for the 17-year-old to negotiate at this time. He couldn't pitch.

Once again, the experience of the Greens development staff had allowed them to anticipate this development; discussion of this eventuality had already taken place and a new plan was in the works. Player development tends to stray from the script, and teams that are adaptable, especially when it comes to the needs of the individual, are the teams most likely to maximize the potential of that individual. The Greens had made a sizeable investment in José's future. Despite a plume of black smoke coming from their initial developmental strategy, the team wiped the canvas clean and decided to start again. José, a $2 million top-of-the-rotation dream, was on his way back to the Dominican Republic to work out at the team facility, a short car ride from the sandlots of his youth.

Professional season number two: José hadn't been ready for stateside baseball and wouldn't pitch in a professional game in his debut season. Nobody outside of the Greens knew the truth about the circumstances. A sore shoulder was the explanation fed to the media.

After the reassignment to the Dominican Republic, the Greens development staff played detective, looking for clues leading up to the collapse but arriving at more questions than answers. The intensity of the disappointment had more to do with the specific parties involved than the scenario itself; some in the organization (the majority of the developmental staff) had pushed for José, a seemingly mature talent, to start his career in short-season Low-A, a league heavily augmented with college-age players. They were left questioning their own evaluations and convictions, having put a fragile teenager in a foreign environment and asked him to execute as a professional.

After spending the rest of the summer and fall of his debut season at the team facility, José grew even more attached to the comforts provided by proximity to his family, and his professional progress stalled.

His second year would find the soon-to-be 18-year-old starting over at square one, only this time the decision was made to proceed with extreme caution, keeping the hurler in the Dominican Republic and building up his trust and confidence before sending him back to the United States. For the foreseeable future, José would be encouraged to crawl before being made to walk. The investment might take longer to mature, but the payout would be worth the diligence, or so the Greens were betting.

José's spring workouts mirrored those of the Dominican Instructional League the previous winter, with a focus on establishing fastball command through fluid and repeatable mechanics. The blanket developmental philosophy for young pitchers was still very much in effect despite the setbacks from year one. His arms would become familiar with daily routine including stretching and strength exercises, throwing (long toss and bullpens). There would be education—English language classes, financial lessons, situational awareness (how to function as an adult in the country, how to order in restaurants, how to deal with fans, how to handle yourself when approached by women who seek your companionship, and how to protect yourself against other forms of personal and professional manipulation)—and the disciplinary structure put in place by the coaching staff. José would begin again at the lowest level of instruction offered by the Greens, no longer the youngest player on the circuit. A few months away from turning 18, the pitcher was now considered a veteran because of his stateside experience.

With a more familiar structure in terms of personnel and familial proximity, José was a different player in the Dominican Republic; he took his role as "elder statesmen" seriously and worked with some of the fresh faces brought into camp, both on and off the field. The failures of his first year hadn't affected the currency he held with the region's next wave of talent; his amateur star and subsequent bonus still held a fantastic shine, especially when reflected in the eyes of fellow Dominican pitchers. This was a good time for the projectable right-hander, who had sprouted a tad since signing and now stood closer to six-foot-three and, thanks to regular home cooking and a less than strenuous off-season workout regimen, weighed nearly 180 pounds. His stuff still provoked a Pavlovian response, especially from those who wanted to see the fastball tick up: the pitch that once worked in the mid-1980s now sat comfortably at 88–90, touching as high as 93 in off-season bullpens.

The development of the fastball (and fastball command) took away some repetitions from the once highly touted off-speed stuff, but all in good time. Building arm strength through the establishment of a four-seam fastball is a central part of most developmental strategies, particularly with players as young and physically immature as Latin-American signees. For José, this was the first step in the process. Given the observed quality of the secondary arsenal, it was reasonable to expect that the pieces should eventually fit back into the puzzle.

As spring workouts gave way to summer games, the now 18-year-old José finally took to the mound. His first appearance lasted two innings, and despite giving up a few walks and a few hits, he left the game without allowing a runner to cross the plate. He sent three hitters back to the bench on swinging strikeouts. The pitch sequence was predominately fastballs, thrown anywhere from 85 to 91 mph, and showing a good feel for the strike zone; however, Dominican Summer League strike zones are notoriously expansive, and a get-it-near-the-plate approach can often result in a favorable call. José mixed in a few curveballs, but didn't offer much snap in the delivery, those curves arriving at the plate as ineffective slurves. The one 85 mph fastball was described as a failed changeup by a member of the coaching staff, although José denied throwing any such pitch. All in all, the first start was a very positive step, and the organization couldn't have been happier with the results. Nearly two years after signing as a free agent, the lottery ticket had scratched off his first number.

The remainder of the short season went according to plan. José built up his innings and arm strength, and continued to focus on the development of his fastball and fastball command. His secondary offerings made sporadic appearances but always sat comfortably in the back of the developmental queue. The focus on his command began to bear tangible fruit toward the end of the campaign, his ability to hit his spots leading to a 3:1 strikeout-walk ratio. Separation from the familial tit, to put it rather crudely, was still an area of concern for the developmental staff, but they hoped that on-field success would reignite José's competitive fire and propel him beyond the familiar complex. Numerous internal debates swirled around possibly sending him to the stateside complex to finish out the season, but the conservative approach again won out and José remained near his family for the duration of his second season. It wasn't time to push him, but that time was rapidly approaching.

Professional season number three: The Greens were ready to turn up the heat on José. Before the start of the fall instructional league campaign they informed him that not only would he be participating in the state-side developmental league, but also would go into the following spring training with an opportunity to emerge at the full-season level. The plan was to reinforce his confidence at every available turn, even if the full-season assignment wasn't a likely outcome; setting a goal, however bold, was designed to push the player in a positive direction, out of his comfort zone. José was still very much a child, and the basic construct of year three would test the limits of his emotional strength.

With José, set to turn 19 in the first quarter of year three, the Greens were asking the Dominican teenager to assimilate into a strange culture, navigate his surroundings with an ear to a foreign tongue, receive professional instruction, and participate in a professional environment—and find success in all facets of the process. Factoring in the cost of feeding, housing, coaching, medical care, and more, the team had now invested far more in José than the initial $2 million bonus. After a few years of marginal progress, they were ready to see some answers.

The Greens development staff couldn't have been happier with his performance during the nearly six weeks he was at the team facility, as the on-the-field stuff continued to improve and his emotional maturity off of it impressed as well. By the time spring training rolled around, the third-year vet was poised for a breakout, having broken his adolescent tether to familiarity. His focus had never been more finely tuned. He had clearly been motivated by the possibility of a full-season assignment and seemed to treat every pitch, every class, every incremental improvement as a step toward that goal.

During the instructional league, José had spent time working on a slider, a pitch he would only show as an amateur; it was really just an overthrown curve that happened to find the plate during workout sessions. The Greens pondered which breaking ball to isolate and focus on, with José's long-arm action and three-quarter release making the slider a nice fit with his mechanical profile. For the most part, sliders are easier pitches to learn and command than curves; because of the angle of the arm and the release point from a three-quarter slot, a pitcher can stay on top of the slider more easily than he can snap a curve. For year three, José would do without the curve and feature a three-pitch mix; he would rely heavily on the fastball early in counts, using the slider as his feature breaking ball and mixing in some changeups. The changeup is a feel pitch that takes time to properly utilize in relation to the fastball, but one that the Greens development staff felt had even more promise than the slider for José.

Stateside spring training found José paired with a bullpen group consisting of much older players, the majority of whom had pitched at the full-season level. The group of eight, carefully selected for compatibility, would arrive at the back fields together, stretch together, warm up together, throw either bullpens or toss together, run together, and, finally, eat together. As February slid into March and minor league exhibition games fast approached, José was turning heads like he had back in his first stateside instructional league. His fastball was crisp and his command sharp, with the newfound slider showing two-plane movement and tilt. His body had lost some of the bulk added by the home cooking of the past year; José was starting to look the part of a young ace. The Greens development staff was quite satisfied by the transformation.

José was brilliant in his first two games, pitching two innings in each start, allowing only one hit, zero walks, and zero runs while striking out five in total. His fastball was working comfortably in the 90–92 mph range, although it was unclear if the increased working velocity was real or just a short-burst phenomenon. The slider wasn't used in his first appearance, as the fastball was effective without complement. In the second appearance, however, the slider was used as a swing-and-miss offering in standard sequencing; to the delight of the development staff, it looked nasty in the process, missing bats. José's confidence was never higher than after the second outing. Spotted on the back fields: a few members of the Greens development staff trying to hide their smiles—and stifling expressions of relief.

The rest of camp progressed without setback. As affiliate assignments were in the process of being made, the development staff faced a serious dilemma regarding José's destination. His performance in camp warranted an assignment to a full-season league, but despite the physical and emotional transformation that had taken place, his limited professional experience gave some pause. With every member of the scouting and developmental departments present for the conclusion of camp, the Greens took the opportunity both to showcase José and test their convictions by putting him in a high-pressure situation against superior competition, scheduling him to pitch in a Double-A-level game.

The Greens wanted to see how José would handle the opportunity; specifically, they wanted to see how he would respond to failure, as the exposure to the higher level of talent (and the pressure of pitching in front of all eyes in the organization) was designed to produce a less than positive result on the field. Not many teenagers without a stateside résumé, two years younger than most Double-A players, would face such a crucible, but the Greens hoped that a special talent would rise to the challenge. That night, back at the hotel, away from the prying eyes of the development staff, José felt the need to speak to his family.

José was informed he would pitch five innings or 80 pitches, whichever happened to come first, and the game was his to control. He was told to have fun. The first batter stepped into the box, and before the first pitch could be thrown José noticed the Dominican scout (employed by the Greens) that he had first met when he was 14 years old. The scout was the man who witnessed him signing his professional contract, and now he was about to see the most important appearance of his brief baseball career.

What happened next set a high bar for all those set to follow a similar path, as José responded to the possibility of failure in the purest way possible: he didn't fail. Over five innings, the young starter was nearly perfect, locating a lively low-90s fastball with an easy and fluid release, whipping his slider into the zone (and out of the zone when necessary), and even dropping a few heavily pronated changeups in for called strikes. Only requiring 70 pitches to go five, José sent four Double-A-level hitters back to the bench on strikes while allowing only one hit and one free pass.

The emotional release from the pressure-filled performance resulted in tears for José, especially when he heard his father's voice over the phone. He was able to tell his humble and hardworking father—a man who worked with his hands from dawn until dusk as a *campesino* (farm laborer), only to return home to play catch with his son until near exhaustion—that he was set to join a full-season affiliate in May, after building up his innings during an extra month of extended spring training. He had successfully reached his overambitious goal, and after his performance in camp was now considered one of the top pitching prospects in the entire system.

Despite the healthy bonus acquired when he signed his professional deal, his father never left his place of employment, wanting to instill in his son the value of hard work even in the face of excess reward. The family home remained in the same location, although with the new renovations and the new automobile parked out front, it looked slightly incongruous in the surrounding neighborhood. That aside, José's financial windfall wasn't on display, with the majority of the funds set aside for the education of his four younger siblings and the security of his family. The money wasn't worn around José's neck or in his ear, he wasn't riding in style, and he wasn't sending lavish gifts to his girl.

José wasn't your standard teenager, and the Greens were quite aware of his characteristics when they decided to invest in a 16-year-old from the outskirts of Santo Domingo. Teenagers and money can be a dangerous cocktail, and when available funds exceed pedestrian allowances, an appetite for frivolous spending can bleed a player's bank account in short order.

Imagine the typical American 16-year-old: for attending school and keeping his room clean, he receives a $10 weekly allowance that he immediately spends, seduced by the bright lights of the mall or the Internet. Now take a Latin-American player of nearly the same age: he has money in his pocket, a world of products within reach (products unavailable in his region of birth), and the same adolescent impulsiveness as the American kid—except that his urges have not been tempered by the slightest hint of cynicism inculcated in our children by a lifetime of experience with commercial come-ons, spending money on toys that don't work like they do in the commercials, and movies that aren't as good as their trailers. When a player is finally afforded the opportunity to participate in first-world consumerism, staying in control often takes a backseat to pure indulgence exacerbated by naïveté.

The season itself never saw a high as fantastical as the one experienced that night on the spring-training back fields, but José's progress was steady. His cultural acclimation was made easier by a coaching staff familiar with him, as well as a roster heavy on Latin-American talent. The phone calls back home continued, but the voice originating in the States sounded more like a man with every passing exchange in terms not only of an adult's vocal depth but also maturity and sophistication; the pitcher displayed his educational progress by giving his younger siblings English lessons over the phone.

But what happens when cultural assimilation fails? Simply put, not only will the player fail on the field, but also quite often the player will fail off of it. Imagine a young player from a rough background who possesses little in the way of education or social skills. In his native region, the basic laws we adhere to in the United States are, at best, guidelines, so some distinctions between right and wrong have not been learned. When the player is introduced to the United States, a land of "freedom," it is natural for him to maintain the adaptive behavior of his youth, and perhaps even step beyond established lines because of what that aforementioned "freedom" seems to imply—that this is the land of "do as you please." This can end very poorly, with outcomes ranging from basic indiscretions (petty theft, inappropriate language, or sexual advances) to felonious acts like rape or assault. This isn't unique to any one region or group of people, and it should be noted that not every player who originates from a difficult socioeconomic background will fail to comprehend the basic tenets of right and wrong. Rather, it is players—of any background—who reject education and/or the assimilation process, who can suffer negative effects that have consequences beyond their professional development.

On-field results were often mixed, but José's stuff was constantly improving. His fastball was now consistently working in the 91–94 range, touching 96 mph on a few occasions; the slider would get slurvy at times, but he never abandoned it, working hard to throw the pitch without deliberation and with fastball arm speed. When the results weren't there, he didn't wear the failure and never lost his focus. The changeup was starting to emerge as a future plus-pitch, with excellent splitter-like vertical depth and enough deception from the fastball to keep left-handers out in front of the pitch. Working mostly out of the rotation, José made 19 starts, logged over 90 innings, struck out more hitters than innings pitched, walked more than he would have liked but maintained a solid 2:1 strikeout-walk ratio, and wasn't overly hittable. Scouts and team officials alike championed José as one of the top prospects in the organization, and many national publications listed the righty as one of the top prospects in all of the minors. The Greens development staff worked to temper expectation created by such lofty praise by keeping the pitcher grounded in reality, working him as hard as everyone else, reminding him that his next goal was to reach the Double-A level at some point in year four. His command still needed refinement, his slider needed more velocity and tilt, and his feel for sequencing and situation wasn't ready for prime time. In other words, José might have a bright future, and scouts and prognosticators might adore his projection, but the present was anything but perfect and the developmental process still had a long road ahead.

Professional season number four: After a successful full-season debut, José would not participate in stateside instructional; he would spend the offseason with his family, using their proximity to the team facility to his advantage. The Greens development staff informed José before spring training that his most likely destination to start year four would be the team's High-A affiliate, where he would be one step closer to his next big professional goal: reaching the Double-A level.

Unfortunately, year four wasn't the step forward he (or the Greens development staff) had scripted, as the move to High-A baseball brought uneven results, depressed stuff, and mechanical inconsistency. With José struggling to adjust to yet another new environment and a new set of coaches, it wasn't surprising that the psychological elements at play were beginning to expand in size and sizzle. By the summer, the development staff was debating a demotion back to Low-A. Because of the aforementioned mechanical problems, the stuff just wasn't up to snuff, with the fastball wild and fluctuating in velocity from the mid-80s to the low 90s. The slider had become a soft slurve with more sweep than sharp break, showing hitters a beach ball over the plate when José missed his spots. As a pitch designed to play off the fastball, the changeup suffered the most from inconsistency; it was thrown with too much firmness and had lost the depth and deception of last season's version. A decision was made to demote the now 20-year-old from the High-A level and send him back to the team facility, in order to smooth out his mechanics hurdles and give him a break from the beating he was receiving every fifth day.

At the team facility, José worked with the organization's roving pitching coordinator, watched video of his starts, and tried to rediscover his delivery and release point. The national media was quick to write the 20-year-old pitcher off, calling the mechanical setback and subsequent demotion a telltale sign of injury; some went as far as to suggest surgery was on the horizon, confirming for those in the know just how often media speculation is based on innuendo, lazy inferences, and secondhand gossip. In fact, the arm itself was fine, just as it had been fine during year one, with the true culprit lying between José's ears. That said, the situation in year four wasn't as extreme or provocative; mechanical hiccups are ubiquitous in the developmental process, and despite José's previous difficulty in coping, the development staff wasn't overly concerned.

After two weeks on the shelf, really just two weeks of hyper-focused instruction at the team's complex, José returned to the High-A affiliate to pitch out of the bullpen for the remainder of the season. The move to the bullpen was to get José into more games, thereby giving him more opportunities to rediscover his fastball command as well as the overall consistency of his delivery. The Greens development staff wanted to restore muscle memory through repetition. Pitchers get into trouble when they think about the individual characteristics of the physical process, rather than executing based on muscle memory.

With scouts and national publications still propagating the injury meme, José returned to baseball action with the same electric stuff he had showcased last season, only the command component had yet to join the party. As is typical with starting pitchers working in relief, the fastball showed more giddyup than previously seen, working in bursts in the 93–96 mph range with comfort, although the movement on the pitch wasn't as exciting. The slider had more velocity as well, thrown around 82–84 mph with tilt, but as with the fastball, the command just wasn't sharp. Initially, José's changeup was deemphasized with the move to relief pitching, but he started mixing in the offering to left-handed hitters, showing more feel as the season neared its conclusion. Like the rest of his arsenal, the pitch was thrown with more velocity and as a result often arrived at the plate too firm. The results still weren't overly impressive and command that once stood alongside the stuff itself was dragging down the overall effectiveness of the arsenal.

On the season, walks eclipsed strikeout totals, and Jose's hits-allowed total nearly doubled. The final line didn't reflect the talent. A few positive outings at the end of the season gave the Greens some hope for the future, but on the whole, year four was a step back. The polished three-pitch pitcher lost his polish, turning into a hard-throwing hit-or-miss reliever. José was pressing, thinking when the game requires execution without reflection. Still, the Greens development staff knew a major league starting pitcher could still be had, and the results of year four weren't going to dissuade them; they just hoped the grip-it-and-rip-it mentality encouraged from the bullpen in order to quiet the mind hadn't created another problem, one that would be just as difficult to reform.

Professional season number five: José's mind had lost its connection to his body, and his mechanics and release point followed suit. It was a testament to his makeup that he didn't seek sanctuary within himself, maintaining a willingness to accept criticism and instruction, taking his demotion to the bullpen as a step in the developmental process. For that reason alone, the Greens saw the disaster that was José's year four as a positive, a series of on-the-field failures that would, they hoped, be followed by redemption. The developmental plan would not be altered.

It's not uncommon for players to take criticism personally, using any pejorative connotation as material to build a barrier between themselves and the developmental staff. The more personal the perception the higher the barrier becomes, starting with on-the-field clashes that sometimes steamroll into the clubhouse, affecting others in their path. It's the job of the development staff to find the right approach for each player, and to continue to refine that approach in order to reach that player. Every player's lock will require a specifically designed key, but it's a two-way street: the developmental staff can't unlock a door that isn't willing to open. Those unwilling to accept and participate in the process will fail to maximize their potential.

After a brief respite from baseball back in the Dominican Republic, José returned to the team's stateside facility to continue his search for the fluid delivery that had originally brought the buscones to his doorstep. A brief growth spurt had left the no longer quite so young Dominican standing just over six-foot-four, with a frame that now supported a healthy 195 pounds. You couldn't ask for a better starter's physique, although now the question arose as to whether the prospect was better suited for relief or rotation. When asked, members of the development staff were adamant that José possessed a starter's skillset, ranging from his three-pitch mix, easy arm action, smooth delivery, and a body capable of eventually carrying 200-plus innings a season. The proponents of a bullpen assignment had fallen in love with the small-burst arsenal, including plus (borderline plus-plus) fastball velocity and a hard, biting slider to compensate for shaky command and a limited track record of success in the rotation. A legitimate case for either eventuality could have been made.

Months of extra work had helped refine not only José's delivery but his body as well, adding the strength necessary for the increased workload of year five. In countless bullpen sessions, the Greens development staff introduced a hybrid drop-and-drive delivery; they encouraged more lower body (stride) in order to put less stress on the arm, but didn't encourage an exaggerated drop in the launch phase, opting to utilize José's height and downhill plane. In other words, the delivery was more rock-and-drive than drop-and-drive, with a rocking trigger and a longer stride. The goal was to establish an easy rhythm and maintain a good line to the plate, while also better utilizing the strengthened lower body in the delivery. The arm angle would remain in its standard three-quarter slot, as its action was natural and unencumbered.

In addition, the development staff added a fastball variation to the mix, slowly adding a cut fastball to José's repertoire, but limiting the number of cutters thrown at any given time. The coaching staff believed that too many cutters, despite the potential effectiveness of the pitch, would weaken the arm strength established by throwing the four-seam fastball. José had always been a heavy four-seam pitcher, fooling around with a two-seam grip sporadically throughout his career, but always going back to his bread-and-butter four-seamer, a pitch that had some natural run to it, and thanks to his height and release point, arrived at the plate on a steep plane. The cutter wasn't added to replace the changeup against lefties, but rather to add another velocity pitch to the mix in order to induce weak contact and to help enhance the overall effectiveness of the much slower changeup, a pitch that wasn't utilized as often in year four. Not wanting to overwhelm José with a complete arsenal overhaul, the plan to bring the curveball back was put on the back burner, focusing instead on the development of the cutter and the refinement of the slider and changeup. The arsenal would still work off of the four-seamer, with the changeup and slider utilized as "out-pitches" and the cutter used as a contact pitch designed to miss the good part of the barrel.

Starting year five back in the High-A rotation, José didn't show any hangover affects from the previous campaign, bringing his much smoother and more effective delivery into game action. His arsenal was much more powerful than before, his fastball sitting in the 92–94 range and holding that velocity beyond the 70-pitch mark. His slider was becoming his best pitch, thrown in the 84–86 range with a sharp two-plane break with excellent overall depth. It would flash as a plus-plus offering, absolutely dominating right-handed hitters who struggled to distinguish the slider from the fastball. The changeup was the velocity variance pitch, and thanks to the power arsenal surrounding it, played nicely at 78–81 mph, with some natural weight and some fading action. The team graded the pitch in the 50/55 range, with projections of its becoming another plus pitch. The cutter wasn't deployed very often, and when it was the results were mixed; the movement of the pitch itself was very good, but the delivery was a little more deliberate and it didn't play off the fastball as effectively as it should have. More often than not, it looked more like a poor slider than a proper cut fastball. It was a work in progress. José's overall command of his arsenal had greatly improved, although he was still quite loose within the zone, avoiding exploitation because of the makeup of the arsenal itself; his stuff was nasty enough to live in the zone yet find a way to avoid hard contact. The 21-year-old was once again one of the top arms in the system, and the national prospect prognosticators rejoiced at his return to glory.

After ten starts in High-A, it became apparent that a new challenge was in order, so José was promoted to the Double-A level and another professional goal was achieved, although much later than the Dominican hurler had first envisioned. He kept reminding himself not to think. The transition to the new level went smoothly, and several members of the Greens development staff were on hand for his first start; a start that saw him go six innings, allowing five hits and one run, while striking out seven. The big Dominican, now affectionately dubbed "Astro" by some of his teammates, handled the pressure of the promotion without much visible effect, taking the ball every fifth day and going to work. His cultural assimilation was almost complete. His English was nearly fluent, his awareness of the culture around him was superior to that of some of his North American teammates, and his place within that culture was firmly established. José was a man, both in body and in mind; the scared 17-year-old who couldn't navigate the professional landscape was gone forever. For the rest of the minor league season, José's results were finally consistent with his ability. His feel for sequence and situation enhanced the raw stuff beyond its grade, and as his command continued to improve, the competition was overwhelmed by the complete package. The prospect-mongers were back on board, never failing to miss an opportunity to take credit for maintaining their faith in him. José was once again considered a top-tier prospect, the real deal.

A few days before August became September, the phone rang at the home of José's family in the Dominican Republic. It was one of the more personable members of the Greens staff, a former player who now oversaw player development and had been an instrumental figure in José's progress, dating back to José's first professional workouts. He was calling to inform the family that their son had been promoted to major league level was being placed on the 40-man roster. With a slight tremble in his voice, he thanked José's parents for their commitment to their son and for all the sacrifices they had made in order to push him beyond the surroundings he was born into. The director's heartfelt statements were met with sobs, as both José's mother and father wept uncontrollably, overwhelmed with pride and excitement for their eldest son. Although a more detailed call regarding logistics would need to be made later that day, this call was the director's first priority. Without them, this day would not have been possible, and it was only fair that the father who had worked until his hands bled, day after day, year after year, should be the one to call his son and tell him, "Son, you did it."

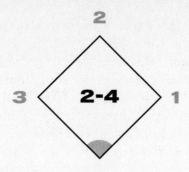

How Can We Evaluate
General Managers?

REBECCA GLASS

Baseball is a sport that values experience. No college or Japanese or Cuban league experience compares to major league experience; the ranks of baseball managers are filled with former players, and proven players command higher salaries than prospects, no matter the potential of the latter. Given the game's long-standing embrace of graybeards over green youth, Boston's 2002 hiring of Theo Epstein, then 28 years old, to serve as general manager stands out as a dramatic break with history. It still does, even now, after the subsequent hiring of other young general managers (including current Rangers GM Jon Daniels, 28 at the time he was engaged) has been received with less controversy.

What might have occurred to the Red Sox and Rangers on the way to hiring Epstein and Daniels is that experience only matters if one has a tangible method of evaluating how experience affects performance. Unlike with players, who can be gauged by everything from the 20 to 80 scouting scale to advanced statistics, there is no accepted method by which we can measure how and why a GM is successful. It might be tempting to assume that the number of World Series won is an indicator of how good or bad a general manager is; indeed, winning the World Series is (or is supposed to be) the goal of every major league franchise. However, that is a very high bar; in many cases, winning a World Series is not a realistic goal or expectation depending on the team's stage of the competitive life cycle, the financial commitment of the owners, and other details—though both would likely wish it otherwise, the general manager of the Pittsburgh Pirates must be considered to be performing a different job than the general manager of the New York Yankees; a general manager's immediate goals will differ based on the needs of the team in question.

How can we, then, find a way to evaluate general managers objectively within their own context? One of the central tenets of sabermetrics is that you only evaluate players on factors that they can control: a player creates his own hits and walks, or, for a pitcher, his own strikeouts and walks. A hitter can't control the actions of another team's defenders; a pitcher can't control whether or not his shortstop can catch a ball in the hole. Similarly, there are certain things that are under a general manager's control, and many more that are not. If one wants to discuss how to statistically evaluate a GM's success or failure, one must first be able to evaluate the parts of a game that the GM—and no one but the GM—can influence. A GM is responsible for not just a major league team's roster; he is also responsible for a team's farm system, the amateur draft, and any other method in which players may be acquired or released. Here's the problem: a GM will rarely, if ever, make these decisions alone. A good GM will, one expects, hire the best people to work for him, but even the smartest sage can occasionally offer faulty advice.

We can, at best, attempt to gauge where a general manager will have the most influence on his team. Trades, good or poor, are usually attributed to a GM; the same with free agent signings. We know for sure that a GM has no control over whether or not a player gets injured under his watch (although, perhaps, a good GM will hire competent people to review a player's medicals before approving a signing or trade, and then to treat them after), or whether an owner will or will not be generous with his budget. What we do not have, however, is a single statistic that can evaluate how a GM will influence his team, for good or ill.

There are some statistics that can help, even if they cannot provide us with a definitive evaluation. One such statistic created by Doug Pappas at Baseball Prospectus is marginal payroll dollars per marginal win (or M$/MW), which attempts to measure a front office's efficiency by comparing its payroll and record to the performance it could expect to attain by fielding a roster of replacement-level players, all of whom are paid the major league minimum salary.

The benefit of this particular measure is that teams that produce the best players for the least amount of money will rank high; the drawback is that teams with players such as Albert Pujols and Alex Rodriguez on the roster may be unfairly penalized. Players of a Pujols and in-his-prime Rodriguez caliber are rarities, which means that even though they might provide tremendous value to their team, they will likely never be worth as much to their team their salary suggests. Another problem with M$/MW is that as players gain experience, so, too, do they gain in salary. Shawn Hoffman at Baseball Prospectus addressed some of these concerns, noting that a team's 90th win is inherently more valuable than, say, a team's 60th win, and that the issue shouldn't be whether a team such as the Yankees has a payroll of $200 million or $100 million, but rather, if it *is* the higher figure, how well the $200 million is spent.

Still, concerns remain. A player might make the major league minimum one season and in the next earn significantly more after winning an arbitration case, while he still provides the same value. Penalizing a general manager for sticking with a productive player just because that player has become expensive is putting too broad an emphasis on the GM's delivering savings versus his building a quality roster.

Too much of the former can be counterproductive, at least in terms of wooing and winning a fan base. In the years since their 2003 championship, the Florida Marlins have been best known for playing in an empty football stadium (a new stadium will open in spring 2012) and having a front office that, at least until quite recently, was notably tight-fisted. In December 2007, the Marlins traded Miguel Cabrera and Dontrelle Willis to the Tigers for then-prospects Cameron Maybin, Andrew Miller, Mike Rabelo, Eulogio De La Cruz, Dallas Trahern, and Burke Badenhop. While Maybin and Miller were considered strong prospects, Cabrera was a four-time All-Star who'd hit 30 home runs in more than one season and after his rookie season had played in at least 157 games each year, and Willis was a former Rookie of the Year and Cy Young Award candidate. Neither Maybin nor Miller have reached the ceiling once projected for them, and indeed, neither of the two are still with the Marlins. On the other hand, though Willis collapsed as a pitcher, Cabrera's Tigers came within a game of going to the 2011 World Series—in large part due to Cabrera's offense. The issue of the Marlins' front office trading away players just before they were due a substantial payday got so bad (and so obvious) that MLB and the MLBPA issued a joint statement in January 2010 saying that they were concerned the Marlins were not in compliance with Article

XXIV (B)(5)(a) of the Collective Bargaining Agreement, regarding the reinvestment of revenue sharing funds in the team (Josh Johnson was signed to a $39 million four-year extension that same January week).

In one sense, the Marlins, with their super-low payroll, were successful; by at least one measure they were the most profitable team in baseball. However, they were a failure on the field, where their best record from 2004 on was .537, and at the gate, where they drew a total of just 11,911,899 between 2004 and 2011. They were also an aesthetic failure, as exemplified by center field, where the Fish could not be bothered to hire a quality center fielder. Since trading Juan Pierre in December, 2005, the club has employed one patchwork solution after another, kicking the position from Reggie Abercrombie to Alfredo Amezaga, Cody Ross, Maybin, and Chris Coghlan, with occasional side trips to Emilio Bonifacio, DeWayne Wise, and more.

By bailing out on the arbitration process, the Marlins cut themselves out from both continuity and, in some cases, the best part of a player's career. The league's best players, especially internationally signed ones who have not entered the draft, don't always reach their peak within the first four years of their major league career—for example, by OPS+, Carlos Peña's best seasons have been 2007 and 2009—even though Peña has been playing in the majors since 2001. While GMs are certainly not immune to handing out less than well thought out contracts (exhibit A: see Ruben Amaro and Ryan Howard), to remain competitive, spending cannot be anathema to teams in the appropriate circumstances.

Another possible approach to evaluating general managers is MORP (Market Value Over Replacement Player), developed by Baseball Prospectus's Nate Silver. MORP translates a player's WARP into a dollar value in order to find out how a win by a player is valued monetarily in the current market. Unfortunately, doing so may result in more uncertainty than clarity. The most common method involves looking at the actual production of players and comparing them to their salaries earned as free agents. The trouble is that general managers must offer a contract in advance of the player's actual production, and such cumulative measures count contracts that look awful in hindsight as part of the average value. If the free agent market was fully rational, this would be fine, but free agents do not accept the most reasonable contract, but the contract from the GM who makes the biggest mistake in overestimating a player's value. (Economists refer to this phenomenon as the "winner's curse.") As such, a GM that hands out contracts at the going rate for MORP may not be doing his team any favors. More importantly, MORP treats the value of each win as linear, which is to say that if a player who supplies 1.0 WARP to his team was worth (to use a simplified example) $1 on the open market, a player who is worth 5.0 WARP would be worth $5 and a player that contributed 10.0 WARP would be worth $10. Indeed, this seems to accurately reflect the way teams pay for talent. However, the market's valuation is not necessarily correct or ideal. There is reason to believe that a player who contributes 5.0 WARP has far greater utility to his team than is conveyed by the 4.0-WARP advantage he has over a player who can only generate 1.0 WARP because he is granting his team greater value for his roster spot and playing time. Similarly, that 5.0 WARP player is more valuable than two 2.5-WARP players, because he has contained their production in one spot—despite what MORP says, no general manager in the game would trade Matt Kemp (roughly 9.0 WARP in 2011) for nine Darwin Barneys (approximately 1.0 WARP in 2011). MORP captures how teams behave economically, but not how they *should* behave; in studying general managers, we are looking for those who can transcend the conventional wisdom, not hew to it.

There is also no single statistic currently in existence that can adequately measure the value of a trade; while one can attempt to use WARP to measure which team "won" a trade, this too has its faults. For example, in December 2009, the Yankees traded right-handed pitcher Ian Kennedy, left-hander Phil Coke, and outfielder Austin Jackson for Tigers outfielder Curtis Granderson as part of a three-team deal. Two years later, the Yankees had surrendered 13.8 WARP for 8.9 WARP, but this is deceiving: when 13.8 WARP is split among three players, it becomes that much less impressive. More important, at the time the trade was made, Granderson was a player with major league experience—indeed, a former All-Star—at a premium position the Yankees needed to fill. On the other hand, Jackson was still a prospect (albeit a good one), Kennedy a pitcher in a rotation who had yet to experience A.J. Burnett's implosion, and Coke, a LOOGY, hardly central to the Yankees' needs. Kennedy, Coke, and Jackson all filled important needs for *their* new teams; in a sense, every team involved in this particular trade benefited. All three teams involved—the Yankees, the Diamondbacks, and the Tigers—made the postseason in 2011. While Kennedy, Coke, and Jackson may have combined for more WARP than Granderson, it was Granderson who filled the team's needs at that particular time.

Likewise, there is no single way to evaluate the success or failure of a free agent acquisition. We say a signing is good if the player is worth the contract he has signed for, but as discussed above, not only is this something that is perhaps ultimately subjective, a player's value changes from year to year, and so a player worth a four-year, $56 million contract one year may not be worth it the next (here's looking at you, Adam Dunn). In many, if not most cases, a free agent signing can only truly be evaluated after that contract ends, by which time the general manager who originally signed the player may have long since moved on.

The draft, the third major method of player acquisition, might be the hardest of all by which to judge a general manager's performance. Players enter the draft after either high school or college, and often are years away from actually appearing in a major league game. In the intervening time, players can and do sustain career-threatening injuries, find out that they can't compete with the major or even the minor league talent pool, or perhaps decide altogether that they are not interested in pursuing a baseball career. While players taken in the first round of the draft are statistically more likely to reach their ceiling, there is no guarantee that they will pan out, nor is it set in stone that the 10th-rounder will never step on a major league field. General managers are supposed to work with their team's scouting and player development personnel for the draft, and while the GM may ultimately make the final decision on top picks, he is in most cases reliant on his scouting staff and, to a large degree, on the team's draft position, the actions of other drafting teams, and the limitations of his budget (not to mention those set by the new collective bargaining agreement).

Even if we can't yet put an exact number on a general manager's performance, we can at least begin the process by asking the questions that need to be answered in order to understand the parameters under which a GM must function. After all, the expectations of a GM in New York, Philadelphia, or Boston will be different than the expectations of Andrew Friedman in Tampa Bay or Terry Ryan in Minnesota. We need to know how much freedom a general manager has been given to operate, and how he has used that freedom. Inspired by Bill James's "manager in a box" rubric, we came up with a set of questions to ask in order to gauge some of the peculiarities of general managers and their situations. We will begin with Epstein, newly named GM of the Chicago Cubs, and see how our answers to these questions color our evaluation of the job he did with the Boston Red Sox. We begin with some basic matters of background and record.

◆

Theo Epstein

Who Is the General Manager, and What Is His Background?

Theo Epstein was only 28 years old when he became general manager of the Red Sox—at the time the youngest to have ever been selected for a major-league job. Epstein comes from a fascinating family background. His grandfather and great-uncle wrote the screenplay for *Casablanca*, his father is a successful novelist, and his older sister a writer for such noted series as *Homicide: Life on the Streets* and *In Treatment*. He grew up not far from Fenway Park and played on the Brookline High School baseball team. After graduating from Yale with a degree in American Studies (and with an internship with the Baltimore Orioles under his belt) he worked for the San Diego Padres while taking a law degree. During this time, his work habits impressed Padres president and CEO Larry Lucchino, and within five years he had risen to the position of director of baseball operations, a job he held from 1997 to 2001. In 1998, the Padres represented the National League in the World Series. When Lucchino took on an identical role with the Red Sox in 2002, he brought Epstein across the country to serve as an assistant general manager.

Epstein initially worked under interim GM Mike Port. During the 2002–2003 offseason, he was in the strange position of helping to search for Port's replacement, the man who would become his new

---

Theo Epstein in a Box

Teams: Boston Red Sox (2003–2011)

Overall record: 839-619 (.575).
During Epstein's tenure, the Red Sox never finished below .500.

Postseason teams: 2003, 2004, 2005, 2007, 2008, 2009

Advanced to League Championship Series: 2003, 2004, 2007, 2008

Advanced to World Series:
2004 (won), 2007 (won). The 2004 championship was Boston's first since 1918, breaking a legendary streak of failure and frustration.

Team budget rankings:

2003: 6th
2004: 2nd
2005: 2nd
2006: 2nd
2007: 2nd
2008: 4th
2009: 4th
2010: 2nd
2011: 3rd

boss. The team initially invested its hopes in luring away Oakland GM Billy Beane, hopes that initially seemed to bear fruit. When Beane balked at the last minute, the Sox turned to Epstein.

Was This General Manager Able to Work Independently of Ownership, or Does Ownership Interfere in Baseball Operations?

During the 2011–2012 offseason, the Baltimore Orioles' GM job was turned down more than once, and while many reasons might be given, the meddling of Peter Angelos in his team's affairs is widely held to be one of the top reasons the Orioles went from 98–64 in 1997 to a team that could lose a game 30–3 in 2007 and still has yet to post a winning season in this century. George Steinbrenner, too, was known as an interfering owner, and disagreements between Steinbrenner's sycophantic court and the so-called baseball people were such that it almost cost the Yankees their current GM, Brian Cashman. A GM is in some ways a glorified middle manager. He takes both the kudos and the brickbats for his team's moves, but at times he is not the sole author of those transactions.

This was, at least initially, the case with Epstein. From 2003 to 2005, Epstein was never truly independent—indeed, a disagreement with Lucchino caused Epstein to resign in October 2005—an event that involved donning a gorilla suit at one point to avoid the press. Epstein did return to the Red Sox, in January 2006, but only after owner John Henry granted him greater independence.

While Epstein had his advisers, including his eventual successor, Ben Cherington, and future Padres and Cubs GM Jed Hoyer, the decisions were ultimately his.

Did He Generally Work for Teams That Spent Money, or Was He Controlled by a Tight Budget?

In a sport without a salary cap, money is the single most valuable resource a general manager can have at his disposal. In recent years, the Red Sox have ranked among the top teams in payroll—after ranking sixth in budget among major league franchises in 2003, the Red Sox have yet to fall out of the top five—so unlike, say, Andrew Friedman with the Rays or Billy Beane with the Athletics, Epstein should not be evaluated on his ability to do more with less; Epstein did not need to make a dollar go further or cut corners in other areas of management to afford his star player. Only four teams have ever exceeded the payroll threshold that triggers Major League Baseball's punitive "luxury tax," and only two have done so more than once, the New York Yankees and Epstein's Red Sox, who were taxed from 2004 to 2007 and again from 2010 to 2011.

Was He a Big Player in the Free Agent Market?
Did He Spend Wisely?

That said, just because a GM has significant resources at his disposal does not mean he should get carried away with using them. In this case, the most egregious example might be the John Lackey contract. A year after the rival Yankees signed both C.C. Sabathia and A.J. Burnett, the Red Sox went all in on a pitcher who at the time had a career 3.81 ERA and 4.47 FIP, signing Lackey to a five-year $82.5 million contract (the same deal Burnett received), making him one of the highest-paid pitchers in baseball. In his two years thus far in Boston, Lackey has gone 26–23, with a 5.26 ERA and FIP of 4.80. At the end of the 2011 season, it was discovered that Lackey would need Tommy John surgery (which he had in November 2011) and was cited in a clubhouse conditioning controversy involving consuming fried chicken and beer during games. Most, if not all, of 2012 is shot for the pitcher. Whether the Red Sox signed Lackey as a move in the arms race with the Yankees or because they truly believed he could become an ace alongside Josh Becket and John Lester might be up for debate, but what isn't is that thus far it has been a less than stellar signing for the Red Sox.

Epstein has on occasion used his financial resources well; under his tenure Adrian Beltre, Dustin Pedroia, and Jon Lester have all been successful free agent signings or contract extensions, but Julio Lugo, Daisuke Matsuzaka, Jason Varitek, and Lackey may be moves he wishes he could have back (although resigning Varitek was an avowedly emotional decision). Edgar Renteria, Keith Foulke, Lugo, Matsuzaka, J.D. Drew, and Lackey combined for a WARP of just 17.5 while costing $301 million, not insignificant investments even for the Red Sox.

Epstein's front office has had success with smaller signings; Marco Scutaro signed a two-year, $12.5 million deal and has accumulated 5.6 WARP over the past two seasons; in 2010 his 3.0 WARP landed him in the top 10 among all major league shortstops—by comparison, Jose Reyes was 10th (2.8) and Derek Jeter 27th (0.7).

Matsuzaka is worthy of further examination: signed to a six-year $52 million contract in the 2006–2007 offseason, Matsuzaka was reasonably successful in his first two seasons with Boston (4.7 WARP

TABLE 2-4.1 Free Agent Gazetteer: Best Signings

Date	Player	$ (millions) /Years	WARP
1/03	DH David Ortiz	1.25/1	36.3 (2003–2011)
1/10/03	3B Bill Mueller	6.7/3	9.3
11/30/06	RP Hideki Okajima	4.25 /2 plus option	4.2 (initial three years only)
1/4/10	3B Adrian Beltre	10.0 /1	7.5

TABLE 2-4.2 Free Agent Gazetteer: Worst Signings

Date	Player	$ (millions)/Years	WARP
12/19/04	SS Edgar Renteria	40.0 /4	1.1 (traded after 1 year)
1/7/04	RP Keith Foulke	20.5 /3	2.3
12/18/04	SP Matt Clement	25.0/3	1.7
12/5/06	SS Julio Lugo	36.0/4	0.1
12/14/06	SP Daisuke Matsuzaka	52.0/6	9.1
2/14/07	OF J.D. Drew	70.0 /5	10.9
12/28/08	SP Brad Penny	5.0/1	1.1
12/14/09	SP John Lackey	82.5 /5	3.0
12/14/09	OF Mike Cameron	15.5 /2	0.1

combined), but has been a below average pitcher every season since. He missed significant time with arm injuries in 2009 and 2011; in the latter of those two seasons he ended up with almost as many walks (23) as strikeouts (26) on his way to Tommy John surgery. Matsuzaka is a cautionary tale of the care a team needs to take when acquiring a player whose experience is not college or minor league baseball, but instead another league entirely.

Who Were the (Field) Managers Who Held the Job under the General Manager's Tenure? Were They Strategic Innovators or Quieter Types?

Grady Little (2003) and Terry Francona (2004–2011) were the only Red Sox managers under Epstein's tenure, and Little had been managing the team before Epstein joined the organization. Little's firing after failing to lift an exhausted Pedro Martinez from Game 7 of the 2003 American League Division Series has entered baseball parlance as one of the worst managerial blunders in postseason history. Francona, Epstein's only actual managerial hire, had considerably more success, winning two World Series in his first four seasons with the team. Francona, better known as a player's manager than as a tacti-cian, had spent four seasons as the skipper of the Philadelphia Phillies, a tenure that resulted in four losing records and a seemingly overly deferential attitude towards ace pitcher Curt Schilling. How-ever, he had just spent a season as a bench coach with Beane's A's and had observed that organization's sabermetric model of managing, which emphasized on-base percentage and denigrated small-ball tac-tics. Francona's willingness to yield the spotlight and let his players play made him an ideal candidate for Epstein's new-model Sox orga-nization.

What Types of Baseball Players Does the General Manager Prefer to Acquire—Good Hitters or Good Defenders, Flamethrowers or Finesse Artists?

Just as fans and managers will have their favorite types of players, so, too, will general managers have a type of player they prefer more than another. The trick here, then, might be not to laud the general man-ager who consistently signs flamethrowers or bashers, but the one who is most able to evaluate his team's needs and sign the appropriate players. Once again, we happen upon the theme: the resources that a GM has to work with are not nearly as important as *how* the general manager uses them.

Many of the players acquired by Epstein were considered the best or near the best available talent at the time. Curt Schilling had had three 300-strikeout seasons and a series of dominating postseason appear-ances; Adrian Gonzalez was probably the best hitter available in the 2010–2011 offseason. The acquisition of Josh Beckett was *not* a deal authored by Epstein—it came during his temporary resignation during the 2005–2006 offseason—but it speaks to the quality of the players the team pursued during his tenure. Beckett became the staff ace after he was acquired, and veteran third baseman Mike Lowell, also part of the deal, gave the Sox four years of solid work as well. (One can debate if the price paid, principally for Hanley Ramirez and pitcher Anibal Sanchez, was worth it given the team's difficulties in finding a short-stop prior to signing Scutaro.) Eric Gagne was the most sought after relief pitching candidate at the deadline in the 2007 season.

As with all Red Sox GMs, Epstein seemed to keep the Green Mon-ster in mind when making moves; in a park that plays small like Fen-way, pitchers, such as Schilling and Beckett, who can keep batters from making contact—strikeout pitchers—would be more beneficial than pitch-to-contact types. Thus, Epstein's moves can be understood not just as attempting to nab the best talent possible, but also as attempting to have his lineup and rotation cater to a park well known for its quirks. Not every move has succeeded—no general manager is *that* good at his craft—but most of the moves Epstein made seemed to make sense at the time.

How Much Emphasis Did He Put on Gloves? Given a Choice between a Slugger and a Glove Man, Which Would He Pick?

Epstein tended to go for all-around players. The Red Sox rarely played a pure glove man during his tenure, but also rarely sacrificed defense for offense, coming closest in 2008 when he traded for Jason Bay to replace Manny Ramirez rather than keep speedster Jacoby Ellsbury in left field, and in 2011, when the acquisition of Adrian Gonzalez meant pushing Kevin Youkilis to third base. When Epstein felt he had more to gain from playing a glove over a bat or vice versa he would do that; Todd Walker and Mark Bellhorn, both bat-first infielders, were among his early second basemen, and he signed Edgar Renteria, a shortstop better known for his bat than his glove. Conversely, he acquired Doug Mientkiewicz, a slick-fielding first baseman, for the 2004 stretch run. As part of that deal, Nomar Garciaparra's superior bat went to the Cubs while Orlando Cabrera's glove and superior durability came to Boston. On the whole, though, Epstein courted players who could do both.

In Building a Pitching Staff, Did He Favor Fireballers or Pitch-to-Contact Types?

From 2003 to 2011, the Red Sox ranked sixth in the majors and first in the AL in team strikeout rate of 7.2; the AL average in that time was 6.6. Over this period, the Red Sox had six 200-K seasons: Pedro Martinez (who was with the team prior to Epstein) did it twice, as did Jon Lester; Curt Schilling and Matsuzaka did it once each. Those are six of the 37 200-strikeout seasons in the American League between 2003 and 2011. This makes some sense because, in a park that plays small like Fenway, keeping the ball from being in play (especially as it could end up in the triangle in right field, curling around the Pesky Pole or bouncing off the Green Monster) becomes that much more of an imperative.

How Successful Was He at Building Bullpens?

In his first season as general manager of the Red Sox, Epstein attempted to put the bullpen-by-committee theory to work and promptly ended up with Byung-Hyung Kim in the closer's role on the way to signing Keith Foulke as a free agent the following January. Relievers are a volatile lot, and all teams see a good deal of turnover in the bullpen. During Epstein's tenure, the Sox maintained two pitchers, Jonathan Papelbon and Mike Timlin, long enough for them to throw over 300 games, with another, Manny Delcarmen, coming close with 289. With the exception of an exceptionally stable Twins team, which had four pitchers clear the 300-game threshold during this time, this was about par for the course in the American League. Otherwise, Epstein bullpens struggled with consistency and effectiveness. His two strongest pens came in 2009 and 2011; both finished second in the league in fair run average for relievers. In all other seasons, the Red Sox ranked somewhere between eighth and 12th.

How Much Emphasis Did He Put on Stocking His Benches?

In 2004, the American League Championship Series turned around for the Red Sox because an outfielder with just two home runs in about 100 at-bats stole a base at the right moment. In the 2004 and 2007 World Series–winning seasons for the Red Sox, the bench was mostly filled with a combination of journeymen veterans, like Eric Hinske and Dave McCarty, and homegrown prospects, like Kevin Youkilis and Jacoby Ellsbury, who were not yet necessarily ready for a full-time role but came up when injuries presented them with opportunities. A rash of injuries in 2010 and 2011 meant that the bench appeared thinner than it actually was—as players such as Youkilis, Ellsbury, Dustin Pedroia, and Victor Martinez all missed significant time. Players who would have otherwise been the second-string backups were thrust into starting roles, and fringe major-leaguers such as Eric Patterson and Jonathan Van Every received significant playing time they might have otherwise not been granted.

When it came to filling the bench and insuring some of his other gambles, Epstein's bravura performance came during his first months on the job. The Sox had gone through the 2002 season without a regular first baseman or designated hitter, using a combination of Tony Clark, Brian Daubach, and Jose Offerman at the former position and Manny Ramirez, Carlo Baerga, Cliff Floyd, Daubach, and Offerman at the latter. Epstein began by trading for Oakland's Jeremy Giambi (Jason's younger brother), who had spent the previous two seasons bouncing between left field, right field, first base, and DH while hitting an excellent .272/.402/.475. About a month later, Epstein added another bat when he signed free agent first baseman-DH David Ortiz. The Minnesota Twins had released the man the world would come to know as Big Papi rather than pay him an arbitration-appropriate salary. They had failed to appreciate his power-hitting skills (Ortiz was a career .266/.348/.461 hitter to that point) or potential as an everyday player—something that Epstein pointed out on the very day Ortiz was signed.

Still not satisfied, Epstein made an audacious move by violating one of baseball's oldest informal rules. Kevin Millar was a late-blooming four-corner utilityman who had hit .296/.367/.504 in four seasons of regular play for the Florida Marlins. The penurious Fish had no interest in paying Millar appropriately and so had allowed him to sign a two-year deal with Japan's Chunichi Dragons. To complete the transaction, the Marlins had to place Millar on waivers, normally a formality—teams have historically allowed each other the courtesy of completing these kinds of deals without interference—at which point Epstein claimed Millar. Though Millar initially refused the deal, Epstein was eventually able to negotiate a deal that satisfied all of the parties involved—Millar, the Marlins, and the very aggrieved Dragons.

The Red Sox now had three solid candidates for two spots, but Epstein brought in more insurance in the form of non-roster invitee Dave Nilsson, a career .284/.356/.461 hitter who had left the majors after the 1999 season to represent his native Australia in the Olympics, and minor-league slugger Earl Snyder, who had slugged .494 in a five-year journey through the Mets and Indians systems. In addition, the signing of free-agent third baseman Bill Mueller freed carryover infielder Shea Hillenbrand to take turns at first base as well. The Red Sox had gone from having no depth at first base and DH to a surplus of possible solutions.

When the season began, Grady Little juggled Millar, Ortiz, and Hillenbrand at first, while Giambi and Ortiz got most of the starts at DH. Giambi failed to hit, was remanded to the bench, and, found to be suffering from a torn labrum, disappeared to the disabled list after August 1. He would never again play in the majors. Millar established himself as the every-day first baseman, and Ortiz as the every-day DH. These roles were confirmed when Hillenbrand was traded at the end of May for a needed reliever in Byung-Hyun Kim—another way that Epstein's thoroughness paid off.

Did He Try to Solve His Problems with Proven Players or with Youngsters Who Still Have Something to Prove?

Over Epstein's tenure, the trend has been to acquire the larger names when possible—John Lackey, Adrien Gonzalez, Adrian Beltre, Jason

Bay, Daisuke Matsuzaka, and J.D. Drew—but relying on production from the farm system, which he reportedly called a "player development machine," has not been fruitless, either. Jon Lester, Jonathan Papelbon, and Daniel Bard were all home-grown products, as were Jacoby Ellsbury and Dustin Pedroia. Epstein's front office went after the best possible player for the position in need; whether the player was a youngster or a veteran seems to have been of secondary importance to the player's talent or potential.

Did He Make Many Trades?
What Was a Typical Trade for This GM?

Epstein's Red Sox pulled off a significant number of high-profile trades, and, as tables 2-4.3 and 2-4.4 show, the front office was not afraid to trade the team's best prospects or even their biggest veteran names if it meant acquiring significant help, even in just the short term. The Red Sox were willing to trade Manny Ramirez and Nomar Garciaparra—two of baseball's biggest names and, at more than one point, two of the Red Sox' best players—despite being in the midst of a pennant race at the time of each deal. Shortstop Garciaparra was a two-time batting champion for the Red Sox who could clearly still hit in 2004, but his increasing fragility had meant the decay of his defensive abilities and long absences when the team was forced to live with Pokey Reese's miserable bat for weeks at a time. Epstein gambled that it would be better to have a clearly inferior but more durable shortstop in Orlando Cabrera than the offense Garciaparra would provide when and if he was healthy enough to play. Nomar hit the road on the July 31 trading deadline, a key moment in the eventual championship.

TABLE 2-4.3 Trade Gazetteer: Best Trades

Date	Acquired	For	5-Year WARP In	5-Year WARP Out
2/15/03	Kevin Millar	Cash	6.6	0.0
11/28/03	Curt Schilling	Casey Fossum, Brandon Lyon, Jorge de la Rosa	15.0	6.9
7/31/08	Jason Bay	Manny Ramirez, Craig Hansen, Brandon Moss	7.9	6.9
12/4/10	Adrian Gonzalez	Casey Kelly, Anthony Rizzo, Reymond Fuentes, Eric Patterson	5.9	-1.2 (but many still just prospects)

TABLE 2-4.4 Trade Gazetteer: Worst Trades

Date	Acquired	For	5-Year WARP In	5-Year WARP Out
7/31/04	Orlando Cabrera, Doug Mientkiewicz	Nomar Garciaparra, Matt Murton	1.2	8.1
3/20/06	Wily Mo Pena	Bronson Arroyo	0.8	8.4
7/31/07	Eric Gagne	Kason Gabbard, David Murphy, Engel Beltre	0.7	7.7
11/19/08	Ramon Ramirez	Coco Crisp	1.9	7.2
7/31/09	Victor Martinez	Nick Hagadone, Bryan Price, Justin Masterson	6.9	8.0

Were His Teams Successful in the Draft and International Scouting?

Epstein didn't just depend on free agent signings; Clay Buchholz, Lester, and Pedroia are all among players who came up through the Red Sox farm system, and are, as of November 2011, all important pieces of the team. Caveat: when discussing the importance of the draft, one has to be careful not to get carried away—just because the Angels developed Jeff Mathis and gave him a chance to be a starter doesn't mean he *should* start. A team's front office and GM don't need to produce major leaguers; they need to produce *good* major leaguers who can help the team just as much, if not more, than would a free agent at the same position. Epstein's Red Sox have by and large done this; under his watch, Beckett, Pedroia, Jacoby Ellsbury, Kevin Youkilis, and Jonathan Papelbon all became stars, while Hanley Ramirez, Anibal Sanchez, and Justin Masterson have all become regular players on their current MLB teams.

Was This GM an Old-School Thinker, or Did He Also Incorporate Sabermetric Ideas into His Decisions?

Sabermetric pioneer Bill James was hired by the Red Sox prior to Epstein's ascension, but it was the latter who tried to carry James's theories about bullpen by committee into effect in 2003 (and he who pulled the plug on the experiment as well). More substantively, Epstein hired Terry Francona as his manager. With the Phillies, Francona was restrained with one-run strategies, but largely abandoned them with the Red Sox, the team usually far behind the average American league team in sacrifice bunts. During Epstein's tenure, the Sox ran powerful high-OBP offenses consistent with the sabermetric approach; they led the majors in isolated power during that period, tied for first in OBP (.354), and were second in walks by precisely one. Conversely, they were 24th in stolen base attempts and last in sacrifice bunts.

Were There Any Long-standing Problems This GM Could Not Solve?

Throughout Epstein's tenure, shortstop has been something of a black hole for the Red Sox. Julio Lugo, Jed Lowrie, and Marco Scutaro are some of the names that have tried to take up the shortstop mantle; none has thus far been more than a stopgap. Scutaro, with an OPS+ of 110 in 2011, has been the most successful; however, 2012 will be his age-36 season, so it is unlikely he will be a long term solution. With Epstein gone to the Cubs, this is no longer his problem to solve, but it is one of the small areas in which he left the team no legacy (as opposed to the more important and lasting legacy of two championships). The Red Sox *did* have the potential solution to their shortstop problems in Hanley Ramirez, but during Epstein's absence, Ramirez was traded in a package that landed the Red Sox Josh Beckett and Mike Lowell. Beckett and Lowell would be critical to the Red Sox' 2007 World Series win.

Was There Anything Unusual in the Way This GM Did His Job?

Epstein was not afraid to trade or release anyone on the team who was no longer helping it—for example, the trade of Manny Ramirez in a three-way deal that ultimately landed the Red Sox Jason Bay. Furthermore, Epstein had a bit of a rebellious streak: he walked out on the job for about four months in 2005–2006, and then, after 2011, left the Red Sox to go and take the helm of another legendarily cursed baseball team. Epstein also embraced sabermetrics earlier than many other GMs did, and should receive appropriate credit for his willingness to use new and/or advanced metrics to evaluate players.

What Was His Strongest Quality as GM?

As stated above, Epstein's willingness to trade away or else not resign his team's biggest names—Pedro Martinez, Nomar Garciaparra, and Manny Ramirez among them—points to a general manager unafraid to cut bait when said stars are becoming detriments instead of assets. One would have a much harder time imagining the Yankees refusing to resign Derek Jeter or the Phillies parting with Ryan Howard, but with the exception of his commitment to Varitek, Epstein appears to lack the sentimentality gene. This was perhaps most visible in his allowing Martinez, Orlando Cabrera, and Derek Lowe to depart as free agents after the 2004 championship, a time when many teams are handing out foolish contracts to incumbent players as part of the World Series afterglow. The compensatory draft picks received as a result netted the team, among others, Jacoby Ellsbury and Clay Buchholz. Similarly, Epstein's refusal to over-commit to championship favorite Johnny Damon when he became a free agent following the 2005 season brought a compensation pick from the Yankees that the Red Sox used on Daniel Bard.

If There Was No Professional Baseball, What Would He Be Doing?

Epstein does have a law degree, so saying he would be a lawyer is probably accurate—though it seems more likely that he might work in business law than, say, as a trial lawyer a là *Law and Order*. Of course, having put together a roster in 2004 that labeled itself the "idiots," and having dealt with the larger-than-life personalities involved in Boston baseball, he would probably do just fine as a psychologist.

◆

Based on our answers to these questions, we come up with a portrait of a GM who used his deep financial resources to no small degree, but whose main strength is his ability to use his farm system well (for the most part), keeping the players who will provide value at their positions for the Red Sox, and finding a way to trade those who will not. The numeric answer may not be necessary.

The Red Sox haven't been past the first round of the playoffs since 2008, but the last two seasons (2010 and 2011), in which the Red Sox did not make the playoffs, have involved factors outside of Epstein's control, namely a slew of injuries such that in the heat of the September 2011 race, the club was forced to start Kyle Weiland and an injury-diminished Erik Bedard (not to mention the supremely miserable John Lackey, who was himself nursing a bad ulnar collateral ligament). At the end of the 2011 season, marred by the potentially greatest collapse in baseball history, allegations of beer and fried chicken in the clubhouse painted a portrait of a clubhouse not wholly united, a front that Epstein could not entirely control.

Epstein should not be penalized because the roster he put together got bit by the injury bug equivalent of the 1918 Spanish flu pandemic. On the other hand, should he bear responsibility for the John Lackey signing, which, as of this writing, has been a bust? If it's true that ownership (as represented by either Henry or Lucchino) allowed Epstein greater latitude in the post-2005 period, was not bound by a limited purse, and the decision to sign Lackey was ultimately his, then, yes, Epstein deserves his share of the blame.

At the beginning of this chapter, we asked for the reasons as to why Theo Epstein could be so successful with the Boston Red Sox, and the answer thus appears to be that it is a combination of the various aspects we've looked at—considerable monetary resources, an ownership that keeps its influence in baseball operations limited, an appreciation for a well-stocked farm system, and an ability to build a roster centered around his team's current needs. Epstein's youth and appreciation of sabermetrics may have given him an edge over other general managers when he first started; *Moneyball* had yet to go mainstream. As the years have progressed and OBP is no longer a saber-stat but instead something routinely noted on broadcasts of a baseball game and on the DiamondVision at the ballpark, so general managers can no longer expect to get away with an advanced knowledge of sabermetrics as their specific talent. Indeed, a general manager who does not take sabermetrics seriously would be just as incompetent as one who refused to use the farm system as a way to develop players or another who avoided the free agent market at all costs, not for a lack of money but because of a lack of inclination.

Baseball Prospectus's Ben Lindbergh recently argued that the days of a general manager making such a significant difference like Branch Rickey or (in a smaller way) Theo Epstein may, in fact, already be numbered, and such a conclusion is not far-fetched. Sabermetrics have gone mainstream. With the greater accessibility to its statistics and arguments fostered by the Internet, breakthroughs in theories as to how to assemble a World Series-winning team are no longer solely limited to insiders. Even though Theo Epstein left the Red Sox, the process, as Lindbergh argues, that he helped create is so well-established that the Red Sox might not suffer for his absence, and in fact might not miss a beat at all. In short, we may have reached the age of parity in general managers—an organization with a deep and talented staff that adheres to established procedure can make up for most shortcomings in its titular executive.

Because there is so much that needs to be taken into account when evaluating a general manager, it's unlikely that there will ever be a single, objective, all-encompassing statistic—a WARP or true average for GMs—that will tell us everything we need to know about a general manager. What we *can* have, however, is an understanding of the different factors that comprise the framework in which a GM must work, and then we can evaluate that GM's talent within that framework. General managers don't play the game on the field, but no team can succeed for long with a GM who cannot put his resources, varied or few, to good use.

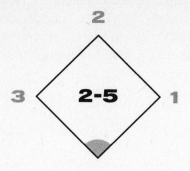

How Do Teams Like the Orioles, Pirates, and Royals Get Broken, and How Can They Be Fixed?

BEN LINDBERGH

For baseball fans, unlike occupants of late-18th-century France, the best and worst of times don't often overlap. Most fans are familiar with the feeling of sitting in a mostly empty stadium cheering on a dead-end team stocked with too-young and too-old players whose only collective motivation is the prospect of playing "spoiler" to a squad that might be going somewhere. Stick it out for a few years of losing baseball, though, and in most cases the former sad sack's fortunes start to turn; the stands once more fill up with "fair weather" fans, ticket prices rise in response to increased demand, and the airwaves and message boards start buzzing with the echo of elevated expectations. Yankees fans of recent vintage haven't known anything but the best of times; the 27-time world champions have made the playoffs in 17 of the last 18 years and haven't finished a season with a winning percentage below .500 since 1992 (though even they have occasionally suffered a few consecutive losing campaigns in the long history of the franchise). However, with the possible exception of the deep-pocketed team from the Bronx, which now seems to exist in a perpetual state of winning 95-plus games, the good times and bad times are easy to tell apart. In baseball, neither the boom years nor the lean years tend to last for very long.

In 2002, former *Baseball Prospectus* author and *Baseball Between the Numbers* editor Jonah Keri coined the term "the success cycle" to describe this continual waxing and waning of major league teams. The success cycle, Keri contended, is "a baseball continuum on which every team resides." A team contends when it assembles a competitive, cost-effective core of players in their primes, but over time, cracks begin to appear in the roster's foundation. Perhaps advancing age renders some of its stars injured, ineffective, or too expensive to retain, exposing the team's lack of ready replacements. Maybe another organization mounts a challenge and leaves it with less margin for error. Whatever the cause, when enough of those cracks accumulate, the team—which in many cases is populated primarily by players with the same names as the ones who carried it a couple of years earlier—can no longer succeed with the same core and falls out of contention. The only questions are how long it can delay that decline, how far it will fall, and how long it will take to rejoin the race.

Fortunately, for most teams, falling out of the first division is only a temporary setback, an ugly record that is not an omen of more bad times to come, but a sign that the next success is just around the corner. Ideally, a losing season sends the signal to rebuild, not to abandon all hope for the future; by the time the old core is on its last legs, the new core is already taking baby steps in the lower levels of the minors, with just a brief unsuccessful span to separate them. From 1900 through 2011, the average duration of a losing streak was 2.99 years, meaning that the average team that dipped below .500 following a season or seasons at or above .500 could expect to reach or surpass .500 again in just three seasons, hardly long enough for the natives to grow restless. Often the drought was even shorter: 55 percent of teams returned to .500, at least fleetingly, in the very next season, and two (the 1965 Twins and 1999 Diamondbacks) bounced back from failure to top 100 wins.

But what happens when the record, so to speak, gets stuck, producing the same losing tune for so long that babies born in the first year of a sub-.500 streak can go from terrible twos to teenage tantrums without seeing a single winner? Table 2-5.1 lists the teams that suffered from the longest sustained, well, sucking. In the century-plus history of the World Series, 14 teams have managed to repeat as world champions by winning back-to-back fall classics. Sixteen have accomplished an almost equally rare feat on the opposite end of the spectrum: losing more games than they won for more than 10 consecutive seasons. What went wrong for these teams and continued to go wrong for so long that they couldn't right themselves for over a decade—or,

TABLE 2-5.1 I've Fallen and I Can't Get Up: Teams with 10-plus Consecutive Losing Seasons (active streaks in bold)

Team	Years	Losing Seasons
Pirates	**1993-2011**	**19**
Phillies	1933-1941	16
Red Sox	1919-1933	15
Athletics	1953-1967	15
Orioles	**1998-2011**	**14**
Phillies	1918-1931	14
Mariners	1977-1990	14
Athletics	1934-1946	13
Browns	1930-1941	12
Tigers	1994-2005	12
Brewers	1993-2004	12
Braves	1903-1913	11
Browns	1946-1956	11
Reds	1945-1955	11
Dodgers	1904-1914	11
Senators	1901-1911	11

in the cases of the Orioles and Pirates, still can't? Can their sordid pasts tell us anything about the tactics that teams should avoid if they hope to regain their winning ways quickly?

As one might expect of a collection of teams connected only by a lack of success and separated, in some cases, by a century, no single cause can explain all of their ills. However, certain examples are instructive, and there are some common themes. I mentioned earlier that age is often a factor in a formerly successful team's exit from the winner's circle. In 1940, about to embark on his third season as the skipper of the Boston Bees—a team that (beginning as the Bees and bottoming out as the Braves) strung together seven consecutive losing seasons starting on his watch—future Hall of Famer Casey Stengel stated, "I've made up my mind that from now on we're going to have a team of young players. We've monkeyed around with older players in the belief that they would help us while we were finding young stars. Where do you get, sticking along with the veterans? The second division." But does youth always equal success? (See Table 2-5.2.)

TABLE 2-5.2 Oldies but Goodies: Average Ages of Good and Bad Teams

100-Plus Wins	100-Plus Losses	.500 or Better	Under .500
28.8	27.5	28.6	28.0

As it turns out, too much inexperience can be even more toxic to a team than too much experience. On the whole, when weighted by playing time, the average age of extremely successful teams since 1915 has tended to be higher than that of extremely unsuccessful teams, and the same has held true for teams over .500 as opposed to teams under .500. All else being equal, a younger team is preferable to an older one, since younger players generally cost less and offer more room for improvement, but a roster composed of players who haven't yet hit their primes is at least as unlikely to succeed as a team of players who've left their primes behind.

What can we uncover if we examine the *origins* of each group of teams' players instead of their ages? Table 2-5.3 reveals the percentage of playing time awarded to homegrown players (defined as those who hadn't first appeared in the majors with any other team) on teams at several different levels of success since 1950. These figures suggest that while successful teams may not give the bulk of their available playing time to fresh-faced rookies, they do tend to produce and retain more of their own talent. In today's game, with the reserve clause long since discarded and arbitration and free agency frameworks in place to compensate players at a level commensurate with their service time, building from within has become the only cost-effective way to assemble a contender. Even when the reserve clause was still in effect, young talent reigned supreme.

TABLE 2-5.3 Home Cooking: Percentage of WARP Generated by Homegrown Players on Good and Bad Teams

100-Plus Wins	<100 Wins	100-Plus Losses	<100 Losses	.500 or Better	Under .500
52.6	47.5	27.0	48.9	53.9	41.0

In his later incarnation as the manager of the wildly successful Yankees, Stengel again put his Bees-era plan to replace veterans into action. The difference this time was that he had similarly talented players in line to replace them. As he remarked in 1955, dismissing other teams' deference to the success cycle, "That's a lot of bunk about them five-year building plans. Look at us, we build and win at the same time." Stengel's boast wasn't mere bravado. Under Stengel and Yankees general manager George Weiss, the Yankees never succumbed to the fatal entropy that so often dooms good teams, because almost year by year they integrated at least one young player per season into the lineup at the expense of a veteran. This is what the lineup looked like in 1950, Stengel's second season at the helm (see Table 2-5.4). Not content to be complacent despite his squad's

TABLE 2-5.4 Before . . . World Champion Yankees Lineup in 1950

Name	Position	Age
Yogi Berra	C	25
Joe Collins	1B	27
Jerry Coleman	2B	25
Billy Johnson	3B	31
Phil Rizzuto	SS	32
Hank Bauer	OF	27
Joe DiMaggio	OF	35
Gene Woodling	OF	27

TABLE 2-5.5 Out with the Old, In with the New: Yankees Turnover Under Casey Stengel

Year	Player In	Position	Age	Player Out	Position	Age
1951	Gil McDougald	INF	24	Billy Johnson	3B	32
1952	Billy Martin	2B	24	Jerry Coleman	2B	27
	Mickey Mantle	OF	20	Joe DiMaggio	OF	36
1954	Andy Carey	3B	22	Replaced player in military		
1955	Bill Skowron	1B	24	Joe Collins	1B	32
	Billy Hunter	SS	27	Phil Rizzuto	SS	37
	Elston Howard	OF	26	Gene Woodling	OF	31
1957	B. Richardson	2B	21	Billy Martin	2B	29
	Tony Kubek	INF/OF	20	Acted as supersub		
1958	Norm Seibern	OF	24	Enos Slaughter	OF	42
1960	Clete Boyer	3B	23	Andy Carey	3B	28
	Roger Maris	OF	28	Hank Bauer	OF	36

success, Stengel continued to tinker, injecting youth into the lineup with each successive season (see Table 2-5.5). By 1960, not a single lineup spot looked the same, though Berra was still around and had begun to split time in the outfield (see Table 2-5.6). In 1950, the Yankees won 98 games and a World Series with an average batter age of 29.2. Ten years later, they had dropped all of one game from the win column and won the World Series again—this time with an average batter age of 28.0. Stengel had succeeded in reshaping his team without breaking the underlying mold of a winner.

Obviously, most teams don't have an older star like Joe DiMaggio to begin with, and even fewer can pull an even brighter, younger star like Mickey Mantle out of the professional firmament just as the older star fades. A glance at some of the names that Stengel's Yankees assimilated hints at the reason for one of our long-suffering losers' struggles. Boyer and Maris, who joined the Yankees' lineup in 1960 and combined for nearly nine wins above replacement (WARP), mostly due to Maris's MVP performance, were traded to the Yankees by the Kansas City Athletics, who at the time were owned by a successful businessman named Arnold Johnson. Johnson had gotten into baseball in 1953 by purchasing both Yan-

TABLE 2-5.6 . . . and After: American League Champion Yankees Lineup in 1960

Name	Position	Age
Elston Howard	C	31
Bill Skowron	1B	29
Bobby Richardson	2B	24
Clete Boyer	3B	23
Tony Kubek	SS	23
Roger Maris	OF	25
Mickey Mantle	OF	28
Hector Lopez	OF	30

kee Stadium and Blues Stadium, the home of the Kansas City Blues, the Yankees' top farm team. Johnson's business relationship with Yankees owners Del Webb and Dan Topping extended to a one-sided baseball relationship in which Johnson would funnel talent to the Yankees for—almost without exception—an uneven return, creating a perception that the Athletics, not the Blues, were the primary source of Yankees talent in Kansas City.

It's impossible to pin the blame for a 15-year losing streak on a single source—Johnson's predecessor, Connie Mack, suffered some long stretches in which he wasn't much better than the guy who gave away Maris. As one of the few owners whose income derived solely from baseball, he was hit hard by the Depression, he avoided building a farm system or delegating any responsibility for running the club long after most owners had invested in the minors and hired general managers, and he was fast approaching senility by the time he relinquished the team after half a century of some form of ownership. Still, it's no coincidence that the first half of the A's *second* decade-long losing streak unfolded under Johnson, who presided over the Yankees' cleverly disguised meat market until March of 1960, when he suffered a somewhat understandable cerebral hemorrhage after watching the soon-to-be 58-win team play in spring training.

Unsatisfactory ownership or undesirable geographical situations and their attendant evils—meager payrolls, inadequate playing conditions, poor decision-making—sunk several of the long-term losers on our list. The Phillies of the first half of the 20th century were so underfinanced that they couldn't afford to maintain their park, let alone pay good players—the team used sheep to trim the grass at its oddly shaped park, the Baker Bowl, until 1925. In 1926, the right-field grandstand collapsed (possibly owing to an act of sabotage by the newly out-of-work animals), forcing the team to move to Shibe Park, home of Mack's then successful A's. Following a 43-win season in 1941, the Phillies had to take out a loan from the league just to stage spring training, and by 1943, owner Gerald Nugent had no choice but to sell the team back to the league. Nugent's predecessor, William Baker, had money but hated to spend it; Nugent himself would have liked to field a competitive team but lacked the means. Without an owner who could and would pump up the team's payroll, the Phillies were doomed to suffer two streaks of over 10 consecutive losing seasons. When they were sold to the vastly more wealthy William B. Cox, and later to DuPont heir Robert R. M. Carpenter, their fortunes predictably improved.

Nugent wasn't alone among owners in finding his finances unequal to the expenditures required to maintain a major league team. Boston Braves owner Emil Fuchs was so strapped for cash by the mid-1930s that he hatched a plan to host dog racing at Braves Field while the Braves played in Fenway Park as a ploy to be bailed out by the other National League owners. Not surprisingly, this was not a particularly successful period for the Braves, who went 38–115 in 1935, but it wasn't their worst. The 1903–1913 struggles that landed them on our list came about because much of the talent on the team (at that time dubbed the "Beaneaters") jumped ship and joined Boston's new American League franchise, the Americans (later to be renamed the Red Sox), which was offering far more lucrative contracts.

Other perennial losers on our list were handicapped by equally onerous ownership situations. The Red Sox lost more often than they won for 15 straight seasons from 1919 to 1933, and the primary culprit was infamous owner Harry Frazee. To keep his franchise afloat, Frazee orchestrated a series of lopsided deals with—who else?—the Yankees, often receiving only cash in return. The most notable player to serve as a human sacrifice to Frazee's checkbook, of course, was Babe Ruth, but he also sold off future Hall of Famers Herb Pennock and Waite Hoyt, among other valuable contributors. The end of the Red Sox' streak coincided with Tom Yawkey's purchase of the team, which wasn't a coincidence.

Elsewhere, the stories were similar. The Browns, whose inventive owner Bill Veeck tried everything from signing popular former Cardinals to putting a midget in uniform, struggled to compete with the Cards in the St. Louis market and ultimately relocated to Baltimore in order to corner a market of their own. The Senators stumbled out of the gate under penny-pinching owners as one of the American Leagues' charter franchises before achieving some success under Clark Griffith, who later became quite adept at pinching pennies (while also clinging tightly to the color line) himself. Clearly, the first key to avoiding a decade of failure is having an owner who wants to win and puts his money where his mouth is, as well as a market that can comfortably support a team.

The era of privately owned teams beholden to miserly owners probably went out with Carl Pohlad, who kept a tight rein on Minnesota Twins payrolls, despite his considerable personal fortune, until his death in 2009. While financial disparities among teams are hardly a thing of the past, an environment in which teams are often underwritten by large conglomerates or a multitude of investors makes men like

Mack, whose sole business was baseball, seem hopelessly quaint. To-day's owners are expected to put capable people with baseball experi-ence in place to administer their investments, rather than pull the strings themselves. Thus, while declining to ante up in the payroll de-partment still results in a competitive disadvantage and recrimination from fans, meddling in baseball operations directly or installing in-competent leadership can be perceived as even more serious sins.

Of course, running a successful team was always about more than signing sizeable checks. Consider the case of the post-war Cubs, who (if it's any consolation to their long-suffering fans) escaped our list on a technicality: they finished with a .500 record in 1952, coming in at 77–77, which limited their losing streak to 10 seasons—but failed to post a single winning season for 16 straight years, from 1947 to 1963. Cubs owner Philip K. Wrigley was a wealthy man—you may have heard of his father's chewing gum—but not always a forward-looking one. As Joe Posnanski wrote, "Wrigley is probably the only owner in baseball history who actually WANTED there to be another major league—no matter how much it might hurt his business—because he thought it would provide more opportunity for fans and players." While other teams followed Branch Rickey's example and cultivated their own farm systems to serve as pipelines for young talent, Wrigley did all he could to preserve the independence of the minor leagues. He may have been correct from a moral perspective, but not from a com-petitive one: by clinging to his old-fashioned operation while his rivals embraced the latest and greatest approach to team-building, Wrigley deprived the Cubs of a vital source of talent. Wins were scarce until he reluctantly went with the flow, allowing the Cubs to rebuild with play-ers like Billy Williams, Ron Santo, and—briefly—Lou Brock.

All of today's teams have farm systems, but that doesn't make them immune to mismanagement. Compare Stengel's pattern of promoting young players to take the places of fading veterans to the Pirates' 2007 trade for Matt Morris, perhaps the move most emblematic of that hap-less organization's mistakes under misguided general managers Cam Bonifay (1993–2001) and Dave Littlefield (2001–2007). In his early to mid-twenties, Morris was a valuable pitcher; the righty was the runner-up for the Rookie of the Year Award in 1997, made two All-Star teams, and finished third in the NL Cy Young Award voting in 2001, when he went 22–8 with a 3.16 ERA for the Cardinals. By the time he caught the Pirates' eyes in 2007, he was 32 and had been a below-average starter for the better part of four seasons. Worse still, he was making over $10 million, with another season at the same rate to come. Undaunted by both his hefty price tag and his declining performance, the Pirates—at the time 42–62 and hopelessly out of the race, 14.5 games behind the first-place Brewers in the NL Central—traded for him and light-hitting outfielder Rajai Davis on July 31, parting with an insignificant prospect and, more important, assuming the entirety of the $13.7 million remaining on Morris's contract. The righty pitched all of 84 1/3 innings for the Pirates with a horrific 7.04 ERA before being released and retiring the following April.

The Pirates are an object lesson in how not to run a franchise. Granted, Pittsburgh is one of Major League Baseball's smaller markets, which tends to suppress the Pirates' payrolls, but as their large outlay in the Morris trade suggests, their failures aren't solely attributable to insufficient spending. In 2011, the Pirates' Opening Day payroll was a shade over $44 million, the third-lowest sum in the majors. They would win just 72 games. Meanwhile, the Tampa Bay Rays, despite being limited by baseball's *second*-lowest payroll (at just over $43 million), won 91 games and beat out the big-spending Red Sox for a playoff spot in the ultra-competitive AL East. How much you spend matters, but how you spend it is also a significant factor. Over the course of their 19 consecutive seasons with records in the red, the Pirates have spent it as poorly as any team.

The acquisition of Morris may have been the organization's most baffling move, but backing the wrong horse had been par for the course in Pittsburgh since the early 1990s, even before the team fell apart on the field. In 1992, Barry Bonds was the most productive player in the majors, amassing 9.3 WARP for the Pirates. In 1993, he was again by far the best player in baseball, totaling 10.5 WARP and winning his second straight MVP award, but this time he did it for the San Francisco Giants, who had signed him to a six-year, $43 million contract prior to the season. That might have been too rich for the Pirates' blood regardless of their other commitments, but they killed any chance of keeping him that they might have possessed by signing center fielder Andy Van Slyke to a three-year, $16 million deal after the 1991 season. Van Slyke was a good player, but rarely a great one, and unlike Bonds, he was already over 30 by the time he hit the market. He had a fine season for the Pirates in 1992, but he contributed under two wins in 1993 and 1994 combined while Bonds wrought havoc on the West Coast. Casting their lot with Van Slyke instead of breaking the bank for Bonds (or, for that matter, locking him up to a long-term extension when he would have been affordable instead of engaging him in a bitter arbitration battle) was the beginning of almost two decades of Pirates mismanagement.

Morris was just one in a long line of Pirates trade targets or signees whose bubbles had already burst or were in the process of bursting by the time they donned the black and orange. The Pirates' last-place finish in 1998 after a deceptively encouraging 79–83 showing in 1997 prompted the team to blame its young players for underperforming and waste more money on soon to be washed up veterans like Kevin Young, Pat Meares, and Derek Bell, whose contracts hamstrung the team for years. Littlefield, too, got in on this act, bringing in the likes of Jeromy Burnitz and Joe Randa, each of whom predictably cratered. As we wrote in *Baseball Prospectus 2007*, "It's one thing to bring in a player at the top of his game and have him take an uncharacteristic powder. It's another to bring him in after he's already demonstrated that he's taking on water and watch him continue to sink."

While the Pirates were busily shooting themselves in the foot with their ill-considered acquisitions of established players, they were also failing to establish any of their own. Although they've made plenty of trades to swap veterans for other teams' prospects, very few of the proceeds (with the notable exceptions of Brian Giles and Jason Bay, whom they later got for Giles) have panned out. Moreover, while their extended occupancy of the NL Central cellar has given them squatter's rights to a perennially high pick in the amateur draft, the Pirates have hardly distinguished themselves with their selections. After striking gold with Jason Kendall in 1992—which later backfired when he fell off a metaphorical cliff immediately after signing a six-year extension with the team, thereby strongly suggesting that some higher power hates the Pirates—the organization drafted conservatively, tending toward low-ceiling players whom they nonetheless often proved unable to develop (see Table 2-5.7).

In the 10 drafts after the one that produced Kendall, six of the Pirates' first-rounders made the majors, but only Kris Benson made any kind of impact, and even he fell well short of the heroics a team hopes for from a first overall pick. Lately, things have looked up: since 2003, the team's first-round selections have produced two productive major leaguers (Paul Maholm and Neil Walker), one legitimate

TABLE 2-5.7 No Stars in Sight: Pirates First-Round Picks Post-Kendall

Year	Name	Pick	Career WARP
1993	Charles Peterson	22	N/A
1994	Mark Farris	11	N/A
1995	Chad Hermansen	10	-2.6
1996	Kris Benson	1	7.5
1997	J.J. Davis	8	-0.9
1998	Clinton Johnston	15	N/A
1999	Bobby Bradley	8	N/A
2000	Sean Burnett	19	1.3
2001	John Van Benschoten	8	-1.2
2002	Bryan Bullington	1	0.2

superstar (Andrew McCutchen), and one potential star who followed a promising debut with a disappointing sophomore season (Pedro Alvarez). Even more encouraging, the Pirates have clearly come to see the wisdom of aiming high, spending a major-league-leading $48 million in current GM Neil Huntington's first four drafts, including a record-breaking $17 million last season. Those investments might take time to pay dividends, but for the first time in years, there is some hope on the horizon.

As one might expect, the teams that have experienced losing-season streaks almost as long as the Pirates' in the last 20 years—the Orioles, the Tigers, and the Brewers—have gone wrong in many of the same ways. Unlike the Pirates and Brewers, the Orioles have at times spent lavishly with little return, and even as their payrolls have diminished in recent seasons, they've remained above the level of the league's true skinflints. After taking Mike Mussina with the 20th pick of the 1990 draft, the O's got almost nothing from their first-rounders until they selected Nick Markakis seventh overall in 2003 (see Table 2-5.8).

The Orioles hit on only one substantial contributor here, Jayson Werth, who was destined never to appear in a Baltimore uniform; he was traded in 2000 for lefty reliever John Bale, who gave the O's all of 27 2/3 innings. Pair that poor draft performance with a meddlesome owner in Peter Angelos, a repeated reluctance to trade veterans (such as Ty Wigginton in 2010) when their value was at its peak, and a spotty record of free agent signings (three years and $19 million for Danys Baez, for example), and it's easy to see why the O's have been easy prey for the beasts of the AL East, as well as why four candidates to fill their GM vacancy last winter reportedly withdrew from consideration before Dan Duquette seized the unexpected opportunity to return to baseball.

The Tigers' system suffered a similar talent outage after producing Kirk Gibson, Jack Morris, Lance Parrish, Alan Trammell, and Lou Whitaker in a burst of fertility

TABLE 2-5.8 O's-for-15: Orioles First-Round Picks Post-Mussina

Year	Name	Pick	Career WARP
1991	Mark Smith	9	0.9
1992	Jeffrey Hammonds	4	11.3
1993	Jay Powell	19	4.3
1995	Alvie Shepherd	21	N/A
1997	Jayson Werth	22	22.3
1997	Darnell McDonald	26	0.4
1998	Rick Elder	26	N/A
1999	Keith Reed	23	-0.2
1999	Larry Bigbie	21	4.4
1999	Richard Stahl	18	N/A
1999	Mike Paradis	13	N/A
2000	Beau Hale	14	N/A
2001	Mike Fontenot	19	4.0
2001	Chris Smith	7	N/A
2002	Adam Loewen	4	1.0

between 1977 and 1979. It took until stars like Justin Verlander and Curtis Granderson arrived in the mid-aughts for the team to reach a new era of respectability. During that drought, the team's forays into the free agent market and its tendency to award regrettable extensions to its own players often came back to haunt it in a big way. The 2003 team that lost 119 games paid nine players $2 million or more, which constituted an enormous waste of resources in light of how little the Tigers received in return for their investments in players like Bobby Higginson, Dean Palmer, Damion Easley (who didn't play for Detroit that season, thus managing to be one of the *better* deals), Steve Sparks, Matt Anderson, Craig Paquette, Danny Patterson, and Shane Halter. As we noted in *Baseball Prospectus 2004*, "For over $48 million—about $4 million less than the World Champion Marlins spent on their whole roster—the Tigers got Dmitri Young and eight players who would have been overpaid at the major league minimum." Things would have been even uglier if Juan Gonzalez had taken then-GM Randy Smith up on the eight-year, $140 million offer he dangled in front of the slugger after trading six players in exchange for his one inconsistent, injury-plagued season in Detroit.

Through their decade-plus in major league limbo, the Brewers seemed to lack any awareness of their position in the success cycle, failing to develop or stick to a coherent long-term plan. They cut payroll, neglected the international market, and showed little of the ingenuity needed to overcome the handicap of playing in one of MLB's smallest markets. Not until the farm system's engine caught, sputtered, and then roared to life thanks to better drafting beginning in 2001, producing J.J. Hardy, Prince Fielder, Rickie Weeks, Yovani Gallardo, and Ryan Braun in quick succession, did the Brewers begin to climb out of the second-division slums, aided by some shrewd trades and signings orchestrated by GM Doug Melvin.

The Royals' absence from the sour 16 is conspicuous in light of their lack of success since the late 1980s, but their false spring of 2003 took what could have been a 17-year streak of losing seasons had a few wins gone the other way and turned it into two marginally less depressing eight-year streaks, extending from 1995 to 2002 and from 2004 to 2011. The small size of the Kansas City market has kept the Royals' payroll in check, periodically forcing them to part with homegrown stars like Johnny Damon and Carlos Beltran. A better-managed team might have made the most of the hand it was dealt by bringing in some blue-chippers in exchange for all that outgoing offense, but the Royals received almost nothing of use in return for either player.

The Royals passed up a similar opportunity to restock their system when they traded Jermaine Dye, a player whom they'd stolen from the Braves after his 1996 rookie season but who by 2001 was about to get expensive, for Neifi Perez, who could charitably be described as a waste of a perfectly good roster spot.

When the Royals have sprung for a big-ticket item, they've generally had cause to regret it. In late 2007, they signed inconsistent outfielder Jose Guillen, whose bad temper was far more dependable than his bat, to a three-year, $37 million contract. They got nothing but headaches in return, as Guillen provided negative value over the life of the deal. The perpetrator of that pact, current GM Dayton Moore, was brought on board largely because of his amateur scouting acumen, which became apparent as soon as he started signing major leaguers. He also handed out a five-year, $55 million bounty to starter Gil Meche, who started out strong but fell apart after the first two seasons and retired after the fourth. (In an unusual display of either integrity or insanity, he gave the Royals a reprieve by retiring rather than collecting the $12 million remaining on his contract.) However, slowly but surely, while frittering away wins at the big-league level—like the Pirates, they were bitten by the Kendall bug, though in their case, he was bad before they signed him—Moore and his staff assembled what was almost universally hailed as the strongest collection of prospects in at least a decade, which might bail them out before long. Many of those highly touted tyros, including Eric Hosmer, Mike Moustakas, Johnny Giavotella, and Danny Duffy, debuted in 2011, though the Royals' infusion of youth (with an average age of 25.8, their unseasoned batters were almost two years younger than those of the next-youngest team) didn't lead to immediate success.

Today's struggling teams can avail themselves of opportunities unavailable to the entrenched losers of earlier eras; as we noted two years ago, baseball has entered "the age of the great correctives to competitive failings," even if the Pirates have only just noticed. No longer is the pool of potential big-league talent restricted to certain races or hemispheres—a team that has been stymied in the States can establish a presence in one of baseball's well-developed foreign markets, or even build an academy on virgin territory, as the Rays recently did in Brazil. Unsuccessful seasons result in high draft picks, which can turn a team around quickly if judiciously employed. With the reserve clause no longer binding players to the teams they came up with, stars often become available to the highest bidder, and role players can easily be acquired to plug holes a farm system hasn't been able to fill. Granted, there is a large component of luck attached to all of these endeavors, especially in drafting amateurs and in signing 16-year-olds who may or may not be 16. Still, today's system encourages creativity, and the potential is there for such sustained losing streaks to be consigned to the past. Just make sure you think twice before making a move for the next Matt Morris.

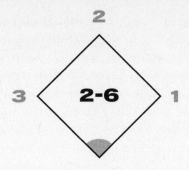

How Can We Evaluate Managers?

STEVEN GOLDMAN

He had never dreamed of managing a major-league club. He was too modest and introspective, he had never been considered as potential big-league material as a manager. He could take a boy after others failed, and bring that boy to the highest possible degree of ability; he could handle problem players with patience or harshness; he was thoroughly rounded in all departments of the game; but no one had ever mentioned his name as a big-league manager. He worked from, and with, a twenty-year supply of knowledge, he knew baseball as well as any man in the game, but had someone asked if he had desired to manage a club, he would have said honestly, "Who'd want me?"

And if the questioner was a close friend, he might add with a knowing, sober wink, "And besides, only a damned fool takes that job."

—Frank O'Rourke, *The Manager* (1953)

This is a bit awkward, doing this here in this time and place, but there is a confession that I need to make: Our specialty, this thing that we do with numbers, it's applicable to many, many things. It's applicable to *most* things, but it's not applicable to everything. The mission of sabermetrics should be to ask of each aspect of baseball that we encounter, "What is it? How does it truly work? Is the conventional wisdom accurate?" It should not be to try to answer each of those questions with one-size-fits-all solutions. We have many tools at our disposal, and sometimes wisdom does not come with a decimal place.

The real value of a manager to the winning effort is one of those soft areas of baseball analysis where only some of the answer is approachable via the statistics. To get closer to the answer, we have to go deeper into the misty, insubstantial realms of history, personality, and psychology; and we have to abandon simplistic notions such as that a plan that doesn't work should automatically be classified as a bad plan and one that works should be viewed as a good plan, regardless of its faulty conceptualization. Managers can control their own intentions, but not execution or outcomes. As Orioles Hall of Fame manager Earl Weaver wrote, "If I send Terry Crowley in with the bases loaded to hit for Mark Belanger and Crowley strikes out, that's not a mistake. Or if I bring in Tippy Martinez to face Graig Nettles and Nettles homers, that's not a mistake. Those are moves that didn't work. There is nothing to apologize about."

Management in action: on the first day of the battle of Gettysburg in 1863, it was recognized by both sides that a large hill that overlooked the town was going to be a key feature of the ensuing conflict. Confederate general Robert E. Lee issued a command to Lieutenant. General Richard Ewell to take the hill "if practicable." Ewell, who had only recently been promoted to his position upon the death of the legendary "Stonewall" Jackson, decided that such an attack was not, in fact, "practicable"; the Union occupied the heights, commanded the superior position over the next two days of battle, and the Army of Northern Virginia suffered a devastating loss from which it never recovered. Whatever subsequent decisions Lee made during the course of the battle, they took place under conditions determined by Ewell's failure to take Cemetery Hill.

There is no record of Lee anticipating Weaver and saying, "Those are moves that didn't work. There is nothing to apologize about." In fact, he tendered his resignation. However, the same decisions and failures of execution take place in every baseball game, except the manager's orders are far less ambiguous than Lee's were. "Hit and run." "Bunt that runner over." "Steal that base." "Retire that batter." Table 2-6.1 sums up the results of such decisions.

Here we have a series of numbers that reflect some of the decisions made by AL skippers in 2011. NPS is the average number of pitches compiled by the manager's starters. With good starters like James Shields, David Price, and eventual Rookie of the Year Jeremy Hellick-

TABLE 2-6.1 American League Managers in 2011

MGR	TM	G	NPS	120+	QS%	IBB	#PH	PH AVG	SBA	SB PCT	SAC ATT	SAC Rate	PN SH
Mike Scioscia	ANA	162	101.0	11	92%	34	75	.154	187	72	78	.81	59
Buck Showalter	BAL	162	91.8	0	91%	42	57	.309	106	76	41	.66	26
Terry Francona	BOS	162	96.8	4	93%	11	83	.176	144	71	33	.73	24
Ozzie Guillen	CHA	160	99.5	2	92%	49	67	.250	133	61	76	.83	61
Manny Acta	CLE	162	95.6	0	89%	34	65	.211	131	68	43	.86	32
Jim Leyland	DET	162	98.2	9	97%	34	79	.300	69	71	72	.79	57
Ned Yost	KCA	162	96.9	0	94%	42	36	.152	211	73	75	.84	58
Ron Gardenhire	MIN	162	95.2	2	90%	37	87	.175	131	70	52	.87	45
Joe Girardi	NYA	162	95.7	2	93%	43	54	.196	193	76	54	.83	38
Bob Melvin	OAK	99	100.4	1	95%	9	30	.276	103	73	38	.79	28
Bob Geren	OAK	63	97.4	0	95%	15	41	.273	57	74	20	.80	15
Eric Wedge	SEA	162	99.7	6	90%	27	49	.209	165	76	49	.92	44
Joe Maddon	TBA	162	102.1	5	91%	38	129	.252	217	71	63	.78	47
Ron Washington	TEX	162	99.2	3	95%	21	59	.204	188	76	63	.73	45
John Farrell	TOR	162	97.7	4	96%	28	58	.185	183	72	54	.81	44

son and a bullpen that had just been rebuilt out of spare parts, Rays manager Joe Maddon was understandably reluctant to turn over the game to a reliever. Intriguingly, the "120+" column suggests he was still more concerned with pitch counts than some of his brethren, letting his starter throw 120 or more pitches in just five games, an above-average number but still less than half of the long starts that Mike Scioscia permitted in Anaheim. Scioscia, too, had three strong starters and question marks in the bullpen.

We can view such choices by Scioscia and Maddon as reflecting their strategic preferences, and if we study their careers, this may well prove to be the case. In the short term, however, such tactics are often a reaction to available personnel. In other words, in his ideal world, Buck Showalter might have preferred to let his starters throw more than 92 pitches a start, but they were so often thrashed that he didn't have any choice but to make a move.

One key skill for a manager is having some insight into when to remove a starting pitcher from the game. Although pundits typically contend that the National League is the more difficult league to manage due to pitchers hitting (as well as the foolish pretension that the double switch is tantamount to brain surgery), the AL pitcher has to remove the starting pitcher when it *feels* right rather than having the pitcher's second or third time at-bat make the decision for him. One way we can track this is by noting how often a manager not only received a quality start from his pitcher, but kept it. The quality start is a statistic conceived of by Bill James as a shorthand way of counting how many times a starting pitcher did an acceptably adequate job. In order to be credited with a quality start, a pitcher must throw at least six innings and allow three or fewer earned runs. Last season, AL teams averaged about 86 quality starts apiece. The Rays led with 99 quality starts, while the Orioles brought up the rear with 60.

Sometimes, a manager guesses wrong. He gives the pitcher an extra batter when he should be waving in a fresh arm from the pen. In those instances, a pitcher who had already qualified for a quality start can quickly lose that status by allowing more runs. The manager has allowed his starter to blow his quality start. As the quality start percentage ("QS%") column above shows, managers got this decision right almost 95 percent of the time in 2011. Jim Leyland led the junior circuit in this category, watching his starters—who after Justin Verlander and midseason acquisition Doug Fister were not all that impressive— blow just three of 93 possible quality starts.

Three years earlier, Leyland had endured 13 blown quality starts, more than any other manager in the league. That year, his pitchers blew 13 percent of their possible quality start opportunities. All of his other Tigers teams have been roughly in harmony with the league average. Was Leyland simply less intuitive in 2008, or was he hamstrung by a Tigers staff that was among the worst in the league? Was White Sox manager Ozzie Guillen crazy to ask non-pitchers to bunt a league-leading 61 times ("PN SH" column) in a league with the designated hitter, or was it the proper response to having Juan Pierre, Gordon Beckham, and other confirmed non-hitters on the roster? Similarly, was Guillen's tolerance of a miserable stolen base percentage by his players the mark of a manager who was not willing to acknowledge his club's shortcomings, or another attempt to create offense where none might have existed regardless?

Even when recent events are concerned, these evaluations are difficult to make from a great height, and all but impossible to make when we are talking about the distant past. Statistics are by their nature a birds'-eye view. They are collections of hundreds or thousands of discrete events that are then converted into averages and other numbers that are easier for us to manage intellectually. In statistics like these, we have captured the results of managerial decision making and perhaps infer some of the thinking behind it, but we are a long distance from being able to assign credit and blame for outcomes. To do that, we need history, biography, a granular view of game conditions, and the wisdom to understand that a failure of execution does not always imply a similar failure of conception.

Hall of Fame manager Casey Stengel described managing as "getting paid for home runs someone else hits." This is, in a nutshell, why it is very difficult to evaluate managers. A manager can make the right move from the correct motives and still have it come out wrong—or vice versa. Even when a manager does push a button for a bunt or call for a particular reliever, just because it worked out doesn't mean he was right, and if it a given move doesn't pay off it doesn't mean he was wrong. "After therefore because" is a logical fallacy. The best the manager (and we) can hope for is to have a good rationale for his decisions, because the intention is more revealing than the outcome. The actual execution is up to the player, but the manager gets the credit or the blame. As Stengel once said when the pinch-hitter he called on failed to deliver, "If [he had] got a hit, you'd say I was the smartest manager in the world. But he didn't get a hit, so now you're saying I'm the dumbest." Hall of Fame manager Tommy Lasorda put the problem of judging intentions against results this way: "The hardest part of managing is that you only get one guess." Prior to Game of the 2011 World Series, Tony La Russa echoed these sentiments: "It comes down to you make a move, and if it works, 'Hey, what a good move.' If it doesn't work, 'What was he thinking?' That's just the name of the game."

We delved into these issues in this book's predecessor, *Baseball Between the Numbers*, and came to roughly the same conclusion. James Click wrote:

> In the end, we may be forced to concede that the evaluation of managers is one area of analysis in which the numbers cannot provide any useful insight. Through a slew of different analytical techniques, no evidence of managerial influence has been found. We have seen that most managers overuse strategies like sacrifice bunts, stolen bases, and intentional walks, but it's unclear if they are the instigators or if the personnel involved escape the analysis of the Win Expectancy framework. Managers show no consistent ability to exceed their team's projected record based on runs scored and runs allowed. There is, as yet, no viable way to evaluate on a macro level how a manager distributes playing time, nor does there appear to be any consistent ability to improve a team's batting performance over the

course of the season. The use of either pinch hitters or relief pitchers does not reveal any skippers who show an ability to deploy their available resources better than others, and the benefit of late-inning defensive replacements is so small that attempting to find superior managers in that regard is nearly impossible. Finally, managers show no consistent ability to improve batter performance.

The singular problem with statistical analysis of managerial ability is that there are too many factors in play that are not measured by any available numbers. Not only do individual managerial decisions take into account a wide variety of factors—the individual players involved, unreported injuries or fatigue, the particular aspects of the park or weather, other available options—but the very choices normally attributed to the manager may not be his decision or influence at all . . . The analysis of managers may instead be best undertaken through a more historical approach, as opposed to an analytic tack. While this methodology is filled with nearly as many pitfalls as the ones already undertaken, it does allow many more factors to be explored in terms of actually contributing wins on the field, the influence of managers remains clouded by auxiliary factors, hidden somewhere beneath the numbers.

Though this was the correct answer, it did not sit well with us at the time. It also bothered historian Chris Jaffe, who was moved to write a fine book in response, *Evaluating Baseball's Managers: A History and Analysis of Performance in the Major Leagues, 1876–2008*. In it, Jaffe explained how Click's conclusions inspired his own study of managers:

In the book *Baseball Between the Numbers*, Click performed a brief study about what impact managers have on their players, ultimately concluding that skippers had no meaningful effect on player performance. However, whatever the study's merits, he spent barely one page introducing, summarizing, and concluding the entire matter before moving on. Dismissing the existence of coaching requires a bit more time than that.

. . . I have an admitted bias: I believe managers matter. To convince me otherwise would take more than an equation, no matter how brilliant its math. I need a clear and coherent argument based on ideas and thoughts instead of double regression studies and metrics. It takes words, not numbers, to convince me otherwise. Paragraphs make better arguments about human interactions than equations. . . . I reject his approach. I do not take issue with his formulas (in fact, I cannot even rebut them) as much as I do his mindset.

Jaffe has badly misunderstood both Click's methodology and his point. He did not say that managers have no meaningful effect on player performance; rather, he said that we cannot *document* its existence statistically. The key to making an argument about any subject, be it managers or murderers, is to present evidence. In the case of managers, a skipper who possessed the skill to consistently alter some attribute of his clubs would manifest that ability consistently and in a way we could document. While many managers do tend to mold their teams in certain characteristic ways over time (something that Jaffe's book excels in demonstrating), there is no evidence that over time managers can have more than a small positive influence on the outcome of a given contest or season in terms of his on-field impact, be it through his tactical choices or in some Svengali-like effect that hypnotizes batters or pitchers to perform in a way that was dramatically different than they might have otherwise. This is distinct from how a manager might positively influence a club through the way he shapes the work environment or psychologically affects certain players, but these are impossible to pin down statistically. Ironically, there is stronger statistical evidence that shows a manager can have a negative impact on his team's fortunes.

Jaffe tries to have it both ways, insisting that managers are about human interactions and not equations, but then offering his own equations in defense of managers (we will get to those shortly). In truth, human interactions trump the manager's preferences every time the two come into conflict, making the manager a much more passive figure than we like to imagine. It doesn't take much in the way of "formulas" to see it. In the days of John McGraw and Connie Mack, the manager was a unitary executive, functioning as both coach and general manager, and so his sway over personnel and playing time was absolute. Those days are gone; modern managers no longer possess that level of control over their rosters, and this is only right; most of them are not the most qualified members of their organizations to evaluate talent or project future performance.

In addition, the game's strategies and tactics were still being felt out, and so there was room for bold experimentation and quick thinking to swing a few decisions. Today, the opportunities for decisive action are far more limited, in part because most managers have become a conservative and cowardly lot, cowed by second-guessing in the media and an unimaginative reliance on received wisdom. The managerial playbook is far more restrained today than it has been anytime in history. As Click wrote, "Modern managers make [their] strategic decisions within strict limits. Virtually all of them follow the same ground rules. The best reliever pitches to start the ninth inning only with the team leading by between one and three runs; the best two hitters bat third and fourth in the lineup; and so on. Because of this lack of variation, there is only a small difference between even the best and worst managers in terms of applied strategic decisions."

A look at some key strategy areas where managers have the most leeway—stolen base attempts, innings pitched by starters, intentional walks, and long saves—in terms of standard deviation from the mean shows an increasing likeness down the generations from 1950 until today, with little separating managers from each other. Only in the area of sacrifice bunts, where the general decline in offensive levels of recent seasons seems to have caused a split between managers who have taken retrograde recourse in giving up outs and those who hew to the sabermetric line that an out is a terrible thing to waste, do we see a divergence that is greater than it was 60 years ago (see Table 2-6.2).

TABLE 2-6.2 Bunting the Blues Away: Most Sacrifices by Position Players, 2009–2011

Manager	POS SH
Ron Washington	208
Jim Leyland	208
Ozzie Guillen	205
Mike Scioscia	200
Joe Maddon	187
Bud Black	176
Tony La Russa	169
Ron Gardenhire	167
Dusty Baker	154
Jerry Manuel	153

Because of both the homogenization of strategy and the inherently limited nature of its impact—you can't bunt runners who never reached base in the first place—team architecture is far more important than team strategy. Many managers don't play their optimal batting order, but none play the least optimal, either. As we have seen, all have a basic competence in yanking a pitcher from the game at the right time. Talent is the great determinant of team fortune, and in modern baseball, talent is determined by ownership and the general manager, not the manager. As the celebrated sportswriter Leonard Koppett put it, "Most managers have little effect on the team's won-lost record, because most clubs reflect their basic talent over the course of a full season."

What Koppett meant by this is that no manager would have been able to solve the problems of the 1962 Mets or completely wreck the 1998 Yankees. If Joe Torre had been manager of the former and Casey Stengel manager of the latter, there would have been minor differences in the way those teams utilized their resources, but the outcome would have been largely the same. Ultimately, those teams were expressions of their aggregate talents as assembled by their general managers, not their field managers. As Stengel himself said upon being let go as manager of the Brooklyn Dodgers in 1936, "We are not occupied with games in October like the better ball clubs and when that happens, ownership commences to looking for a new manager—when maybe they oughta commence looking for players like Joe DiMaggio and them fellows [manager Joe] McCarthy has over there in Yankee Stadium." Given that, Earl Weaver was only being honest when he said, "My best game plan is to sit on the bench and call out specific instructions like, 'C'mon Boog,' 'Get hold of one, Frank' or 'Let's go, Brooks.'"

Despite this, we would not deny that managers can have a significant impact on their players, not when we are aware of decisive interactions such as that between Giants manager Leo Durocher and rookie outfielder Willie Mays in 1951. In his autobiography, Mays recounts the famous story of his getting off to a slow start after being called up to the majors and tearfully asking Durocher to send him back to the minors. Durocher's response: "Ever occur to you tomorrow's another day? And you're going to be playing center field tomorrow, and the day after that, and the day after that. So get used to the idea!" Mays stayed and a Hall of Fame career was launched. The value of such a moment is impossible to quantify, except in the 659 home runs that Mays hit from that point onward. Durocher wasn't finished, though. He went on, adding to the inspirational with a practical bit of advice. As recounted by Mays:

> He turned to leave, then turned back. "And by the way—who do you think you are? [Hall of Fame pitcher Carl] Hubbell?"
>
> I stared at him. "Hubbell?"
>
> "The way you wear the leg of your pants, down nearly to the ankles," he said. "Pull them up."
>
> "Why?"
>
> "Because," he said, "you're making the umpires think your strike zone's down where the knees of your pants are. They're hurting you on the low pitch. Pull up your pants. If you do, you'll get two hits tomorrow."
>
> I pulled up my pants. I got two hits.

Flash forward four years: Mays was established as a star in the majors, having already won the Rookie of the Year (1951) and Most Valuable Player awards (1954). At the end of that season, Durocher took Mays aside.

"I want to tell you something," he began. "You know I love you, so I'm prejudiced. But you're the best ballplayer I ever saw. There are other great ones, sure. But to me you're the best ever. Having you on my team made everything worthwhile. I'm telling you this now, because I won't be back next season."

Mays had tears in his eyes. "But Mr. Leo, it's going to be different with you gone. You won't be here to help me."

Then Durocher told him something he would never forget. "Willie Mays doesn't need help from anyone," he said, then leaned over and kissed him on the cheek.

Mays later described it as his saddest moment in baseball.

This tender man was the same Durocher who, by dissembling in the press in 1943, alienated his players—at one point the situation was so bad that Durocher had to say, "If nine of you fellows want to play, we'll play. If not, we'll forfeit the game"—and cost the Dodgers the services of all-time great shortstop Arky Vaughan. The normally placid player preferred sudden retirement to continued coexistence with a man he did not like and could not respect.

Similarly, the human impact of players on managers is also real, complicating their plans considerably. In *Evaluating Baseball's Managers*, Jaffe uses the unceremonious departure of fireman Joe Page, an MVP candidate in both the 1947 and 1949 seasons, from the Yankees in 1951 as an example of Casey Stengel's cold-blooded attitude toward his players, saying, "When he stumbled Stengel quickly sent him packing." Even Page would have agreed. "Shake my hand?" Page responded when asked about how Stengel handled his release. "He wasn't even there to say good-bye."

Yet, while the depiction of Stengel's overall attitude is correct, the details are wrong and change the interpretation of the story significantly: Page was a problem drinker and this, combined with an elbow injury, ended Page's effectiveness. "Page burned himself out," his teammate Jerry Coleman said. "He was drunk all the time for God's sakes." Another teammate put it best: "You can't relax," Allie Reynolds said. "He did." When the Yankees cut Page, he was a 33-year-old with physical problems and an addiction coming off of a bad year. It was what any team would have done, then or now. Additionally, the move came after the Yankees had put Page on the trading block and received no offers from the 15 other teams in baseball, then also offered him for free on waivers. Given Page's demonstrated value in winning the 1947 and 1949 championships—he was a decisive factor in each, particularly in the latter season—the Yankees surely would have kept him had his value not been destroyed.

Similarly, Jaffe writes of other Yankees moves during this period:

> Examples of the "what have you done for me lately" attitude abounded on Stengel's Yankees. Second baseman Billy Martin had as close a relationship to Stengel as anyone on the team, having played for him as a teen in Oakland. In 1956, his career peaked when he earned a selection to that year's All-Star Game. The following year he got off to a slow start, so the Yankees traded him to the pathologically pathetic Kansas City A's . . . Hank Bauer had an off year in 1959. He was in another uniform in 1960. Phil Rizzuto was the anchor for Stengel's first teams, but once his skills diminished, Stengel would not give him many plate appearances for old time's sake.

Speaking of his signature strategy of platooning, Stengel once said that people alter percentages. They also dictate a manager's plans far more often than the manager dictates theirs. All three of these examples are indicative of a manager being forced to action by his players. In an era in which player contracts were inexpensive and were good for only a year at a time, the Yankees kept Rizzuto on the roster for nearly two full seasons after he hit .195/.291/.251 as a 36-year-old. He no longer played every day during that period, but he was no longer worthy of starting. He was finally cut only when the Yankees, confronted with a glut of reserve infielders, needed to claim what had become a wasted roster spot prior to the World Series. Bauer is a similar story. He had done excellent work for the Yankees for 10 years, but in 1959 he had hit .238/.307/.375 in 114 games, a contributing factor in the team posting its worst record since 1925. The Yankees did trade him at that point, but three facts are important to observe: (1) even today, no team wins by betting on a 37-year-old right fielder who has just posted a .307 OBP; (2) Bauer was finished, hitting only .271/.324/.377 in the 138 games remaining in his career; (3) the Yankees were able to bring back a 25-year-old Roger Maris in the deal.

Both of the foregoing are examples of a player hitting the end of the road. The Martin situation was far more complex. He was indeed "Casey's boy," as it says on his plaque at Yankee Stadium, having essentially apprenticed himself to Stengel with the Oakland Oaks of the Pacific Coast League in the late 1940s. It was a sentiment Stengel echoed: "That little punk," he crowed. "How I love him!" It was he who made sure the Yankees acquired Martin four days after the 1949 World Series, when his own position had been assured. Martin's departure from the Yankees came not after he had been superseded at second base by the young Bobby Richardson; that had already happened, but Stengel had been prepared to use the 29-year-old in a utility role. However, Martin was involved with two controversial brawls, one on field, one off (the infamous "Copacabana incident") early in the 1957 season that undermined his position.

General manager George Weiss had always been less than enamored of Stengel's rough-edged protégé, calling him an "un-Yankee-like Yankee" and worrying that he had been a bad influence on his younger roommate, Mickey Mantle. It was Weiss who ordered Stengel to play the kid ahead of Martin despite the manager's concerns that Richardson wouldn't hit. "I think Richardson can be a very good player [but] suppose this young fellow is my regular," he asked that May, "and the pitchers have him striking out for a month or so when they get on to him?" Though Stengel had previously blocked, in his words, "three or four" other attempts to deal Martin, after the two fights, the manager knew he was licked, remembering, "The owners and Mr. Weiss didn't like that at all, and didn't think the manager was handling his players right." The matter was out of his hands. When Stengel was asked his opinion about fines imposed on the players in the aftermath of the scrap at the Copa, he answered, with some bitterness, "What I thought wouldn't make a difference."

In fact, Stengel hadn't even been consulted. As *The Sporting News* reported after Martin was dealt, "George Weiss insists there is no feud between him and Casey Stengel. The Yankee dictator is right, as usual. It's no feud when you take the gun out of the other fellow's hands. Martin was safe under Stengel's protection until the Copa floor show busted that. Casey said he was going to study the affair and deal out punishment as warranted. Weiss moved in and Martin's number was up."

Even before Weiss had completed a trade, a sorrowful Stengel told Martin, "Well, you're gone. You were the best little player I ever had. You did everything I ever asked." When the deal was finally done, Stengel was too pained to confront his protégé. "Casey just didn't have the heart to face Billy," remembered team executive Lee MacPhail. "I had to tell Billy he was no longer a Yankee. He couldn't stop crying." Yet, his grief was ill concealed. Young pitcher Ralph Terry, who was sent to the A's along with Martin, found Stengel obsessed:

I asked him, "Who else is in the trade?" Then he started talking by saying, "We gave up a helluva lot, we gave up Billy Martin, he's one helluva player, one of the best I'd ever had and you could look it up," and then he just went on and on about Billy for ten or fifteen minutes. I just sat there in his office, not saying a word. I was really upset about my own career and he was talking about Billy. I finally looked up at him, and he had tears in his eyes, he was really in bad shape, and he said, "You're just lucky you're going over there with Billy Martin."

Though the front office insisted that one of the players acquired for Martin, outfielder Harry "Suitcase" Simpson, was to be a regular, Stengel insisted he would be a reserve and initially used him sparingly, snapping, "I'll play who I want," when quizzed by reporters about the dichotomy between the front office's take on the trade and his own actions. "I know what my men can do; I have to find out about all those fellows Weiss sends me," he said. "The team they come from knows all about those fellows; I don't know until I see for myself." He took his time investigating the man who had replaced his favorite.

Similarly, Jaffe misunderstood the great manager John McGraw, writing, "Though McGraw produced a bountiful supply of quality young players, he rarely guided truly great talents. Great players are irreplaceable, and the only man indispensable in McGraw's system was himself." What this leaves out is that McGraw went out of his way to make this a self-fulfilling prophecy both by specializing in difficult personalities such as Turkey Mike Donlin, Bad Bill Dahlen, Bugs Raymond, Shanty Hogan, Buck Herzog, Earl Smith, Hack Wilson, and others, but also by going out of his way to alienate some of those players who would have kept contributing were it not for his abrasive handling.

For example, Jaffe notes, "Aside from [Mel] Ott, McGraw's best position players were Frankie Frisch and Bill Terry. McGraw traded the former away and was not on speaking terms with the latter for several years." Again, the lesson here is in the details, not in the simple fact of the trades themselves. With both Terry and Frisch, McGraw's habit of riding his stars for both the failings of the team as a whole, as well as his own errors and oversights, proved to be punishingly counterproductive. McGraw once said, "With my team I am an absolute czar," but a czar can't make mistakes or his subjects will start doubting key concepts such as infallibility and divine right. Resultantly, McGraw tended to pick scapegoats and whipping boys. This practice became more exaggerated as he became older and had an increasingly difficult time communicating with his charges. Parenthetically, this happens to almost all managers—they begin their careers in their 40s, when their players might be, on average, only 10 to 15 years younger than they are. If they manage long enough, that gap expands, year by year, until man and team are literally generations apart. When Joe Torre managed the 2010 Dodgers, he was 40 years older than his average player. As players change from near contemporaries to young punks, common ground becomes a rare commodity.

As McGraw aged, his ire found unwilling targets in two of his best players. McGraw had brought Frisch directly from college to the major leagues at 20 and slowly worked him into the lineup over two seasons, teaching the tyro the finer points of the game along the way. The two evolved a close relationship, and McGraw eventually made Frisch his team captain. Yet, to the hard-bitten manager, who had come to baseball as a matter of personal and economic survival, this meant that Frisch was responsible not only for his own play, but that of the entire team. After one tirade too many in 1926, Frisch jumped the team and stayed home for three weeks, a daring gesture in an era in which players could be blacklisted for the slightest hint of rebellion. After that, a trade was inevitable. McGraw had some good teams in the six seasons remaining before he burned out in body and spirit, but he would win no more pennants after he had chased Frisch away.

Terry became McGraw's chief antagonist of the post-Frisch years, at least if one discounts porcine catcher Shanty Hogan, who turned McGraw's last seasons into a black comedy in which the obsessive, prematurely old manager drove himself to distraction scrutinizing Hogan's restaurant bills for signs that an entry for broccoli was not actually a coded reference to pie à la mode (it was), then fining Hogan when he failed to lose weight. Not only did this futile ritual drain what little energy McGraw had left for baseball (or living), it left the two locked in a perpetual stalemate. "Any time I was on the bench and the Giants messed up a play on the field," Hogan said, "McGraw would turn to me and snarl, 'Where were you last night?'"

Terry, a slugging first baseman from Georgia, was a more spirited opponent who rejected McGraw's hostility even more directly than Frisch did. "You've been blaming other people for the mistakes you've made for 30 years," Terry told McGraw after the latter ripped him for a fielding miscue that was less important to the outcome of the game than McGraw's tardiness in pulling a faltering pitcher. When McGraw attempted to respond, Terry cut him off with, "Aw, nuts!" to which McGraw replied, "No one can say 'Aw, nuts,' to me."—Well, it was reported as "Aw, nuts," but one imagines something more colorful, even among refined gentlemen ballplayers in 1930. Whatever the actual words, the two did not speak for the next two years.

The tiffs with Frisch and Terry were nothing new for McGraw;

another future Hall of Famer, Edd Roush, couldn't get along with McGraw and had to be given up not once but twice, the second time after the outfielder sat out a whole season rather than report. These partings are not examples of any "system," but rather evidence of how McGraw's own failings could defeat any system he might have had, particularly in his later years, when he had become embittered and ill. Again, the manager's on-field proclivities are interesting, but not nearly as instructive as who is on the field—or, in this case, who he has prevented from being there.

Whitey Herzog's disavowal of slugging first baseman John Mayberry is another example of why you can't have it both ways, can't say that managers' choices are dictated both by their preferences and by human interaction. Jaffe writes of Herzog, "Due to his fixation on movement-based baseball, Herzog was disinterested in the long ball. He allowed sluggers John Mayberry and Ted Simmons to depart Kansas City and St. Louis respectively."

"Allowed" is so bland a term as to be deceptive. In Mayberry's case, Herzog didn't allow, he *insisted* he be traded, and not because he disdained the home run. For a few short years, from 1972 through 1975, Mayberry had been one of the most productive hitters in baseball. In those seasons he hit .277/.399/.493, ranked second in the AL in home runs (behind Reggie Jackson), second in on-base percentage (after Rod Carew), fifth in slugging percentage, and twice led the league in walks (see Table 2-6.3). In his autobiography, Herzog called him, "a wonderful young man. I always loved the way he played. The only thing he ever wanted to know was whether he was in the lineup or not, and then he'd go out and play the best he could. What a great first baseman he was—a big, big man who could dance around out there like Vic Power and use his hands like a surgeon."

By 1977, when Herzog had become disenchanted with Mayberry, things had changed. In 1976, Mayberry dropped from .291/.416/.547 with 34 home runs to .233/.322/.342 with 13 home runs despite playing every day. His 1977 wasn't much better. He compounded this decline with dereliction of duty. The preseason guides for 1978 carry this note: "Missed final game of playoffs with toothache." This was only half true, a cover story for the press. Mayberry showed

TABLE 2-6.3 Best Hitters in Baseball by True Average, 1972–1975

Name	PA	TAv
Willie Stargell	2309	.343
Joe Morgan	2658	.339
Reggie Jackson	2474	.329
Cesar Cedeno	2465	.322
John Mayberry	2421	.322
Dick Allen	1903	.321
Jimmy Wynn	2418	.320
Bob Watson	2408	.317
Reggie Smith	2186	.316
Willie McCovey	1716	.315

up for Game Four of the American League Championship Series against the Yankees somewhat the worse for wear after a late-night party. Herzog put him in the lineup anyway, but Mayberry wasn't capable of playing, twice striking out ("missing the ball by a foot each time," Herzog said) and dropped a popup, his one official error among other misplays. Herzog pulled him. "I finally sat him down in the dugout and asked what the hell was wrong. The man couldn't even talk, and I knew what was wrong . . . I told [the press] that Mayberry had a toothache and was in a lot of pain, so he'd taken painkillers, which had made him dizzy."

Thus was Mayberry sold, which is to say more or less given away, to the Toronto Blue Jays. "I told you before," Herzog said to the owner, "it's him or me, and I mean it. Either he's out of here or I am." Mayberry went. Herzog liked speed-based offenses, but he never deluded himself into thinking he was playing in the deadball era. His teams were not powerful, but not power*less*. They always had at least some sources of power. With the Cardinals, those sources included George Hendrick, Darrell Porter, and Jack Clark. With the Royals, Herzog had Porter, as well as George Brett, Hal McRae, and others, especially Mayberry. When Herzog didn't have those power sources, such as in 1979, when the forced departure of Mayberry meant his first baseman was the light-hitting Pete LaCock, or in 1985, when Clark was hurt, he didn't win. Herzog knew that as well as anybody, but his chief characteristic as a manager had nothing to do with stolen bases or switch-hitters, but rather that if you weren't prepared to give 100 percent, for whatever reason, he wanted you the hell out of town:

> If I knew a guy had a problem, I gave him a chance to come forward and let the ballclub help him. That's a guy you can work with, because he's honest with himself and still willing to be honest with you . . . But other guys, if you give 'em the same chance, stay in the shadows. That's when you call off the hunt. It's less a chemical problem than it is a trust problem; trust is the glue of any organization, top to bottom, and if a guy won't look you or himself in the eye, he's trouble. Get him off the reservation.

Stengel put the same idea more succinctly: "No ballplayer should ever get into the habit where he drinks before a ball game . . . When I had one of those boys, I said, 'Well, this man is limited . . . if he doesn't want to change—why, disappear him.'" All managers have faced these same issues, albeit regarding different substances, going back to the beginning of baseball, and they have always been of over-riding concern.

These are examples of a manager's preferences and tactical hobby-horses being utterly irrelevant to his personnel choices, which have been eviscerated by entropy. Since players create all decision-making possibilities, a manager cannot choose to bat Albert Pujols cleanup if Pujols plays for another team, cannot press his stolen base strategies if he has Victor Martinez on base instead of Brett Gardner, and he cannot go long with his starters if he has Daisuke Matsuzka instead of Roy Halladay. As Stengel said, "Percentage isn't just strategy. It's execution. If a situation calls for a bunt and you have a batter who can't bunt, what's the percentage of bunting?" Miller Huggins might have added, "Managing is not so difficult. You just figure out the things of which your players are capable and then try to get them to do those things." Quite often, though, once these limitations are established, they are impossible to transcend.

What makes evaluation even more difficult is that even if a manager has Pujols, Gardner, and Halladay, he might not get the desired results. Knowing a manager's preferences is an extremely useful thing in terms of characterizing his approach and what impact he might have, or have had, on a team (and Jaffe excels at this); making more than tentative feints toward enumerating a manager's effect on a team's record is to ignore the complexities of managing itself.

Managers being fallible human beings, sometimes they just plain miss. Bobby Bragan, who managed over 900 games in the majors, remembered the 1958 season this way:

> The Indian center fielder I inherited didn't impress me at all. Roger Maris had difficulty catching fly balls close to the wall. He was the most wall-shy outfielder I ever saw. In spring training, one of my coaches was assigned to spend 30 minutes every day hitting balls over Maris's head so he'd get rid of his fear of colliding with the wall. Excessive effort was not Maris's problem. He didn't look very impressive with the bat either, and in his own words, 'I was born surly.' He would not have won any personality contests. I didn't find much playing time for him once the season started.

There is no comment as to how Bragan felt when Maris, only 23 and a major league sophomore at the time recalled above, won two MVP awards and a Gold Glove with the Yankees. Establishing young players is a key part of a manager's job, and Bragan failed with the future single-season home run leader.

Similarly, Cito Gaston won two championships with a mostly veteran Blue Jays club in 1992 and 1993, but clashed with younger players John Olerud and Shawn Green. These disagreements helped end the Jays' run at the top of the AL East and ultimately led to Gaston's dismissal. Hank Greenberg, Indians general manager for most of the 1950s, warned against having this kind of manager:

> Each new player delivered in the spring to a big league manager under [the] farm system method represents upwards of $100,000 of corporate spending for bonus and salary, scouting, study, optioning, supervision, transportation, teaching and even medical bills . . . Extension of front office operation, then, comes as the manager tests the new player under big league conditions. A single look, a few innings of competition in a game already lost will not suffice. He represents a small fortune. Was it wasted or not?
>
> If a big league manager's pride and ego thrive upon his unique ability to detect talent or lack of it when others can't, he'll never get along with the front office . . . Decisions based on whim or caprice are useless. As a corporate employee, the manager must return a fair and concrete appraisal of the rookie's value . . . He must get results from players handed over to him or give a valid reason for their failure.

The Yankees narrowly averted the waste of Greenberg's small fortune when they hired the veteran-loving Joe Torre as their manager in the winter of 1995 with Derek Jeter on the cusp of a 3,000-hit career. Torre initially ordained Jeter as his starter, but reportedly "less than thrilled" about playing a rookie shortstop, began to backtrack, insisting that Jeter would only be given an "opportunity" to win a job. Further, he made a point of saying that Jeter needed "a safety net" and that "Tony Fernandez hopefully will be there in the event we need him to back up for us." Fortunately, Fernandez suffered a season-ending injury, preventing Torre from giving in to his worst instincts. A dynasty was born in that moment, perhaps in spite of its manager. The human element of managing is *everything*.

In contrast, the strategic element is painfully, pitifully small. As stated earlier, Whitey Herzog has long since been retired, and his go-go tactics went with him. Rosters are too swollen with relievers for a Stengel or Earl Weaver to have much impact through platooning—Joe Maddon is the only real practitioner as of 2011. Managerial tactics all come in one flavor: vanilla. Even when they have not, when managers have taken risks, they have not often worked.

Al Lopez, managing the Indians in 1951, tried to hold off a charging Yankees team by going to a three-man starting rotation. This prompted Stengel to observe, "They say you can't do it, but sometimes it doesn't always work." It didn't. The Yankees won. Three years later, the situation had reversed and the Yankees were chasing the Indians. Stengel briefly tried a "power lineup" in which Yogi Berra played third and Mickey Mantle shortstop, but it accomplished nothing. In 1964, Gene Mauch tried to staunch what would become a historic bout of bleeding by his Phillies team by starting Jim Bunning and Chris Short on two days' rest. These outlandish gestures had little more impact than does the daily effect of a bunt here and a bunt there.

The club's basic assembly counts for much more, and the manager's ability to evaluate talent—what Greenberg described applies to veterans as well as rookies—is where he can make the greatest impact. Leo Durocher created the "Miracle of Coogan's Bluff" when he realized he could win the 1951 pennant by playing his ex–center fielder at third base and an outfielder at first. Making bunt signs and calling for the hit and run had little to do with it, as much as Durocher might have preferred to think otherwise. This is painfully apparent when we look at managers from the point of view of one-run strategies and their impact on win expectancy. Using play-by-play information, we can look at each managerial move in the context of its game and see how the team's chances of winning were altered as a result of that decision. The results, which consider sacrifice bunts (as well as sacrifices by non-pitchers), stolen base attempts, and intentional walks, are stunning (see Table 2-6.4). Those managers who best utilized these tactical tools influenced their team by an average of about half a win in the standings. Not coincidentally, those who used those tactics best were also

TABLE 2-6.4 Best Manager Seasons by Strategic Decisions, 1950–2011

Manager	Year	Team	SAC ATT	N-P SAC ATT	IBB	SBA	WX
Charlie Manuel	2007	PHI	94	36	62	157	0.80
Ron Washington	2007	TEX	83	79	38	113	0.71
Earl Weaver	1980	BAL	64	64	33	149	0.58
Dick Williams/Jim Fanning	1981	MON	73	37	21	178	0.58
Chuck Tanner	1972	CHA	99	50	29	152	0.53
Willie Randolph	2007	NYN	107	47	40	246	0.48
Sparky Anderson	1976	CIN	93	24	56	267	0.47
Walter Alston	1962	LAN	143	101	66	241	0.44
Tony La Russa	1983	CHA	62	62	32	215	0.44
Joe Maddon	2009	TBA	41	39	22	255	0.43
Average			**86**	**54**	**40**	**197**	**0.55**

TABLE 2-6.5 Worst Manager Seasons by Strategic Decisions, 1950–2011

Manager	Year	Team	SAC ATT	N-P SAC ATT	IBB	SBA	WX
Bobby Winkles/Jack McKeon	1978	OAK	122	122	59	261	-6.17
Jeff Torborg	1978	CLE	114	114	38	127	-5.81
Frank Robinson	1975	CLE	70	70	78	195	-5.67
Roger Craig	1987	SFN	90	41	86	223	-5.35
Joe Torre	1992	SLN	90	43	46	326	-4.89
Lou Piniella	1993	SEA	93	93	56	159	-4.81
Roger Craig	1986	SFN	120	75	78	241	-4.68
Gene Mauch	1973	MON	134	97	74	144	-4.68
Bruce Bochy	1996	SDN	74	26	47	164	-4.65
Tony La Russa	1980	CHA	78	78	44	122	-4.62
Average			**99**	**76**	**61**	**196**	**-5.13**

those who used them least. Conversely, the most enthusiastic practitioners did the most damage to their club's chances (see Table 2-6.5).

The one exception to the rule here is in the stolen base ("SBA") column. All managers were burned by intentional walks, but in their best seasons managers gave themselves fewer chances to be hurt by this tactic. Bunting was a break-even proposition at best even for the good managers, but the bad ones (or the good ones having bad seasons) tended to bunt at the wrong times and minimize their chances of scoring—Frank Robinson reduced his expected wins by three games with ill-timed bunts in 1978. It was poor use of the running game, though, that really defines the managers in Table 2-6.6. One of the worst things a manager can do is force a team without speed to run.

TABLE 2-6.6 Is This Trip Really Necessary? Worst WX Stolen Base Seasons by Teams

Manager	Year	Team	SBA	SB	CS	Really?	WX SB	WX
Roger Craig	1987	SFN	223	126	97	Will Clark, 5 SB/17CS	-3.54	-5.35
Bobby Winkles/Jack McKeon	1978	OAK	261	144	117	Mike Edwards 27/21	-3.32	-6.17
Frank Robinson	1975	CLE	195	106	89	Duane Kuiper 19/18	-3.11	-5.67
Joe Adcock	1967	CLE	120	53	65	Max Alvis 3/10	-3.09	-4.25
Joe Torre	1992	SLN	326	208	118	Bernard Gilkey 18/12	-3.09	-4.89
Bobby Valentine	1986	TEX	188	103	85	Scott Fletcher 12/11	-2.84	-3.63
Butch Hobson	1992	BOS	92	44	48	Tom Brunansky 2/5	-2.66	-4.52
Bobby Bragan/Joe Gordon	1958	CLE	104	50	49	Minnie Minoso 14/14	-2.64	-3.83
Phil Garner	1993	MIL	231	138	93	Darryl Hamilton 21/13	-2.63	-4.60
Tony La Russa	1980	CHA	122	68	54	Mike Squires 8/9	-2.61	-4.62

These findings, while basic, suggest that a manager having his best season for instinct and mental acuity can help steady a properly constructed team but otherwise should restrict his actions to those soft areas we have discussed, mainly creating a harmonious work environment. Button-pressing can only lead to trouble. We have finally found areas in which managers can have a dramatic influence on their teams, but it is a negative one. This is one reason why teams such as the A's and Red Sox have made an effort not only to find the correct manager for their teams, but also to restrict his strategic palate ahead of time so these one-run strategies could not be abused.

Note that in Table 2-6.6 we have not grappled with broader concepts like optimal lineup construction, knowing when to pull or pinch hit for a starting pitcher, or rational usage of relievers; all of these, if done perfectly, would impact our best-season list in a small way, but if done poorly would add additional losses to our worst-of list. Consider something as basic as making sure that a team's leadoff spot represents one of a team's best on-base percentage threats instead of its worst. Excluding cases of the pitcher batting in the National League, since 1950 104 teams have had the leadoff spot trail every other spot in the lineup in OBP, with more than half getting an OBP below .300 from their leadoff men on the season. Among recent managers, Clint Hurdle achieved this counterproductive feat in four of his six full seasons as manager with the Rockies, while Dusty Baker has done it three times for three different teams. Both managers continue to be employed, suggesting that skills other than a facility with the Xs and Os of baseball carry a greater weight with general managers when choosing a skipper.

Jaffe attempts to evaluate managers statistically not through win expectancy, but by measuring them against a database created by statistician Phil Birnbaum "to measure the ways teams under- or overachieve in a given year, most notably performances by individual hitters and pitchers":

> For both batters and hurlers, Birnbaum created algorithms that determined how they *should have done* in a given season based on what they did in surrounding years . . . Running everyone who played under a manager through these algorithms should provide an idea of how well he did at coaching and leading his men [emphasis added].

The logic bounds like a gazelle on the savannah. Hitters' careers are largely linear (pitchers not so much), and so we can form a reasonable estimate of how they might have done in a given year of their careers or should do in the future. However, such estimates or projections, as the very name implies, are purely hypothetical. If a player over- or underperformed his projection, the problem is with the projection, not with the player or his manager—or more accurately, it is the result of that messy business Douglas Adams called "life, the universe, and everything," which tends not to conform to expected patterns. When we penalize a player for failing to live up to our projection it is misunderstanding what a projection is; when we criticize a third party, the manager, for that player failing to achieve what was an estimate in the first place, we have departed from the recognized boundaries of reality. Paraphrasing Shakespeare, the fault is not in our baseball stars, but in ourselves. If the projections were gospel, they wouldn't have to play the games.

Yet, play the games they do, and players exceed or fall below projections for many reasons: injury, a happy new marriage, a nasty divorce, a taste of one of the magical elixirs in the PED cabinet. None of these elements reflect in any way on the manager. Jaffe, though, is married to this notion, saying that though his analysis may be imperfect, "I do not believe in limiting myself to mathematic rationales. This evidence beautifully corresponds to long-lasting and widely held notions that managers can and do have an impact on player performance. I therefore accept it." This is a textbook definition of confirmation bias; Jaffe excepts the results because they confirm his beliefs, not because they are illustrative of reality.

Jaffe's method assigns managers responsibility for things that have nothing to do with them, including the volatility of teams under certain conditions, be they maniacal or impoverished owners or simply the vagaries of the modern free agent market. Today, teams are rewritten each winter in a way inconceivable only 30 years ago. Yet, the more static days of the reserve clause offer evocative testimony of the wisdom of not giving managers overmuch credit for the records of their teams. The Dodgers changed managers five times in six seasons from 1946 to 1951. Whether the manager was Durocher, Burt Shotton, Durocher again, Shotton once more, or Chuck Dressen, the outcome for the club wasn't much different. Durocher won 96 games in 1946, Shotton won 94 (with two wins by an interim skipper) in 1947, won another 97 in 1949, and Dressen won his own 97 in 1951. The only continuity that mattered was that of the roster and general manager Branch Rickey, who did the most to create it.

Knowing this, how can we evaluate:

- Fred Clarke, manager of the Pittsburgh Pirates from 1900 to 1915, whose great records and four pennants were the direct result of a National League contraction that gave him the pick of the best players of two teams (Louisville and Pittsburgh), including Honus Wagner, perhaps the best player in the game at that time?

- Miller Huggins, who was relentlessly hounded, second-guessed, and overruled, particularly in matters of discipline, by warring owners Jacob Ruppert and Tillinghast L'Hommedieu Huston during his first half-dozen years as manager of the Yankees? "It is a matter of common gossip that Huggins seldom wins a decision, verbal or otherwise, over Ruth," wrote Joe Williams of the *New York World-Telegram* in 1928. "The standing at present is 53 disputes, with Ruth winning them all." This did not change until general manager Ed Barrow banned the owners from the clubhouse and Huston sold out after announcing to the press that "Miller Huggins has managed his last game as a Yankee," only to find out he could not make the firing stick. Huggins confessed to Barrow, "I wouldn't go through the years from 1919 to 1923 again for all the money in the world." Huggins later argued that the Yankees could have won five straight pennants, from 1920 to 1924, "if they hadn't loafed," a reference to his being undermined in matters of discipline.

- Paul Richards, manager of the White Sox from 1951 to 1954, when he worked under general manager Frank Lane, a compulsive trader who made 49 deals just in those four years, thereby stretching the definition of "team" as something resembling an identifiable unit? Richards's last White Sox team had three starting position players and one starting pitcher in common with his first.

- Hank Bauer, manager of the championship 1966 Baltimore Orioles, who had negotiated with the Cubs to bolster his team by trading first baseman Mike Epstein for future Hall of Famer Billy Williams only to be blocked by ownership. Asked almost 40 years later about the deal, Bauer shouted, "That bastard in Baltimore wouldn't do it! That son of a bitch! Later they traded Epstein even up for Pete Richert. I had my lineup all written out: Williams, left field, Blair in center, Frank Robinson in right. Boog Powell at first, Brooks Robinson, Aparicio, Davey Johnson—I might have *still* been there!"

- Earl Weaver, manager of the 1974 iteration of those same Orioles, who found his tactics overruled by his own players when they found that his trademark three-run homers just weren't coming fast enough that August. With the team trailing by eight games and only a month to play, the veterans decided to play inside baseball with their own set of signals. Second baseman Bobby Grich recalled, "Earl did have a strategy for that year . . . to sit back and wait for the three-run home run and it wasn't happening for us. We didn't have Frank Robinson and Boog Powell and that was what Earl was used to in the previous four, five, six years. We recognized it and just thought, 'We've got to get more along a small-ball type of program here.' We did say, 'Guys, put on a hit and run with the guy in front of you or behind you. If you know you can do this, Earl might not realize you have the confidence to do a hit and run, so work a sign with the guy on first base.'" Weaver, said Grich, had momentarily misjudged the team. "It was one month out of his career . . . he kept thinking [the home run power] was going to happen, but it just continued to not happen." Said Don Baylor, "There I was, my third year in the big leagues and about to enter into rebellion against Weaver and take orders from Brooks [Robinson], [Paul] Blair and [Jim] Palmer." Utilizing this system, the Orioles played .800 ball down the stretch, passing three teams to win the AL East.
- Bob Lemon, Yankees manager in 1978–1979 and 1981–1982, whose decision to remove Tommy John from a World Series start, and lord knows how much else, was dictated or heavily influenced by owner George Steinbrenner? As Reggie Jackson said of Steinbrenner after he was inexplicably held out of a postseason game, "That sonofabitch. He's so determined to take me down, now he's even taking October from Mr. October."
- Jim Leyland, who had his 1997 championship Marlins built by a spending spree and then unceremoniously yanked out from under him via a fire sale?
- Managers as diverse and separated by time as Bill Carrigan, Burt Shotton, Wilbert Robinson, Casey Stengel, and Don Mattingly, who at different points in their careers were tasked with commanding ballclubs that were literally and sometimes legally bankrupt?

In some ways, managers are the game's most pathetic creatures, held responsible for all kinds of events that are out of their control, while their most dramatic and direct actions have negligible or a negative impact. As such, managers are simultaneously given too much credit and not enough—so few aspects of the game are under their control, and the few that they can interfere with are often approached incompetently. As Baseball Prospectus's Ben Lindbergh has written, "A GM can go out and spend $30 million or so for six wins on the free agent market and watch it all go down the drain because his manager, whom he's paying a fraction of that, doesn't know what a win expectancy table says." Thus managers get too much credit for outcomes that are dependent on talent assembled by the general manager, and not enough blame for bunting and stealing their way out of runs, not to mention calling on his 12th-best pitcher in a key situation when his best pitcher sleeps in the dugout just because ol' 12th-best is left-handed. Recognizing that a right-hander who can pitch stands a better chance of recording an out against a left-handed hitter than a left-handed pitcher who can't pitch is a simple test of intelligence that almost every manager fails once a game.

In 1948, Billy Meyer took over a Pirates club that had lost over 90 games in 1946 and 1947 and finished at 83–71. For this shocking fourth-place finish, he was voted *The Sporting News* manager of the year award. The next season his team reversed its record, something he would not be able to undo in three more seasons of futile effort. Stengel, who had won the 1949 championship with an aging Yankees team that had been predicted to finish a faint third, inherited the *Sporting News* award. Meeting Meyer that winter, Stengel quipped, "Ain't it funny, Bill, how all of a sudden I got so smart and you got so dumb?" The Ol' Perfesser had been around long enough to understand that there is only so much in life that can be controlled by man or manager, and that it's the ballclub that makes the man. The search for objective knowledge in baseball will go on forever, but this is one truth that we may be forced to accept *without* numbers.

PART 3
Questions of Pitching

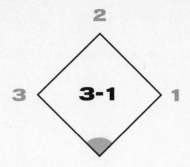

Why Is Building a Bullpen the Hardest Task a General Manager Can Undertake?

BEN LINDBERGH

In his first 12 starts of the 2011 season—a span of 68 1/3 innings—Milwaukee's presumptive ace Zack Greinke recorded a 5.66 ERA, prompting Brewers fans to fear the worst for a player acquired with much fanfare (and at a high price) during the previous offseason. In his next nine starts—a total of 59 2/3 innings—he pitched to a 2.56 ERA, helping to move Milwaukee into a comfortable first-place position in the NL Central. Same pitcher, same environment, vastly different results. It might seem as if Greinke flipped a switch and salvaged his season at the start of July, but his underlying performance tells a different tale.

Over that first small-sample chunk, Greinke struck out nearly 12 batters per nine innings while walking fewer than two. In the second, seemingly more successful small sample, he struck out just under 10 batters per nine innings and walked almost 2 1/2—still stellar figures, but not up to his early-season standards. In other words, Greinke actually pitched better at the start of the year, despite the inflated ERA he had to show for his efforts. The culprit was an elevated .347 batting average on balls in play (BABIP), which fell to .286 during the second stretch. Whether the Brewers' defense stepped up behind him as the season progressed or opposing batters simply found fewer holes,

Greinke's apparent resurgence stemmed from unpredictable factors outside his own control.

What does this have to do with relievers? Consider that in the age of the seven-man bullpen, many relievers amass fewer innings in an entire season than Greinke did during his first 12 hard-luck starts. If a reliever suffered from the same bad bounces that Greinke did in his first 60-plus frames, he wouldn't have another two-thirds of the schedule remaining to restore his numbers to the realm of respectability; his season would simply be over, consigned to the back of his baseball card with an exorbitant ERA intact.

Couple that unavoidable variability with the typical reliever's comparatively modest talent—most relievers washed out of a starting rotation or three before switching to shorter outings—and the problem of building a dependable bullpen becomes clear. Before a manager can go about earning the ire of sports radio callers with his *handling* of the bullpen, a general manager faces the far trickier task of *constructing* one without being bewitched by BABIP, succumbing to small-sample mirages, and overpaying for a flash in the pan.

For years, owners and general managers have been shelling out millions to bolster their bullpens without seeing a substantial return on their investment. Investing in relievers is the sport's equivalent of subprime lending; it's simply not a safe proposition. Table 3-1.1 shows how much teams paid players at each position per win above replacement players (WARP) from 2001 to 2010. Over the last decade, teams paid nearly twice as much per win in the bullpen as they did at any other position, and the longer the contract, the worse the return; according to research by Baseball Prospectus alum Eric Seidman, relievers signed to multi-year deals cost almost twice as much per win as those signed for a single year. Even among the elite (and theoretically most dependable) pitchers at the position, the closers, bargains are few and far between: in overpaying for relievers, teams are often overpaying for saves, one of the less meaningful statistics in baseball's canon.

Over the 2001–2010 time period, teams paid $3.55 million per win from the relievers who earned the most saves for their respective teams—a better return than they got from the unwashed bullpen masses, but still worse than the going rate at every other position. Thanks to

TABLE 3-1.1 $/WARP by Position, 2001–2010

Position	$ Million/WARP
RP	4.33
1B	2.84
RF	2.43
C	2.42
LF	2.18
3B	2.17
SP	2.16
SS	1.91
2B	1.73

the position's prestige, closers often enjoy some of the most egregious overpays; that figure includes single-season outlays above $10 million for Mariano Rivera, Francisco Rodriguez, Brad Lidge, Joe Nathan, Billy Wagner, and John Smoltz, excellent pitchers who nonetheless struggled to top two WARP in their most productive campaigns, since modern usage patterns make closing an occupation that no longer allows for enough innings to justify that kind of cash.

Despite the fetishization of the save statistic, a good deal of evidence suggests that earning saves is something most pitchers could do with a high degree of regularity if given the chance. The small edge in save percentage that employing an elite reliever as closer confers doesn't justify an extra expenditure to obtain a player who has been employed in that role in the past.

In 2003, the Cubs' Joe Borowski saved 32 games with a 2.63 ERA and a 3.24 fair run average (FRA, a statistic on the RA scale that measures the effect of a pitcher's sequencing without unduly crediting him for the performance of his fielders). Four years later, Borowski, by then wearing an Indians uniform, took another crack at closing, this time struggling to the tune of a 5.07 ERA and 4.89 FRA. The result? Forty-two saves. Borowski had a slightly higher save percentage in the earlier, more successful season—88.9 percent, compared to 83.7—but the fact that he converted more than four-fifths of his chances despite his poor pitching supports what historical seasons have to say about the likelihood of pitchers of varying talent levels locking down leads.

Figure 3-1.1 shows the empirically derived expected save percentage for pitchers at RA increments of 0.5. Expected save percentage declines quite slowly as RA increases; a pitcher who allows two runs per nine innings, like the richly rewarded Rivera in his prime, would be expected to convert 90.8 percent of his save opportunities, while a dime-a-dozen arm with a 4.00 RA would lock things down 84.9 percent of the time. That means that team can get by without established closers, but while it should avoid paying a premium for past saves, it also needn't necessarily settle for mediocrity.

From 2009 to 2010, the Brewers paid Trevor Hoffman $13.5 million to serve as their closer as he marched toward 600 saves. The 41-year-old was effective, if a bit brittle, in his first season on the job, but the wheels came off at 42, as Hoffman allowed 13 runs in nine innings to start 2010. Although he settled down some in the second half, he'd already been stripped of his original role in mid-May and demoted to setup duty. To replace him, the Brewers turned to John Axford, a 27-year-old castoff from the Yankees system who had fewer than 10 major

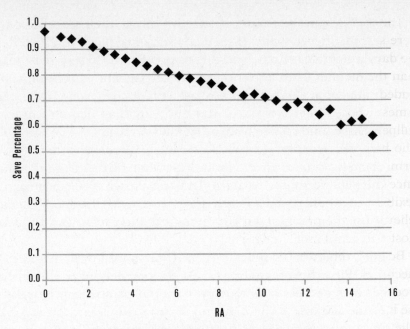

FIGURE 3-1.1 Estimated Save Percentage by RA

league innings under his belt before that spring. Axford had impressed the organization by striking out 19 batters in 13 1/3 innings at Triple-A Nashville before being promoted to take Hoffman's place. He didn't miss a beat after getting back to the bigs, posting a 2.48 ERA with 24 saves in 27 attempts for the major league minimum salary while the high-priced Hoffman looked on. As Hoffman enjoyed retirement, his successor outdid himself in his first full season, pitching 72 2/3 innings with a sub-2.00 ERA and leading the NL with 46 saves. Of course, even once they identify their best relievers, managers tend not to use them optimally, reserving them for save situations that don't properly leverage their talents.

This counterproductive closer-oriented system has become so deeply ingrained that only the most courageous and iconoclastic of managers and general managers, or maybe just those least in need of their jobs, dare challenge it. Any GM or skipper who takes on the sacred cow of closers, call him Moo-riano Rivera, exposes himself to rabid criticism from fans and media members, not to mention players and rival executives. The outcome of the last serious attempt to replace the status quo with a system that has come to be known as a "closer by committee," undertaken by the 2003 Red Sox, makes it unlikely that we'll see another such effort soon.

The Red Sox in the season before they broke their so-called curse were seemingly well positioned to roll back bullpen management to the days when reliever usage was determined by a team's needs rather than the dictates of an arbitrary save rule. The club's front office included influential thinker and senior baseball operations adviser Bill James, whose *New Historical Baseball Abstract* had deplored modern bullpen usage, and was led by progressive young GM Theo Epstein, who had been weaned on James's insights. "Closer by committee," a term coined by the Boston media, was something of a misnomer, since the plan depended on having no true closer at all. Instead, the flexible pen would adapt to each game state, with the most talented reliever (or the one best suited for the situation) called upon at the most crucial moment, whenever it might arise.

Boston's otherwise sound strategy was sabotaged by two failures of execution. First, Epstein entrusted this late-model bullpen to an old-model manager in Grady Little, who was either unwilling or unable to use it as the GM had envisioned. Second, the Sox didn't have the right relievers to put their plan into action: Chad Fox predictably pitched well only until he got hurt, and Bobby Howry, Ramiro Mendoza, and an assortment of other journeyman arms pitched poorly. When the personnel failed, the plan took the blame, and before long, Boston was back to depending on a closer like the rest of the league. As Alan Embree, a lefty who pitched fairly well out of that pen, later remarked, "We lost four of those guys and had to make do with what we had. Then after that, you're being criticized for anything that goes wrong. The manager's getting hammered by people asking 'How could you have the nerve to go and do that?'" Part of the problem with building bullpens, then, is that risk-averse teams shoot themselves in the feet by caving to peer pressure and failing to get the most out of the arms they've assembled.

Another culprit behind the exorbitant going rate for bullpen help is the high rate of turnover among leading relievers. Top players at every position are susceptible to a statistical phenomenon known as regression to the mean, the tendency of extreme observations to become less extreme with repeated trials. Any group of league-leading players in one season is likely to decline in the following season, as the confluence of factors that enabled them to excel—luck, health, an unusually weak crop of opponents—fails to provide the same level of support in the succeeding campaign. However, relievers, dependent as they are on the vagaries of good and bad bounces, stand to suffer even more after enjoying a successful season. The top five relievers in each season

TABLE 3-1.2 Year-to-Year Declines among Top Players by Position

Position	Avg. Year n WARP	AVG. Year n+1 WARP	% Decline
RP	2.37	0.89	62.5
2B	6.14	2.42	60.5
LF	5.79	2.33	59.7
C	5.70	2.50	56.1
RF	5.65	2.67	52.7
CF	5.69	2.70	52.6
SP	3.65	0.58	42.0
1B	6.61	4.43	32.9

from 2007 to 2009 produced only 37.5 percent of the WARP they'd just managed in the following year, the greatest decline among top five players at any position (see Table 3-1.2).

This year-to-year instability of relief arms also manifests itself in a more macroscopic view of players at the position. Table 3-1.3 reveals how many of the top 50 relievers (by WARP) in each season from 1980 to 2010 also placed in the top 50 in each of the preceding three seasons. On average, over 60 percent of the bullpen top 50 turns over in a single season. That percentage has only increased in recent years, as more relievers have crowded major league rosters, pitching even fewer innings apiece. In any given era, only a few elite relievers can be counted on to number among the top players at the position with any regularity. In 2010, only four relievers—Rivera, Jonathan Papelbon, Jonathan Broxton, and Heath Bell—could claim to have been one of baseball's 50 most valuable relievers for at least four consecutive seasons. Lower the bar to three seasons, and only three more players—Matt Thornton, Scott Downs, and Darren Oliver—join the list. If so few players can be regarded as near-guarantees to perform among even the top 50 of their kind, a not inconsiderable portion of relievers in the game, it makes little sense to guarantee so many of them millions.

Between 1977 and 2010, almost 70 pitchers placed among the top 25 relievers in WARP once without ever again cracking the top 50. A list of the top 10 WARP scorers among those one-hit wonders yields a number of names who produced a single season that could have tricked a team into making an unwise commitment (see Table 3-1.4).

Another way of looking at the low reliability of relievers also offers a potential solution to the problem of building a bullpen. Consider how many of the top 50 relievers each season were complete non-entities in the preceding campaign (Table 3-1.5). On average, more than a tenth of the 50 most valuable relievers in baseball in a given season didn't appear in the majors in the previous season; an even higher percentage pitched fewer than 10 innings, like our old pal John Axford. (Consider also that WARP is a cumulative statistic, and that pitchers with little or no prior experience often don't earn a roster spot right out of spring training; it's likely that even more unproven pitchers pace their position on a rate basis.) Some of these found talents are established arms who lost a season to injury; others are recent high-profile draft picks or international signees. In many cases, though, these "free talent" finds are unearthed from within organizations where they had languished in obscurity while bigger names earned multi-year contracts without meeting any more success. While these rags-to-riches relievers underscore the fungibility of most players at their position, they also offer the solution to penetrating the fog that permeates bullpen construction.

If some uncertainty is unavoidable and all but a few players are as likely to fall out of favor as they are to repeat their success, the secret to building a capable bullpen might lie in embracing the constraints of prognostication at the position. When evaluating a re-

TABLE 3-1.3 Turnover among Top 50 Relievers

Year	Year 1	Year 2	Year 3
1980	23	16	15
1981	27	17	15
1982	22	18	13
1983	25	19	15
1984	19	16	16
1985	18	17	13
1986	17	16	9
1987	20	11	11
1988	23	17	14
1989	21	20	13
1990	23	18	12
1991	19	16	17
1992	22	17	17
1993	20	15	12
1994	12	11	13
1995	18	16	13
1996	21	20	11
1997	22	14	14
1998	19	12	8
1999	17	16	9
2000	20	13	10
2001	16	17	13
2002	17	15	13
2003	15	13	9
2004	20	10	11
2005	16	15	5
2006	16	14	10
2007	18	11	6
2008	11	13	7
2009	12	11	10
2010	16	12	14
2011	19	13	7
AVG	**19.7**	**15.5**	**12.8**
Post-2000 AVG	**17.9**	**13.9**	**11.4**

liever over the inherently small samples in which he works, it's best to focus on indicators that stabilize quickly instead of more macroscopic metrics like ERA, which tend to take longer to provide an accurate picture of a pitcher's performance. Table 3-1.6 shows the thresholds, according to research by BP's Derek Carty, at which half of the observed performance according to the given metrics is attributable to a

TABLE 3-1.4 The Top 10 One-and-Done Relievers

Name	Year	WARP
Lance McCullers	1987	2.8
Joel Zumaya	2006	2.5
Steve Foucault	1977	2.0
Aaron Heilman	2005	2.0
Juan Gutierrez	2009	2.0
Rick White	1999	1.9
Tom Johnson	1977	1.9
Jason Christiansen	1998	1.8
Justin Miller	2007	1.8
Blas Minor	1993	1.8

player's true talent. The values in the "Seasons" column are based on the average season length for one of a team's top five relievers in 2011—just under 59 innings and 250 plate appearances. At that rate, it can take several seasons to ascertain anything meaningful about a reliever's performance. Most relievers retire before we can draw any conclusions about their ability to suppress hits on balls in play. However, focusing on strikeout rate is often the best way to identify an effective reliever early on, since an ability to miss bats is both the easiest attribute to discern and the surest route to a pitcher's success.

One of the most successful bullpens of 2010 (a mere .02 WARP "worse" than the best-in-majors White Sox) belonged to the San Diego Padres, who also paid the fourth-lowest amount of money in the majors for the privilege of owning an airtight pen. At a mere $1.2 million per WARP accrued in relief, the Padres were easily the most financially efficient team at building a bullpen, and they didn't sacrifice any success in the process. How did they do it?

As is the case with most teams, the most expensive member of the San Diego bullpen was the closer, Heath Bell, who made $4 million. However, Bell wasn't recruited as a high-priced free agent in an attempt to elicit a repeat performance at the back end of the bullpen; he was added via trade (along with another reliever, Royce Ring) for two players who produced a grand total of 4 2/3 innings and 30 plate appearances after the trade. At the time of the exchange, Bell's sole major league experience was contained within 108 innings distributed over three seasons with the Mets. In those innings, he'd recorded an underwhelming 4.92 ERA, well below average for any pitcher, let alone a reliever with the benefit of working in short bursts.

The Padres were perceptive enough to see what Bell had going for him: in addition to strong minor league stats, he'd struck out 8.8 batters per nine innings while walking only 2.5. The culprit behind the inflated ERA was a fluky .371 BABIP that hadn't even come close to being stabilized. Since putting on a Padres uniform, Bell has posted close approximations of the strikeout and walk rates he managed with the Mets (9.3 and 3.2, respectively), but his BABIP has been only .285. As a result, his ERA has been a mere 2.56, just over half of what it was in Flushing. Bell's success was predictable, by relief standards at least, but the Mets, who would less than two years later go on to guarantee Francisco Rodriguez $37 million over three years for less value than Bell provided the Padres, failed to see it coming.

The Padres rounded out the rest of their bullpen on a budget with a passel of similarly undervalued pitchers. They acquired Bell's sterling setup men, Mike Adams and Luke Gregerson via further highway robbery; Adams came from Cleveland for an over-30 reliever, Brian Sikorski, who would pitch under 20 innings for his new team, while Gregerson was a throw-in sent from St. Louis to complete a prior trade. Lefty specialist Joe Thatcher was another astute trade target, stolen from the Brewers in a trade that sent Scott Linebrink, a formerly elite reliever whose best days were already behind him, to Milwaukee. Control specialist Edward Mujica, who walked just 25 batters over two seasons and 163 1/3 innings for the Friars, came from Cleveland in a conditional deal, and middle man Ryan Webb was plucked from Oakland in mid-2009. Tim Stauffer was a 2003 Padres draftee who was taking a temporary break between assignments in the starting rotation, and Ernesto Frieri was signed as an amateur free agent the same year. None of these names had been well known when Padres GM Kevin Towers rolled the dice, but the ingredients for success were already present.

Once they had excavated these diamonds in the rough, the Padres also showed a willingness to deal them for more dependable properties before they'd passed their expiration dates, rather than become victims of the belief that bullpen performance is eternal. Mujica and Webb were shipped to the Marlins over the winter for former top outfield prospect Cameron Maybin, who had had trouble making contact in Florida but was worth nearly four wins to San Diego in his first season with the team. (Mujica and Webb combined

TABLE 3-1.5 Out-of-Nowhere Top 50 Relievers

Year	DNP	<10 IP
1980	3	4
1981	6	8
1982	4	5
1983	5	6
1984	6	8
1985	6	10
1986	7	10
1987	9	9
1988	5	7
1989	3	7
1990	7	8
1991	11	14
1992	0	1
1993	5	8
1994	7	8
1995	7	8
1996	2	4
1997	5	6
1998	4	5
1999	4	5
2000	2	4
2001	6	7
2002	7	10
2003	8	9
2004	4	10
2005	6	7
2006	6	11
2007	6	7
2008	4	8
2009	10	14
2010	6	7
2011	5	6
AVG	5.1	6.9

TABLE 3-1.6 How Fast Pitching Stats
Stabilize

Stat	Stabilizes (PA)	Stabilizes (Seasons)
K	126	0.5
UIBB	303	1.2
HR/FB	1239	5.1
HR	1271	5.2
HBP	1346	5.5
BABIP	3729	15.4

for under a win in Miami.) With the Padres out of contention, Adams fetched a high price in pitching prospects from the Rangers at the deadline. Stauffer successfully transitioned back to the rotation, and Thatcher lost most of his season to shoulder surgery. Even after those subtractions, both planned and otherwise, the Padres still finished with the third-best bullpen ERA in baseball, as Bell, Adams (for half a season), Gregerson, and Frieri continued to pitch well, and the team plugged holes from within with recent draftees Anthony Bass and Josh Spence.

The Padres' pattern wasn't exclusive to San Diego. From 2008 to 2010, the total WARP produced by teams' bullpens was only weakly tied to the amount of money it took to secure that performance; bullpen salary and WARP had only a 0.18 correlation. Over the same period, and not coincidentally, bullpen WARP and the percentage of non-starter innings thrown by "homegrown" relievers (defined as pitchers who hadn't appeared previously in the majors with another team) yielded a much stronger 0.51 correlation. (The *lowest* 2011 bullpen ERA belonged to the Braves, who also paid the second-least per-relief win, largely because their closer, Craig Kimbrel, was an Atlanta draftee, a rookie, and the most valuable reliever in the majors, and their all-star setup man Johnny Venters was another homegrown pitcher in his sophomore season.) The implication, then, is that uncovering previously unproven pitchers well suited for relief, whether they be young players at the outset of their careers or unfairly overlooked minor league journeymen, is more closely associated with success than buying up arms who have succeeded before—which, as we've seen, is no guarantee that they'll succeed again.

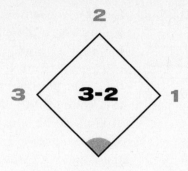

Are Relievers Being Used Properly?

COLIN WYERS

"Alcohol is like love," he said. "The first kiss is magic, the second is intimate, the third is routine. After that you take the girl's clothes off."
—**Raymond Chandler**, *The Long Goodbye*

At first, it truly was magical. Our first kiss was Dennis Eckersley back in 1987. Eckersley, viewed as a washed-up starter in the twilight of his career, ended up with the one manager creative enough to bring his career back to life, Tony La Russa. La Russa, no doubt with an assist from pitching coach Dave Duncan, tailored a role just for Eckersley, one that we now recognize as that of the modern closer: the pitcher would appear only at the end of the game, only to protect a lead, and almost never for more than an inning at a time. Eckersley credited the move with revitalizing his career:

"It was a hell of an idea, and I was the lucky recipient," says The Eck. "I was 32. Starting was getting to be difficult. I couldn't go six or seven innings, wade through all those left-handers anymore. But just pitching one inning, my fastball came back. I was throwing like I was 25 again. One inning suited me very well. I never would have lasted if I had to pitch two or three innings all the time. Plus, I would have had my head knocked off."

269

The results were bewitching. Eckersley ended up with a Cy Young and MVP award in the same season, and every team in baseball decided they had to have a pitcher just like him. Like a virus, the fever spread, the limited role designed for Eckersley evolving to include other pitchers.

Now it's routine. La Russa, not content to simply have a designated ninth-inning guy, added pitchers devoted solely to retiring left-handed hitters late in the game. Most managers have followed La Russa in form if not in creativity; managers enter a game with a set plan for how they want to use their bullpen, and some are unwilling to deviate from it. Yankees manager Joe Girardi is notable for his inflexibility. After an eighth-inning meltdown by Rafael Soriano, Girardi told the press why he was allowed to pitch long enough to squander a four-run lead: "Soriano's our eighth-inning guy," Girardi said. "And by no means is four runs a game in the bag, as we just saw."

Baseball Prospectus's Steven Goldman responded:

[Girardi's] is a nice thought, except that a manager can't go through life worrying about protecting four-run leads; in 2010 and 2011, when the home team carried a four-run lead into the top of the eighth, it won roughly 98 percent of the time. Girardi also argued that he had to use Soriano there because he would have been second-guessed if he hadn't. "If a guy gets on or a couple guys get on, and I have to get Soriano up, then I'm asked the question, 'Why didn't you just have him to start the inning?'" This seems to suggest that only your eighth-inning guy can pitch the eighth inning, all 162 of them, because the consequences of using a non-eighth-inning guy in the eighth-inning spot are too frightening to contemplate. Someone might yell at you. Fans. Owners. Mom.

Similarly, Girardi had to use his eighth-inning guy because had he not, he might have had to use his closer: "If we get through the eighth without giving up a run, then I don't have to get up [Mariano Rivera,] my 41-year-old closer who, I think, is quite important to us in the course of the year." Again, by this reasoning, no lead is so safe that you don't have to take all possible precautions to ensure that your closer does not ever have to pitch.

Yet, even had the Yankees given up a run in that eighth inning, the game wouldn't truly have been in jeopardy, it just would have been in jeopardy according to the saves rule, which is a different matter. The manager of the Yankees does not dictate when to use Mariano Rivera, but the arbitrarily defined "save situation" does. He is powerless before it. Even had he deemed it wiser to skip Rivera that day so that he might be available for some future clash with the Red Sox, he would have had to use him.

FIGURE 3-2.1 Percentage of Innings Thrown by Starting Pitchers, 1871–2011

The closer, once an invention based upon creativity, is now either an excuse or a mandate to avoid creativity in how a manager applies his relief pitchers in the search for team wins. How did we end up where we are now? And is it truly benefiting the game of baseball?

Relief pitchers were so rare in the early days of baseball that it didn't occur to those keeping the records to track pitchers' performance both as starters and relievers. We can, however, estimate the split of a pitcher's playing time in each role, which gives us a useful starting point for analysis. While the historical record is unclear for individual pitchers, it is relatively simple to estimate the number of innings pitched by all starters for a season, as well as the number of relief appearances per game. Using these league-wide estimates, as well as a pitcher's games and games started, lets us estimate how much of a pitcher's work came from starting versus relief pitching.

For the modern era we have play-by-play data and can calculate these things precisely, but I have chosen to continue presenting the estimates so as to make it easier to identify trends without worrying if a shift is caused by changes in what happened versus changes in how the numbers are tabulated. See Figure 3-2.1 for the percentage of innings thrown by starting pitchers.

It is not until about 1908 that we see a decline, settling at 90 percent for a few years and then drifting almost inexorably downward, so

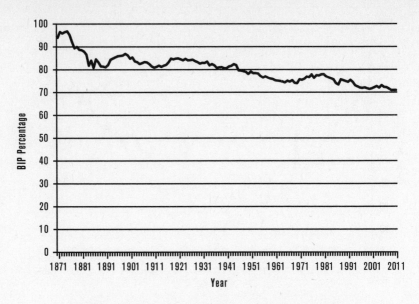

FIGURE 3-2.2 Balls in Play per Plate Appearance, 1871–2011

that in the modern game less than 70 percent of all innings are thrown by starting pitchers.

What is fascinating about the downward slope is that it is unimpeded by almost anything that would affect pitcher usage. The second deadball era doesn't seem to arrest the decline at all; the 1960s actually saw a slight drop in starter innings, while shaving nearly a full run per game in comparison to the 1950s. As a whole, the correlation between the percentage of innings thrown by starting pitchers and the runs scored per game is only 0.4. If we eliminate the evolving game of the late 1800s and early 1900s and start with 1920 (the first year starters threw less than 90 percent of all innings) we get a correlation of only 0.16.

The arrow of correlation is counterintuitive in that it suggests the more runs scored per game, the more innings thrown by starting pitchers. At the very least this causes us to reconsider the commonly held belief that pitchers don't throw as deep into games because they have to face tougher lineups than pitchers of old used to. It has often been said that replacing slap-hitting shortstops with Cal Ripken types means fewer spots in the lineup to pitch around, but even replacing the pitcher with the designated hitter—in essence a second first baseman—doesn't seem to affect the magnitude of the downward slope.

What accounts for the change in pitcher usage? We can neatly divide the outcomes of a plate appearance into two groups—balls in

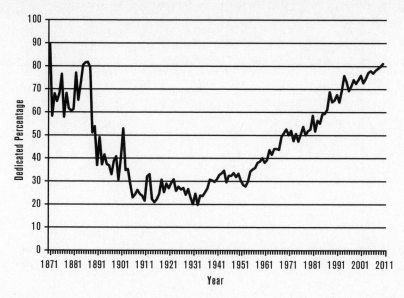

FIGURE 3-2.3 Percentage of Relief Innings Thrown by Dedicated Relievers, 1871–2011

play, which require action by the defense, and the so-called three true outcomes of walks, strikeouts, and home runs. Figure 3-2.2 gives us a look at the rate of balls in play as a percentage of plate appearances over time.

The two graphs are strikingly similar. The BIP rate and starter IP rate have a correlation of .88. What this suggests is that pitching has gotten harder over the years because more and more of the burden has shifted to the pitcher alone, with less and less reliance on the defense. This has created an increased need for relief pitchers. It took some time, however, for this to lead to the rise of dedicated relief specialists. Figure 3-2.3 shows the percentage of relief innings thrown by pitchers who never started a game over time.

We actually see that baseball started with "dedicated" relievers, but that can be misleading—there weren't many relief innings to go around, and so teams pressed position players into pitching on the rare occasions where a starter couldn't finish a game. Using pitchers as relief pitchers seems to start in the 1890s, and by 1910 or so teams relied on pitchers nearly exclusively for relief pitching appearances. Teams still hadn't moved to using pitchers whose primary job was to pitch in relief, however; the majority of relief appearances went to starting pitchers, or at the very least, swingmen who could be counted upon to work both roles. This began to change around 1936, when teams began a gradual transition toward pitchers who specialize in relief.

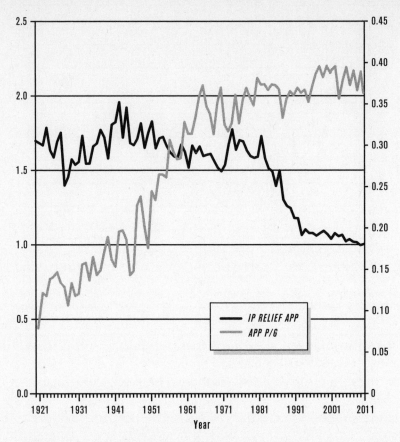

FIGURE 3-2.4 Closer Innings per Appearance and Appearances per Game, 1920–2011

Once you have dedicated relief pitchers, you're going to notice that some of them are better than others. And you're going to try and use your better pitchers in tight games at the expense of your lesser pitchers. This is where we see the first manifestations of what we'd now call a "closer," but which at the time were often called "firemen," relief pitchers who are supposed to come in with the game on the line and finish it off. By the end of the 1960s, we see most (if not all) teams having a relief ace. If we define a team's closer as the pitcher with the most saves for his team that year, we can look for historical trends in closer usage. We'll look at two measures: how many IP a closer pitches per appearance, and how many appearances a closer makes per team game (see Figure 3-2.4).

From 1920 through to 1960, the percentage of games where a closer makes an appearance rises dramatically from 8 percent to 33 percent. After, we see a much subtler rise up to an average of 38 percent for the

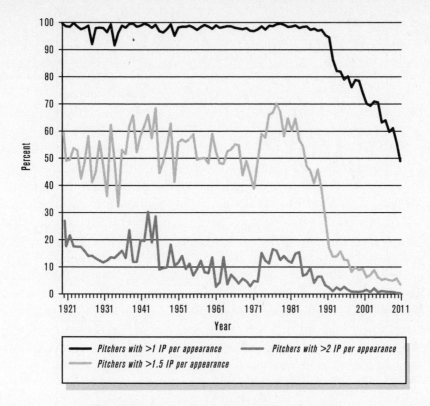

FIGURE 3-2.5 Rate of Multi-Inning Outings, 1920–2011

past decade. The frequency with which teams used their relief ace has been relatively stable since 1960 or so. But right around 1988 we see a dramatic change in how many innings a team's relief ace pitches each appearance. Up to that point you have a pretty stable equilibrium around 1 and 1.2 innings per outing. After a five-year decline, though, you hit a new equilibrium at just over an inning pitched per game, one that's even more stable than the old equilibrium.

We don't just see this change among relief aces. Looking at the percentage of innings thrown by relievers with at least one, one and a half (half-innings are the result of averaging, whereas in actuality pitchers only throw in multiples of one-third), and two innings per outing over time shows us how drastically total bullpen usage has changed (see Figure 3-2.5).

We see the same late 1980s, early '90s inflection point for the dramatic change in closer utilization. Before that point, nearly every relief pitcher threw at least an inning per outing; as of 2010 only half of all relief innings were thrown by pitchers who averaged an inning or more per outing. Pitchers who average at least an inning and a half of work per outing have gone from representing between 40 and 60 percent of innings pitched to representing less than 10 percent. True long relievers—pitchers who threw two or more innings per outing—experienced an extinction-level event akin to that which met the dinosaurs.

We can quibble a bit about the exact moment that comet struck—maybe it was 1988, maybe 1989—but it came soon after Eckersley's first season in Oakland. In terms of impact on the game, the creation of the modern closer by La Russa seems as influential as Babe Ruth's home run prowess ending the primacy of the bunt and stolen base.

Having identified where the change began, it falls to us to assess if the change itself has been a positive development. We can't answer that question directly, unfortunately; baseball is a zero sum game, and if all teams change strategies, then in the end the average team doesn't benefit at all from the shift. Still, a change in strategy of this magnitude should have one noticeable impact: by putting a team's best pitchers in late to finish close games, we should expect all teams to be better at holding leads in such situations. After all, there is no strategy out there that has allowed managers to get their best hitters to face the other team's closer a disproportionate amount of the time.

To find this evidence, let's focus on situations resembling the archetypal save, with one team leading by one to three runs at the start of the ninth inning or later. (These won't all be save situations; sometimes a pitcher other than the closer will be called upon to start the inning, but most of them will be.)

In the 1950s, a team in such a situation would win its game 90 percent of the time; in the 2000s, a team would win such a game 91 percent of the time. Assuming 44 such chances a season (the average for the past decade), that means modern teams will win an additional game every two to three seasons due to changes in relief pitcher usage. There is a slight countervailing impact from increased run scoring, but with a correlation of just –0.28 between runs per game and these win rates, such an effect shouldn't be expected to significantly alter these conclusions. In short, baseball has contorted its roster and raised a small class of pitchers up to be multi-millionaires for a very small benefit.

In an additional bit of irony, the rise of pitchers designed to pitch in these sorts of situations has coincided with a decline in these sorts of chances. The primary driver seems to be the rise in offense, not the change in pitcher usage. There is a .81 correlation between the rate of potential ninth-inning saves and the seasonal average for runs per game. From 1950 through 2011, 29.1 percent of games resulted in a potential ninth-inning save chance, while from 1988 through 2011, only 27.9 percent did. That decline in possible save chances, at the least, provides a countervailing effect to the ability of ace relievers to come in and close a game.

The paucity of ninth-inning save chances points out another flaw in saving your best reliever for that inning. If you only have 44 ninth-inning save chances a season, but your best reliever can pitch 60 or 70 innings in one-inning stints, you end up having more than a few wasted innings from your closer. For the moment, let's define a close game as one where the fielding team leads by two or less, is tied, or trails by one run. From 1988 through 2011, at the point when the closer first enters the game, he finds himself in a close game only 59 percent of the time. Twenty-one percent of all games pitched by a team's closer happen when the run differential is four runs or greater. This is because managers have to "find work" for their team's supposedly most valuable reliever, and thus must resort to putting him into a game that's essentially already decided just so he can get his innings in. (In fairness, earlier managers were little better, with 60 percent of appearances in close games and 17 percent in blowouts of four or more runs.)

Fans in the stands would be surprised to hear this, of course; if the closer wasn't achieving something special, would he need a special entrance song? Would he send chills up our spine when he delivered his first pitch? The cold, raw numbers feel inadequate to explain how it feels to watch a dominant closer. You can hear the familiar refrain already: "Get your head out of your spreadsheets and watch a ballgame sometime." Yet, as it turns out, spreadsheets are in fact capable of recognizing the heightened excitement that occurs when a closer enters the game. In order to capture this feeling, sabermetricians have often turned to what Dave Studeman has called "the story stat," win probability added (WPA). I'll let him explain:

> Here's the basic idea. An average team, at any point in a game, has a certain likelihood of winning the game. For instance, if you're leading by two runs in the ninth inning, your chances of winning the game are much greater than if you're leading by three runs in the first inning. With each change in the score, inning, number of outs, base situation or even pitch, there is a change in the average team's probability of winning the game.
>
> . . . Bottom of the ninth, score tied, runner on first, no one out. The home team has a 71% chance of winning according to the Win Expectancy

Finder (in this situation, the home team won 1,878 of 2,631 games between 1979 and 1990). Let's say the batter bunts the runner to second. Good idea, right? Well, after a successful bunt, with a runner on second and one out, the Win Probability actually decreases slightly to 70% (home team won 1300 of 1,848 games), according to the WE Finder. The bunter hasn't really helped or hurt his team; his bunt was a neutral event.

. . . To really have fun with this system, you can take it one step further and track something [called] "Win Probability Added" (WPA). Once again, the concept is simple. Let's say our batter in the bottom of the ninth hits a single to put runners on first and third with no outs. This increases the Win Probability from 71% to 87%, for a gain of 16%. So, in a WPA system you credit the batter +.16 and debit the pitcher/fielder –.16. If you add up every positive and negative event from the beginning to the end of a game, you wind up with a total for the winning team of .5, and a total for the losing team of –.5. And the player with the most points will have contributed the most to his team's win.

Related to win expectancy is the concept of "leverage," which is simply a measure of the possible change in win expectancy given the context. For our purposes, we will fix the leverage index of each event at one, so that a situation with a leverage index of two would have twice the average change in win expectancy compared to the average plate appearance.

Examining all events from 1950 through 2011, we find the average plate appearance in the ninth inning and later has a leverage index of 1.33, compared to .96 for the first eight innings. In a model based upon win expectancy and leverage index, those late-game situations are worth 37 percent more than events earlier in the game.

Contrast this to a more traditional model of how events contribute to team wins and losses—the Pythagorean theorem, which has been revised countless times but takes the basic form of

$$\frac{RS2}{RS^2 + RA^2}$$

where RS is runs scored and RA is runs allowed, and the result is an estimated win percentage. The Pythagorean model doesn't care about the order of events. It doesn't matter if a run is allowed in the first inning or the ninth; the formula treats them exactly the same.

How can we tell if the leverage model of pitcher evaluation is better than our Pythagorean model? What we can do is come up with a prediction based upon the ideas behind the leverage model, and test them at the team level. One thing we find, if we do a little digging, is that relief pitchers tend to pitch in slightly higher leverage spots than starting pitchers. The greatest concentration of leverage occurs in the ninth inning or later, with the average ninth-inning leverage from 1988 to 2011 at 1.33. Extra innings have even more leverage. (We'll look at the reasons for this in a little bit.) In the language of leverage, what this means is that each batter faced by a pitcher in the ninth inning is more important in deciding the outcome of a ballgame than each batter faced by a starting pitcher.

If true, this suggests that we could beat the Pythagorean theorem at estimating team wins by putting a greater emphasis on a team's pitching performance in the ninth inning. To see if this is true, we can break Pythagorean wins down into two components: a team's expected win percentage given only the performance of its pitchers through the first eight innings, compared to its record after. We can use these two variables to predict both a team's Pythagorean and actual win percentages. We can then compare them to see how close the two models are, and if the Pythagorean method is underweighting a team's pitching performance in the ninth inning.

What we see instead is incredible consistency between the two models; the difference between the weight for relief pitching in the Pythagorean model and the observed wins model is only .03. In other words, there is little practical difference in the amount of emphasis on relief pitcher performance when predicting actual wins versus Pythagorean wins—the Pythagorean model is a much more realistic model of the impacts of pitching performance than the leveraged model. A .03 change means that for a team with a ninth-inning-and-later performance of half the league run average, you would expect it to win roughly one more game than predicted by the Pythagorean model per season. (Teams pitching that well occur less than one percent of the time.) In a more realistic scenario, a team that has an RA in the ninth and later that's 75 percent of league average (teams pitching that well or better occur about 16 percent of the time) wins one more game than predicted by the Pythagorean model every two seasons.

What the win expectancy model is truly capturing is not how much a play contributes to team wins, but how well an event predicts the outcome of the game itself. There is, of course, going to be some substantial overlap between the two, as things that lead to wins also tend to be good predictors of wins. What complicates things is that at the end of the game, the music stops and everyone has to find a chair—

the winning team is at one and the losing team at zero. This is what's known as an "assuming state"; once you enter it, it's impossible to leave. Late-game events are more predictive in terms of win expectancy due to their proximity to the end of the game.

To this end, WPA is truly the story stat. It captures very well how exciting a game is close-and-late. A blown save is tremendously upsetting emotionally, because it takes what was very nearly a sure win and turns it into a sure loss. WPA captures this change very well. But what it does not capture nearly as well is the fact that, indeed, the closer enters the game when it is already very nearly a sure win.

Consider the toughest save spot a closer would see to start the ninth inning—the pitcher comes in with three outs left in the game and a one-run lead. In order for his team to win, all he has to do is pitch one scoreless inning. The reality is most innings in MLB are scoreless; from 1988 through 2011, 72 percent of all innings had zero runs scored. Because we're already dealing with a high probability of success, it's difficult to improve on this rate; the average pitcher coming into a ninth-inning save chance allowed no runs only 75 percent of the time.

Emotionally, the final inning is an assuming state as well; the pitcher on the mound when a team wins or loses the game tends to bask in the reflected glory of the triumph or wallow in the agony of the defeat. However, in reality all that matters is the final score. If the starter pitches a scoreless fifth, that's just as meaningful to deciding the outcome of a one-run game as it is if the closer pitches a scoreless ninth. Win expectancy may tell a better story than the Pythagorean analysis, but it tells us less about the relative contributions of closers versus starting pitchers to team wins and losses.

If the change in reliever usage hasn't altered how effective teams are pitching late in games, it has changed how managers handle their tactical choices, and by doing so has affected the way we watch the game. The shift to relievers pitching fewer innings per appearance did nothing to arrest the decline of innings pitched by starting pitchers. The result of this change has been more pitching changes per game; in the 1980s there were 3.4 relief appearances per game, while in the 2000s there were 5.6 relief appearances per game. This has meant less space on the roster for position players (see Figure 3-2.6).

After a sharp jump up to the levels of the late 1890s, we see a gradual rise until the late 1980s, where again we see a dramatic increase. Teams are increasingly using more pitchers to fill their roster spots.

A manager's chief strategic weapon is no longer the position player,

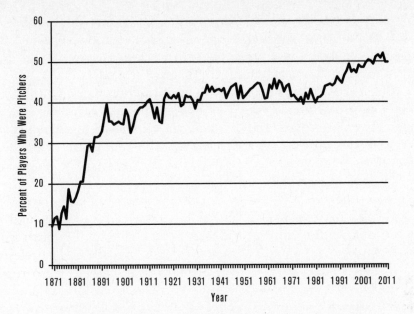

FIGURE 3-2.6 Percentage of Players Who Were Pitchers, 1871–2011

but the relief pitcher. While specialization came naturally to position players, it had to be created for relievers. A manager can probably tell which player is his pinch-hitter and which is his pinch-runner just by looking at the him, but can't tell which pitcher is which without some sort of guidance. Thus, managers have created increasingly narrow pitching roles to help them make those decisions: one pitcher is your closer, one your setup man, one your seventh-inning guy, one guy goes after tough lefties.

This increasing parade of relievers may not make it any easier to hold leads late in games, but they do in fact make the "late" in games more accurate. Looking at all seasons from 1950 through 2011, each reliever used per game adds an additional 10 minutes to the length of the game. This holds even after you control for increased run scoring (which is not a significant predictor of game length once you control for the number of relievers used). And changes in reliever usage account for over 70 percent of the variance in game length over that time period.

What this means is that, from 1950 through the present, we've added more than half an hour to the length of a ballgame. If this addition meant more play, it might be worth it. But for the most part, it's an addition of seeing managers coming out of the dugout with an arm in the air, warm-up pitches from the mound, and catchers jawing with their starters to give the fresh arm in the pen a little more time to loosen up. Seeking ephemeral advantages, managers have instead colluded to add 30 minutes of tedium to our national pastime.

If history teaches us anything, it's that nothing lasts forever. Someday, some enterprising manager will decide to eschew the staid traditions of the closer for something new—after all, this is how the notion of the closer got its start, and so it's how it will meet its inevitable end. Just don't expect it to happen anytime soon.

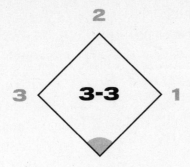

Could Stephen Strasburg's Injury Have Been Predicted or Prevented?

COREY DAWKINS

In late July 2010, after the ninth start of Nationals pitcher Stephen Strasburg's rookie season, he was placed on the disabled list with inflammation in his right shoulder. This would have been a disappointing development for any young pitcher, but Strasburg was the most-anticipated phenom in years. The news was greeted with predictable anguish. Before the injury, Strasburg had been billed as a once-in-a-lifetime talent. Before the start of the 2010 season, Baseball Prospectus's prospect expert Kevin Goldstein wrote:

The Good: Strasburg's talent is historic. His fastball sits at 95–98 miles per hour, touches triple digits regularly, and features the pinpoint accuracy of a top-notch finesse pitcher. His power breaking ball is a plus-plus offering that can be an absolute wipeout offering when it's on, and even his changeup is above average with excellent depth and fade. He's a big, physical pitcher who maintains his velocity all night.

The Bad: He's a perfectly sized righty with pitches that rate as an 80, 70-plus, and 60 on the 20-to-80 scouting scale to go along with plus-plus command and control, so it's really hard to criticize any aspect of his game.

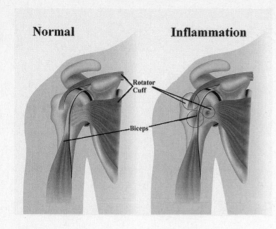

Normal   **Inflammation**

FIGURE 3-3.1 The Shoulder and Its Miseries

In his major league debut, Strasburg struck out 14 while walking none. Over his next nine starts, Strasburg continued to impress, striking out 75 over 54 innings, but shoulder inflammation would cause him to miss 19 days. The news would get worse from there: in late August, Strasburg was found to be in need of Tommy John surgery and the repair of his common flexor tendon.

What could have caused a young, otherwise healthy pitcher to need surgery that would cause him to miss nearly a whole season? Could it have been prevented? Why is it that Strasburg needed an operation only a few months into his major league debut while Felix Hernandez, with 1388.1 innings to his name through his 25th birthday, has never needed any arm or shoulder surgery? (See Figure 3-3.1.)

What Causes Pitching Injuries?

The Baseball Prospectus injury database, which contains nine seasons of major league injury information as well as data from the minor leagues, winter leagues, and spring training, was created several years ago for the purpose of evaluating a pitcher's risk of injury on a pitch-by-pitch basis. Once the information was assembled, however, it became apparent that all games of a given pitch count are not created alike. Relief pitchers are injured and end up on the disabled list more often than starting pitchers. Some pitchers don't tire as quickly as others, so the 100-pitch mark should not be treated as a one-size-fits-all danger indicator. Injuries occur not because a pitcher went beyond 100 pitches, but because he threw too many pitches for his body to handle without harm, whatever his count happened to be. This is one of the core principles of strength, conditioning, and rehabilitation programs, which demand that everything be tailored to the individual. (See Tables 3-3.1 and 3-3.2.)

The tables reveal that pitchers are more prone to upper-extremity injuries than they are to injuries in any other region in the body. The vast majority of these upper-extremity injuries have an overuse com-

TABLE 3-3.1 All Injury Database Entries Since 2005

Position	Upper Ext	Lower Ext	Trunk/Back	Abdomen	Head	Gen Med	Total
SP	561	161	110	6	7	15	860
RP	606	152	113	8	6	19	905

TABLE 3-3.2 DL-Only Entries Since 2005

Position	Upper Ext	Lower Ext	Trunk/Back	Abdomen	Head	Gen Med	Total
SP	561	161	110	6	7	15	860
RP	606	152	113	8	6	19	905

ponent, which is often the result of pitching through fatigue. Pitching through fatigue can lead to rotator cuff strains in the shoulder, which diminish the stability of the joint and can lead to labrum damage. This creates a self-perpetuating cycle of fatigue, weakness, and instability until failure results. In the elbow, fatigue of the flexor pronator muscles can increase the amount of force that is transmitted to the ulnar collateral ligament of Tommy John surgery fame.

The symptoms of fatigue are just as individualized as its causes. Power pitchers respond differently than finesse pitchers. Power pitchers with an excellent curveball respond differently than power pitchers who rely on the changeup, and so on. How a pitcher becomes fatigued is akin to his "tell" in poker: it is an individual response, but it tends to be similar each time he tires.

Pitching can be broken down into six phases: windup, stride/early cocking, late arm cocking, arm acceleration, arm deceleration, and follow-through. During the windup and stride stages, especially, the risk of injury is low because little forceful activity is taking place. The follow-through stage also carries a fairly minimal risk of injury. Most of the potential injury risk is concentrated in the middle three stages. The late arm cocking phase starts when the front foot makes contact with the ground and ends when the shoulder reaches maximum external rotation. Arm acceleration follows and lasts until the ball is released. Arm deceleration occurs from ball release to maximal internal rotation of the shoulder, before the follow-through phase begins.

There are two key moments in the pitching motion at which the pitcher faces an elevated risk of injury. During the arm-cocking phase, the shoulder blade moves to keep the humeral head centralized so that the shoulder can progress into the next stages without instability. Concurrently, the biceps is firing to manipulate the shoulder and elbow into the famous "Flex-T" position. At the end of the arm-cocking phase, the shoulder reaches its maximum amount of external rotation and often approaches 180 degrees in professional pitchers. Components of the rotator cuff must also contract forcefully to resist anterior forces that place the shoulder at risk for subluxation (partial dislocation), full dislocation, or labrum injuries.

As the arm lags further behind the body, the humeral head bangs up against the top back edge of the labrum, leading to internal impingement in the shoulder, which can cause tears in the labrum. Then, when the muscles are already eccentrically contracting to provide stability, the latissimus dorsi, pectoralis muscles, and other components of the rotator cuff concentrically contract to accelerate the arm and transfer energy to the ball. To get some idea of the velocity attained by professional pitchers, swing your arm in a full circle twenty times as fast as you can. Pretty hard, right? If you could do that in one second, you'd approach the angular velocity of over 7,000 degrees per second achieved by professional pitchers during arm acceleration.

The next critical moment with an increased risk of injury occurs immediately after ball release, during the arm deceleration phase. After its sudden acceleration, the arm has a tremendous amount of kinetic energy that must be dissipated (assuming, of course, that the pitcher would prefer to keep it attached to the rest of his body). The joint loads are highest during this stage, with roughly 90 pounds of posterior shear force and almost 70 pounds of inferior shear force generated in the shoulder with each pitch. That alone might sound doable, but factor in the 1,000 pounds of force pulling the arm away from the body, and it quickly becomes apparent why so many injuries occur at this moment. This distraction force is directly related to ball velocity, so the greater the velocity, the greater the force required to keep the shoulder in place.

The way a pitcher is able to complete these motions is known as his mechanics; in Strasburg's case questions about his mechanics even in college abounded, but these were not dwelt upon because of his perceived talent and dominance over collegiate hitters. His jerky motion was able to deceive the hitters but not the ligaments and tendons in his arm—imagine again, the scenario above, and the way a stop-start motion will add additional stress to an already stressed shoulder.

When Strasburg's stride leg made contact with the mound, his forearm and elbow were often horizontal to the ground at shoulder level and with his elbow behind his back. According to medical studies, this late external rotation increases the load on his shoulder but decreases the load on the elbow. A pitcher having his elbow behind his back in a hyperangulated position at foot contact also increases the forces on his shoulder.

All of the musculature is in jeopardy of tensile failure during this stage, and it seems that the rotator cuff and posterior shoulder musculature are especially at risk. The prime function of the rotator cuff muscles is to keep the glenohumeral head in proper position in the shoulder joint. The rotator cuff is already contracting to resist the distraction force in the shoulder during arm deceleration, so when the extremely large muscles like the latissimus dorsi, trapezius, and pectoralis muscles contract near maximal effort, the rotator cuff is often overloaded and cannot do its job properly, resulting in injury. If the rotator cuff is already fatigued and cannot produce enough force, significant acute injuries can occur.

Strasburg's peculiar mechanics also had implications for his elbow. There were two main factors in his mechanics that likely led to Tommy John surgery. Research has found that an increased amount of maximal external rotation of the shoulder (critical instant number one) and decreased elbow flexion at ball release (critical instant number two) is associated with greater valgus forces. High-speed video analysis reveals that Strasburg has an extreme amount of maximum shoulder external rotation—a positive factor for his high velocity, but not for healthy elbows—and often very little elbow flexion at ball release, another no-no.

Fatigue

When pitchers wrestle with workloads, they follow a risk-reward model, balancing the risk of injury with the potential payoffs (both on the field and at the bank) of pitching through fatigue. Teams must weigh short-term production gains against the likelihood of further injury and a decrease in long-term effectiveness, especially in the cases of players signed to long-term contracts, whose absences can force a team to pay through the nose without seeing any return (as the Orioles did with Albert Belle from 2001 to 2003). It's in everyone's best interest to isolate the point of fatigue and determine when it begins to affect production.

Fatigue in musculoskeletal tissue is similar to structural fatigue in buildings. In the human body, fatigue often manifests itself in muscle weakness, slowed movements and reaction times, lack of energy, or a combination of any of the above. Through repeated loading and unloading of forces approaching the maximum tissue tensile strength, fatigue causes damage on a microscopic level without exhibiting any clear outward symptoms, such as cracks or mechanical deformation. Continued cyclic force loading can cause that microscopic damage to progress to visible damage, which in the human body involves partial tears of ligaments, cartilage, or tendons.

How can we measure fatigue without taking a page from structural engineers and sampling musculoskeletal tissue every time we think a pitcher is tiring? In research studies, fatigue is often subjectively measured on a visual analog scale, much like the medical practice of asking a patient to rate his or her pain from one to 10. However, competitive pitchers are hesitant to admit to being fatigued until their discomfort becomes painfully obvious. In the laboratory, torque is most often determined either by measuring force produced against a device moving at a constant speed or calculating by means of biomechanical analysis using a high-speed camera system. The maximal torque is the average of three or five measurements taken prior to the start of the official testing sequence. Depending on the research study, protocols define fatigue as 30–60 percent of the peak torque or maximal force production level. In baseball, this threshold is unrealistic, since no pitcher would be left in to throw a 60-mile-per-hour fastball when he normally throws 90. There has to be some other way to recognize fatigue without relying on these methods.

When 100 Pitches Isn't 100 Pitches, and When It Is

Over 20 years ago, John Tudor said that there was no mystery as to when he should be removed from a start: "The hitters would tell me when I'm done," and there is certainly some truth to that. Not all pitchers are fatigued after throwing 100 pitches. Being able to recognize fatigue is of paramount importance in preventing pitching injuries. One major misconception is that fatigue does not set in until we have seen a drop in velocity. What often occurs is that the pitcher actually gains a little velocity as he tries to compensate for the relative weakness or neurological delay caused by fatigue. If this continues, the structures can become compromised.

Before the pitcher's velocity drops, we often see that the movement and control of his pitches suffer. Instead of delivering a pitch on the back of the inside corner, it's an inch or two into the zone, allowing a hitter to reach it. Instead of diving out of the zone, a breaking ball rolls into the middle of the plate. When pitchers start to fatigue, they may also lose the Flex-T position or become delayed in reaching it. In the Flex-T position, which should occur during the arm-cocking phase with the arms at 90 degrees of abduction to the side, the shoulders and elbows are aligned. If this position is delayed until the arm acceleration phase, increased stresses will be placed upon the shoulder and elbow. It has been shown that fatigue decreases the body's ability to replicate the position of the hand in space. When the arm angle deviates from 90 degrees of abduction consistently, the arm is at a higher risk of injury.

The hips also play an important role in the pitching motion and in injury prevention, so by looking at the hips, we can gain some valuable information. When the pitcher starts to fatigue and reaches back in an effort to restore his lost velocity, he increases his maximal shoulder external rotation and also brings the arm farther behind the shoulder. At the same time, he often takes a longer stride, resulting in increased amounts of hip extension on the dominant leg. This relationship of increased hip extension and increased shoulder external rotation has been associated with shoulder injuries in professional pitchers. In addition to hip extension, rotational characteristics of the hips are important. If the pitcher lands in a more open position, increased external rotation of the hips and pelvis occurs. The arm-cocking phase occurs earlier and causes a disconnect between the upper and lower extremities. As a result, the upper extremity needs to generate more force instead of leaving the task to the lower extremities and core, which plays a role in injuries.

Can We Use Trajectory Analysis to Estimate Fatigue and Tie It to Injuries in Professional Players?

PITCHf/x, a system created by Sportvision that is now in place in every major league stadium, may be able to help us identify fatigue points. Since 2006, the PITCHf/x system has used fixed-position cameras to take snapshots of the ball in mid-flight until it crosses the plate. Those snapshots are run through algorithms to determine each pitch's velocity and release point. Baseball pitchers generally consider two factors when evaluating themselves for fatigue: velocity and loss of proprioception, or their sense of where their hands are in space. A 2001 study noted a five-mile-per-hour drop in velocity among major league pitchers as their games progressed, although self-preservation was also advanced as a possible cause. Another study six years later reported similar findings among college pitchers, despite the majority of pitching mechanics remaining consistent. Still another observed that proprioception suffered in the setting of muscle fatigue.

When pitchers lose proprioception, they lose the ability to repeat their delivery. Both reductions in velocity and variations in release point resulting from decreased proprioception should show up in the PITCHf/x data. When the ball crosses the plate, PITCHf/x is accurate to within one inch and 0.5 of a mile per hour, but the error can easily be twice as large at the release point. Therefore, we need to exercise some caution when hunting for injury indicators with PITCHf/x, since small variations of one inch can dramatically change the way the body handles the stresses placed upon it.

Analysts have had a difficult time linking PITCHf/x data to pitching injuries in the past. The main obstacles are the amount of measurement error and the fact that PITCHf/x does not truly measure the pitcher's release point. The PITCHf/x system assumes that all pitchers release 50 feet from home plate, so the ball is often 10 feet out of the pitcher's hand at first measurement, requiring some relatively imprecise backward engineering to estimate an actual point of release. Consequently, the defining characteristics of injuries, precise joint angles, and hand height at the moment of release are likely not contained within the data set.

Some analysts have posited that release point changes are indicative of an upcoming injury. While it is true that certain individuals have shown changes in release point prior to suffering injuries, that pattern proves irrelevant when applied to a larger sample. For every Phil Hughes in 2008 and 2011, when PITCHf/x changes preceded injuries, there are countless other pitchers for whom similar shifts were not ill omens.

When we look at the correlations between factors assumed to be associated with injury—namely, changes in velocity and release point—we must be sure to compare pitchers to themselves rather than to all pitchers as a group. Given our theory, we can form a hypothesis that large variations in the standard deviations of velocity and vertical release point could serve as injury warning signs.

To test this hypothesis, we limited our sample to starting pitchers, since the smaller sample sizes associated with relief pitchers would skew the numbers. Unfortunately, there is no significant correlation between any of these factors.

Multiple culprits could be to blame for the lack of correlation, but the most likely reason is that PITCHf/x doesn't actually measure anything prior to the 50-foot mark. Given the limitations of PITCHf/x, it's possible that other systems could offer more effective means of evaluating injuries. Although it's not yet available to the public, the innovative system used by a Danish company called TrackMan represents one such potential solution. TrackMan has been used in golf for some time, but it has started to make its way into baseball in the last few years. Using Doppler radar situated high above and behind home plate, Track-Man measures the location, spin, angle, velocity, and trajectory of all balls in flight, both pitched and batted. This allows a recording of the true release point of the pitch to replace a PITCHf/x-based estimate, increasing accuracy significantly.

Non-Trajectory Analysis Models

Due to the limitations of PITCHf/x and the unavailability of TrackMan data, we have to rely on alternative methods to discover why (and when) pitchers become more prone to injury. The consensus over the last couple of decades has increasingly shifted toward settling on 100 pitches as the point beyond which further work increases the odds of injury. Teams began limiting the number of pitches thrown by starters in the 1990s, but it was not until Rany Jazayerli introduced the concept of "pitcher abuse points" (PAP) at Baseball Prospectus in 1998 that the 100th pitch began to be regarded as the baseball equivalent of the boogeyman under the bed. In 2011, only 12 outings of 133 pitches or more were made by major league starters. Just 20 years earlier, in 1991, there were 168 such outings.

Jazayerli's original pitching abuse points was one of the first systems to examine the effects of pitch counts and quantify "stress" to a pitcher's arm on an individual game and cumulative basis. Each start was categorized based on the number of pitches thrown (see Table 3-3.3).

Pitching abuse points represented a significant step forward in examining the possibility of pitcher injuries and decreased production from a quantitative standpoint. The message that inning and pitch totals were related to injuries (as Figure 3-3.2 illustrates) quickly started to spread.

TABLE 3-3.3 Rany Jazayerli's Pitching Abuse Points Scale

Situation	PAP/Pitch	Category
Pitches 1–100	0	1
Pitches 101–110	1	2
Pitches 111–120	2	3
Pitches 121–130	3	4
Pitches 131–140	4	5
Pitches 141–150	5	5
Pitches 151+	6	5

Figure 3-3.2 also reveals that beginning in 2008, there has been an increase in the number of category 2, category 3, and category 4 starts. Part of this trend is attributable to established veterans like C. C. Sabathia and Carlos Zambrano, but it also has to do with the emergence of a new class of pitchers that began to arrive in the major

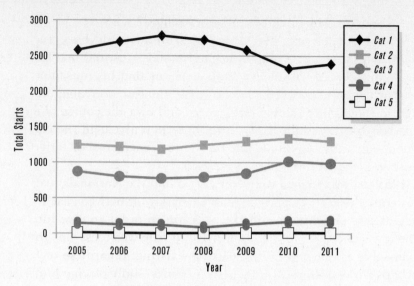

FIGURE 3-3.2 Total Starts by PAP Category

leagues in 2007 and 2008, including Tim Lincecum, Justin Verlander, Felix Hernandez, and Jon Lester. Since 2007, these six pitchers have been responsible for 7.9 percent of category 4 starts and 9.2 percent of category 5 starts.

PAP was refined further by Keith Woolner and others since its original implementation, but does the system really work? PAP has a number of limitations for the purposes of injury analysis. First and foremost, it largely excludes relief pitchers. Again, relief pitchers have actually ended up on the disabled list more often than starting pitchers since 2007. Second, if a greater number of pitches per start is indeed more dangerous, why have the four pitchers listed above not broken down more often, and why are the vast majority of the pitchers who appear in the top 10 PAP counts healthy year in and year out? Fewer than 30 percent of the pitchers who cracked the top 10 in PAP in 2009 and 2010 ended up on the disabled list in the same year or the year after.

Using the injury database, we investigated how closely PAP correlates to injuries, looking at the system's connection to days missed and times on the disabled list in year x and year $x + 1$ to find out whether PAP can be used in short-term or long-term injury prediction. Once again, we failed to find a significant correlation between PAP and injuries.

Could Strasburg's Injury Have Been Prevented?

The answer as to whether Strasburg's injury could have been predicted, and thus prevented is, unfortunately, yes and no. The most likely cause for his physical breakdown was that his musculoskeletal system was not able to perfectly balance the forces created and dissipated throughout pitching in the game and over the course of the season. Though Strasburg had not yet had even a year in the Nationals system, key muscles could have been either weakened or fatigued because of the longer professional season.

If fatigue was indeed the culprit, and had the Nationals realized it, they could have given Strasburg an extra day off between each start or periodically skipped him in the rotation in order to give him extra time to recuperate. On the other hand, if true weakness was the main issue—that is, weakness that was preexisting, regardless of fatigue, perhaps derived from Strasburg's mechanics—only placing him on the disabled list prior to experiencing shoulder inflammation would have been enough to save him from incurring additional damage. However, that does not mean that the preexisting damage would not have required surgery anyway.

The Nationals might have considered changing Strasburg's mechanics, but had they done so they would have risked curtailing those traits that had made him special in the first place. Part of what makes Strasburg so dominant is his ability to rotate his shoulder as externally as is humanly possible, and thus achieve the velocity that makes his pitches so hard to hit. The movement on his pitches, too, is related to his elbow position at ball release. If either of these were changed, especially if done quickly, not only would Strasburg potentially lose effectiveness, but other structures in his arm and shoulder would be at risk for injury as well.

Changes would have had to have been made over a long period of time, something the Nationals did not have in 2010 because of public interest. Even if Strasburg was taught the proper techniques, the body's muscle memory is very long and it would likely have been some time before on-field results were noticed.

Pitching injuries will never be banished entirely, nor will they ever be completely predictable. It's clear that the incidence of injuries has risen in the last decade and could remain at an elevated level for the foreseeable future. Upper-extremity injuries to pitchers, which make up the vast majority of overall pitching injuries, generally have a component of overuse and chronicity to them, so anyone who is dependent on a pitcher's performance should be mindful of ways to monitor workloads with injuries in mind.

This is not to say that things can't be done to decrease the risk of injury. Players need to perform strength and conditioning exercises as prescribed both during the season and in the offseason. Pitchers need to focus on proper mechanics of the entire body, not just the arm slot. They need to be honest with the coaching and medical staff regarding their soreness or fatigue on days that they pitch and also on off days. Full disclosure on the part of the players at risk would allow teams to design individualized programs more effectively. Pitchers should avoid "gutting it out" and reaching back when they feel tired or sore. Common reports of difficulties getting loose, tightness in the back of the shoulder, or soreness that lasts longer than usual can be indications of an internal injury to the labrum. By pushing through discomfort, pitchers risk further weakening and, eventually, significant injury.

Coaches and organizations also share responsibility. In addition to their roles in looking for signs of fatigue, they are crucial to the development of a throwing program. The best results occur when the coaching and medical staffs work together to individualize the programs. Many discussions on long tossing have taken place, since it has been shown to be an effective strengthening technique. The concern over long toss is that it does not replicate game conditions and employs different mechanics than throwing off the mound. Studies have proven that strength can safely be improved despite the different mechanics because forces on the shoulder are decreased when pitchers throw with less intensity. It is not until the pitcher is using maximum effort in his long toss that the forces and torques in the arm become greater than they do when he is pitching off a mound, increasing the risk of injury.

Coaches and teams should not force every pitcher to conform to set methods, especially if they come from teams with wildly different methods and throwing programs. The body is great at adapting to demands placed on it; in fact, there are two scientific laws that describe this tendency. Wolff's law states that bone will adapt its structure to be able to withstand the forces applied to it, and Davis's law applies similar reasoning to soft tissues. As a result, any changes must be made slowly.

Monitoring pitch counts on an inning-by-inning and per-game basis while making real-world adjustments when necessary can be crucial. Extra days' rest should be given in cases of several high pitch-count innings, even if the game pitch count remains relatively low. This would help to monitor relief pitcher workloads objectively. Organizationally, more emphasis can be placed on pitching to contact in proper situations, which can keep inning pitch counts lower, a style of energy conservation on the mound that goes back to the days of Christy Mathewson. Any forceful throwing—long-toss and bullpen sessions—should also be factored in when determining extra rest.

As new medical research is released, it is up to teams and their medical staffs to evaluate how to integrate it into their systems. Training methods need to be individualized—not just in the weight room, but also in throwing programs. These throwing programs should include a long-toss component that avoids extreme distances to minimize excessive torques. This needs to be done from the top of an organization all the way down to rookie ball, as well as in high school and college programs, because that is where the foundation is laid for major injuries such as Stephen Strasburg's Tommy John surgery.

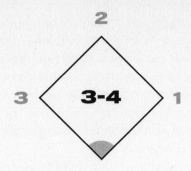

What Has PITCHf/x Taught Us?

MIKE FAST

A love for the game, a sense of curiosity, and access to data are all a person needs to be a baseball analyst. Generations of players and families have handed down a love for baseball for at least a century and a half. For almost as long, people have been recording and counting information about the game, going back to men like Henry Chadwick and Al Spalding. Information gatherers, organizers, and distributors have played a prominent role in how fans have understood the game throughout its history. If you are the type of fan who wants to know why things happen and how baseball works, there is no better time to be alive than now.

This is the age when we are progressively figuring out how to track everything that happens in a baseball game. At the forefront of this advance is Sportvision, a company whose engineers were responsible a decade ago for tracking hockey pucks across television screens with glowing auras and imposing virtual first-down lines for football viewers. Sportvision also developed television special effects for baseball, including ESPN's K-Zone virtual strike zone. In October 2006, it unveiled a technology that was to transform the baseball information world.

As Jason Kendall led off for the Minnesota Twins against Esteban Loaiza of the Oakland Athletics in Game Two of the American League Division Series, two Sportvision cameras were poised to track the trajectory of each pitch. Software processed the images from these cameras to determine the speed of the pitch, its movement, and its location; this information was then transmitted to Major League Baseball (MLB) Advanced Media headquarters in New York City for display in MLB's online Gameday application. For the first time, baseball fans had precise knowledge of the trajectories of the pitches thrown by major league pitchers in game action. Few of us recognized it at the time, and those who did may not have fully understood the event as the revelatory development it was.

Sportvision called its new system PITCHf/x. In collaboration with MLB, Sportvision expanded its PITCHf/x camera installations throughout the league during the 2007 season. Twenty-eight stadiums had PITCHf/x setups by the end of 2007, and the final two installations were completed prior to 2008. The system tracked almost half of the pitches thrown in the majors during 2007 and over 95 percent of pitches thrown in 2008. In an incredible boon for amateur analysts, and a brilliant marketing move for Sportvision as well, the data collected on these pitches were made freely available on the MLB website.

Baseball players, coaches, and fans at every level of the game have observed pitchers and their pitches for decades. The lore is extensive: a Walter Johnson fastball hissed when it passed, a Sandy Koufax curveball dropped off a table, and a Hoyt Wilhelm knuckleball leapt and quivered. In that sense, PITCHf/x data offered us nothing that was not also available to the eyes. What it did was to digitize this information, making it widely and cheaply available, precisely quantified, and no longer subject to privileged access of the observer.

This gold mine of information has greatly increased our understanding in such diverse areas as the physics of baseball, pitch types and pitcher repertoires, and the strike zone.

Baseball is a game that has always fascinated physicists. It has moving objects, collisions, and invisible forces at play. One of the classic puzzles of the game is a physics question: Does a curveball really curve, and if so, why?

In 1990, at the urging of Commissioner Bart Giamatti, Dr. Robert Adair researched and published a book called *The Physics of Baseball*. He condensed in one small volume a wealth of knowledge about how the ball, bat, and players moved and interacted. In some cases, he based his explanations upon the results of laboratory experiments conducted by scientists on baseballs and baseball bats. These scientists were often fans who had found a spare moment to investigate the physical principles of the game they loved. In other cases when experimental data were unavailable, Adair drew conclusions from careful observations of the game or from mental exercises through which he determined the most likely sequence of the constituent parts of the baseball event in question.

Within the space of a year after its introduction, the data compiled by PITCHf/x systems dwarfed that compiled by most of the previous physics experiments combined. Does a curveball curve? We have now been able to measure the curvature of several hundred thousand curveballs within an accuracy of a couple of inches. How does air resistance affect the movement of the baseball? Previously conflicting findings by scientists based upon dozens of wind tunnel measurements have been surpassed by findings from millions of data points collected by PITCHf/x cameras.

Dr. Alan Nathan has succeeded Dr. Adair as the foremost teacher of the physics of baseball; both Nathan and Adair assisted Sportvision in their development of the PITCHf/x system. Nathan has led the effort to learn about the aerodynamics of a baseball from the resulting data. The improved understanding of the physical forces involved has provided a foundation for a great deal of the subsequent analysis done with the data.

One of the most interesting areas of study is learning how pitchers make the ball move by the forces they apply to the ball in their grip and during release. The pitcher's arm, wrist, and fingers send the ball on its way to the batter with a particular velocity and set it spinning at some rate and orientation. Gravity pulls the pitch down toward the ground, and the forces of air resistance slow the ball and deflect it one direction or another based upon the spin on the ball.

There are eight commonly used pitch types in baseball today: the four-seam fastball, sinking fastball, cut fastball, curve, changeup, split-finger fastball, slider, and knuckleball. There are also hybrids and variations of these basic types and a few rarer types like the screwball and forkball. PITCHf/x data has helped us learn a great deal about the typical usage and behavior of these pitch types.

PITCHf/x data itself does not tell us anything directly about what grip a pitcher used on a particular pitch, nor has it led us to discover heretofore unknown pitch types, but it has given us the information we needed to develop a scientific understanding of how pitch grips produce pitch movement. Much of what was speculation, lore, and snippets of observation is now scientifically established from evidence, physics, and mountains of data. PITCHf/x data has allowed us to settle many of the arguments people have had about how pitches move and why. Observations from slow-motion game video, still photographs, and pitcher interviews can now be combined with precise information about how a pitch moved. That combination has greatly improved the precision and accuracy of our understanding of how pitches work, moving us away from a fog of imprecise descriptions, where it was one person's word against another, and toward a unified scientific theory based upon common evidence available to the public.

In *The Neyer/James Guide to Pitchers*, published in 2004, Rob Neyer argued that a forkball was an off-speed pitch, while Bill James believed it was a faster pitch. Since the introduction of PITCHf/x, we have observed detailed data on the forkballs thrown by three pitchers—Jose Contreras, Scott Linebrink, and Justin Speier—and have learned that the forkball is a distinct pitch type from the splitter, rather than simply a variation. PITCHf/x data showed that the forkballs thrown by Contreras, Linebrink, and Speier were dropping more than they would based upon gravity alone, indicating that the pitchers were applying topspin to the ball. In addition, unlike curveballs with topspin, the forkball pitches mostly broke toward the pitcher's throwing-arm side. They also were thrown at roughly curveball speed and had fairly low spin rates.

The combination of evidence about spin direction and video evidence of forkball grip and release allowed us to determine how the forkball pitchers were producing their unique speed and movement on the pitch. The forkball is gripped similarly to the splitter, although wedged deeper between the fingers. A true forkball is gripped with the index and middle fingertips below the center of the ball and released with a flip over the fingers to induce topspin. This is a unique way to produce topspin without turning the wrist, either around the outside of the ball as with a curveball or around the inside of the ball as with a screwball. True forkballs are a unique type of off-speed pitch, as Neyer believed.

Neyer and James also discussed the question of whether a pitcher must turn his wrist to throw a slider. In one section of the book they quoted veteran pitcher Tom Candiotti: "The grip on a slider is similar to a curveball grip—it's released with a break of the wrist." In another section of the book, longtime pitching coach Bob Cluck is quoted as saying, "[Like the cut fastball,] the slider is also gripped off-center and simply thrown like a fastball . . . Remember, if you twist the ball, it is not only tough on your elbow but the break will never be the same from pitch to pitch." Who is correct, Cluck or Candiotti? Do you have to turn your wrist to throw a slider, or is that a bad idea that will kill the consistency of the pitch and injure your elbow?

The beauty of the PITCHf/x system is that we have data on hundreds of pitchers who have each thrown sliders in game action. We have combined this data with game photos of slider grips and slow-motion video of pitchers releasing sliders, and we have learned how variations in grips and releases produce different movement. The classic slider is gripped as Candiotti described, in a manner very similar to a curveball, and the pitcher's hand turns around the side of the ball on release. This motion produces bullet spin around the direction of travel and leads to the typical slider break and a speed differential from the fastball of about eight miles per hour. If the ball is gripped like a fastball, but off-center, backspin combined with sidespin produces cut fastball movement and speed differential of two to five miles per hour off the fastball. In addition, some pitchers use variations that produce results somewhere in between that of a cut fastball and a slider.

Some pitches have particularly controversial or confusing names. Take the split-finger fastball. It turns out that the pitch isn't really a fastball at all. Rather, it belongs squarely in the family of changeups. PITCHf/x data has demonstrated that the splitter is usually thrown with speed similar to a changeup, about seven miles per hour slower than the fastball on average. Like any other pitch type, various pitchers have their own variations on the splitter, but in general, the movement is also similar to a changeup.

Confusion also surrounds the *shuuto*. Throughout the period when PITCHf/x data has been collected, a number of pitchers from Japan have played in the major leagues. Several of these pitchers have thrown a pitch described as a shuuto. Based upon the detailed pitch data for these pitches, shuuto appears to be a general description that can be applied to several pitch types with arm-side movement, such as the sinking fastball, the splitter, and the circle change, rather than describing a pitch type unique to Japanese baseball.

Another pitch with Japanese origins that has generated controversy and contradictory descriptions is the gyroball, allegedly thrown by several pitchers. However, a pitch with bullet spin is not particularly unusual in the majors. For example, Hideki Okajima's rainbow curve and Francisco Liriano's slider meet this description, though these pitchers do not call their pitches gyroballs. In fact, many pitchers have sliders with bullet spin and only a small amount of sidespin.

Let's look at an example of the detailed pitch data from PITCHf/x. In Figure 4-1.1 we have a plot of the movement of all the pitches Cliff Lee threw in his June 16, 2001, start against the Florida Marlins. Each point on the plot shows the deflection of that pitch from its initial tra-

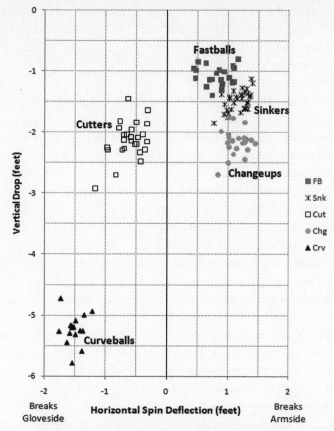

FIGURE 3-4.1 Cliff Lee, June 16, 2011, Pitch Deflection

jectory out of Lee's hand to the point where it reached home plate, as viewed from the catcher's perspective.

Because curveballs drop so much from their initial trajectory—between five and six feet in Lee's case—pitchers usually launch them on a slightly upward path in order to let them drop into the bottom of the strike zone.

The movement of Lee's various fastball types is evident from the PITCHf/x data. His cut fastball moves toward his glove side (the third-base side). His four-seam fastball and sinking fastball, along with his changeup, move toward his throwing-arm side (the first-base side).

This type of detailed pitch tracking data has also taught us a lot about how pitchers use their pitches. Fastballs are the easiest pitches for pitchers to throw for a strike. However, fastballs are also the least likely pitches to generate a swing and a miss, and four-seam fastballs and cutters are vulnerable to the home-run ball. Changeups and split-

TABLE 3-4.1 The Art of Pitching: Pitch Types and Their Results

Pitch Type	In-Zone%	Swing%	Whiff/ Swing	Groundball%	Home Run%	Height (ft.)
Four-seam fastball	55%	45%	17%	38%	3.7%	2.6
Sinking fastball	53%	44%	14%	50%	2.9%	2.4
Cut fastball	52%	49%	21%	40%	3.6%	2.5
Changeup	42%	50%	30%	48%	3.3%	2.0
Split-finger fastball	41%	49%	31%	50%	3.7%	2.0
Slider	46%	48%	31%	45%	3.4%	2.1
Curveball	43%	40%	29%	50%	3.0%	2.0
Knuckleball	53%	50%	21%	46%	3.5%	2.6

ters tend to be thrown down and away where they are likely to miss the zone if the batter lays off the pitch, but batters are often fooled and swing and miss, more than for any other pitch type. Pitchers are willing to use sliders in the zone a little more often, but they are also good at generating whiffs. Curves, too, are good swing-and-miss pitches, but batters take more often with curveballs than with any other pitch type. Sinkers and curveballs are the best pitch types for avoiding the home run. (See Table 3-4.1.)

Pitchers tend to throw pitches toward the side of the plate where the break of the pitch will carry it off the plate and away from the sweet spot of the bat. That means that right-handed pitchers tend to throw sinkers, changeups, and splitters to the third-base side of the plate and sliders and cutters to the first-base side of the plate. Left-handed pitchers tend to do the opposite. Because curveballs are the hardest pitch to control, pitchers often aim them toward the middle of the plate. If a pitcher has good command of his four-seam fastball, he can throw it to both sides of the plate.

We can use the detailed pitch type and location data from PITCHf/x to get an idea of a pitcher's strategy and pitch usage patterns to right-handed and left-handed hitters. When we split the data this way, we can also get an idea of how consistent the pitcher's mechanics are by how tightly grouped his pitches are near the edges of the plate. Mariano Rivera is one pitcher who has excelled in this department. For example, look at the plate locations of all Rivera's pitches to right-handed batters in 2011 (see Figure 3-4.2).

Rivera did an excellent job of putting cut fastballs on the outside edge against right-handed batters and jamming lefties with cutters in on their hands.

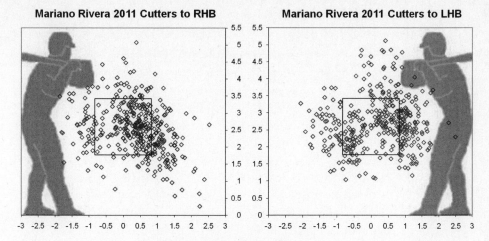

FIGURE 3-4.2 Rivera Cutters Locations

Mechanics are one of the most important parts of the pitching craft, but they have historically been among the most difficult subjects to study. PITCHf/x provides data on the release points and arm angles used by pitchers. This data could also be useful in understanding pitcher injury and fatigue. In addition, we have observed that some pitchers change their arm angles or shift on the pitching rubber based upon the handedness of the batter they are facing.

Our knowledge of the strike zone, the heart of the confrontation between the pitcher and the batter, has also been changed by PITCHf/x, with the data on pitch locations for hundreds of thousands of umpire strike-calls shedding light on its true nature. At the most basic level, we have learned the average dimensions of the zone. Umpires typically call strikes on pitches over the plate between about 1.75 and 3.4 feet high, on average. The height and stance of the batter also shifts the zone up or down slightly.

In the horizontal dimension, batters of different handedness see different strike zones. Umpires call strikes about one foot in either direction from the center of the plate with right-handed batters at the plate. Lefty batters, on the other hand, have a strike zone also about two feet wide but shifted toward the outside by two inches. This is due to the large influence on the umpire's call at the edge of the zone by the location of the pitch relative to the target set by the catcher. Left-handed batters see more pitches on the outside part of the plate than right-handed batters do. The average pitch location to a lefty is about two inches farther outside than the average pitch location to a righty.

Umpires typically set up in the slot between batter and catcher in line with the inside edge of the plate. When the catcher slides outside, calling for a pitch on the outside corner, the umpire also tends to shift outside very slightly. The effect is small, but it may be enough to influence his line of sight to the outside edge of the plate. In addition, catcher mechanics in receiving the pitch cleanly and without unnecessary glove or body movements have been shown to affect the likelihood of a strike call. This helps to explain why umpires are more likely to give strike calls to pitches that hit the catcher target, even if they are a couple of inches off the edge of the plate.

There are many other areas of research and many analysts using PITCHf/x data, and our knowledge continues to grow as these investigations proceed. PITCHf/x is not the only advanced data set being collected, though it is the only one currently being made available publicly. Marv White, the former chief technical officer of Sportvision, talked of creating a complete digital record of a baseball game. Toward that end, Sportvision has developed two additional tracking products, HITf/x and FIELDf/x. The HITf/x data record the initial speed and direction of every batted ball, which is useful for determining the quality of contact. The HITf/x data is collected from the same camera footage used for PITCHf/x and is thus available everywhere PITCHf/x is installed. However, HITf/x data has not been made free to the public except for a one-month sample from April 2009. FIELDf/x data records the position tracks for every person on the field and the full trajectory of the baseball after contact. It offers the promise of accurate fielding evaluation. The FIELDf/x system is currently installed only in AT&T Park in San Francisco for evaluation, and there are plans to install the system in additional ballparks.

The TrackMan radar system is a pitched- and batted-ball tracking system developed by a Danish company and introduced to Major League Baseball in 2009. Several clubs have installed TrackMan radar in their stadiums and are analyzing the resulting data. Both PITCHf/x and TrackMan systems have been installed in various minor league stadiums to collect data for the parent clubs. None of this data is currently available to the public.

All of this new digitized information on pitch trajectories has greatly expanded our understanding of the craft of pitching. We know in detail how pitches move and how pitchers choose to use them. We know the repertoire of every pitcher in the majors to an amazing degree of certainty. We are in the process of a gaining a much better understanding of the battle between the pitcher and the batter. We are learning about the strike zone and its effect on that confrontation. The data has potential to teach us about pitcher mechanics and injury prevention, and it holds promise for improving our projections of future player performance. The batted-ball tracking data currently being collected may also become revolutionary, particularly if it is someday released to the public for analysis.

This avalanche of data has unleashed a transformation in our understanding of our beloved game of baseball, and what we know about players' skills and the minute details of their game performances is only likely to increase over time. Analytical techniques based upon these data have made their way into many front offices as clubs hire amateur PITCHf/x analysts and baseball operations personnel absorb the public discussion of analysis.

Challenges remain, not only in learning how to understand the data and what it says about the game, but also in learning how to present the information in formats that are useful to fan and player alike. Nonetheless, knowledge is power, and the power of a curious fan to understand how the game of baseball works has never been greater. We live in interesting times.

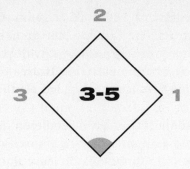

Is Jack Morris a Hall of Famer?

JAY JAFFE

On October 27, 1991, Jack Morris squared off against John Smoltz in the Game Seven of the World Series. Even for a fall classic that had gone the distance, the series had been an unusually exciting one, with Morris's Twins and Smoltz's Braves combining to win three games in their final at-bats. The Braves took Games Two and Three on close plays at the plate, while the Twins' Kirby Puckett ended Game Six with an 11th-inning walk-off home run capped by Jack Buck's immortal signoff, "And we'll see you tomorrow night!" As riveting as all that had been, the best was yet to come.

Enriching the narrative even further, this marked a chance for the hometown boy to prove a point. A native of St. Paul, Minneapolis's twin city across the river, Morris had departed the Tigers after 14 seasons as a new-look free agent. A victim of the owners' collusive effort to hold down player salaries during his free agency following a stellar 1986 season (21–8, 3.27 ERA), Morris had been allowed to opt out or renegotiate his existing contract as part of the settlement. Hampered by elbow woes, his previous two years as a Tiger had been dismal; he'd gone a combined 21–32 with a 4.65 ERA for a pair of sub-.500 teams. At 35 years old, he had chosen a fresh start in a familiar locale, agreeing to a three-year deal with two player options, lest he rebound and desire to test the market again.

Before a raucous crowd of 55,118 packed into the most artificial environment of any venue in major league history—Minneapolis's

Metrodome, with its record 125-decibel peak—Morris and Smoltz produced a duel that harkened back to the game's earliest days. The two aces swapped zeroes for seven innings, with both teams stranding six runners. In the top of the eighth, the Braves missed a golden opportunity when Lonnie Smith, who had led off the frame with a single, was decked by Twins second baseman Chuck Knoblauch, who feigned a double play throw as Terry Pendleton doubled to deep left center field. Smith slid, and after dusting himself off was only able to advance to third base. The Braves would leave the bases loaded without scoring, as would the Twins in the bottom half of the inning, even as they chased Smoltz. The two teams went into the ninth still tied. Morris mowed down the Braves 1–2–3, striking out Mark Lemke to end the inning. The Twins led off with consecutive singles against reliever Mike Stanton but failed to get a run across.

Morris came out for the 10th inning. On the television and radio broadcasts, neither Buck nor Vin Scully—both witness to far more baseball than most of us in their lifetimes—would be moved to remark immediately upon the starter's stamina. Only later would it loom larger than life; not until 2003 would anyone else throw an extra-inning shutout. Morris, who had thrown 118 pitches to that point, set the Braves down in order on just eight pitches, then watched as Dan Gladden doubled, advanced to third on a Knoblauch bunt, and waited through two intentional walks before pinch-hitter Gene Larkin looped a single to left center to bring home the Series-winning run.

Given the context, Morris's 10-inning shutout was arguably the greatest pitching performance of postseason history. A world championship wasn't on the line when Don Larsen threw his perfect game for the Yankees in 1956; that was a Game Five. Pitchers had thrown shutouts in Game Seven of the World Series before, with the Yankees' Ralph Terry doing so in a 1–0 game to close out the 1962 World Series, but never before had a pitcher taken a shutout beyond nine innings in the deciding game.

That performance was the apex of Morris's 18-year career. The right hander won 254 games pitching for the Tigers, Twins, Blue Jays, and Indians. He reached the 20-win plateau three times, made five All-Star teams, threw a no-hitter in 1984, and helped Detroit win a championship that year by throwing two complete game victories in the World Series. Indeed, Morris gained a reputation for his postseason prowess; through that Game Seven shutout, he had accumulated a 7–1 record with a 2.60 ERA in nine postseason starts. Despite returning to the playoffs the following year with the Blue Jays after another

21 wins—he had opted out and upped his salary—his October magic suddenly wore off; he was tagged for a 7.43 ERA while going 0–3 in four starts, though the Blue Jays won the World Series nonetheless. Morris would win another ring with the Jays in 1993, but elbow trouble led to a 7–12 record, 6.19 ERA and shut him down in mid-September. He would struggle through the strike-shortened 1994 season with Cleveland, drawing his release just two days before players walked out, and retired during spring training the following April after an unsuccessful run at the Reds' roster. A brief comeback attempt that began with a half season with the hometown St. Paul Saints of the independent Northern League in 1996 was thwarted when he squabbled over how many starts he would have to make for the Yankees' Triple-A team.

That Seventies Group

On the surface, Morris's credentials might appear worthy of the Hall of Fame. Of the 46 pitchers with at least 250 wins, 33 are enshrined. Four others with at least 300 wins—Greg Maddux, Roger Clemens, Tom Glavine, and Randy Johnson—await ballot eligibility at this writing; nobody with 300 wins is outside the Hall, though steroid-related allegations concerning Clemens threaten that perfect record. Removing the 24 300-game winners from the equation, 13 of the other 22 pitchers in the 250–299 win range are enshrined.

Even so, it has become an uphill battle for such pitchers to gain entry. Between the 1991 election of Fergie Jenkins (284 wins) and the 2011 election of Bert Blyleven (287 wins), no starting pitcher with less than 300 wins was elected by the Baseball Writers' Association of America (BBWAA). Dennis Eckersley, Rich Gossage, and Bruce Sutter were elected for their merits as relievers, while 300-winners Gaylord Perry (1991), Tom Seaver (1992), Steve Carlton (1994), Phil Niekro (1997), Don Sutton (1998), and Nolan Ryan (1999) gained entry as well. A wave of tremendously accomplished and exceptionally durable contemporaries, the latter group—which snapped up 12 of the 20 Cy Young awards from 1971 to 1980—set an extremely high standard against which two decades worth of candidates, Blyleven and Morris included, have been measured and generally found wanting, at least according to conventional thinking (see Table 3-5.1).

While the first seven pitchers listed above pitched into their forties, Hunter and Palmer—younger than everyone in that group besides Ryan—retired at ages 33 and 39, respectively; they thus avoided direct comparison with their cohorts as candidates and beat them to Coop-

TABLE 3-5.1 That Seventies Group

Pitcher	Years	W-L	IP	SO	ERA
Steve Carlton	1965–1988	329–244	5218	4136	3.22
Nolan Ryan	1966–1993	324–292	5386	5714	3.19
Don Sutton	1966–1988	324–256	5282	3574	3.26
Phil Niekro	1964–1987	318–274	5404	3342	3.35
Gaylord Perry	1962–1983	314–265	5350	3534	3.11
Tom Seaver	1967–1986	311–205	4783	3640	2.86
Fergie Jenkins	1965–1983	284–226	4501	3192	3.34
Jim Palmer	1965–1984	268–152	3948	2212	2.86
Catfish Hunter	1965–1979	224–166	3449	2012	3.26
Average (300 winners)		320–256	5238	3990	3.17
Average (all of above)		300–231	4813	3484	3.16
Bert Blyleven	1970–1992	287–250	4970	3701	3.31
Jack Morris	1977–1994	254–186	3824	2478	3.90

erstown due to the strength of their supporting credentials beyond career win totals. Hunter won 20 games for five straight seasons (1971–1975), took home a Cy Young, and helped the A's and Yankees win five world championships and six pennants in a seven-year span (1972–1978); he went 9–6 with a 3.26 ERA in the postseason as well. He reached 200 wins at age 30; among 20th-century pitchers, only Christy Mathewson and Walter Johnson did so at younger ages. He was forced into retirement at 33 due to shoulder troubles and diabetes, but the concentration of his accomplishments registered with BBWAA voters, as he gained entry in 1987, his third year on the ballot. Palmer reached the 20-win plateau eight times; among post–World War II starters, only Warren Spahn did so more often. He also won three Cy Youngs while helping the Orioles to three world championships and six pennants, a resume that earned him first-ballot election in 1990.

Those two pitchers' elections were in line with the well-decorated but non-300-win starters whom the BBWAA had elected over the previous decade, namely Bob Gibson (251–174, 2.91 ERA, elected in 1981), Juan Marichal (243–142, 2.89 ERA, elected in 1983), and Don Drysdale (209–166, 2.95 ERA, elected in 1984); but after the 300 Club had stormed the shores of Otsego Lake, the writers rejected Tommy John (288–231, 3.34 ERA), Jim Kaat (283–235, 3.44 ERA), Luis Tiant (229–172, 3.30 ERA) and Mickey Lolich (217–191, 3.44 ERA), all of whom lasted the maximum 15 years on the ballot without getting even half the votes needed for election. Since Jenkins's election in 1991, the only other sub-300-win starters besides Morris, Blyleven, and the aforementioned quartet to last more than one year on the ballot are Fernando Valenzuela, Dave Stewart, and Orel Hershiser, each of whom lasted two years.

Blyleven and Morris spent the better part of their first decade on the ballot looking as though their candidacies would play out the string as well. The former, stuck with bad ballclubs in the seventies and eighties, allowed his heyday to be so overshadowed by his contemporaries that he made just two All-Star teams and never won a Cy Young. He debuted on the 1998 ballot; despite his high win total and the number three all-time ranking in strikeouts (he's now fifth), he received just 17.5 percent of the vote. The next two years saw that support erode slightly, but his candidacy slowly climbed up off the canvas. Aided by a groundswell of support from statheads (including yours truly, more on which momentarily), he climbed to 29.2 percent in 2003, and by 2006 reached 53.3 percent, a significant milestone; besides Gil Hodges, no player had ever received more than 50 percent and not eventually gained entry via either the BBWAA or the Veterans Committee. Blyleven fell below 50 percent the following year, but rebounded to 61.9 percent in 2008, and finally topped 75 percent in 2011, his penultimate year of eligibility, after falling a mere five votes short the year before.

Morris debuted with 22.2 percent of the vote in 2000. Like Blyleven, it took him three years to clear that initial showing. His climb has been more gradual, but in 2010 he reached 52.3 percent. He gained just 1.2 percent the following year while Blyleven went over the top; at this writing he faces something of a now-or-never situation on a relatively weak 2012 ballot, with Bernie Williams the top new candidate and shortstop Barry Larkin (62.1 percent in his second year) the only other holdover to have cleared 50 percent. The 2013 ballot will introduce a backlog of candidates that threatens to obscure the twilight of Morris's candidacy; in addition to Barry Bonds, Roger Clemens, Sammy Sosa, and Mike Piazza, all with performance-enhancing drug-related allegations attached to their candidacies (see Chapter 1-2), Craig Biggio (3,060 hits) and Curt Schilling (216 wins and a sterling postseason record) will be eligible as well. The 2014 ballot will add 300-game winners Tom Glavine and Greg Maddux to the mix as well as Mike Mussina (270 wins) and Jeff Kent (377 home runs, a record 355 of them as a second baseman). Throw in holdovers Lee Smith, Tim Raines, Jeff Bagwell, and Edgar Martinez, all of whom polled between 32.9 and 45.3 percent in 2011, and who have plenty of eligibility left, and it's conceivable that Morris's support could erode given the 10-candidate maximum on the ballot. Despite Morris's high win total, his candidacy for Cooperstown may well have stalled.

Similar, but Different

At the Baseball-Reference.com website, Morris's page lists the 10 most similar pitchers according to Bill James's Similarity Scores, a method of comparing players according to career statistics introduced in the *1986 Baseball Abstract*. Each comparison starts with 1,000 points, with one point subtracted for each difference of one win, another point subtracted for each difference of two losses, one for each difference of 0.02 in ERA, one for each 20 starts, and so on. An additional penalty of 10 points is applied if a player threw with the opposite hand. James used Similarity Scores as a tool to gauge uniqueness and worthiness for the Hall of Fame; two players with a similarity of 950 or above are said to be "unusually similar," while a pair 900 or above is "truly similar," and a pair 850 or above is "essentially similar." Morris's closest comparable scores a 903, while his 10th-closest comp scores 854; nobody's a statistical dead ringer for him, but nine of the 10 players are essentially similar, with the closest comp, Dennis Martinez, truly similar.

That, in and of itself, is telling, as it says Morris is not terribly unique; many players put up similar career totals. Walter Johnson's closest Similarity Score is Warren Spahn at 795, a level that James would classify as "vaguely similar"; nobody's career numbers truly resemble his. Still, the fact that six of Morris's 10 comparables are Hall of Famers is a point in his favor as far as a case for Cooperstown is concerned. Table 3-5.2 shows that top 10, with an abbreviated statistical thumbnail.

Pore over that table and several things become apparent. One is that Morris's brethren range from an even 200 wins in just under 3,200 innings to 273 wins in over 4,300 innings—a fairly wide spread that has much to do with the way the job of a starting pitcher changed in the 62-year gap between the beginnings of the careers of Ruffing and Finley. Ruffing was generally expected to finish what he started; he completed 62 percent of his 538 career starts, and averaged 7.7 innings per start. Finley, backed by a specialized bullpen designed to take advantage of late-inning matchups, generally including a closer whose job it was to nail down the ninth inning, completed just 13 percent of his 467 starts and averaged 6.6 innings per start. Those two

TABLE 3-5.2 The Jack Morris Group

Pitcher	Sim	Years	W	ERA	SO	ERA+	SUP+
Jack Morris		1977–1994	254–186	3.90	2478	104	106
Dennis Martinez	903	1976–1998	245–193	3.70	2149	106	105
Bob Gibson*	885	1959–1975	251–174	2.91	3117	127	97
Luis Tiant	873	1964–1982	229–172	3.30	2416	114	104
Jamie Moyer	873	1986–2010	267–204	4.24	2405	104	104
Red Ruffing*	860	1924–1947	273–225	3.80	1987	109	112
Amos Rusie*	859	1889–1901	246–174	3.07	1950	129	103
Chuck Finley	859	1986–2002	200–173	3.85	2610	115	95
Burleigh Grimes*	855	1916–1934	270–212	3.53	1512	107	109
Bob Feller*	855	1936–1956	266–162	3.25	2581	122	107
Jim Bunning*	854	1955–1971	224–184	3.27	2855	114	100
Average			**247–187**	**3.50**	**2358**	**114**	**104**

* Hall of Famer

don't even represent the extremes from this group; Rusie completed 92 percent of his starts and averaged 8.2 innings per appearance (no starter/reliever breakdown is available), while Moyer completed 5 percent of his starts and averaged 6.2 innings per start. Morris, who completed 33 percent of his starts and averaged 7.1 innings per start, is somewhere in the middle.

The changing game is also apparent in the gap between Grimes's 1,512 strikeouts and Gibson's 3,117. The former struck out just 3.3 hitters per nine innings, though that put him ahead of the National League average in most years of his career; he led the league with 4.0 strikeouts per nine in 1921, and finished in the top 10 eight times. Gibson struck out 7.2 per nine at a time when the NL average was generally between 5.5 and 6.0 per nine; he never led his league in strikeout rate, but his 268 K's did lead the league in 1968. Morris struck out 5.8 per nine at a time when the AL average grew from 4.5 to 6.0; like Gibson, he never led in strikeout rate, but did lead in K's in 1983, with 232. Finley, whose 7.3 strikeouts per nine is tops in this group, never led the league in either total or rate, but had years when he struck out more than 8.0 per nine.

The far right column of the table represents the level of offensive support each pitcher received—simply the number of runs scored by a pitcher's team on the day he pitched, regardless of how deep into the game he went—adjusted for park and league scoring levels, and normalized such that 100 is average, a concept borrowed from Pete

Palmer and Gary Gillette in the *ESPN Baseball Encyclopedia* but using Baseball Prospectus park factors. The highest of the group is Ruffing, whose teams scored 12 percent more runs than average overall, albeit in a fairly drastic split. With some terrible Boston teams from 1925 to 1930, his SUP+ was 78, 22 percent below average; he went 33–96 for those teams. Traded to the Yankees in mid-1930, his SUP+ was 123 over his next 15 seasons (through 1942, and then in 1945–1946) as he had the likes of Babe Ruth, Lou Gehrig, Joe DiMaggio, and Joe Gordon putting runs on the board for him at different times. In those 15 seasons, the Yankees led the AL in scoring 10 times, ranked second three times, and third twice; Ruffing went 231–127, for a .645 winning percentage.

What's rather alarming about that group above is that despite their widely varying innings totals and run prevention abilities—a topic to which we haven't even gotten yet—the level of run support and the total number of wins match up extremely well. Ruffing has the best support and the most wins, followed by Grimes, Feller, and Morris, with Finley, who has the worst support, bringing up the rear, and Bunning, whose support was almost exactly average, near the bottom. Moyer and Gibson are the most out of step with the rankings, because run prevention *does* matter; those two are the extremes in terms of ERA, separated by 1.33 runs per nine innings.

Still, it should be apparent from this the extent to which offensive support drives those win totals. Via the Pythagorean theorem, each extra percentage point difference in run support translates roughly to a .005 gain in winning percentage, or an extra win for every 200 decisions. All else being equal, Morris's 6.3 percent advantage would translate to a record of 233–207 over the course of 440 decisions, and again, we have not yet delved into run prevention.

An Ounce of Prevention Is Worth a Pound of Wins

Run prevention is where Morris's problem relative to the Hall of Fame really begins. His 3.90 ERA would be the highest in Cooperstown, supplanting Ruffing's 3.80. His 104 ERA+—an expression of how much better than the park-adjusted league average a pitcher's career ERA is, with 100 being average—means that he was just four percent better than average during his career, neck and neck with Moyer for the low man of the group; none of that is accounted for in the Similarity Score. Deadball era hurler Rusie was the furthest ahead of his leagues at 29 percent better, followed by Gibson, who pitched when scoring was at its low ebb in the 1960s, at 27 percent better.

Scoring levels have fluctuated widely throughout baseball history. The average major league team scored 5.96 runs per game in 1889 (Rusie's debut), 3.56 per game in 1916 (Grimes's debut), 4.75 runs per game in 1924 (Ruffing's debut), 4.38 per game in 1959 (Gibson's debut), 4.04 per game in 1964 (Tiant's debut), 4.47 per game in 1977 (Morris's debut), and 4.41 per game in 1986 (Moyer's and Finley's debuts). ERA+ helps to level the playing field when comparing run prevention across eras.

For Morris, the problem is that of the 63 pitchers in the Hall of Fame (excluding pioneers Al Spalding and Candy Cummings, as well as Satchel Paige, who is in primarily for his Negro League career), only one has an ERA+ lower than 104 (Rube Marquard at 103), and just eight are at 110 or below, including Ruffing and Grimes. Marquard pitched from 1908 to 1925 in some low-scoring times; his raw ERA was 3.08, more than three-quarters of a run better than Morris, yet worse in the context of his own leagues. The next lowest ERA+ in the Hall belongs to Hunter; his 3.26 ERA is almost two-thirds of a run lower than Morris's, and yet his 105 ERA+ means he was just one percent better relative to his leagues.

Morris's supporters dismiss his high career ERA by noting that it's distorted by the 5.91 mark he put up over his final two seasons; through 1992, he stood at 3.73, with a 109 ERA+ and "only" 237 wins. This is hardly unique among pitchers, Hall of Famer or otherwise. Hunter was hit for a 4.52 ERA and an 86 ERA+ while battling injuries over his final three seasons. Carlton was rocked for a 5.72 ERA over his final three seasons while passing through five teams. Niekro was lit for a 6.30 mark in his final year while pitching for three teams. Blyleven posted a 4.35 ERA and just a 90 ERA+ over his final four seasons, a span that included a full year missed with injury; he had one stellar year (17–5, 2.73 ERA, fourth place in the Cy Young voting) and two with ERAs above 5.00 in that span. All of them elevated their win totals by hanging on, but with the possible exception of Blyleven, none enhanced their Hall of Fame cases.

Another way that Morris's supporters wave off his high ERAs is by claiming that he "pitched to the score," which is to say that because of a changed approach, he pitched better in closer games and worse in games where he had a big lead or was further behind, making his ERA an inaccurate measure of his performance. Morris himself has taken this tack; in 2011 he said, "I know one of the huge knocks is my high E.R.A. (3.90), and I've said it a hundred times, and I can't say it any more simple: I never pitched to win an E.R.A. title. I pitched to win.

And I did that, I won more than anybody else when I was there. I don't know how to put it any other way."

Over the years, researchers have sought this white whale of pitching to the score. For the *Baseball Prospectus 1997* annual, Greg Spira examined the annual won-loss records and offensive support levels for a handful of pitchers, deriving expected won-loss records for each using the Pythagorean theorem. His analysis of Morris's record from 1979 (his first year as a rotation regular) through 1993, a span over which he was 240–174, showed that the pitcher was four wins ahead of his projected record based upon what his teams gave him—and 16 wins ahead of his expected record based upon league average offensive support. None of the other pitchers he examined (Dwight Gooden, Jose DeLeon, Catfish Hunter, Sandy Koufax, Jack McDowell, Dave Stieb, and Dave Stewart) showed any pattern of significantly outpitching their team-level offensive support (none of the others were compared to league average).

In 2003, Joe Sheehan took a start-by-start look at Morris's entire career in search of further evidence that he pitched to the score. He compared the pitcher's record when receiving a given number of runs of support in a game to that of his teammates and found little difference except at the higher ends:

> Given five runs—Morris' team scored five runs in nearly half his career starts—Morris was nearly a lock, going 177–19. Ninety-nine of Morris' 254 career wins came in games in which his team scored at least seven runs. Not to disparage that—the run support isn't his fault—but if Random Teammate can win 65.9% of his starts with that kind of run support, Morris winning 74.4% of his starts at that level doesn't look so impressive.

Sheehan found that Morris's rate of runs allowed per nine innings was 10.5 percent higher when his team was ahead or behind by one run than if the score was tied (4.39 to 3.97) and seven percent higher than if the margin was two runs in either direction (4.10)—a fairly damning contradiction of any "pitch to the score" claim. He did find that Morris got the win more often than his teammates when allowing five or six runs; both did so in 21 percent of their starts. Morris went 27–64 in those games, for a .296 winning percentage, while his teammates went 47–324 for a .127 winning percentage. Left in to allow five or more runs, which happened 30 percent of the time, he went 29–101 (.223), while his teammates went 52–407 (.113).

Morris surely netted extra wins that way; among pitchers since

1960, his 113 starts allowing five or six runs ranks 11th; Niekro is first at 138, followed by a mostly familiar cast: Sutton, Frank Tanana, Ryan, Carlton, Perry, Blyleven, Moyer, John, and Jenkins. Morris's 27 wins under such circumstances are nine more than anybody else's. When you expand the latter criteria to include all pitchers for whom we have game logs (1919 onward) and consider all games in which a starter allowed five or more runs, Morris's 159 games rank ninth, his 29 wins eighth, his 101 losses 20th, and his .223 winning percentage a less impressive 44th, suggesting that while he grubbed a few extra wins, he did more harm than good to his overall record.

A pitcher's job isn't to collect wins, however. Far from measuring an individual pitcher's brilliance or intestinal fortitude on a given day, wins are simply statistical cookies owed in large part to teammates for the confluence of adequate offensive, defensive, and bullpen support on a given day. On those days when Morris got the win despite allowing five or more runs, he owed more of those cookies to his teammates. A pitcher's job is to prevent runs, and the vast wealth of raw data we have says that Morris wasn't particularly special at doing so.

Advancing the Argument

When comparing run prevention abilities, a stat like ERA+ can help to even things out across eras, but the two competing trends mentioned above related to starting pitching—fewer innings and higher strikeout rates—have caused the level of defensive support required for each pitcher to vary considerably over time as well. Those changes over time are one argument in favor of turning to more advanced metrics to gauge player value more accurately; the distortional effect of offensive support on those won-loss records is another. We can get better measures of what these pitchers' performances were really worth using stats like fair run average (FRA), FRA+, and wins above replacement player.

As noted in the introduction to this book, FRA adjusts for some of the shortcomings of ERA. Going through the play-by-play record with a fine-toothed comb, it does a better job of dividing up the responsibility when a pitcher departs with men on base by taking into account the run expectancy of the situation—the expected yield given the number of outs and the location of baserunners. While it does away with the distinction between earned and unearned runs—and thus scales about nine percent higher, pegged to the league scoring rate—it adjusts for the quality of defensive support received, and for the pitcher's sequencing; a walk issued with the bases empty is less costly than one

TABLE 3-5.3 Extremes in FRA+ among Hall of Fame Starting Pitchers

Rank	Player	Years	FRA	FRA+
1	Lefty Grove	1925–1941	3.75	128
2	Dizzy Dean	1930–1947	3.59	123
3	Rube Waddell	1897–1910	3.18	122
4	Walter Johnson	1907–1927	3.24	121
5	Grover Alexander	1911–1930	3.47	121
6	Christy Mathewson	1900–1916	3.16	121
7	Sandy Koufax	1955–1966	3.35	121
8	Dazzy Vance	1915–1935	3.85	119
9	Eddie Plank	1901–1917	3.27	118
10	Cy Young	1890–1911	4.20	118
49	Jesse Haines	1918–1937	4.51	104
50	Jim Palmer	1965–1984	3.93	104
51	Amos Rusie	1889–1901	5.55	104
52	Red Ruffing	1924–1947	4.71	103
53	Mickey Welch	1880–1892	5.13	103
54	Burleigh Grimes	1916–1934	4.40	103
55	Phil Niekro	1964–1987	4.17	101
56	Whitey Ford	1950–1967	4.13	101
57	Catfish Hunter	1965–1979	4.00	99
58	Bob Lemon	1941–1958	4.66	94

with the bases loaded. FRA+ is analogous to ERA+ or SUP+, adjusting for park and league scoring levels and normalizing to a scale where 100 is average.

Morris's career fair run average is 4.54, higher than all but 11 Hall of Fame starters, eight of whom spent all or significant parts of their careers in the 19th century, when scoring levels were regularly above 5.0 runs per game and could climb higher than 7.0; even Cy Young (1890–1911) is at 4.20. The other three whom Morris tops are Bob Lemon (4.66), Ted Lyons (4.70), and Ruffing (4.71). Again, it's helpful to switch to the indexed format of FRA+ for cross-era comparisons, but even so, Morris is at a very average 100 (99.52, actually). Among Hall starters, only two are lower (see Table 3-5.3 for the top and bottom 10 among Hall of Fame starters).

The ultimate Hall of Fame measuring tool, at least as far as Baseball Prospectus goes, is one I introduced at greater length in Chapter 1-2, the Jaffe WARP Score (JAWS) system. JAWS is a tool used to evaluate Hall of Fame candidates by measuring them against the average enshrined player at their position in terms of career and peak value, the latter defined as a player's best seven seasons. Those values are de-nominated in WARP so as to incorporate hitting, fielding, and pitch-ing contributions. JAWS is the average of those career and peak totals, an attempt to recognize that longevity is not the sole determinant of Hall-worthiness, and that peak performance has a nonlinear effect on a team's results in the standings and on the bottom line.

The average Hall of Fame starting pitcher accumulated 53.0 WARP during his career, with a seven-year peak of 37.1 WARP (an average of 5.3 per year), for a JAWS of 45.1. That's lower than all of the other po-sitions, because pitching and defense together share the responsibility for the other half of the game that's not offense. Catchers, who have shorter careers than other players and who generally play only about three-quarters of a full season's games, are very close at 54.9 career WARP, 35.7 peak WARP, and 45.3 JAWS, while at the other positions, the latter score ranges from the low 50s to the low 60s; see Table 1-2.1 for the full breakdown.

Though our methodology for computing WARP has continued to evolve over the years, Blyleven was well above the JAWS standard when the system was introduced in 2004, and his showing remained strong enough to place him on par with his 300-win cohorts, and among the top 20 pitchers of all time, a powerful argument in his fa-vor. (See Table 3-5.4.)

Morris does not look very strong in this light. Because of his merely average ability to prevent runs as figured by FRA, he accumulated just 33.3 career WARP and 21.4 in his best seven seasons, with a high of 4.0 in 1983, when he went 20–13 with a 3.34 ERA and a career-best 4.01 FRA. Only four other times was he above 3.0 (1985, 1986, 1988 and 1991), and only one other time was he above 2.0, in 1980. Some of his big-win seasons delivered surprisingly unremarkable values; his 1984 season (19–11, 3.60 ERA, 4.34 FRA) was worth 1.9 WARP, while his 1992 season with Toronto (21–6, 4.04 ERA, 4.40 FRA) was worth 1.8 WARP. With that relatively low peak, his JAWS is just 27.3, far short of the Hall standard for starting pitchers. In fact, he would rank as the sixth-lowest starter. (See Table 3-5.5.)

Morris doesn't even stack up well among his Similarity Score play-mates, who are, after all, 60 percent Hall of Famers. The spread of the Morris group's run prevention abilities is narrower as measured by FRA+ than by ERA+, but even so, Morris winds up below the group average and near the bottom. As the WARP values show, he was a hair less than half as valuable as Gibson over his career at his peak, and he

TABLE 3-5.4 Top 25 Pitchers According to JAWS

Rank	Pitcher	Years	FRA	FRA+	Career	Peak	JAWS
1	Walter Johnson*	1907–1927	3.24	121	125.3	72.3	98.8
2	Cy Young*	1890–1911	4.20	118	112.9	56.7	84.8
3	Grover Alexander*	1911–1930	3.47	121	99.4	61.3	80.3
4	Roger Clemens	1984–2007	3.80	122	110.3	46.3	78.3
5	Christy Mathewson*	1900–1916	3.16	121	91.5	60.3	75.9
6	Randy Johnson	1988–2009	3.66	123	95.8	54.1	75.0
7	Lefty Grove*	1925–1941	3.75	128	84.3	52.8	68.6
8T	Greg Maddux	1986–2008	4.31	105	86.9	40.0	63.4
8T	Kid Nichols*	1890–1906	4.94	116	74.4	52.5	63.4
10	Al Spalding*	1871–1878	6.27	122	61.0	61.0	61.0
11	Pedro Martinez	1992–2009	3.50	128	72.3	46.3	59.3
12	Eddie Plank*	1901–1917	3.27	118	73.3	41.3	57.3
13	Bob Gibson*	1959–1975	3.53	115	67.6	44.7	56.1
14	Curt Schilling	1988–2007	3.82	120	68.5	41.0	54.8
15	Bob Caruthers	1884–1893	4.95	113	55.6	51.8	53.7
16	John Clarkson*	1882–1894	5.07	113	55.4	50.5	53.0
17	John Smoltz	1988–2009	3.93	114	67.7	36.7	52.2
18	Tom Seaver*	1967–1986	3.62	110	65.4	38.7	52.0
19	Bert Blyleven*	1970–1992	3.93	111	66.5	36.9	51.7
20	Steve Carlton*	1965–1988	3.78	108	66.6	36.4	51.5
21	Tom Glavine	1987–2008	4.58	100	65.8	35.1	50.5
22	Mike Mussina	1991–2008	4.29	112	65.7	35.1	50.4
23	Early Wynn*	1939–1963	3.98	107	60.3	36.8	48.5
24	Nolan Ryan*	1966–1993	3.66	109	64.1	32.3	48.2
25	Don Drysdale*	1956–1969	3.69	110	56.8	38.8	47.8

* Hall of Famer

comes nowhere close to the Hall's high-ERA man Ruffing. Also worth noting is that Morris would be even further below the Hall and group averages had military service not robbed Feller of his age-23 through age-25 seasons and most of his age-26 season as well. He averaged 6.4 WARP per year in the four seasons surrounding that gap, all of them incorporated into his peak score; a reasonable estimate of what he might have produced would push his JAWS 15 points higher, to 58.3, and he's hardly the only Hall of Famer who would stand to gain from such a method. (See Table 3-5.6.)

As noted in Chapter 1-2, for all that goes into JAWS, the system does not cover every aspect of a player's Hall of Fame case. It makes no attempt to account for postseason performance, awards won,

TABLE 3-5.5 Lowest JAWS among Hall of Fame Starters

Pitcher	Years	FRA	FRA+	Career	Peak	JAWS
Jesse Haines	1918–1937	4.51	104	22.7	14.7	18.7
Catfish Hunter	1965–1979	4.00	99	25.0	21.6	23.3
Addie Joss	1902–1910	3.37	111	24.4	23.1	23.7
Lefty Gomez	1930–1943	4.38	111	26.7	24.8	25.8
Bob Lemon	1941–1958	4.66	94	28.3	24.2	26.3
Jack Morris	1977–1994	4.54	100	33.4	21.2	27.3
Jack Chesbro	1899–1909	3.92	106	26.7	28.0	27.4
Amos Rusie	1889–1901	5.55	104	27.6	30.1	28.9
Joe McGinnity	1899–1908	4.07	110	32.0	25.9	28.9
Mickey Welch	1880–1892	5.13	103	28.6	31.0	29.8
Rube Marquard	1908–1925	3.83	106	32.0	27.8	29.9

TABLE 3-5.6 JAWS and the Jack Morris Group

Pitcher	Years	FRA	FRA+	Career	Peak	JAWS
Bob Gibson*	1959–1975	3.53	115	67.6	44.7	56.1
Jim Bunning*	1955–1971	3.66	112	52.8	40.3	46.6
Bob Feller*	1936–1956	4.00	112	49.0	37.8	43.4
Red Ruffing*	1924–1947	4.71	103	51.2	32.5	41.9
Jamie Moyer	1986–2010	4.91	97	48.4	26.5	37.4
Burleigh Grimes*	1916–1934	4.40	103	38.4	30.5	34.5
Luis Tiant	1964–1982	3.97	108	40.8	25.6	33.2
Chuck Finley	1986–2002	4.51	104	40.7	24.2	32.4
Amos Rusie*	1889–1901	5.55	104	27.6	30.1	28.9
Jack Morris	1977–1994	4.54	100	33.4	21.2	27.3
Dennis Martinez	1976–1998	4.67	93	25.4	16.7	21.0
Average		**4.40**	**104**	**44.2**	**30.9**	**37.5**

*Hall of Famer

leagues led, milestone plateaus reached in significant categories, or historical importance. Morris's credentials beyond his high win total and low JAWS are not overwhelming. He never won a Cy Young award, though he finished in the top five five times, including third-place showings in 1981 and 1983. He led his league in wins twice and finished in the top five nine times, but only led in strikeouts once (with four top five finishes) and never in ERA (with two top five finishes). While he had his postseason highlights, most notably Game Seven in 1991, his overall postseason record over 13 starts (7–4, 3.80

ERA) is a microcosm of his career numbers, much as Andy Pettitte's 19–10, 3.83 ERA over 42 postseason starts is for his career (240–138, 3.88 ERA). Both had the occasional dud of a start to offset some gems.

Like Morris, Pettitte was well supported by his offenses (111 SUP+), and he, too, would have the Hall's highest career ERA if elected, but his 117 ERA+ puts him a significant cut above Morris. His 4.38 FRA seems bloated, but given the high-scoring era in which he played, it's 11 percent above average. As noted in Chapter 1-2, he's much closer to the Hall standard with 55.2 career WARP, 32.1 peak WARP, and a 43.7 JAWS. He led his league in wins once, finished second in ERA once, and was on the fringes in both categories a small handful of times. He never finished higher than sixth in strikeouts, and while he never won a Cy Young, he finished an extremely close second to Pat Hentgen in 1996, losing by four points. He's nowhere near a slam-dunk candidate; his Hall case is complicated by his admission of having used human growth hormone, so he can expect to linger on the BBWAA ballot once he reaches it in 2016.

One other postseason hero of the past quarter century who comes to mind for comparison to Morris is Schilling, who finished his career with a 216–146 record, a 3.46 ERA, and six All-Star appearances. A closer look shows that he blows Morris away as a candidate despite not establishing himself as a starter until age 25. His 128 ERA+ is stellar, and his 3,116 strikeouts ranks 15th all time and puts him in an elite club filled with 10 Hall of Famers and five contemporaries with strong cases (Johnson, Clemens, Maddux, Pedro Martinez, and Smoltz). He led his league in strikeouts and wins twice, and while he never won a Cy Young, he finished second three times in a four-year span (2001, 2002, 2004). Additionally, he has the second-best strike-out-to-walk ratio of all time at 4.38; the only pitcher better, Tommy Bond, pitched from 1874 to 1884, when the number of balls needed for a walk ranged from nine to six. Schilling's career postseason line (11–2, 2.23 ERA) includes the famous "Bloody Sock" game in the 2003 AL Championship Series and lacks the occasional flop of Morris or Petitte. His FRA (3.82), FRA+ (120), career (68.5 WARP), peak (41.0), and JAWS (54.8) are well above the Hall standard, and vastly superior to Morris's. Likewise, all of the upcoming candidates with 3,000 strikeouts have better cases both on the traditional and JAWS sides, and Mussina clears the JAWS standard as well.

Jack Morris was a very good pitcher for a very long time, a durable workhorse who ate a ton of innings, racked up a heap of wins, helped multiple teams win championships, and produced some indelible moments on the field. Superficially, his statistics bear a resemblance to many a Hall of Famer, but the more one places his performance in the proper context with advanced metrics, the less convincing his case becomes. His Game Seven 1991 performance will be remembered for as long as baseball is played; unlike World Series of a century ago that are still discussed but seldom seen even in photographs, we have the entirety of his gritty, spellbinding performance preserved on video for posterity. That's a level of immortality that Cooperstown can't even top. It should be enough.

PART 4
Questions of Fielding

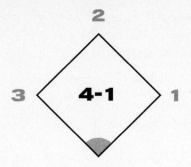

Is It Possible to Accurately Measure Fielding without Shoving a GPS Device Up Derek Jeter's Ass?

COLIN WYERS

The official record of baseball throughout history has been an astonishingly detailed accounting of the events on the field. Batting, pitching, and baserunning have all been recorded with ever-increasing levels of care and precision. Seemingly the only area in baseball exempt from this fastidiousness has been fielding, which has ever lagged behind other areas of study. Many were, and are, content to evaluate fielders based on little more than putouts, assists, and errors made.

Much of our system of baseball scorekeeping has been handed down to us from sportswriter Henry Chadwick, whose plaque in Cooperstown reads "the father of baseball." It's not at all surprising that we inherited our most basic fielding stats from his efforts. It's more than a little surprising that he was one of the first to propose reform, suggesting an alternative:

The new score sheet for score books, which we have copyrighted, is prepared in such form as to insure a correct analysis of each man's play in a match, both at the bat and in the field, to the extent necessary to arrive at a true estimate of his skill as a player in both departments. The best player in a nine is he who makes the most good plays in a match, not the one who commits the fewest errors, and it is in the record of his good plays that we are to look for the most correct data for an estimate of his skill in the position be occupies.

(It took over 100 years for his suggestion to take root; a company called Baseball Info Solutions started tracking what they called "Good Fielding Plays" in 2004.)

Then, as now, the hardest part of fielding analysis hasn't been tabulating how many plays a player has made, but figuring out his opportunities to have made a play. The form of the formula for fielding percentage (also known as fielding average) is as simple as it is flawed:

$$\frac{\text{Putouts} + \text{Assists}}{\text{Putouts} + \text{Assists} + \text{Errors}}$$

Aside from the silliness of having a formula to measure fielding prowess that is identical for each fielding position, the fundamental problem behind fielding percentage is that it only considers times when a fielder gets to a ball as an opportunity. General manager Branch Rickey perfectly summarized the problems with this measure of fielding:

Fielding averages? Utterly worthless as a yardstick. They are not only misleading, but deceiving. Take Zeke Bonura, the old White Sox first baseman, generally regarded as a poor fielder. The fielding averages showed that he led the American League in fielding for three years. Why? Zeke had "good hands"! Anything he reached, he held. Result: an absence of errors. But he was also slow moving and did not cover much territory. Balls that a quicker man may have fielded went for base hits, but the fielding averages do not reflect this.

Rickey's conclusion? "There is nothing on earth anybody can do with fielding." For years, that was the state of the art of fielding analysis.

It should surprise no one that Bill James was one of the first to come up with a novel system of fielding analysis. For teams, he came up with the idea of measuring defensive efficiency, which was simply the number of fielding outs divided by the number of balls in play. For individual fielders, he devised "range factor," a player's putouts plus assists divided by games played (or for later seasons, innings divided by nine).

Range factor wasn't without its problems, of course. The largest problem is that range factor was utterly worthless for teams, because it used games and innings as its measure of playing time. For a team season, those quantities are fixed. Every team has the same number of fielding opportunities according to range factor, but in real life we know teams have different numbers of balls in play (primarily depending on how efficient the pitchers are at striking out batters). Furthermore, we can tell from observing baseball games that teams have different distributions of batted balls. People like Tom Tippett (creator of the Diamond Mind baseball simulator, now working for the Red Sox) and Pete Palmer have created revised versions of range factor that attempt to address these concerns, with varying degrees of success.

Sabermetricians have often been of the belief that the typical fan (as opposed to a trained observer, such as a scout) is unable to discern the difference between good and bad fielders. Bill James likened the problem to that of discerning between good and bad hitters through casual observation:

> One absolutely cannot tell, by watching, the difference between a .300 hitter and a .275 hitter. The difference is one hit every two weeks. It might be that a reporter, seeing every game the team plays, could sense the difference over the course of the year if no records were kept, but I doubt it . . . the difference between a good hitter and an average hitter is simply not visible.
>
> A fielder's visible fielding range, which is his ability to move to the ball after it is hit, is vastly less important than his invisible fielding range, which is a matter of adjusting his position a step or two before the ball is hit.

What of systemic observation, though? Instead of observing a fielder and observing how well you think he performs, or scoring "good plays" as per Chadwick's suggestion, you try to record objectively the location of the batted ball as it lands (or for grounders, where it passes through the infield). The first systemic effort at this was undertaken by the non-profit Baseball Project, but now that sort of recordkeeping is undertaken primarily by commercial concerns, such as Baseball Info Solutions (BIS) and STATS, Inc. What is typically recorded is a ball's location in feet from home plate, the angle from the landing point to the back of home plate, and a description of the trajectory (typically ground ball, line drive, or fly ball).

If data providers were able to furnish reports with a high level of accuracy, we would see consistency between datasets. In reality, data providers can and will differ substantially even in the aggregate. Peter Jensen compared data from STATS and BIS and found that the root mean square error between the two providers for outfield flies was 11 feet of distance traveled and three degrees of "spray" angle.

Mitchel Lichtman compared rates of ground balls and fly balls and found differences there as well. He also compared how well the two datasets agreed when fed to the same system of fielding evaluation, his "ultimate zone rating" (UZR). He found that the root mean square error between UZR figured with BIS data and STATS data was 6.75 runs a season, with a correlation of only .702 (a respectable correlation for measurements of two different variables, but a rather poor correlation for two measurements of the exact same events).

A lack of accuracy in and of itself is worrying, but in theory it ought to be overcome by a larger sample size. Comparing UZR based on two different data sources even over a five-year period reveals significant differences. For instance, Andruw Jones can rate at 112 runs above average when measured using BIS data, but at –5 runs using STATS data, from the same period. That suggests that there's some sort of bias preventing the data sources from coalescing around similar figures over a long time span.

One potential source of bias is the position of the observer when recording the data. MLB Advanced Media (MLBAM) collects batted-ball trajectories (ground balls, line drives, fly balls, and popups) for their Gameday live scoring system. The data is collected by stringers seated in the press boxes at all 30 major league parks. Using stadium diagrams, photographs, and a little bit of trigonometry I was able to estimate press box heights for 27 major league parks. They range from a low of 38 feet in Oakland to a high of 92 feet in Pittsburgh. As it turns out, there is a relationship between press box heights and line drive rates as measured by Gameday stringers. For every additional foot of press box height, we see an increase in line drive rates of .002. While that seems small, it can be significant in practice. Consider the two Chicago parks. U.S. Cellular Field has a press box height of 47 feet, while at Wrigley Field the press box is 67 feet off the ground. Given that, we can expect a player with a line drive rate of 22 percent at the Cell to have a line drive rate of 26 percent at Wrigley.

This is the sort of issue that can cause problems with defensive metrics based on stringer-provided data; those systems will use batted ball type to establish which fielders were responsible for each batted ball and the difficulty assigned to it. Having systemic differences between batted ball rates that persist over long periods of time is one

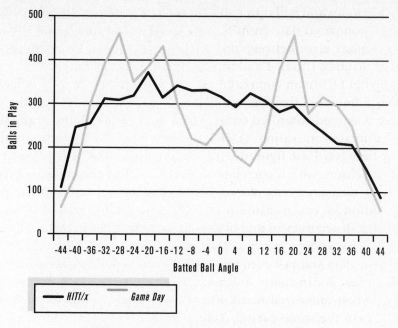

FIGURE 4-1.1 HITf/x vs. Gameday on Balls in Play

thing that may be preventing different data sources from reaching agreement even in larger samples. (There is some overlap between data providers in terms of vantage points. MLBAM and STATS both score from press boxes, while BIS scores from game broadcasts. Some of the broadcast cameras are located in or at the level of the press box. Not all are, which could lead to differences in batted ball classification at certain parks between providers, depending on where cameras are positioned relative to the press box.)

We can also compare stringer-collected data to more objectively sourced data. Sportvision has a set of dedicated cameras in the ballpark to collect very precise estimates of the pitched ball, typically within about an inch at home plate. (For more on PITCHf/x, see Chapter 3-4.) Sportvision has adopted the PITCHf/x technology to provide information on the batted ball as well, called HITf/x. Sportvision released one month's worth of HITf/x data for the public to evaluate. We can compare the angle of batted ball landing points collected by Gameday stringers to the estimates of a batted ball's horizontal angle collected by HITf/x over the same time period, looking only at ground balls (left axis is quantity, right axis is batted ball angle, see Figure 4-1.1).

What we tend to see in the stringer-collected data is that hit locations tend to cluster around the typical locations of the four infielders (five if you count the slight increase around the pitcher in the middle of the large trough up the center of the graph). We instead see a very smooth curve in the HITf/x data (slightly higher over on the left-hand side of the graph, because that's where right-handed hitters tend to hit ground balls).

What could be causing these differences between the precise estimates of HITf/x and the human stringer data? After all, this is not simply evidence of a lack of accuracy but of a systemic difference in how batted balls are recorded. The simplest explanation is that stringers are unable to score the absolute position of a batted ball. Instead, the stringer determines the position of the batted ball relative to one or more landmarks, and uses that to assign the position of the ball on the field. What this data suggests is that one of the landmarks the stringers use is *the position of the fielders themselves*.

(Before we assume that this finding is limited to Gameday data, data provided by Lichtman suggests that it also occurs in STATS batted ball data, while data provided by Shane Jensen seems to indicate it also occurs in BIS batted ball data.)

This has three effects:

- Stringer-provided batted ball locations will overstate the importance of horizontal angle in determining the difficulty of converting a batted ball into an out.
- Stringer-provided batted ball locations will overstate the fielding chances of good fielders and understate the chances of bad fielders.
- Stringer-provided batted ball locations will overstate the fielding chances of players who play adjacent to bad fielders and understate the fielding chances of players who play adjacent to good fielders.

We have two problems with stringer-collected data: random measurement error and systemic bias. The cure for the first problem is increased sample size, but that has the perverse effect of exacerbating the second problem.

The third problem is that the most popular methods (such as UZR, BIS's own defensive runs saved, and so forth) are proprietary both in raw data and in method. We know there are biases and discrepancies, but we are unable to evaluate each particular method to see exactly the magnitude of those effects. So far we lack an objective criterion by which we can evaluate each method to determine which is correct (or more likely, which *parts* of each are correct).

Batted ball data has become so pervasive that it is difficult to conceive of evaluating fielding without it. From that point of view, the problems with batted ball data seem intractable (like HITf/x, which outside of samples like the one referenced above has been restricted to teams willing to pay for the data). If we allow ourselves to take a step back, though, we can recall that there were efforts to estimate fielding analysis before we had batted ball data. Is there anything there that might shed some light on how best to evaluate fielding?

Once again, we turn to Bill James, who was dissatisfied with his own range factor, as well as attempts to improve upon it. Finally he came upon a fundamental change to how we consider fielding stats:

> Batting success of individuals may be successfully related to team wins because there is a natural relationship between individual batting statistics and team success. Pitching statistics of individuals may be successfully related to team wins because there is a natural relationship between individual pitching statistics and team wins. But fielding statistics of individuals are difficult to relate to team wins because there is no natural relationship between individual fielding statistics and team success. How do you fix that?
>
> You fix that by starting in a different place. You don't start with the individual fielding statistics. You start with the performance of the team. First, before you do anything else, establish the overall defensive quality of the team. Then you can transfer credit (or blame) for that performance to the individuals on the team—but without an implicit assumption that all teams are defensively equal or nearly equal.

This observation has languished largely unnoticed, partly because the advent of systems relying on batted ball data seemed to supersede it and partly because it was part of his arcane and confusing "win shares" system. The fundamental insight behind "fielding win shares" was buried in baggage like "claim points" and other mathematical gyrations, and separating them would take a fair amount of effort. James's proposal turned traditional fielding analysis on its head. To that point, fielding analysis began with what a player did and then proceeded to a comparison with that player's peers. Instead of attempting a seemingly apples-to-apples comparison of one team's shortstop to another, James started with the team, considered how many runs that team's fielders saved relative to other teams, and then apportioned the credit among the team's fielders.

This is a key insight because in looking at the totality of a team's fielding chances and the distribution thereof, we can see when a player's fielding performance is actually helping his team save runs, as opposed to simply taking fielding chances that would otherwise be going to another player. An example chosen at random from many: in 1984, Gary Matthews, the starting left fielder for the National League East–winning Chicago Cubs, had 223 putouts (fourth in the NL) but still rates as a negative defender because the Cubs were simply allowing an above-average number of balls to be batted in his direction. More recently, the 2011 Oakland A's tied for last in the American League in outfield putouts despite having, according to the metrics, two above-average outfielders (Coco Crisp and David DeJesus) and another who was only slightly below average (Josh Willingham). With a pitching staff that was heavy on strikeouts and ground balls, the outfielders simply didn't see many flies, but they largely caught what came their way.

Our "fielding runs above average" attempts to recreate the "top down" approach of "fielding win shares" with play-by-play data (wherever possible), giving us plays and runs saved relative to the average player at that position. This allows us to separate ability from opportunity. The biggest indicator that a player is simply hogging chances rather than contributing is if his performance comes when the team itself is having little defensive success. We start by comparing infield to outfield and then break down between the positions in each unit. If the outfielders are making a lot of plays as a unit, but the team's defense is not appreciably above average, that's an indicator outfielders are simply getting more balls hit to them than would normally be the case. Conversely, if a team's outfielders are making relatively few plays and the team's defense isn't noticeably suffering as a result, the more likely explanation is fewer chances, not poor performance. The same process of evaluation applies to the infield—a fielder should not be penalized for failing to field a certain number of balls in a given amount of playing time if he had a dearth of opportunities; nor should he be credited with making an abnormally large number of plays if he lines up behind a staff of Greg Maddux–Tommy John types whose style leads to his receiving a generous helping of chances.

Once we know what has been hit where and how often, we can make a reasonable estimate of an expected number of plays on those balls. At that point, it is much easier to isolate individual player skill. Consider hypothetical versions of the Yankees and the Cardinals. The

Yankees have Derek Jeter at shortstop. The Cardinals have Ozzie Smith. Both teams see an equal number of defensive chances, with a typical distribution of balls to each position. In most seasons, a vastly greater percentage of balls hit toward the Yankees' shortstop position are going to go for hits based on the disparate abilities of the short-stops. An exceptional third baseman playing next to a Jeter, a Nettles, Brooks Robinson, or Mike Schmidt, might save some of those grounders from going through, but never enough to change the team's overall defensive outlook to disguise the impact of the lesser fielder (see Table 4-1.1). In the short run, it's an open question as to whether or not FRAA improves upon metrics based upon batted ball data; to establish this would require a more precise estimate of the accuracy of the batted ball data than the data providers have given us, and until the data providers either take it upon themselves to do that work or provide independent analysts the ability to do this for them, it will re-main an unsolved question (see Table 4-1.2).

TABLE 4-1.1 Best FRAA Seasons by Position

Player	Pos.	Year	Team	FRAA
Greg Maddux	1	2000	ATL	14.0
Yorvit Torrealba	2	2007	COL	7.4*
Albert Pujols	3	2007	SLN	26.7
Rennie Stennett	4	1975	PIT	27.5
Graig Nettles	5	1971	CLE	33.6
Ivan DeJesus	6	1977	CHN	31.3
Willie Wilson	7	1982	KCA	26.6
Andruw Jones	8	1999	ATL	37.8
Jesse Barfield	9	1987	TOR	24.2

*FRAA covers what happens on batted balls, not defensive tasks specific to the catcher position such as framing.

TABLE 4-1.2 Worst FRAA Seasons by Position

Player	Pos.	Year	Team	FRAA
Jim Bunning	1	1966	PHI	-8.7
Sandy Alomar Jr.	2	1997	CLE	-3.7
Fred McGriff	3	2000	TBA	-32.3
Bobby Richardson	4	1961	NYA	-27.5
Chipper Jones	5	1999	ATL	-27.5
Derek Jeter	6	2000	NYA	-24.4
Greg Luzinski	7	1979	PHI	-24.9
Dale Murphy	8	1986	ATL	-32.3
Brad Hawpe	9	2008	COL	-25.8

At a career level, things become different. Biases will keep batted ball data from coalescing to similar conclusions over large sample sizes, so we know that increases in sample size will not necessarily improve our understanding. Metrics that eschew batted ball data don't have that same concern. Consider, for instance, Derek Jeter. In his career he's played behind 181 different pitchers, in dozens of different parks, and alongside 51 different third basemen and 35 different second basemen. The only constant throughout his career is Derek Jeter—and while Derek Jeter the hitter may have the ability to control where his grounders go, Derek Jeter the fielder certainly does not.

Derek Jeter is one of the most controversial players when it comes to fielding analysis. He's well regarded by many for his fielding prowess at shortstop, having won five Gold Gloves in his career, but practically every accounting method of fielding prowess based on the numbers disdains his glove. If you consider balls that Jeter gets to, he seems to be roughly equal to his peers—his career fielding percentage is .976, just a tick above the league average of .971 through his career to date. That means that in Jeter's 9,710 fielding chances, he's made 41.5 fewer errors than the average shortstop in the same number of chances, or 2.4 fewer errors per year. However, there is little differentiation among shortstops in terms of fielding percentage—the standard deviation of fielding percentage is only .008, so 68 percent of shortstops have a fielding percentage between .963 and .979 over that time span. Flashy plays are more likely to stick with voters and fans than an extra error here or there.

The key to evaluating Jeter's fielding isn't what he does with balls he fields, but counting how many balls he gets to in the first place. Looking at traditional fielding chances (putouts plus assists plus errors), Jeter has .47 chances per inning played; the average shortstop over that time has .51 chances per inning played. That's almost 1,000 fewer chances over his career, or 59 fewer chances per season. Derek Jeter's skill at avoiding errors is fundamentally a skill at avoiding baseballs.

Why don't we notice this shortage of fielding chances? Because we aren't watching Jeter (or any shortstop) early enough. We start off watching the pitcher, then the batter, and then finally we watch the fielder. But before we finally turn our attention to the shortstop, he's already positioned himself, read the ball coming off the bat, and started moving to where he thinks the ball is going to be. All of that is a vital element of fielding, and all of it happens while we're watching someone else. Once we have finally turned our attention to where the fielder is, a ball to which he has reacted poorly during those crucial first few seconds will seem as if it had been out of his range all along.

Defensive metrics may disagree on how many of those missed chances are due to Jeter and how many are due to his circumstances, but all agree that Jeter deserves at least some blame for how few balls he gets to, rather than assuming that he was truly an above-average defender who somehow repelled batted balls like a magnet of the opposite polarity.

The utility of batted ball data, over thousands of balls in play over the course of a career, is greatly diminished. Given a large sample, we expect the range of expected outs for different players at the same position to diminish substantially. There is still some variance in chances even over the course of a career, but the contributing factors (playing behind a ground-ball or a fly-ball pitching staff, or playing in a park that benefits fielders) can often be deduced from play-by-play records without use of batted ball data.

Having metrics that work well for careers but less for individual seasons is an unsatisfactory solution, but it's preferable to having metrics that work well for neither. There is hope that measurements such as HITf/x will allow us to refine our metrics to do better in analyzing single seasons. Waiting upon commercial data providers of any stripe to solve our analysis problems for us means turning away from the spirit of inquiry that defines sabermetrics. As a Russian proverb tells us, we pray, but we also keep rowing toward the shore.

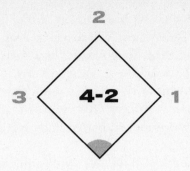

How Do We Value
Hitting vs. Fielding?

DAN TURKENKOPF

*Defense to me is the key to playing baseball. I know people
say, "Well, you've got to score runs," but you've got to stop
them before you can score runs.*
—Willie Mays

As Ralph Kiner is reputed to have said, home run hitters drive Cadillacs. One-dimensional sluggers like Ryan Howard get big bucks, while defensive stalwarts like Adam Everett toil in relative obscurity. In a good year, a Howard will put a lot of runs on the scoreboard with his bat while preventing few from scoring on defense, or even costing his team runs; glove men like Everett prevent runs from appearing on the scoreboard when in the field while creating relatively few when at bat. Baseball has clearly delineated how it values each kind of player by their vastly divergent levels of compensation and job security, but is it correct? What is the relative value of offense and defense, and how does it affect team building?

Pretend you're the general manager of a team that finished last season with a .500 record. What's more, your team scored exactly as many runs as it allowed, 700 in both cases. Your third baseman, Aaron Average, has decided to retire and you need to find a replacement for his precisely average performance.

To replace him, you've got your choice of two players: Bobby Bats and George Gloves. Either one will cost you $5 million. Bobby Bats will contribute 20 more runs offensively than Aaron Average, and will match him defensively. George Gloves will save 20 runs more than Aaron Average would have on defense, while contributing identical value with the bat. Which player should you select?

The easiest way to answer this question is to use baseball's version of the Pythagorean theorem. Originally developed by Bill James, it uses runs scored and runs allowed to estimate a team's winning percentage. There have been some improvements since the formula's creation that improve its accuracy, but for simplicity's sake, we'll use James's original:

$$Win\% = RS^2 / (RS^2 + RA^2)$$

Based on the Pythagorean theorem, your team last season had an expected winning percentage of .500. It's funny how contrived examples work out, isn't it? Now let's look at the team's expected winning percentage next season under each scenario.

Bobby Bats:

$$Win\% = 720^2 / (720^2 + 700^2) = .5141$$

George Gloves:

$$Win\% = 700^2 / (700^2 + 680^2) = .5145$$

Adding George Gloves to your team increases your expected winning percentage just a little bit more than adding Bobby Bats does. For a balanced team, each run saved is slightly more valuable than each run added.

What about teams that aren't as balanced? For a offensive juggernaut that scored 900 runs and allowed 700, saving 20 additional runs is worth almost half a win more than scoring 20. A similarly effective defensive team might have scored 700 runs and allowed 550. Saving 20 runs is even more valuable in this case; the difference is about 0.7 wins. It's the other way around for losing teams: most losing teams will do better adding 20 runs scored than reducing their runs allowed by 20 runs. As Table 4-2.1 shows, for good teams, reducing your overall runs allowed means it's less likely for the opponents to sneak out a win on those days when your offense doesn't play up to its abilities.

TABLE 4-2.1 Win Difference between Scoring 20 More Runs and Giving Up 20 More Runs for Various Teams

Runs Scored	Runs Allowed	Pythag. Record	Win Delta ± 20 runs
900	700	101–61	0.52
850	750	91–71	0.30
800	800	81–81	0.05
750	850	71–91	-0.20
700	900	61–101	-0.44
800	750	86–76	0.19
800	700	91–71	0.34
800	650	98–64	0.50

For bad teams, it's the other way around: you want more runs to take advantage of the days when your pitching somehow manages to shut down the opponent.

The Uncertainty of Fielding Stats

We've got the math, and we've got the logical explanation. Have we uncovered a fundamental principle for team building? Yes and no. The Pythagorean theorem is just an estimate of how many games a team will win based on their runs scored and runs allowed. On average, a team's actual won-loss record is about four wins away from that predicted by the Pythagorean theorem, so the magnitude of difference we're seeing based on switching runs added and saved is small enough to be swamped by the noise in our metric of choice. There is some benefit to tailoring your approach based on your overall team quality, but it's far from clear that it makes sense to base your entire strategy around it.

A far more useful plan is "Get better any way you can." Score one for the obvious. How do we go from that flash of brilliance to actually deciding which players to acquire? The best approach is to look at total value by combining hitting, base running, and fielding. In other words, what we should be looking at is an overall value metric like WARP (wins above replacement player).

The traditional approach to figuring a position player's value is to tally up how he compares to average in batting, running, and fielding, add those numbers together, adjust for position and playing time, and voilà! This process is not perfectly accurate, because it assumes all runs are created equal, but it's a useful starting point for discussion.

A measure like WARP assumes we have equal certainty about each part of a player's game, but that's definitely not the case. Looking at the two biggest areas of impact for a position player, hitting and fielding, we see a big difference in ability to accurately measure value. Hitting measures are driven by objective facts, while fielding tends to rely on estimates on top of estimates. The uncertainty in measuring fielding is compounded how few plays a season there are for a given player to demonstrate his ability. According to Baseball Prospectus's fielding runs above average (FRAA), the fielder who made the most plays above average in 2010, Reds outfielder Jay Bruce, converted 62 more chances than that average player. While 62 plays represents a fairly staggering fielding performance, it is also only one play every 24 innings or so. In 2011, the leader was Braves second baseman Omar Infante, who converted 58 more plays than the average player, equivalent to one extra play every 22 innings. Those added plays, although infrequent, are quite meaningful. Making an extra play in the infield is approximately equivalent to hitting a double at the plate.

Since the most prolific defender only makes two extra plays in five games, and the large majority of players are within eight plays of average over the whole season, it takes time to get enough of a sample to judge a player's ability. The rule of thumb is that two to three years of fielding data is as reliable as one season of hitting data. Of course, by the time you get enough information to make an educated guess at the player's defensive talent, he's gotten older and your conclusion no longer applies.

Despite WARP treating both hitting and fielding as equally reliable components, the more a rating is influenced by its fielding component, the more skeptical we should be. It's much more likely to be the product of uncertain data, or the influences of a small sample. Batting value is much more consistent from year to year. Looking at the top ten batters in 2010 and 2011, we find four players appearing in both seasons—Miguel Cabrera, Joey Votto, Jose Bautista, and Albert Pujols. On the

TABLE 4.2-2 Top 10 Fielding Players in 2010

Player	FRAA
Jay Bruce	23
Alexei Ramirez	21
Jose Lopez	20
Alex Gonzalez	16
Adrian Beltre	16
Albert Pujols	14
Mark Teixeira	14
Nelson Cruz	14
Cliff Pennington	13
Josh Wilson	12

TABLE 4.2-3 Top 10 Fielding Players in 2011

Player	FRAA
Omar Infante	22
Jack Hannahan	17
Gerardo Parra	16
Alberto Callaspo	15
Joey Votto	14
Brett Gardner	14
Albert Pujols	14
Brendan Ryan	13
Placido Polanco	12
Todd Helton	12

fielding side, the same comparison finds only one player, Pujols (see Tables 4-2.2 and 4-2.3).

WARP also treats runs scored and runs allowed as equivalent, which makes sense on the league level when you're comparing players. In terms of judging whether a player is a good addition for a team, it's less useful. As we learned earlier, teams at different levels of competitiveness have different requirements for putting games in the "W" column. For good teams, it's more important to keep runs off the board than to put them there yourself. For bad teams, adding offense should be imperative.

It's Money That Matters

As you can see, it's difficult just to get started. Begin with WARP. Adjust for the uncertainty around fielding. Look at your team's runs scored and runs allowed, and pick the appropriate player. Alas, it's not that simple, particularly when we bring these ideas into the real world. As outside observers we can measure a player's value without looking at his salary, but a general manager doesn't have that luxury. Money has to play a part in the evaluation.

In classical microeconomics, there are two qualities that drive the price of any good: supply and demand. The good is priced at the point where the supply curve and demand curve intersect. Similar (though not perfectly analogous) forces are at play in the baseball talent market. List all the good-field, no-hit backup infielders you can think of. Now do the same for the bats off the bench. It's a lot easier to name the good gloves, isn't it? That's because hitting talent is more scarce than fielding talent. Just about anyone who can hit major league pitching above a certain level can find a spot on a roster, regardless of whether he's the second coming of Dr. Strangeglove in the field, but there are a lot more players who can field at a major league level. Most don't get a chance because they can't hit well enough to earn a spot.

This spread of talent informs our choice of replacement level. We tend to assume the replacement level player is league average with the glove, and some number of runs (around −20, generally) below average with the bat. The scarcity of offensive talent makes it more economically valuable than fielding talent (see Table 4-2.4). The fact that there is some justification for paying more for offense than for defense doesn't mean that teams are necessarily doing a great job at it. Over the past five years or so, we've seen a fair number of players with flashy offensive numbers get contracts that seem like tremendous

TABLE 4-2.4 The Many Ways Center Fielders Can Achieve around 3.0 WARP: 2000–2011

Player	Year	Batting	Fielding	WARP
Ken Griffey	2005	29.9	-15.4	3.1
Torii Hunter	2002	18.9	-11.3	3.2
Marlon Byrd	2010	10.2	6.2	3.3
Mark Kotsay	2003	-3.3	13.5	3.2
Willy Taveras	2006	-16.7	19.2	2.8

TABLE 4-2.5 Ryan Howard vs. Gaby Sanchez, 2011

	AVG	OBP	SLG	TAv	HR	BRR	FRAA	WARP
Howard	.253	.346	.488	.295	33	-9.4	0.7	2.1
Sanchez	.266	.352	.427	.278	19	-2.8	4.3	2.1

overpays. Players like Ryan Howard (5 years/$125 million) and Carlos Lee (6 years/$100 million) have received large contracts despite contributing nowhere but the plate (see Table 4-2.5).

Recently, however, this overvaluation of offense has seen a correction. As teams have gotten better at measuring defense and recognizing its effect on pitchers, they've put more of an emphasis on signing players who can contribute in the field as well as with the bat. This renewed focus on defense is evident from the difficulty iron-gloved players like Pat Burrell and Jason Giambi had finding deals in the winter of 2008–2009. Despite coming off seasons where they were each worth three-plus wins with the bat, both had to wait until January to sign, and received less than might have been expected from their performances. In the past, general managers might have overlooked their negative performance in the field, but the sluggers were paid according to their overall value, and not just their value at the plate.

Leveraging Awareness of Defense

As the cost of defensive skill appears to be rising, is there an opportunity for teams to be creative with their rosters and perhaps uncover a new competitive advantage? Let's look at the 2011 Tampa Bay Rays. Joe Maddon's team began with an overstocked outfield, with Sam Fuld and Johnny Damon in left, B.J. Upton in center, and Matt Joyce in right, with second baseman Ben Zobrist taking over for the latter against left-handed pitching. Waiting in the wings was top prospect

Desmond Jennings, who opened the campaign in the minors due to some combination of needing more seasoning and the Rays wanting to keep his arbitration clock from running.

The middle infield was as shallowly staffed as the outfield was deep. Shortstop was a particular problem. Incumbent Reid Brignac slumped badly in April and never recovered. The club fell back on two journeymen, Sean Rodriguez and Elliot Johnson, neither of whom added much at the plate, with the result that on the season Rays' shortstops combined to hit an execrable .193/.256/.282, over nine runs below replacement level.

Center fielder Upton had been sent to the outfield in 2007 after failing in trials at shortstop and third base by fielding .901 and .908, respectively. What if the Rays had tried to solve their shortstop problem by moving Upton back to the infield, hoping his bat would make up for his miserable defense?

In 2011, Upton was 32 runs above average offensively and two runs above average in center field. He earned a two-run adjustment for playing center field and 17 runs simply by showing up.

Let's assume our hypothetical Upton would have delivered the same offensive performance in the same amount of playing time. Moving to shortstop would have given him an additional five runs of positional value; he would deliver at least the same amount of value as he had in center field if he were better than a –3 fielder at shortstop.

That's not the entire calculation. If Upton had moved to shortstop, the Rays would essentially have been be trading Brignac, Johnson, and Rodriguez for Jennings. Jennings was on pace for a four-plus win season in 2011, while Brignac, Johnson, and Rodriguez combined for only 0.8 wins. Making that move on Opening Day would likely have gained the Rays at least two wins, meaning they wouldn't have needed Dan Johnson's heroics in game 162 to clinch a playoff berth. And if Upton was as bad or worse at shortstop as he used to be? (After all, there is no reason to believe that he learned to play the infield while watching from the outfield.) The Rays would still end up on the positive side of this move as long as he was no worse than about 25 runs below average at shortstop, or the worst in the league by about five runs or so.

For a more outlandish example, what if the Red Sox decided to move Manny Ramirez to shortstop in 2007 to get Jacoby Ellsbury more playing time? After all, Julio Lugo was no great shakes, racking up only 0.4 WARP. Ramirez had a down year by his standards, but still contributed over three wins with the bat. A straight prorating of Ellsbury's .353/.394/.509 season would give him over six wins; let's dial that back to three for realism. Replacing Lugo with Ellsbury would have been worth roughly 2.5 wins to the Red Sox in 2007. How bad could Manny be at shortstop before the move cost the team?

Moving from left field to shortstop would have added about 12 runs to his value, which means he would have been just as valuable overall as a –24 fielder at shortstop. It's fair to say he would have been substantially worse than a –24 shortstop (Derek Jeter has been in that range, pardon the pun, more than once, and Manny would probably have made him look like Ozzie Smith out there), but he still would have had a long way to fall before the move failed to pay off for the Sox. He would have had to be very bad, about a minus-50-run fielder, before Boston lost out on the deal. It's entirely possible he'd have been that bad there, too, but it would have been fun to see him try.

Moving players on paper is fun, but in the real world these shifts would likely have further consequences, including demoralization of a player who daily embarrassed himself on defense and a rebellion by the pitching staff. Thought experiments like these are mainly useful to illustrate the relative value of offense and defense at player level. Value metrics like WARP compare a player to the average player in each of the areas of the game. But average isn't the only number we're interested in. The spread of talent is extremely important to properly valuing a skill.

For 2011, hitting value, as measured by batting runs above average, ranged from Jose Bautista at 73 runs above average, to Alex Rios who was worth 24 runs fewer than average—a nearly 100-run difference. Fielding, on the other hand, was led by Omar Infante at 22 runs above average, while Asdrubal Cabrera brought up the rear, 19 runs worse than the average player—a range of only 40 runs. Infante's plus-22 with the glove, had he achieved it with the bat instead, would have left him as the 42nd-best hitter in the game, ranking between Ryan Howard and Casey Kotchman. Clearly there is a lot more distance between the best hitter and the average hitter than between the best fielder and the average fielder.

If you had a choice between the 10th-best hitter in the game (Joey Votto at 44 runs) and the 10th-best fielder in the game (Todd Helton at 12 runs), all else being equal, you'd be basically three wins better off by focusing on the offense. And in many cases, you might be able to extract more overall value by putting your batting star at a position he might be less than suited for if it enabled you to replace a weak link with a strong one. The goal isn't to maximize the value of any one player, but to maximize the value of the team, which is easier to do by overweighting offense.

Our Upton and Ramirez hypotheticals are intentionally outlandish, but their purpose suggests the same truth implied by Derek Jeter's actual career: given a choice of players, the distribution of defense opportunities is such that there is far more to be gained by playing an above-average hitter/subpar defender, even at a premium defensive position such as shortstop, than there is in sacrificing offense for defense with an above-average defender/subpar hitter. If an unrealistically poor defender like Ramirez works on paper, a real-world player who is merely below average is going to have a relatively small impact—a player who is plus-20 runs on offense and minus-10 on defense is still going to contribute more overall than a player who is plus-10 runs on defense and minus-five on offense.

At the end of the day, general managers are looking for how best to improve their teams while staying within their budget. While there can be some advantage in focusing on runs saved for good teams (and on runs scored for bad ones), overall value is a much more important criterion for evaluating a player. At most, trading off offense and defense should be a secondary factor in a decision. With the current state of affairs, we're much more confident in our ability to measure a player's value at the plate than with the glove. Because of that added confidence, and because it's harder to find a good hitter, teams put a premium on offensive talent. Of course, whether a team can find a good deal on a defensive player or on an offensive player depends on market forces more than anything else. Based on which players are available, and which way the market is trending, offense might cost more than defense, or vice versa. The key for the GM is to recognize both the value of fielding and its associated uncertainty, and price accordingly.

PART 5
Questions of Offense

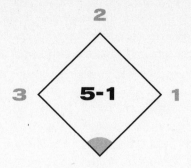

How Did Jose Bautista Become a Star?

COLIN WYERS

It is almost redundant to say that when Jose Bautista first arrived in Toronto as a journeyman utility player, not much was expected of him. This is because "journeyman utility player" is a description that largely negates the possibility of hope and also of disappointment. Indeed, "disappointment" couldn't accurately be applied to the then 27-year-old because it had been years since anyone had any expectations of him at all.

Bautista had been a promising prospect as an amateur, something disguised by his being drafted by the Pittsburgh Pirates in the 20th round of the 2000 draft, a place you're far more likely to find roster filler than a major league star—Bautista fell that far on signability questions and would have rated a pick somewhere in the first three rounds of the 2001 draft had the Pirates not inked him as a draft-and-follow signee. He never made any of *Baseball America*'s top prospect lists, though that publication did rate him the seventh-best player in the Pirates organization after a strong A-ball season in the Sally League. For a long, long while, that ranking would serve as the apex of his professional career.

The club that initially drafted him, the Pittsburgh Pirates, let him go unprotected in the 2003 Rule 5 draft, perhaps because it had become disenchanted with Bautista after a temper tantrum involving a trash can cost him 10 weeks on the disabled list with a broken hand. The Baltimore Orioles bit, starting the young infielder on a bizarre odyssey through five organizations in a single season.

Because Rule 5 picks must spend their entire season in the major leagues, they are a burden to teams that must sacrifice a roster spot to a player who is usually unprepared to play in the majors. When an injury crunch comes, they are usually the first players sacrificed. Bautista was no exception. When the Orioles could no longer maintain a space for a seldom-used rookie, Bautista was placed on waivers and claimed by the Tampa Bay Devil Rays. That same month, after just 12 games and 15 plate appearances, they sold his rights to the Kansas City Royals, who gave him a quick look and traded him to the New York Mets. The Mets held him for a good 10 seconds before he ended up flipped back to the Pirates again.

Given that sequence, it was more likely that Bautista would have been out of baseball entirely in 2010 than arrive as a candidate for an MVP award. Between the broken hand and the roster shuffle, he had played little in two seasons. The Pirates would require him to spend most of a third year in the minors reestablishing that he could play. When he finally did reach the majors for good as a 25-year-old in 2006, the results were unimpressive. Bautista hit only .241/.329/.403 in 400 games with the Bucs. When the Pirates dealt him to the Blue Jays during the 2008 season in return for a very paltry player to be named later (catcher Robinson Diaz), Bautista knew he was almost out of opportunities. "I knew it was probably going to be my last chance to be a starter on a team," Bautista told the *Toronto Star* in the midst of his 2011 season . "I was reaching the age of 30. My time was running out to prove that I was a capable starter. If I didn't prove that, then I was going to fall into a backup, utility role. And that was something I definitely did not want to happen."

At first, Bautista didn't find any more success in Toronto than he had anywhere else. From August of 2008 through the end of the 2009 season, he put up a .261 true average (TAv), just a hair's breadth above league average. All told, Bautista had racked up over 2,000 plate appearances as a below-average hitter in his career so far, posting a true average of .251 on overall rates of .238/.329/.400 with a home run every 30 at-bats.

Bautista's 2010 season hit like a lightning strike. He hit 54 home runs, five shy of his career total to date. His walk rate increased nearly 20 percent. According to batting runs above average (BRAA), Bautista was the third-most valuable hitter in all of baseball that year.

TABLE 5-1.1 Most Improved Players, 1950–2011

Year	Name	Age	PA Prior	TAv Prior	PA	TAv	Improve
2010	Jose Bautista	29	2038	.251	683	.339	59.8
2001	Bret Boone	32	4344	.249	690	.332	57.6
1982	Robin Yount	26	4553	.260	704	.338	55.5
1970	Tommy Harper	29	3541	.258	692	.325	46.4
2001	Rich Aurilia	29	2125	.254	689	.315	42.0
1991	Terry Pendleton	30	3744	.244	644	.305	39.1
1975	Toby Harrah	26	2006	.257	631	.315	37.0
1997	J. T. Snow	29	2003	.255	637	.310	34.7
1980	Robin Yount	24	3495	.250	647	.303	34.4
1969	Don Kessinger	26	2261	.221	737	.267	34.2

For his 2011 encore, Bautista got better by almost any measure you might care to use. His home runs dropped off from 54 to 43, but that was more than offset by a massive boost to both his batting average and his walk rate that led to a stunning .447 on-base percentage. In those two seasons, Bautista was one of baseball's elite hitters, generating 128 batting runs above average—only Miguel Cabrera did more, with a BRAA of 131.

Bautista's 2010 season was unprecedented. A simple way to look at seasons where a player dramatically improved is to look at the change in TAv, multiplied by plate appearances (PA) to ensure that players who show a dramatic improvement over a full season are weighted more heavily than a player who does it in part-time duty. In this case, we're looking at a player's performance in all prior seasons compared to his performance in that season to figure our "improve" score. For non-pitchers with at least 2,000 plate appearances and a career TAv below average, Table 5-1.1 lists the top 10 since 1950. Bautista showed the largest improvement of anybody who meets these qualifications. Looking at the other nine seasons, in all but one case this season represents the best season of that player's career. Robin Yount manages to avoid that by appearing on this list twice, but even so, these represent the best two seasons of his career. Sometimes this represents the best season in a pretty good career—this is much more likely if you're a shortstop or a second baseman. Sometimes this represents the best season in a career that's mediocre at best—this is much more likely if you're a first baseman or a corner outfielder.

Both kinds of players tended to regress after their "banner" year. Taken as a group, there were 77 players who met our criteria, posted an "improve" score of at least 20, and played in at least one more sea-son after their banner year. In their banner year, these hitters had a TAv .045 better than their career-to-date numbers. Looking at per-formance before the banner year compared to the season after the banner year, those same hitters only have a TAv boost of about .017. While they continue to be better than what they were, as a group they fall well short of the improvement they had shown before.

In fact, only seven players showed a greater improvement the sec-ond year than they had the first. Table 5-1.2 shows the change from prior TAv to the first and second year. Once we round out to three dec-imal places, two of these players show no meaningful increase what-soever. The closest anyone comes to Bautista in terms of the magnitude of the year two increase is the juiced Ken Caminiti, and he is still dwarfed by the magnitude of Bautista's evolution. Bautista's leap stands out even among those great sluggers whose performances have been suspected of being generated by performance-enhancing drugs (PEDs)—Barry Bonds, Sammy Sosa, and Mark McGwire—but it is his 2011 topper that ranks, not his 2010 breakthrough (see Table 5-1.3). Jose Bautista's emergence as an elite hitter is essentially with-out precedent in modern baseball history; nobody else has made the same transition he has made. So how did he do it? The explanation is simple enough if you believe Blue Jays hitting coach Dwayne Murphy:

> The change in Jose Bautista from a free-swinging easy out into the leading home run hitter in the major leagues began in the middle of last season, in the weight room at Rogers Centre in Toronto. But not in the way you might think.
>
> One day last summer, Dwayne Murphy, the Blue Jays' hitting coach, said he approached Bautista and brought him over to a mirror. There, Murphy demonstrated Bautista's swing, so long and looping that pitchers routinely overpowered him with fastballs on the inner half of the plate. Murphy told Bautista his swing needed to be shorter and more direct. Bautista took that to heart, and started working on it that day.
>
> "He's always had power," Murphy said Saturday morning in the hallway outside the Jays' clubhouse at Target Field. "He just needed a couple of tweaks."

If the changes in process were mere tweaks, the changes to his out-put certainly were not. Bautista isn't the first player to have made changes to his swing—tweaking a swing or working on a hitch is as

TABLE 5-1.2 Players with Greatest Improvement after Banner Year

Name	Year	Improve 1	Improve 2
Jose Bautista	2010	.088	.122
Ken Caminiti	1995	.051	.090
Roberto Clemente	1960	.046	.078
Alan Trammell	1983	.048	.051
Mark McLemore	2001	.042	.042
Larry Herndon	1982	.031	.042
Ken McMullen	1968	.036	.036

TABLE 5-1.3 Bautista among the Chemistry Sets

Year	Name	Age	PA Prior	TAv Prior	PA	TAv	Improve
2001	Barry Bonds	36	9141	.335	664	.429	62.6
2001	Sammy Sosa	32	6513	.285	711	.380	67.6
1998	Mark McGwire	34	5633	.326	681	.379	35.9
2011	Jose Bautista	30	2721	.273	655	.373	65.7

shopworn a spring training cliché for batters as adding a new breaking ball is for pitchers or weight loss is for pretty much everyone.

Of course, not everyone is content to believe Murphy. Many have cast aspersions upon Bautista's change. Note the veiled retort in the excerpt quoted above—unsubstantiated whispers of chemical enhancement have followed Bautista, without any evidence, since his hitting binge passed the point where it could no longer be written off as a hot streak. For example, *Toronto Star* columnist Damian Cox insisted in August 2010 that "you've got to at least ask the question when it comes to Jose Bautista" about performance-enhancing drugs. This is to be expected in a world conditioned by Bonds, McGwire, and the rest, but it doesn't follow that because some unexpected accomplishments were tainted, they all are.

Indeed, though Cox dismissed as "too funny" assertions that steroids can't help a baseball player hit home runs, "help" is a vague term that does not convey the complexity of baseball in the steroids period. As we pointed out in the first chapter of this book, much of what is thought of as the effect of steroids on home runs was due to environmental factors, such as changes in ballparks and the ball.

(That should not be construed as an apologia; it's just the truth.) Doping was part of the story, but cannot serve as the whole explanation for any player's hitting, particularly a change as dramatic as Bautista's. Nor can we cite those same environmental factors in Bautista's rise, as offense, as measured in runs and home runs, has dropped off across the league rather than risen. Bautista has been sailing into the wind.

It is worth reemphasizing just how far outside of any previous PED narrative Bautista's development has been. If you look at the careers of the most notable home run hitters of the steroid era prior to when they were alleged to start enhancing chemically, they were still exceptional hitters. Even if you believe that steroids alone are enough to turn the Barry Bonds of 1993 into the Barry Bonds of 2001, the Jose Bautista of old was nothing close to a Bonds-caliber hitter. To borrow from fiction, perhaps drugs can turn Dr. Jekyll into Mr. Hyde, but Bautista began further down—his drugs would have had to act in unprecedented fashion, turning an eggplant into Dr. Jekyll into Mr. Hyde.

If not chemical enhancement, is it possible that Bautista received some old-fashioned help? In August 2011, Amy K. Nelson of ESPN reported Bautista being heckled by White Sox relievers over what they thought was assistance in stealing signs:

"Not too easy, is it?"

From the visitors bullpen at Rogers Centre in Toronto, an American League pitcher screamed at Blue Jays right fielder Jose Bautista as he took his position late in a game in the spring of 2010.

"It's not too [f———] easy to hit home runs when you don't know what's coming!"

The enraged player and his teammates could hardly believe what they had seen in the previous inning. As they sat on the perch above the right-field bullpen at Rogers, they caught sight of a man dressed in white about 25 yards to their right, out among the blue center-field seats. And while the players watched, the man in white seemingly signaled the pitches the visiting pitcher was throwing against the Jays, according to four sources in the bullpen that day.

The players weren't exactly sure how the man in white knew what was coming—maybe, they thought, he was receiving messages via his Bluetooth from an ally elsewhere in the stadium who had binoculars or access to the stadium feed. But they quickly picked up the wavelength of his transmissions: He was raising his arms over his head for curveballs, sliders and changeups. In other words, anything besides fastballs.

When Bautista next came up to bat, he struck out. After the inning, he ran to right field, adjacent to the visitors 'pen, and the livid player issued Bautista a warning.

"We know what you're doing," he said, referring to the man in white, according to the player and two witnesses. "If you do it again, I'm going to hit you in the [f——] head."

Our own research into park factors at Baseball Prospectus corroborates the pitcher's allegations. Instead of using park factors that compare runs scored by the team at home and on the road, we compare each player's production at home to his production at every other park in the league. This allows for much more granular comparisons than would otherwise be possible with traditional park factors. When you split the Blue Jays' home run park factor between the home team batting and the visiting team batting, you see the third-largest gap since 1950. Rogers Centre played as a home-run haven for Jays batters but essentially even for their opponents.

Thus there is some cause for suspicion, but even rampant sign-stealing does not account for Jose Bautista becoming Jose Bautista. Presumably, any assistance the man in white was giving Bautista was being dispensed to the other Blue Jays hitters as well, and none of them experienced the sort of radical change Bautista did. And while Bautista has better home stats than road stats, that can be said of most batters (only ones who play their home games in pitcher-friendly parks tend to do otherwise over a reasonable sample). Even if we throw out his home stats altogether, his road stats are impressive enough to tell us that his improvement was not simply a product of his park.

And so we are stymied. No one else has come by this sort of improvement honestly, but no one has come by it by cheating, either. If Bautista's improvement came from a prescription pad, it's a prescription pad to which only he has access. He's about as singular a story as any in baseball's history. We can either accept Dwayne Murphy's account or disbelieve it, but neither course gives us a satisfactory answer. Every spring training brings countless stories about hitters who have shortened their swings, but none have had even half as much to show for their efforts as Bautista has.

In studying the question of Jose Bautista, we quickly come to a branching set of two possibilities:

1. We accept that some phenomena lack simple or convincing explanations or
2. We believe that Jose Bautista simply does not exist.

Since we can't conclude the second possibility, we must conclude the first. That isn't to say that someday we won't understand what Bautista has done, but we certainly don't now.

If sabermetrics is sadly silent on the subject of Jose Bautista, it doesn't mean that Bautista has nothing to tell us about sabermetrics. There are two lessons we can learn from his story if we're willing to be as scrupulous in discussing the craft of studying baseball as we are in discussing the people who play it.

First, we can remember to keep ourselves from becoming fixated on outliers when it comes to predicting future performance. Prior to the 2011 season, ESPN analyst (and Baseball Prospectus alumnus) Keith Law was asked about Bautista's $65 million, five-year contract extension. Was it a good deal for Toronto? Law replied:

> No. Of course not. You have a player with an extremely spotty track record of performance and playing time who has one wildly outlying breakout year. You do not rush to give this guy a five-year contract . . . I mean, it's not like Jose Bautista is 24 or 25 and just kind of emerged as a hitter. He's way past that point. The history of those guys is very poor. He's extremely unlikely to maintain that level of production.

Bautista's 2011 season would seem to have proved Law wrong, but in fact his reasoning was on solid ground given what could have been reasonably known at the time—no one before in the rather extensive and well-documented history of the game had done what we now know Bautista to have accomplished. "Extremely unlikely" is actually a very good way to describe what Bautista did in 2011. In the long run, you end up doing much better as a prognosticator if you don't predict things that are extremely unlikely and do predict things that are extremely likely.

Of course, things that happen rarely do happen sometimes. And in baseball, a lot of things happen, period—there have been over a hundred seasons just in the modern era, with hundreds of players playing every year. While any one rare event is, by definition, unusual, it is actually common for *some* rare events to occur. Predicting which one it will be is nearly impossible, even if the event somehow seems stunningly obvious in hindsight. (That's usually because of "post-hoc rationalization," if you were wondering.)

If you had bet on Bautista to fall short of his 2010 performance, what you have is a false negative: you have failed to affirm a true hypothesis (that Bautista has substantially improved) in favor of the null hypothesis (that no such improvement has occurred).

Law (along with several other analysts) was excoriated by many for "missing" on Bautista. This is valid in a vacuum, but looking at the broader picture it ignores that any system that expected Bautista to do what he did in 2011 would have performed poorly for the vast majority of players who, after a significant improvement, fail to put up similarly improved numbers the following season. In exchange for getting rid of one false negative, you add many more false positives.

This doesn't always have to apply to just a hot season. It can apply equally well to a hitter who's gotten off to a hot start. If you look at how hitters perform in the month of April and compare it to the rest of the season, you find a margin of error of about .060. In other words, a hitter with a TAv of .260 in April would have a TAv between .195 and .314 a total of 68 percent of the time. Looking at just the prior season's stats, you see a margin of error of only .037, so for a player with a .260 TAv, their rest-of-season performance would be between .224 and .298 68 percent of the time.

Trying to pick who will have a good or bad batting season based upon April stats is a fool's errand when compared to just using last season's stats (much less a projection system that accounts for multiple seasons of performance). Yet, if you only remember the false negatives from a more sober analytical approach—being cautious, after all, means missing out on real improvement—then you're emboldened to do bad analysis that picks up many more false positives than it avoids false negatives.

The second thing we can learn, if we attend carefully, is the limit of our knowledge. As you may recall from the introduction, Fox's Ken Rosenthal has railed against what he viewed as "reflexive regurgitation" of stats in voting for postseason awards. Rosenthal is hardly alone in this; his colleague Jason Whitlock offered the following in the wake of the film adaptation of Michael Lewis's book *Moneyball*:

> There's a stat for nearly every action in baseball. Little is left to the imagination. Sports were never intended to be a computer program, stripped to cold, hard, indisputable, statistical facts. Sports—particularly for fans—are not science. Sports, like art, are supposed to be interpreted.
>
> It's difficult to interpret baseball these days. The stat geeks won't let you argue. They quote sabermetrics and end all discussion. Is so-and-so a Hall of Famer? The sabermeticians will punch in the numbers and give you, in their mind, a definitive answer.
>
> It's boring. It's ruining sports.

Sabermetrics may be ruining the ability of gasbags like Whitlock to proffer their arguments with no support but the volume of their own voices, but it's not ruining sports, and it certainly isn't capable of ending all discussion. What sabermetrics does is provide us with a common language for discussion, the language of runs and wins—the core of what baseball is about. It tells us how runs and wins relate to each other, and how everything else in baseball we can measure relates to those things.

More to the point, what sabermetrics does is ground us in reality. Everyone is entitled to their own opinion, but not their own evidence. Sabermetricians certainly argue amongst themselves over a great many things, but the arguments resemble the game of baseball itself: orderly, within a set structure and according to a series of rules. Arguments like the ones Whitlock champions are like a game of Calvinball; whoever wins is the person who can talk the loudest or insult their opponent with the most ferocity.

Reflexive regurgitation happens, not only with advanced metrics, but with the more traditional ones as well. It's far from a tenet of sabermetrics that it should be so. Sabermetrics has, from the beginning, been about the idea that things should be questioned, that nothing is sacred. That's how you get to the idea that a .260 hitter can be more valuable than a .300 hitter, or a guy with 110 RBI might not be as good as a guy with 80 RBI—by being willing to question what the raw numbers say, to investigate and not regurgitate what you're told by somebody else. If everyone believed in reflexive regurgitation, there wouldn't be any sabermetrics.

Sabermetrics cannot definitively answer the question of how Jose Bautista became Jose Bautista. This is a triumph, not a failure, of sabermetrics. Baseball before Bill James was filled with people who had definitive answers to a whole lot of questions that they didn't know the answers to. James's most important role was as the man who would challenge their answers and do his own digging. It would be a pity if his children, so to speak, were to become the kinds of people James tried to sweep away, the kinds of people they are in Rosenthal's and Whitlock's imaginations.

It would also be a pity if skepticism, however well founded, blinded us to the wonder of Bautista's blossoming; like the fans in the aftermath of the 1919 World Series, we are now conditioned to look for cheats, but just because corruption exists doesn't mean that all things are necessarily corrupted. In *Baseball Between the Numbers*, Nate Silver pointed out that unexplained changes in performance are the norm, not the exception. "Inexplicable changes in performance have always been relatively common and may be the result of anything from a new batting stance to LASIK eye surgery to a tippling player finding Jesus and cutting out his drinking and carousing." It might be that, barring evidence to the contrary, Bautista is the most extreme example of unexpected change in the history of baseball. As such, the lessons of Bautista and sabermetrics are one and the same: keep your eyes open and never lose your capacity to be surprised.

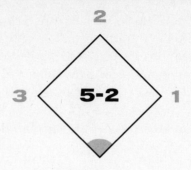

When Does a Hot Start Become Real?

DEREK CARTY

Not much was expected of the Arizona Diamondbacks heading into the 2007 season. Four years removed from their last playoff appearance and having won no more than 77 games in any of the previous three seasons, most prognosticators assumed the D'backs would finish middle of the pack in the NL West, only capable of claiming a top spot by default if the division proved to be as weak as some expected.

There was good reason for this sort of skepticism. The team had been mediocre for years, and had done little to improve itself in the offseason. Randy Johnson was the sole big-name acquisition, but he was 43 years old and coming off a 5.00 ERA season; as unique a talent as Johnson was, the record of outstanding seasons by elderly pitchers was (and is) short enough that there was little reason to expect a return to greatness. Arizona still had then-ace Brandon Webb, but the middle of their rotation was to be filled out with the additions of Doug Davis (off-season) and Livan Hernandez (August waiver deadline), not exactly an imposing duo. The final spot in the rotation was up for grabs among Enrique Gonzalez and Edgar Gonzalez; you're forgiven if you haven't heard of either.

On the offensive side, a changing of the guard was taking place. Four and a half (if you include Miguel Montero, who was to receive a good share of the starts at catcher) of the team's starting eight were either coming off of or entering their rookie seasons. The quintet of Montero, Conor Jackson, Stephen Drew, Chris Young, and Carlos Quentin had accumulated fewer than two seasons' worth of plate appearances (1,068) coming into the season, and if you exclude Jackson—who started for most of 2006 and accounts for 52 percent of that total—they had less than a season's worth of MLB experience between them. Yes, they were all top prospects at one time or another, but top prospects have a much higher failure rate than most realize. Expecting a team of baby-faced youngsters to play like playoff contenders was unreasonable, especially when you consider who the team completed this core with: 2006 holdovers Orlando Hudson, Chad Tracy, and Eric Byrnes—players faintly above average at best.

Despite the improbability of it all, the Diamondbacks roared out of the gate in 2007, winning seven of their first nine games and 10 of their first 16. By the end of the season, the Snakes had won 90 games and the NL West crown.

Even in the midst of this hot start—hot season, really—there was skepticism about Arizona's ability to maintain its pace since contributions were coming from unlikely sources. Byrnes ended up as the offensive leader with a career-best 3.7 WARP. Rookie Micah Owings joined the rotation after the first week of the season, posting his own career-best (to date) 2.2 WARP. B-level prospect Mark Reynolds came off the bus from Triple-A slugging when Tracy got injured. Catcher Chris Snyder pushed Montero aside and compiled a career-best 1.4 WARP.

Conversely, players who were expected to contribute did not. Rookie Montero's share of the catching diminished after July, when he was hitting just .236/.302/.376. Johnson was lost for the season after just 10 starts. Quentin spent much of the year on the disabled list. Youngsters Jackson (1.3 WARP), Young (1.1), and Drew (1.0) played well enough, but underperformed the unrealistically high expectations that accompanied their status as topic prospects. Additionally, the D'backs outperformed their Pythagorean expectation by a substantial 11 wins. Some of this was good managing, including excellent leveraging of the bullpen, but perhaps more was simply the good luck that sometimes elevates average ballclubs into good ones for no discernible reason. God may not play dice with the universe, but he is not above skewing the results of a baseball season.

Still, the fact remains that the D'backs had an excellent 2007 season, slowing down for just a moment in July en route to their first playoff appearance since 2002. At what point was skepticism no longer justified? Sure, a .700 winning percentage after a team's first 10 games is great, but is that enough to say that they're for real? If not, how many games is enough? Do we have to wait until months of games are played before we can really say that a team is legitimate?

Several years ago, former Baseball Prospectus co-founder and writer Rany Jazayerli studied this very topic at our website and in the book *It Ain't Over 'Til It's Over*. Since Jazayerli has done a fine job of it already, I'm not going to cover ground that's already been trodden, instead approaching the topic from a different angle. We will return to Jazayerli's results shortly.

"Real" can be an amorphous concept, especially to those using heavy pharmaceuticals, so we should define what we mean. A team's record is real when its year-to-date performance becomes more predictive of its end-of-season record than simply assuming the team will finish with a .500 record. After one game, of course, a team's year-to-date record isn't going to be a very good predictor of how they will finish the season. Anything can happen in a single game, so after the first game of the year, we're going to be much better off simply assuming that the team will finish 81–81 than trying to pass judgment based on a single victory or defeat. After 161 games, however, we're going to be able to predict a team's final record very well, since there is just one more game left to be played. What we need to do is find the place somewhere in between one game and 161 games that will predict a team's end-of-season record better than a random guess will—the point at which a team's performance becomes "real," and we can trust what it is we are seeing.

To determine how long it takes for a hot start to become "real," I'm going to use a statistical technique known as the "Pearson correlation." The purpose of a correlation is to measure how well two things (termed "variables") predict each other, with a result (termed "R") of 0 meaning they don't predict each other at all and a result of 1 meaning they predict each other perfectly. The higher the number, the stronger the relationship.

Famed baseball analyst Bill James once commented on a phenomenon he dubbed the "whirlpool principle," wherein "all teams are drawn forcefully toward the center. Most of the teams which had winning records in [2010] will decline in [2011]; most of the teams which had losing records in [2010] will improve in [2011]." Today, we call this concept "regression to the mean," which sounds intimidating at first but actually mirrors the whirlpool principle perfectly, even in name, when you work through the words. A team regresses to (or gets drawn toward) the mean (the center of the whirlpool, which is the same thing as league average—always a .500 record). When using regression to the mean to project future performance, we are always going to use some percentage of the team's actual performance (our expectation that it will continue do as it has done) and some percentage of league average (our expectation that it will fall or rise toward .500) to form our projection. How much of each to use is determined by the Pearson correlation (see the endnotes for the specifics of how to do this).

The tables below show the correlation ("R") between a team's winning percentage after a certain number of games have been played ("Games") and the team's end-of-season winning percentage. What we're looking for is the point at which R equals 0.50. It's at this point that the team's year-to-date record will predict its end-of-season record with exactly as much accuracy as assuming the team will finish .500. After that point, the team's actual record becomes more important and, by the definition used here, "real." The correlations in Table 5-2.1 were derived using all seasons since 1962 (the year the 162-game schedule was adopted by both leagues) excluding the strike-shortened years of 1972, 1981, 1994, and 1995. After a single game, a team's record produces an R of 0.12. This means that if we were trying to predict a team's end-of-season record using regression to the mean, we would be best served using 12 percent of the team's performance to date (in that single game) and 88 percent league average (a .500 record). The more games that get played, naturally, the more important actual performance becomes and the more accurate our projection becomes.

After five games, the 2007 Diamondbacks sat at 3–2—a .600 winning percentage. At this point, our projected end-of-season winning percentage for the team would be .528—not very close to their actual .556 end-of-season record. Let's keep going (see Table 5-2.2). Over their next five games, the 2007 D'backs went on a tear, winning four and losing just once in improving to 7–3—a .700 record. Now, our projected end-of-season winning percentage for the Snakes would be .584. That's closer to their actual .556 record than our estimate after five games, but it's still pretty

TABLE 5-2.1 Record for Games One through Five Correlated with End-of-Season Record

Games	R
1	0.12
2	0.20
3	0.21
4	0.25
5	0.28

TABLE 5-2.2 Record for Games Six through Ten Correlated to End-of-Season Record

Games	R
6	0.31
7	0.35
8	0.39
9	0.40
10	0.42

TABLE 5-2.3 Record for
Games 11 Through 19
Correlated to End-of-
Season Record

Games	R
11	0.42
12	0.42
13	0.45
14	0.45
15	0.47
16	0.50
17	0.52
18	0.53
19	0.54

TABLE 5-2.3 Record for Games 11 Through 19 Correlated to End-of-Season Record

far off. Since we haven't reached an R of 0.50 yet, we know we can do better (see Table 5-2.3). There it is. After 16 games, R equals 0.50. After 16 games, the D'backs had won 10 and lost six, good for a .625 winning percentage and an 0.563 expectation—just 0.007 points off of their ultimate 0.556 rate for the season.

This suggests that a hot start becomes real very quickly. After 16 games, just 10 percent of the MLB season has been played. Yet, when we go to estimate a team's end-of-season record, we'll be using 50 percent of the team's year-to-date performance and 50 percent league average. For the 2007 D'backs, after 16 games we would estimate their end-of-season record as such:

$$.625 \times 50\% + .500 \times 50\% = .563$$

While a hot start obviously becomes more real with every successive game, by at least one definition, a hot start becomes "real" after 16 games. If you wish to estimate a team's end-of-season record on your own, you can now do so regardless of how many games have been played. This is the formula I've derived, where "G" is the number of games that have been played and "W%" is the team's win percentage to date:

Projected Winning Percentage = $G/(G + 16)*W\% + (1 - G/(G + 16))*.500$

This formula works well until the 85-game mark, after which the nature of the relationships change, the team in question no longer off to a "hot start," but embarking on a "hot finish," which is beyond this chapter's purview.

Another way that we can tell if a hot start is real is to see how long it takes for a team's hot start to predict its end-of-season record better than our preseason expectation for the team does. After all, a team like the Yankees that wins 95 games in one season is very unlikely to win 70 the next, even if it gets off to a rough start, so to form a basic preseason expectation for a team, we'll use its performance over the past few seasons.

Obviously a team's record from last year is going to be more significant than its record from two years ago, so we should account for this as well. To do this, I'm going to borrow a page from Bill James and use something called a "multivariate regression," which accomplishes the same thing as a Pearson correlation but allows us to use multiple variables (instead of just one) to predict something else.

I initially used a team's past four seasons, but the fourth season ended up not being significant, making our optimal number three. When we include the past three seasons, we see that a team's preseason expectation is composed of four parts:

.500 winning percentage: 48 percent
Record from last season: 35 percent
Record from two seasons ago: 12 percent
Record from three seasons ago: 5 percent

For 2007, the Diamondbacks had won 51, 77, and 76 games from 2004 to 2006, giving them a preseason expectation of 77 wins. From here, all we need to do is find out how well a team's preseason expectation predicts its actual performance. Using a Pearson correlation, we get an R of 0.52 when we do this. If we look back at Table 5-2.3, we see that it takes 17 games for a team's in-season performance to predict its final record with the same amount of accuracy. That means that after 17 games, the in-season record tells us exactly as much as our preseason expectation. Notice anything about that number? It's extremely similar to the 16 games an in-season record takes to become "real." By yet another definition, a hot start becomes "real" after 16–17 games.

While both of my definitions of "real" turned up the same result, it is worthwhile to note that one of Jazayerli's studies—using an equally worthwhile method—found the number to be closer to 48 games. His study employed a multivariate regression, using the team's in-season record at various intervals and a preseason expectation derived the same way mine was, to predict a team's end-of-season record.

While individually a team's in-season 17-game record and its preseason expectation were able to predict its final record with equal accuracy, when the two are combined, Jazayerli found that the preseason expectation is roughly four times more important than the 17-game in-season record. In the formula Jazayerli generated to predict a team's final record at 17 games, the in-season record received a weight of roughly 18 percent while the preseason expectation received a weight of 82 percent. It wasn't until 48 games that the two received equal weight in the formula, because a team's in-season record and its end-of-season record are not completely independent of each other. A team doesn't get off to a hot start as a fluke—at least not wholly. If the team is expected to be good in the preseason, it's more likely to get off to a hot start. When you combine the two to predict end-of-season record, the regression eliminates the "double counting," stripping out the portion of the hot start that was predicted by the preseason expectation and leaving the part that wasn't.

All told, this leaves us with three different points from which to measure a hot start. The first way is the point at which a team's year-to-date performance becomes more predictive of its end-of-season record than simply assuming the team will finish with a .500 record (17 games). The second way is when a team's in-season record and its preseason expectation predicted its end-of-season record with the same level of accuracy (also roughly 17 games). Jazayerli took this second definition a step further, to the point when a team's preseason expectation and the portion of its in-season record that the preseason expectation couldn't predict held equal predictive value over the team's final record.

Which method is preferable depends on the point of the season and what kind of team is being evaluated. The first method is likely best suited to a team that has undergone a major overhaul in the offseason. With such a team, their previous record is going to be much less indicative of their actual talent level since they're largely a different team, so placing more weight on the team's in-season performance will likely be more indicative of its future prospects. That said, preseason expectation is still going to have some importance, even if the team has undergone a complete overhaul, because organizational character will out; even if the Yankees turned over their entire roster in a given offseason, they are still likely to be good the following year because they're working with the same payroll and will have acquired players of comparable value, even if they're different players.

Whether 16 games or 48 games, whether the middle of April or the middle of May, the fact remains that it doesn't take very long for a hot start to become "real." After 16 games had been played in 2007, we would have estimated the hot-start 10–6 Arizona Diamondbacks to have finished with 91 wins; they ultimately finished with 90. While it seems a little hard to believe at first, once those first 16–17 games had been played, we could have made a very good guess as to where they would finish once all 162 were in the books.

The 2007 Diamondbacks are one example of a team's hot start being legitimate. There are plenty of other such examples throughout baseball history. In fact, the 2011 Diamondbacks are actually another such example. Following their tremendous 2007, the Snakes fell to 82 wins in 2008, 70 in 2007, and 65 in 2010. This past season, however, the D'backs rebounded after bringing in Kevin Towers as their new GM. Towers's retooling of the bullpen, Justin Upton's emergence as a true superstar, and an unexpectedly strong 1–2 punch of Ian Kennedy and Dan Hudson pushed he team out to an 11–6 start (an expectation of 93 wins) and an eventual 94 wins. In 1998, the Chicago Cubs rode a wave of three straight sub-80-win seasons straight to a 10–7 start and 88 projected wins; the team parlayed this start into a 90-win season and a Wild Card playoff berth—their first playoff appearance in nine years. In 1996, the St. Louis Cardinals came off their own pair of sub-70-win seasons to win 88 games, which could have been foreseen early on with their .588 record through their first 17 games—which pointed to an eventual 88 wins.

Of course, we need to remember that we're dealing with probability, not certainty. In 2008, the Tampa Bay Rays came into the season having won 66, 61, and 67 games the previous three years and opened the season with just seven wins in their first 17 games. While our formula would have predicted just 74 wins, the team managed to go on a tear to ultimately finish the season with 97 wins. On the back of stellar defense, rookie sensation Evan Longoria, and breakout performances from players like Ben Zobrist, the Rays finished ahead of both the powerhouse Yankees and the Red Sox and won the AL East outright. In 2010, the Cincinnati Reds—having failed to crack 80 wins for the past three years and eight of the past nine—opened the season 7–10, leaving many to expect another long, disappointing season—and that would have been a perfectly acceptable stance given their 74-win expectation at that point. Come October, however, the team had secured 91 wins and their first playoff appearance in 15 years. In 2007, the Colorado Rockies similarly stumbled out of the blocks to their own 7–10 record and 74-win expectation; they wound up with 92 victories and their first-ever World Series birth. In all, when we look at all teams from 1962 to the present (excluding strike-shortened years) from the 16-game mark on, we find that our formula came within seven games of the final record 49 percent of the time.

At the end of April, players, coaches, and the media like to say that there's still a lot of baseball left to be played. While of course this is true, believe it or not, by the end of April we are actually capable of making a very good guess as to how a team will ultimately finish. We'll never be able to say with absolute certainty—that's why they play the games—but we *will* have a lot more to go on than mere conjecture and platitudes.

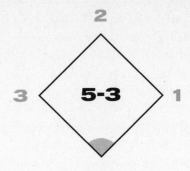

What Is the Effect of the
Increase in Strikeouts?

CHRISTINA KAHRL

You are no doubt aware of the parable of the boiled frog. Toss the unfortunate amphibian into a pot of boiling water and he'll jump out of it. Put him in a pot of water and then slowly raise the temperature to boiling, however, and he'll stick around until he's cooked. Like most parables, it's something you hope people haven't put to the test in the laboratory.

Beyond conjuring up ingenious methods of amphibicide, one of the underlying messages of this particular story is that, if you don't pay attention, a massive change in your environment might be happening. You can see where environmentalists get all worked up about it, but our purpose here is a wee bit more esoteric. It's time to talk about one of the most fundamental changes to the game today, something that has slowly crept up on us, and perhaps on the game as a whole. Quite simply, it's time to notice that we're living in the age of strikeouts, and to take note about the effects of this change on which teams win and why, using which players, and how, and what this means for team-level success in the seasons to come.

Flash back to the 1960s, before and then on into the high-mound era that culminated in the "Year of the Pitcher" in 1968. In 1961, the point at which Roger Maris set the single-season home run record with 61 runs, teams scored 4.53 runs per game. That dropped to 3.42

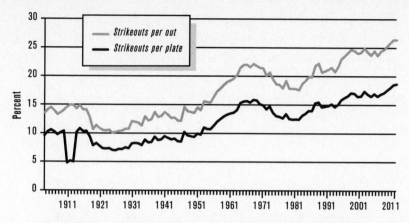

FIGURE 5-3.1 Strikeouts per Out and per Plate Appearance, 1903–2011

runs per game per team in '68. That's a 25 percent drop, where a quarter of runs scored for every team just went away. If you're old enough, you know the names of the pitchers who owned that time: Koufax, Gibson, Drysdale, McLain, even Lonborg. This environmental change helped the pitchers of this era not simply dominate, but generated their statistical impact on record books.

As they did it, one of the things that was part and parcel of their dominance was a spike in the strikeout rates in baseball. In 1955, strikeouts were 11 percent of all plays and 18 percent of all outs. By 1961, those numbers had already moved up to 14 percent of all plays and 22 percent of all outs—steep increases—but by 1968, the number of strikeouts had climbed all the way to 16 percent of all plays (a 45 percent increase across 14 seasons) and 24 percent of all outs (a 25 percent inflation rate).

That's an impressive historic anomaly, one done away with when the mounds were lowered, the strike zone expanded, and (eventually) with the introduction of the designated hitter (DH). It's also a fraction of where strikeout rates are today, because when it comes to getting our results at home plate, we've long since left the Year of the Pitcher in the dust. As of the 2011 season, the rate of strikeouts has reached 19 percent of all plate appearances—nearly a 73 percent increase from Mickey Mantle's heyday—and account for 26 percent of all outs, a 63 percent increase. Both marks are historic highs for baseball as it has been played since 1893, when pitchers had to move out to 60 feet six inches from 50 feet (see Figure 5-3.1).

Now, that's obviously a major environmental change, and you can probably guess at a lot of the contributing factors. Beyond the lower mound or fewer at-bats going to pitchers attempting to hit thanks to the DH, if you've a mind to complain you'll bring up more hitters swinging for the fences, or perhaps the endless tedium of an ever-growing number of relievers putting in appearances in games. If you like parsing pitch data, you'll probably jump to the conclusion that the increasing popularity of the splitter in the 1980s, the changeup in the '90s, or the cut fastball today has something to do with it. Add in video scouting and the contemporary wealth of data, and you might well guess that it's easier than ever to get a strikeout.

This is no doubt pedantic, but keep in mind what a strikeout actually is. Unless you've got a particularly infamous backstop routinely letting guys reach on the strikeout-plus-passed ball or wild pitch play, it's a high-yield event in terms of guaranteeing an outcome: an out. Set against that, you've got an overall decline in the number of balls in play. We'll talk about what that means for the declining significance of defense on a team at greater length shortly, but what has essentially happened is that teams have traded high-percentage play, settling accounts at home plate with a whiff, for fewer total chances for the defense.

On average, it follows that as strikeouts have gone up, the number of balls in play has gone down over time. In 1968, 73 percent of all pitcher-batter outcomes wound up in play, a figure that with the DH batting in one league instead of both nevertheless moved upward of 76 percent in the 1980s. Today, the number of balls in play has dropped to 69 percent in the 2011 season. Again, that's without the higher mound, and with the DH batting in only one of the leagues. It may not sound like much of a difference, but this represents a fairly dramatic change. We've moved from relatively low-yield events for both the batter and pitcher—defensible balls in play that may or may not drop for hits—to a growing number of plays in which the defense has next to no impact on whatsoever: home runs and strikeouts.

Broadly speaking, defensive efficiency (DE) kept pace by going *down*. Going back to the 1950s, major league pitchers could count on 70 to 71 percent of balls in play to be converted into outs. In 1977, DE dipped below 70 percent for the first time since 1940, but that was just to 69.8 percent; but in the '80s it started heading down below 70 as often as not, only briefly bouncing back in 1988–1992. But defenses hit a new low in 1993, an expansion season, with a DE of .693.

Since that year, DE has never gotten back over 70 percent, bouncing around in the 68 percent range in the '90s, in the 69s in the early aughties, dropping back to around 68 percent in 2006–2008 (the immediate aftermath of the so-called steroid era), and only just moving

TABLE 5-3.1 20 Years After

Year	SO%	In Play%	DE	RS/G	HR%
1992	14.7%	73%	.703	4.12	1.9%
2011	18.6%	69%	.694	4.28	2.5%

higher than that 1993 game-wide mark in 2011. For all the attention given to defense in recent years, it's nice to see some small result, but for all of the attention focused on the subject since the Rays' big improvement on defense from 2007 to 2008, defenses in general simply aren't turning as many balls in play into outs as they did in 1992.

Put all that together in terms of what's changed in the last 20 years and you get Table 5-3.1. Relative adjectives like "bad" and "good" don't mean much here; we can't say all fielders in 1992 were better, but with a thorough command of the obvious we can say they were converting more balls in play into outs. Subsequently, pitchers have helped themselves out by settling accounts at home plate, which lowers the overall importance of defense, especially at the positions with the lowest likelihood of seeing a play, like the outfield corners, but generally every position. Indeed, in today's game, you'll find that some teams have headed in the exact opposite direction from the much-ballyhooed lesson of the Rays, punting defense and winning with strikeout-dependent staffs that don't need a top-notch defense to keep runs off the board.

Practically Speaking

Consider the example of the Yankees during the age of Derek Jeter. Year after year, Jeter has rated close to or at the bottom of most of the available defensive metrics, and year after year, the Yankees seem to do just fine without much concern for what that's supposed to mean. Instead, they cash in the benefit of having him in their lineup. Right at the time when sabermetricians were railing about the importance of discovering new and better defensive metrics and treating defense as the new "market inefficiency" to give the nouveau smart a competitive advantage, other teams had already taken the step beyond and figured out that just maybe "bad" or merely competent defenders were entirely affordable risks.

Keep in mind, whatever the available metrics suggest about a player's value relative to his peers (the way a curve-driven metric like ultimate zone rating suggests) or in terms of an absolute historical standard (like the fielding runs calculated by Clay Davenport or Sean

Smith), even a bad big-league defender is among the best players at the position on the planet, indeed, in baseball history. Derek Jeter might be "terrible," and simultaneously playable. Why? Because strikeouts are such an increasingly large part of the game.

That adaptive realization has already had an impact on today's game. Brian Cashman didn't despair over the fact that Derek Jeter has become a living monument at short. Instead, the Yankees' GM used the power of his bankroll to do something after the 2008 season that minimizes the impact Jeter can have on defense. He signed the two best strikeout starters available on the market: the best power lefty workhorse active in the game today in CC Sabathia *and* the American League's reigning strikeout leader, A.J. Burnett. Sabathia's combined 2008 strikeout rate with the Indians and Brewers was 24.5 percent; Burnett was only slightly lower (24.1 percent), but he had topped that with a 25.5 percent clip in 2007.

Few teams could afford that sort of expense, but at a time when Derek Jeter's awful defense was already the stuff of sabermetric canards and snickering references to whatever advanced fielding metric you care to place your faith in, Cashman did. The payoffs were immediate. The Yankees saw their team-wide balls-in-play rate in 2008 drop from a below-average 70 percent to an American League–low 66 percent. Their team-wide strikeout rate jumped from 18.5 percent to a league-leading 20.1 percent.

With lightly regarded defenders up the middle, such as the ancient, indifferent Jorge Posada behind the plate, plus Melky Cabrera's wanderings around center, and Jeter's status as one of the oldest men to ever play short on a contender, the Yankees bludgeoned their way to 103 wins and 915 runs scored, clubbing people to death at the plate while stranding them there on defense.

Come October, the Yankees didn't need depth in the rotation, using just Sabathia, Burnett, and old standby Andy Pettitte to start all 15 of their postseason games. When they beat the Phillies in the 2009 World Series, it wasn't especially elegant as Burnett and Pettitte struggled, but they still managed to get 50 strikeouts in 53 innings, avoiding that defense en route to the win. How did that happen? Not least because the relief corps, armed with Joba Chamberlain, Phil Hughes, David Robertson, lefty Damaso Marte, and the great Mariano Rivera got 11 of their 32 outs on Ks in their four wins over the Phillies.

Maybe the 2009 Yankees used strikeouts to compensate for a few weak defenders, and maybe they were just lucky, but what happened the following season, when the Giants won the 2010 World Series, suggests that the results were anything but random. Here again, you have a lot of the same elements. Aubrey Huff had been a semi-regular DH before joining the Giants; he played first base and a lot of outfield, in particular roaming around in right field in his starts against right-handed pitching during the Giants' hottest stretch of the season, during July and August before they picked up Cody Ross. Opposite Huff in left field was another discarded DH, Pat Burrell. The infield was manned by sub-mediocrities, featuring the then-bloated Panda, Pablo Sandoval, at third base, an aging Edgar Renteria at short, and the limited range of Juan Uribe and Freddy Sanchez up the middle.

None of that mattered all that much, because the Giants' pitching staff was busy leading the major leagues in strikeout rate, erasing 21.6 percent of all batters at home plate. They also managed an MLB-low clip for balls in play of just 65 percent, taking pressure off a defense stocked with the geezers for whom Brian Sabean is famous. Who was getting all those strikeouts? Tim Lincecum and Matt Cain and Jonathan Sanchez, certainly, but the pen could call on Santiago Casilla, who struck out a quarter of all batters faced, rubber-armed Sergio Romo, who terminated 28 percent of all batters, and closer Brian Wilson, who inspired batters to fear the beard not by making them wonder if he'd pillaged the *Gettysburg* hair and makeup department, but by striking out 30 percent of the men who stepped in against him.

The Giants' power out of the pen was critical in propelling them past the Phillies in the NLCS, where Bruce Bochy's frenetic pitching changes and playing matchup games helped produce 22 strikeouts in 19 1/3 relief innings in 21 individual relief appearances in six games, not to mention a series win. That set the Giants up to do the same thing to the Rangers, only much more handily.

This brings us to the next critical point about the age of strikeouts: we're far past the age of individual heroes.

Strikeouts, Strikeouts Everywhere? Isn't Nolan Ryan Retired!?!
Yes, yes, he is, and so is Dwight Gooden. And Sandy Koufax. And Randy Johnson. Bob Feller and Rube Waddell have shuffled off this mortal coil. Yet, none of that matters, because strikeouts are up without them. Instead of individual feats of strength, in today's game of managed and closely monitored workloads and seven- or eight-man bullpens, wiping people out at home plate is very much a team thing.

You didn't need to watch Tony LaRussa's nightly do-si-do over the last three decades to notice the game-wide change in pitcher usage patterns. In 1969, teams averaged less than two relievers per game. In

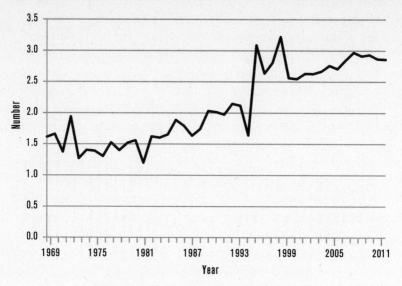

FIGURE 5-3.2 Team Relief Pitchers per Game

the '70s, that dropped to an average of fewer than three relievers total between two opposing teams in any individual game. Things picked up during the '80s with the increasing employment of situational relievers and assorted eighth-inning heroes; teams moved past two relievers per game apiece in 1989, then jumped past three relievers per game in 1995 in the wake of the strike, cresting in 1998 with 3.2 relievers per team per game. Things have come down since, to around 2.9 relievers per game now, but all that means is that we're still sitting through almost three relievers appearing for every team in every game (see Figures 5-3.2 and 5-3.3).

So, managers have adapted in monkey-see, monkey-do fashion, aping not just La Russa's usage pattern for Dennis Eckersley, but also ageless lefty Rick Honeycutt and power setup righties like Eric Plunk. The process accelerated during the offensive boom between 1994 and 2006 as more runs scoring meant more relievers to cope with an increasing workload. They moved past pitching more than a third of every ballgame in 1995, generally staying there . . . until the last two seasons. We'll return to that in a moment.

Generally speaking, the benefits of using more relievers are clear: it makes it hard for the batter to get used to any one pitcher's stuff or pitching pattern, making the accrual of their season stats less and less an aggregation of 162 batter vs. pitcher matchups, and more a matter of two, maybe three at-bats against the starter, then one against some

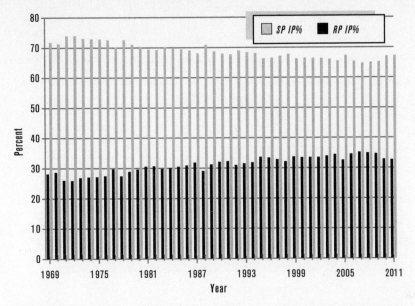

FIGURE 5-3.3 Starters' and Relievers' Innings Pitched as a Percentage of Total Innings

guy you may have never seen before, and then one more against an ace reliever you see twice a month. Even a batter who manages to make contact is not guaranteed to make *hard* contact.

As chicken/egg things go, you can wonder whether the present environment makes record-setting strikeout fiends at the plate like Mark Reynolds possible. And while Reynolds's career 33.2 percent strikeout rate tops that of Rob Deer (31.2 percent), in the context of their eras, Deer's prodigious whiffery at a time when strikeouts were much less common makes his mark the more remarkable feat. It seems quaint to note that Reggie Jackson's career 22.8 percent strikeout rate could generate the all-time record for strikeouts with 2,597. That record will fall to Jim Thome in 2013, assuming Thome decides to play; if not, Alex Rodriguez could put Mr. October in the shade toward the end of this decade, presumably while also gunning to knock Barry Bonds down a peg on the all-time home run list. But A-Rod and Thome have had to cope with something that Reggie never had to confront: a cast of thousands of pitchers instead of hundreds.

That change is directly reflected in today's spike in strikeout rates. Back at the start of the era of divisional play, strikeout rates for starting pitchers and relievers were essentially even, right around 5.8 K/9. Forty-three years later, starters have picked up almost a strikeout per nine without pitching as far into the ballgame.

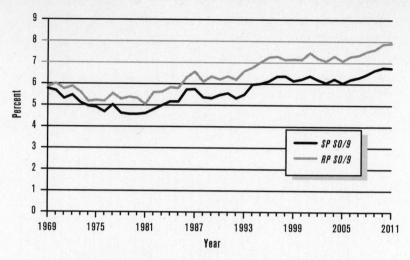

FIGURE 5-3.4 Starters' and Relievers' Strikeouts per Nine Innings

However, the real key to the spike in strikeout rates has been the relievers, as they've reached 7.5 K/9 while pitching a larger portion of every ballgame (see Figure 5-3.4).

So what about the recent drop in the amount of innings relievers are pitching per game—what does that mean? Well, think about it: teams are still carrying seven or eight relievers, but with offense down and starting pitchers going later into ballgames, that means there is a shrinking amount of playing time going to the same number of guys in the bullpen. Relievers are making almost exactly the same number of appearances today that they did before the downturn in the last two years—but those appearances are growing shorter.

That trend was reflected in the Giants' World Series victory in 2010, when Bochy's aggressive use of his pen was much remarked upon. However, that aggressiveness was simply the paragon of a virtue reflected in game-wide trends for using relievers for increasingly short stretches to exploit every incremental advantage, matchup by matchup.

To the 2011 World Series

If the Yankees in 2009 and the Giants in 2010 hadn't already demonstrated the virtues of having the whiffiest of pitching staffs in the age of strikeouts, the 2011 Cardinals flaunted every benefit of the game-wide trends toward more decisions at home plate en route to their own World Series win.

Tony La Russa and company had already made a point of risking their interior defense in 2009 by moving outfielder Skip Schumaker to second base to add an OBP source to the lineup in front of Albert Pujols and Matt Holliday. Schumaker was terrible at the keystone and has remained terrible despite his best efforts, but the Cardinals won the NL Central while Schumaker produced a .364 OBP as their most-regular leadoff man.

In 2011, still counting on Schumaker at second, the Cards defied any thoughtful concerns for their defense by adding Lance Berkman to the lineup to play right field. Berkman was 35 years old and seemed older still with his bulk. He hadn't played the outfield much since 2007, or regularly since 2004. Did the Cardinals care? Hell no. They got Berkman relatively cheap for $8 million, parked him in right, and exerted season-long defensive indifference from the dugout and executive suite. They committed to the equally immobile David Freese at third base. They brought in Ryan Theriot and dared to move him back to short after the Cubs and Dodgers had deemed that unwise.

The penalty? They finished 23rd in the majors in defensive efficiency, led the league in scoring, and—with the help of making a concession to defense by adding shortstop Rafael Furcal at the deadline—raced to the wild card. However, they'd gotten to October without much of a strikeout staff, just 22nd with a 17.7 percent punchout clip. The only above-average starters they had in terms of strikeout rate were Chris Carpenter and Jaime Garcia, but with both shy of striking out batters 20 percent of the time, neither compared to the Yankees' or Giants' wizards of whiffery in postseasons past.

Leave it to La Russa to find the perfect way to compensate—some might say *over*compensate—for the problem and making the term "ball control" relevant to baseball. After squeaking past the Phillies in the League Division Series, he chucked standard operating procedures for staff management. While he had used his starting pitchers normally enough in the LDS, he was forced to deploy Carpenter in the deciding Game 5. Wrong-footed in their rotation even as they advanced, La Russa simply treated every game situation, and perhaps every batter, as a high-leverage moment that might demand a pitching change. Between the two rounds and the 13 games it took to win them, he used 58 relievers over 54 1/3 innings, getting 43 strikeouts while routinely exploiting platoon matchups. If Bochy's flurry of gutsy pitching changes and reliance on his pen in 2010 seemed inspired, La Russa's frenzied churn of relief help kept the Rangers guessing in a blur of changing matchups capped by Jason Motte's triple-digit heat.

Long-Term Implications of the Age of K

First, teams should want what the rising tide of strikeouts affords them. Love the strikeouts not merely for their own sake, but for their impact on team offenses and defenses. Playing slugs like Aubrey Huff or Lance Berkman in an outfield corner, or Derek Jeter or Skip Schumaker up the middle, is an increasingly affordable risk—with the right pitching—and as long as you're getting enough offense.

That might seem obvious, but sabermetric groupthink seems stuck on esoteric notions like the underrated defensive value of left fielders; this at a time when fewer balls are in play, when the rate of how many balls drop safely has also declined, and when runs are nevertheless becoming more scarce. Sometimes it's worth according some measure of respect to old-fashioned mashers at the positions they're traditionally associated with, right and left and first base.

All too often, sabermetrics can be an exercise in documenting the previously observed. For more than a century, perhaps all the way back to the game's earliest days, skippers understood that fewer balls go to right and left field than anywhere else, so they were only too happy to stuff unglovely sluggers in the distant corners of the diamond to reap some offensive benefit. If folks start noticing that teams are winning the World Series with designated hitters in the field, we'll have come full circle from the elaborately exaggerated enthusiasm for the 2008 Rays and their defensive turnaround.

Instead, the lasting lesson from those Rays and life in the age of strikeouts is that bullpen assembly and management is more important than ever. As tedious as the endless shuffle of men from the pen might be to witness, and as much as many of us might lament the loss of a 14th or 15th position player and the impact of that on in-game offensive tactics, the recent success of bad defensive teams with deep pens and strong lineups might provide a template that keeps us exactly where we are for years to come.

In the abstract, the shrinking amount of game time available to relievers as starters pitch deeper into games and run scoring drops ought to trigger a reverse of the industry-wide adoption of the seven- or eight-man pen. But every stathead from Bill James on down has been arguing for a relief reformation of rosters for a good decade now, and after the performances of La Russa and Bochy in the last two World Series, it's becoming something easier to emptily assert than really believe in.

PART 6

Wrapping Up

Epilogue

Catching Up with Baseball's Hilbert Problems

DAN TURKENKOPF

The progress of sabermetrics has always been the result of a close interplay between our concepts of the game and our observations of the action on the field. The former can only evolve out of the latter, and yet the latter is also conditioned greatly by the former. Thus in our exploration of baseball, the interplay between our concepts and our observations may sometimes lead to totally unexpected aspects among already familiar phenomena.

—A bastardization of a quote by
Nobel laureate Tsung-Dao Lee

The study of baseball was once a lonely affair. Many of the progenitors of the sabermetric movement either worked individually (like Earnshaw Cook and Bill James) or in small groups (including Pete Palmer and John Thorn as well as the Mills brothers). Over the past two decades, advances in communication technology have quickened the speed of collaboration and dissemination. The result has been a tremendous outpouring of research from a wide range of investigators, from physicists and statisticians to high school students and computer programmers.

In 1900, the great mathematician David Hilbert gave an address to the International Congress of Mathematicians in which he outlined 23 major problems awaiting solutions in the coming century. In *Baseball*

Prospectus 2000, Keith Woolner (now the manager of Baseball Research and Analytics for the Cleveland Indians) took a page from the great mathematician and posed a list of 23 "Hilbert Problems for the next century" for sabermetricians to dissect in the then-new millennium.

Hilbert's list inspired a generation of mathematicians. Woolner's list likewise served as a challenge, galvanizing a number of influential studies. Now that nearly a dozen years have passed, we can review the progress that has been made toward solving the problems he posed, and see not only how far we have come since he identified these issues in the winter of 1999, but also how much work is left to be done.

Questions of Defense

1. Separating Defense into Pitching and Fielding

How much control does the pitcher have on whether a ball becomes a hit? Can certain pitchers evoke weak contact? At roughly the same moment that Woolner made this the first item on his list, a researcher named Voros McCracken was beginning to publically discuss his ideas about defense-independent pitching. His research, which culminated in a widely cited article at Baseball Prospectus, showed that pitchers had little variability in preventing hits on balls in play. His work literally changed how we study the game. Today, defense-independent pitching statistics (DIPS) are the primary method by which pitchers are evaluated.

McCracken's pioneering work does not mean we can mark this case closed; there are still many questions as to how to identify and treat apparent exceptions to the rule, how to attribute value to fielders, and the best way to leverage the insights of DIPS for measuring "true talent" or a pitcher. **Status: Fairly well understood, but opportunities for further advances remain.**

2. Evaluating Interrelationships among Teammates' Defensive Performances

Did playing next to quality third basemen contribute to Derek Jeter's poor showing in fielding metrics? Could an outfield of Willie Mays, Greg Luzinski, and Pete Incaviglia be anywhere near average defensively? Did John Olerud make the 1999 Mets infield the best ever? While we're becoming fairly good at determining overall team defensive value, and are making progress on individual fielding metrics, we still don't have a good handle on how players can influence each other. For example, while we can calculate how well a first baseman scoops balls in the dirt, it's hard to gauge how that affects the rest of the infielders. Another difficult issue is how to treat discretionary plays (where more than one player could have made the play) in terms of assigning value. **Status: Research in progress.**

3. Measuring the Catcher's Role in Run Prevention

Though Casey Stengel said you have to have a catcher because if you don't you're likely to have a lot of passed balls, quantifying the exact contribution a catcher makes to run prevention remains an elusive goal. Who's the more valuable player, a great hitter with a mediocre glove, like Mike Piazza, or a mediocre hitter but strong reliever such as the various members of the Molina family? Can we even say those defensive reputations are warranted?

Woolner himself took the initial swing at solving this problem in the modern sabermetric era using Catcher ERA as his metric of choice; he found no correlation between catchers and the ERA of their pitchers. Since that time, numerous researchers including Tom Tango, Mike Fast, Max Marchi, and others have leveraged alternative approaches and technological data to develop a more sophisticated componentized look at catcher defense. Aspects of the receiving game like blocking pitches in the dirt and framing pitches are beginning to be understood (most recently Fast showed in a widely cited article at Baseball Prospectus that catchers with good framing skills may have unsuspected value), but we still have a long way to go. **Status: Research in progress, but advancing.**

4. Mapping Career Trajectories for Defensive Performance

What is the aging curve for fielders? Do the fresh legs of the youngster outweigh the experience gained from seeing thousands of fly balls? Much like offensive performance, fielding appears to peak right around age 27. As players age, you'll see their defense suffer, and many will move down the defensive spectrum to an easier position, so you should definitely be wary of a team signing a 36-year-old shortstop to a multi-year contract, even if that player has a sanctified name like "Derek Jeter." **Status: Well understood.**

5. Making an Assessment of Relative Positional Difficulties

Is a first baseman who has an OPS of 1.000 more valuable than a shortstop with an .800 OPS? Having evolved out of Bill James's defensive spectrum concept, concrete adjustment for positions is a key piece of win-value constructs like wins above replacement, but some fine-tuning remains to be done. Tom Tango, co-author of *The Book*, used players who switched positions to measure the value of each position. By comparing their defensive performance at each, he deduced the relative value of the positions. One potentially large flaw in this approach is the small number of players who change positions may not be representative of the entire population. Baseball Prospectus, on the other hand, uses the full sample of players and measures the difference in offensive output between positions. The two approaches tend to be fairly close at most positions, but disagree on second base and third base. Tango's method treats them as roughly the same value despite third basemen being the better hitters. This leads to a difference of five or six runs between the two systems over the course of a full season. **Status: Fairly well understood with some difference of opinion.**

6. Quantifying the Value of Positional Flexibility

Should Ben Zobrist get extra credit for playing multiple positions? Is Mark DeRosa (when healthy) a valuable player? Does it make sense to try to develop a pitcher/pinch-hitter like Brooks Kieschnick? With the reduction of slots for position players on major league rosters due to the proliferation of relief pitchers, it seems reasonable that the ability to fill multiple roles would be of substantial value over and above actual performance. If so, how much value is gained from that flexibility? Should teams be looking to find players who can move between positions on a regular basis? Is there a marginal rate of return where there is a maximum number of this type of player any one team should have? **Status: Wide open.**

7. Measuring the Value of Non-Range-Based Aspects of Defense

Can a first baseman who can scoop really save an error a game? Who has the better arm, Ichiro Suzuki or Jeff Francoeur? John Dewan's Baseball Info Solutions represents the current state of the art in this arena. BIS has a team of video stringers watch every play and classify it into a variety of categories based on difficulty, skill, importance, and so on. While there are questions about the reliability of their batted-ball location data, they appear to do a good job at measuring things like scoops at first and outfield arms. **Status: Fairly well understood.**

Questions of Offense

8. Evaluating the Impact on Offensive Performance of Changing Defensive Positions Up/Down the Defensive Spectrum

Does moving players around on the field affect their offensive performance? Would Joe Mauer be a better hitter if he played first base instead of catcher? Was making Bryce Harper an outfielder a smart move? Is there a direct relationship between raw offensive performance and defensive position? Whether the cause be improved health or the opportunity to bulk up, can moving to a new position catalyze a new level of offensive performance? **Status: Wide open.**

9. Predicting the Impact on Career Length from Changing Positions

Did moving Craig Biggio from catcher to second base make him a Hall of Famer? How much longer would Mickey Mantle have played if he had moved to first base earlier, thereby saving his knees? Beyond the immediate offensive impact from a position change, is there a corresponding change in career length? It seems likely that moving someone from catcher to first base would lengthen his career by saving his knees and removing a bunch of nicks and bruises (and the occasional player trying to run you over). How much of an impact does this make? **Status: Wide open.**

Questions of Pitching

10. Projecting Minor League Pitchers Accurately

How well does minor league performance translate to the big leagues? Are there certain statistics that are better indicators of future success? Projection systems like PECOTA do a fairly good job identifying how minor league pitchers will perform when they reach the majors based on their statistics and those of comparable players. Combining statistical projections with scouting information improves the likelihood of a successful prediction substantially.

Pat Venditte, best known as the switch-pitcher in the Yankees farm system, despite great numbers in the minors, is not considered a prospect because he lacks stuff and is viewed as having succeeded by feasting on inexperienced hitters. On the other hand, Cardinals starter Edwin Jackson has always had tremendous tools, but walked four batters a game in the minors. Despite that statistical record, he continued to be viewed as a quality prospect, and has experienced some success in the majors.

The biggest wild card in projecting pitchers is not ability, but injury. Whoever can predict occurrence and effect of injury will almost certainly achieve his or her place in the sabermetric annals. **Status: In progress.**

11. Creating a Better Way to Analyze Mechanics

Are there pitching motions that increase injury risk? Is height that important? Is there anything at all to the "inverted W"? There are many stories of pitchers who have tweaked (or even entirely rebuilt) their pitching motions to gain speed, control, or to reduce chances of injury. Brewers closer John Axford credits his success (and, in fact, his survival in the game) to mimicking Roy Halladay's approach to throwing.

While the position of pitching coach is an ancient one, analyzing mechanics is a relatively nascent field. Carlos Gomez, who now works for the Diamondbacks, was probably the first person to gain sabermetric exposure by breaking down pitching motions. His work has been carried on by Kyle Boddy and others, but there is still plenty of opportunity for someone to make a mark. **Status: Wide open.**

Questions of Developmental Strategies

12. Identifying and Quantifying Good Coaching

How much is good coaching worth? Can we even determine what makes a good coach? Is good coaching situational? In a much publicized study, J. C. Bradbury attempted to account for the effect of Leo Mazzone on the Braves' pitching staffs of 1990 to 2005. He found Mazzone (or the Braves organization) to be worth over 10 wins per season, an astounding result. Unfortunately for the credibility of the study, Mazzone's staffs didn't respond quite as well in Baltimore in 2006 and 2007, so we still don't have a good way of figuring out the impact of coaching, either in general or in specific situations. **Status: Wide open.**

13. Assessing the "Coachability" of Players

Why hasn't B. J. Upton reached the heights predicted for him? Can effort outweigh talent? History is full of can't-miss prospects who, for whatever reason, missed. And there are plenty of players who have achieved more than was expected based on their "talent." Is there anything to indicate which players won't progress as planned, and which will surpass their ceilings? Is it related to effort and/or the willingness to take instruction and work hard? If so, is there a good way to measure that quality before investing millions of dollars in bonuses and instruction into a player? **Status: Wide open.**

14. Assessing Developmental Strategies for Minor League Pitchers

Are the Rangers and Nolan Ryan on the right track in disdaining pitch counts? Why do so many young pitchers still get hurt? Developing pitchers for long, effective careers in the majors appears to be just as difficult as ever. Pitch counts and innings limits don't seem to have substantially reduced injuries, and may have led to pitchers not being able to pitch as much as their counterparts of yesteryear. Is this true, and if so, can it be fixed? How should teams handle their prospects so as to realize as much value as possible from them? **Status: Wide open.**

Questions of Economics
15. Clarifying the Win/Dollar Trade-Off Preferences for Major League Decision-Makers

Is Albert Pujols worth upward of $200 million? Should the 2011 Rays have called up Desmond Jennings sooner? Clearly Pujols is a once in a lifetime talent, but how much is that really worth? If you take all the free agents on the market, add up their eventual contracts, and figure out how many wins they are worth (generally from projections), you can calculate the average cost of a win. For the 2010–2011 offseason, that value was somewhere in the $4.5 to $5 million range. Generally we've seen an inflation rate for the dollars-per-win mark of roughly 10 percent per year.

Let's assume Pujols is projected for a 10 WARP season in 2012, and that he'll follow that with a fairly shallow decline where he loses one WARP per season. His fair market value can be determined by multiplying his WARP by the free agent cost per win, as shown in Table 6-1.1.

In this scenario, Pujols will generate over $300 million of value for the team that signs him, making a $200 million contract an easy win for the team. That the $200 million is guaranteed while the $300 million-plus in value is hypothetical tilts things in Pujols's favor. On average, though, this looks like a very good deal for the winning bidder. The Angels, who signed Pujols to a 10-year, $254 million contract in December 2011, can only hope this calculus is correct.

But is it a good deal for all teams? Can a team like the Astros, which only won 56 games in 2011 and doesn't have much hope for rapid improvement, justify signing such a big deal? To answer this question, you need to look at the other side of the equation: how much each extra win is worth to

TABLE 6-1.1 Pujols Bucks

Year	WARP	$/WARP	FMV ($)
1	10	5.00	50.0
2	9	5.50	49.5
3	8	6.05	48.4
4	7	6.66	46.6
5	6	7.33	44.0
6	5	8.06	40.3
7	4	8.87	35.5
TOTAL	49		314.3

a team. Nate Silver addressed this topic in the first *Baseball Between the Numbers* and found the marginal value of adding another win to be fairly low unless you're on the cusp of a playoff berth.

Using his values, and adjusting for inflation, a team below 80 wins or above 100 wins only earns about $1.2 million more for each additional win. Between those points, however, the value of an extra win can be much higher. The main reason is that each win (up to about 90) drastically increases a team's chances of entry into the cash cow that is the postseason. Once a team reaches 90 wins, the value of an extra win is still high, but starts to decline because in a lot of years, those extra wins are unnecessary to make the playoffs. By the time a team reaches 100 wins, it is nearly guaranteed a spot in the playoffs (sorry, 1993 San Francisco Giants), so each additional win isn't that helpful.

As a general rule, very bad teams and very good teams should probably steer clear of the big-ticket free agents and focus more on value contributions. For the bad teams, investing in scouting and player development will probably pay off more than buying wins on the free agent market. For the good teams, the added revenue probably isn't worth the cost, although in this case, "good" means true-talent, 100-win teams, something you don't see a lot of. **Status: Well understood.**

16. Creating a Framework for Evaluating Trades
When the Braves acquired Mark Teixeira and Ron Mahay from the Texas Rangers for Elvis Andrus, Jarrod Saltalamacchia, Neftali Feliz, Matt Harrison, and Beau Jones, who won the trade? Did it make sense for the Red Sox to trade Jeff Bagwell for Larry Andersen? The advent of the win value frameworks like WARP has made evaluating trades easier than ever. Based on an estimate of current and future value, and salary, it's possible to determine a net present value for both sides of the deal and determine the likely "winner." While effective in a general sense, this approach to grading trades overlooks the context of a specific trade, and also appears to ignore the risk premium. **Status: In progress.**

17. Determining the Value of Draft Picks, Rule 5 Picks, Player-to-Be-Named-Later Arrangements, and Other Non-specific Forms of Compensation in Transactions
Is it better to sign that free agent or stick with the draft pick? How much value does a soon-to-be free agent have on the trade market? Is Alex Anthopolous a genius?

There are many non-direct forms of compensation that come into play when deciding whether to make a move or not. The most important of these is the draft picks that result from the loss of a free agent, the value of which had been enumerated by Victor Wang, prior to the newly adopted Collective Bargaining Agreement (CBA). The draft picks in return for a Type A free agent averaged out to between $3 and $5 million depending on whether the signing team was bad enough to have a protected first-round pick or not (i.e., the worst 15 teams). In the case of a protected pick, the team losing the player got a sandwich pick between the first and second rounds and the signing team's second-round pick. Otherwise, the free agent's former team got the signing team's first-round pick plus the sandwich pick.

With the new CBA between Major League Baseball and the Players Association, these findings will have to be revisited. The rules for when a team receives compensation have been revamped and the days of paying over slot for draft picks is likely over, with the Type A and B scheme being replaced by a valuation based on the size of the offer from the formerly controlling team and whether it exceeds the average salary of the 125 highest-paid players in the majors. Should the player decline this offer, the team he leaves will receive a "sandwich" pick between the first and second round, while the signing team will forfeit its first-round pick, unless that pick is protected due to its finishing in the bottom third of the league. Those forfeited picks will go into a lottery.

The combined effects of these changes are unknown, but they almost certainly will change the value of a draft pick. While it will likely take some time for the true results to be understood, there's an opportunity for a smart team to take advantage of the shakeout period. **Status: In progress (thanks to the new CBA).**

18. Evaluating the Effect of Short- and Long-Term Competitiveness on Attendance and Demand Elasticity

Why can't the Rays draw fans? Did Jeffrey Loria really kill baseball in Montreal or did the 1994 work stoppage? Flags fly forever, but were the Marlins' fire sales counterproductive? As much as we might hope that the pride of winning would trump all other concerns, owners aren't running a charity. They own teams to make money, whether on a yearly basis or through the eventual sale of the franchise. How a team's success influences the bottom line formed the basis for Vince Gennaro's book *Diamond Dollars*, in which he constructed a win/revenue curve for each team and explored how additional wins, marquee players, and other events lead to added revenue. While Gennaro covered a lot of ground, there remains much that hasn't been investigated, such as the trickle-down effects of structural issues like market size, and the impact of "white flag" trades in both the short and long term. **Status: In progress.**

19. Optimizing the Competitive Ecology of the Game

Can the Pirates or the Royals ever be successful again? Are consistent playoff appearances by the Yankees and Red Sox good for the game? Baseball is more than just a collection of individual teams. As such, economically it is not a zero-sum game despite being one on the field. In recent years, baseball has continued to look for ways to increase the opportunity for so-called small-market teams to compete, including expanded playoffs and revenue sharing. These efforts appear to have paid off as low-payroll teams like the Athletics, Twins, Marlins, and Rays have experienced some level of postseason success in the past decade. Is increased parity the desired result? Is the league better off with an 800-pound gorilla in New York or Los Angeles? What is the best way to grow the entire sport and both improve the quality of play and ensure the best experience for the largest number of people? Teasing out the answer to these questions is a difficult challenge, but one that's ripe for investigation. **Status: Wide open.**

20. Determining Optimal Pitcher Usage Strategies

Was Tony La Russa a genius or were his innovations destructive? Will anyone ever return to the four-man rotation? Over the past few decades, more and more innings have been going to worse and worse pitchers. The trend to fewer starts and shorter relief appearances has reduced the average workload for pitchers. Has it had an impact on the injury rate or the average career length for a pitcher? Do we see better results from the pitchers who are pitching less? **Status: In progress**

21. Determining Optimal Roster Design

Does it make sense for teams to carry 13 pitchers? Is platooning dead? Should it be? As pitchers' workloads drop, teams are carrying more of them. Since roster size has remained constant, that means position players have been traded for pitchers. This reduces the amount of flexibility managers have to platoon, pinch hit, or make defensive replacements. Is there a better strategy that can be employed? **Status: In progress.**

Questions of Tactics

22. Quantifying the Manager's Impact on Winning

Was Joe Torre a horrible manager before he got to the Yankees? What changed? How much of the game is won or lost on the field and how much in the dugout? Disentangling how a manager affects the outcome of a game is a very difficult task. Since the manager's job includes such far-reaching tasks as setting the lineup, determining in-game strategy, maintaining a clubhouse conducive to winning, and instructing players, it's tough to decide how best to measure his impact on a team's ultimate success. Many have studied the problem of how to quantify a manager's impact without satisfying results. **Status: In progress.**

23. Developing a Game-Theoretic Framework for Analyzing Elective Strategies

When should the manager send the runner? Does it make sense to play the infield in? What about pitching out? Managers and players make numerous strategic decisions every game. While many appear to be made with the gut, clearly others are calculated decisions. How should these choices be approached? The quintessential expression of strategic analysis is the chapter exploring the sacrifice bunt in *The Book* by Andy Dolphin, Mitchel Lichtman, and Tom Tango. They examined potential outcomes of a sacrifice, each weighted for batter and context, and then applied a game-theoretic twist to see whether the expectations of the defense change (or can be changed by) the recommended outcome. They found that despite the sacrifice bunt looking like a poor decision in nearly every situation according to a basic run expectancy analysis, it can be a smart percentage play with a poor hitter, an excellent bunter, or sometimes just to keep the defense honest. **Status: Well understood.**

The Road Ahead

Of course, we didn't stop asking questions in 2000. Since then, the sabermetric community has exploded. Where once Bill James, Baseball Prospectus, and Rob Neyer were the standard bearers for sabermetric thought, today just about every media outlet and innumerable blogs espouse at least some of the sabermetric view.

The past decade has also seen tremendous technical advances. With PITCHf/x out in the wild, some HITf/x data available, and the hope of someday seeing FIELDf/x and TrackMan, we have access to information Woolner never could have imagined at the time. To date, researchers such as Mike Fast, Harry Pavlidis, Dave Allen, and many,

many others have had fascinating findings with this new information, but as a community, we're nowhere close to extracting all we can.

This new style of detailed information has led to a bifurcated approach to studying baseball. As Ian Lefkowitz explained:

> There are currently two major schools of sabermetrics operating today. One stream of research involves manipulating the statistical record, and for the last century, it's been the dominant philosophy, from batting average, to OBP, to wOBA, to FIP to WARP and PECOTA. Each advancement has been significant, but they all rely on the same data that's existed for more than a century, all relying upon an aggregation of outcomes.
>
> The other strain of research is vector-based analysis, ranging from the old zone ratings to PITCH and HITf/x. These studies better account for nuance, and in theory could properly allocate credit for the play. I think the problem here has been turning the data we've been collecting into a practicable method of determining value.

He identifies the next stage of evolution as transitioning from "classical" sabermetrics to "quantum" sabermetrics by marrying the macro and micro analysis. To that end, we raise the following seven questions as an invitation to study:

1. What is the most effective way to sequence pitches?

Before Josh Kalk joined the Tampa Bay Rays front office, he investigated how pitchers ordered their various pitches and identified certain patterns that exhibited success. But his analysis was static and, by necessity, backward-looking. Is it possible to derive a game theoretical approach that represents the best way to sequence the various pitches in a given hurler's repertoire?

2. Can pitchers induce weak contact?

One of the biggest mental obstacles to DIPS is the idea that pitchers have little control over whether a ball in play becomes a hit. We see that pitchers who outperform their defense-independent stats over a long period tend to be those who are successful in other aspects of their game. People have found correlations between certain tendencies and a lower-than-expected batting average on balls in play, but can we use more granular pitch data to find more conclusive answers?

3. What percentage of fielding is good positioning?

Today, we combine positioning, reaction time, and actual range into the range category of fielding. With better technology we might be able to break down the fielding components even further and get a better understanding of how big a role coaches play in fielding.

4. Why are there still so many injuries, and can we do anything about it?

Despite pitchers having been treated with kid gloves over the past few decades, they're still getting injured as often as ever. What causes injuries to pitchers? Is there any way to prevent them?

5. How will new medical advances like bionics and gene therapy affect the game?

New technologies in medicine have raised many ethical concerns in everyday life. We've seen that athletes are willing to try illicit means to get ahead, and odds are these new treatments will be much more effective than those of the past. How should baseball handle these new options, and how will they affect our ability to compare players across eras?

6. Do slumps and hot streaks correlate with speed-off-bat?

We know that batters often string together stretches of especially good or poor performance. To date, these are largely considered non-predictive and the result of random fluctuations (especially the hot streaks). Is how the batter strikes the ball more indicative of being locked in than the outcome of the at-bat? Or is "locked in" just a way to explain a string of successes, without any predictive value either?

7. Do teams have certain pitching/hitting philosophies?

Beyond focusing on defense or on-base percentage, do teams teach all their pitchers cutters, or try to get fly ball hitters? Do certain team-wide strategies have more success than others?

The past 11 years have seen the sabermetric community blossom. It's far larger, far more respected, and far more capable of dealing with the questions baseball throws at it. The technological advances that we're just now starting to see the fruits of have created tremendous opportunities for us to gain more insight into the game and to influence the outcomes to a far greater extent. The opportunity is there for analysts of all stripes to make their mark by answering these questions and many, many others. We look forward to recapping their successes in another decade.

Notes

BaseballProspectus.com, July 28, 2010, http://www.baseballprospectus .com/article.php?articleid=11589.

23   *Two examples from the oeuvre:* Steven Goldman, "Babe Ruth's Fat Dead Cats," www.BaseballProspectus.com, March 21, 2011, http://www. baseballprospectus.com/article.php?articleid=13282.

23   *The expected level of performance:* Keri, *Baseball Between the Numbers*, 425.

25   *For over 100 years:* See Keith Woolner, "Why Is Mario Mendoza So Important?" in Keri, *Baseball Between the Numbers*, 165.

25   *We finished last with you:* Lee Lowenfish, "Branch Rickey" (Lincoln: University of Nebraska, 2007), 519.

26   *Since all the players who secure jobs:* Keri, *Baseball Between the Numbers*, 159.

26   *Considering a player in a vacuum:* Goldman, "Babe Ruth's Fat Dead Cats."

27   *Bret Saberhagen is .2 WAR better:* Joe Posanski, "Wins and WAR and MVPs," www.joeposnanski.blogspot.com, September 12, 2011, http:// joeposnanski.blogspot.com/2011/09/wins-and-war-and-mvps.html.

28   *A writer calling him- or herself "Hippeaux":* Hippeaux, "Is WAR the New RBI?," itsaboutthemoney.net, September 6, 2011, http://itsaboutthe money.net/archives/2011/09/06/is-war-the-new-rbi/.

31   *Dodgers general manager Ned Colletti:* Ben Bolch, "Baseball by the Numbers," *Los Angeles Times*, August 20, 2011, http://articles.latimes.com/ 2011/aug/20/sports/la-sp-0821-baseball-stats-20110821.

33   *I have always been against a twirler pitching himself out:* Christy Mathewson, "Pitching in a Pinch" (New York: Putnam, 1912), 64.

35–36 *A statistician named Voros McCracken:* Voros McCracken, "Pitching and Defense: How Much Control Do Hurlers Have?" www.baseball prospectus.com, January 23, 2001, http://www.baseballprospectus .com/article.php?articleid=878.

38   *I've seen guys pitch bad:* Wayne Stewart, ed., *The Gigantic Book of Baseball Quotations* (New York: Skyhorse, 2007), 227.

39   *Have you seen a 420-foot ground ball?:* Stewart, *The Gigantic Book of Baseball Quotations*, 223.

43   *In 1985, Los Angeles Dodgers pitching great Fernando Valenzuela:* John Thorn and John Holway, *The Pitcher* (New York: Prentice Hall, 1987), 186.

44   *If a general manager has been out of touch:* Murray Chass, "The Minority Speaks," November 21, 2010, http://www.murraychass.com/?p=2635.

45   *The conditions it stipulates*: http://mlb.mlb.com/mlb/downloads/y2011/ Official_Baseball_Rules.pdf.

Chapter 1-1. What *Really* Happened in the Juiced Era?

55   *Everything I've done is natural:* Steve Wilstein, "Power at What Price?" *Orlando Sun-Sentinel*, August 22, 1998, http://articles.sun-sentinel.com/

1998-08-22/news/9808220034_1_androstenedione-mark-mcgwire
-lifetime-ban.

55 *Uncertainties about androstenedione's impact on the body:* "Mark Mc-Gwire's Pep Pills," *New York Times*, August 27, 1998, http://www.ny times.com/1998/08/27/opinion/mark-mcgwire-s-pep-pills.html.

55 *Steroids did to baseball what Watergate did to the presidency:* Tom Verducci, "Hard Number," *Sports Illustrated*, May 15, 2006, http://sports illustrated.cnn.com/vault/article/magazine/MAG1111195/index.htm.

57 *Speculation about the hormone's potential:* John M. Hoberman and Charles E. Yesalis, "The History of Synthetic Testosterone," *Scientific American* 272, no. 2, February 1995, 76–81.

58 *After several of its users won championships:* Terry Todd, "The Steroid Predicament," *Sports Illustrated*, August 1, 1983, http://sportsillustrated.cnn.com/vault/article/magazine/MAG1121081/index.htm.

58 *In 1963, strength coach Alvin Roy:* T. J. Quinn, "Pumped-Up Pioneers: The '63 Chargers," February 1, 2009, http://sports.espn.go.com/espn/otl/news/story?id=3866837.

58 *As many as 10,000:* Jere Longman, "East German Steroids' Toll: 'They Killed Heidi,'" *New York Times*, January 26, 2004, http://www.nytimes.com/2004/01/26/sports/drug-testing-east-german-steroids-toll-they-killed-heidi.html.

58 *Dianabol's therapeutic index is in the 2–7 range:* William N. Taylor, *Anabolic Steroids and the Athlete*, 2nd ed. (Jefferson, NC: MacFarlane and Co., 2002), 26.

59 *Nothing has ever come to my attention:* Bil Gilbert, "High Time to Make Some Rules," *Sports Illustrated*, July 7, 1969, http://sportsillustrated.cnn.com/vault/article/magazine/MAG1082583/3/index.htm.

59 *No one knows for certain how many:* James C. Mckinley Jr., "Guessing the Score: Open Secret—A Special Report," *New York Times*, October 11, 2000, http://www.nytimes.com/2000/10/11/sports/guessing-score-open-secret-special-report-steroid-suspicions-abound-major-league.html.

60 *Barrel-chested and thick-necked physique:* Tom Verducci, "Pushing 70," *Sports Illustrated*, October 8, 2001, http://sportsillustrated.cnn.com/vault/article/magazine/MAG1023848/index.htm.

60 *When Bonds was zeroing in:* Murray Chass, "It Doesn't Make Sense to Pitch to Bonds Now," *New York Times*, April 5, 2002, http://www.ny times.com/2002/04/05/sports/baseball-it-doesn-t-make-sense-to-pitch-to-bonds-now.html.

61 *Is Baseball in the Asterisk Era?:* Tom Verducci, "Is Baseball in the Asterisk Era?" *Sports Illustrated*, March 15, 2004, http://sportsillustrated.cnn.com/vault/article/magazine/MAG1031393/index.htm.

61 *Some of the evidence presented by investigators:* Carol J. Williams, "Federal Agents Illegally Seized Ballplayers' Drug-Test Records, Appeals Court Rules," *Los Angeles Times*, September 13, 2010, http://articles.latimes.com/2010/sep/13/sports/la-sp-balco-ballplayers-20100914.

62 *It took four months to get my nuts to drop down:* Tom Verducci, "Totally

Juiced," *Sports Illustrated*, June 3, 2002, http://sportsillustrated.cnn.com/vault/article/magazine/MAG1025902/1/index.htm.

62 *That there is not widespread steroid use in baseball:* Barry M. Bloom, "Mandatory Steroid Testing to Begin," November 13, 2003, http://mlb.mlb.com/news/article.jsp?ymd=20031113&content_id=603458&vkey=news_mlb&fext=.jsp&c_id=mlb.

62 *We will have to act in some way:* Barry M. Bloom, "Selig, Fehr Testify Before Senate," March 10, 2004, http://mlb.mlb.com/content/printer_friendly/mlb/y2004/m03/d10/c648635.jsp.

63 *I'm not here to talk about the past:* Barry M. Bloom, "Players, Execs Testify at Hearing," March 18, 2005, http://mlb.mlb.com/news/article.jsp?ymd=20050317&content_id=969756&vkey=news_mlb&fext=.jsp&c_id=mlb.

65 *A 2004 paper by two Dutch doctors:* Fred Hartgens and Harm Kuipers, "Effects of Androgenic-Anabolic Steroids in Athletes," *Sports Medicine* 34, no. 8 (2004): 513–54.

66 *Since, at most, 10–15% of a dose:* Cynthia M. Kuhn, "Anabolic Steroids," *Recent Progress in Hormone Research* 57 (2002): 411–34.

66 *One study that crops up frequently:* Shalender Bhasin et al, "The Effects of Supraphysiologic Doses of Testosterone on Muscle Size and Strength in Normal Men," *New England Journal of Medicine* 335 (July 4, 1996): 1–7.

67 *A 2008 paper for the* American Journal of Physics: Roger G. Tobin, "On the Potential of a Chemical Bonds: Possible Effects of Steroids on Home Run Production in Baseball," *American Journal of Physics* 76, no. 1 (2008).

68 *Different drag coefficients:* Tobin uses two models to estimate trajectory, one a simple theoretical model by Robert Adair in which there is no "drag crisis" created by the turbulence of the ball flying at a given range of speeds, the other a semi-empirical model by Gregory S. Sawicki in which the drag crisis exists.

68 *Nathan himself arrived at a similar range:* Alan M. Nathan, "The Possible Effect of Steroids on Home Run Production," *American Journal of Physics* 76 (2008): 15–20.

70 *129 players:* The Baseball's Steroid Era website (http://www.baseballssteroidera.com/bse-list-steroid-hgh-users-baseball.html) maintains the most comprehensive list of players alleged to have used steroids and HGH as well as the source of those allegations. As of October 2011, the site lists 129 major league players.

72 *From 4.12 runs per team per game to 4.60:* All per-game scoring and home run figures for this chapter are per team per game, to parallel the convention of translating to a 4.5 run per game environment for purposes of historical comparison.

80 *The average surface temperature in the US:* U.S. Environmental Protection Agency website, http://www.epa.gov/climatechange/science/recenttc.html.

80 *And altitude:* Based upon a rule of thumb in Adair's *Physics of Baseball* (full citation below), an additional 1,000 feet of altitude adds seven feet of distance to a fly ball and increases the probability of a home run by 12 percent. That comes out to an additional 1.6 percent increase in home runs from 1990 to 2010 due to the various altitude changes.

81 *Not lower than the batsman's knee:* "The Strike Zone: A Historical Timeline," http://mlb.mlb.com/mlb/official_info/umpires/strike_zone.jsp.

81 *Today's strike zone basically runs vertically:* Peter Gammons, "What Ever Happened to the Strike Zone?" *Sports Illustrated*, April 6, 1987, http://sportsillustrated.cnn.com/vault/article/magazine/MAG1065780/index.htm.

84 *Revealed no significant performance differences:* Lawrence P. Fallon and James A, Sherwood, "Performance Comparison of the 1999 and 2000 Major League Baseballs," UMass-Lowell Baseball Research Center, http://webusers.npl.illinois.edu/~a-nathan/pob/UML2000.pdf.

85 *A test sponsored by the* Cleveland Plain Dealer: Bil Sloat, "Why Today's Baseballs Go Farther," *Cleveland Plain Dealer*, September 29, 2000, 1A.

85 *Humidity and temperature controls, improved quality control:* University of Rhode Island, "Livelier Balls in Major League Baseball," *Newswise*, October 27, 2000, http://www.newswise.com/articles/livelier-balls-in-major-league-baseball.

86 *The synthetic rubber ring of the modern-day baseball:* University Medical Systems, "McGwire's 70th Home Run Ball Juiced, CT Scan Finds," January 3, 2007, http://www2.prnewswire.com/cgi-bin/stories.pl?ACCT=104&STORY=/www/story/01-03-2007/0004498891&EDATE.

86 *A cardboard washer:* Associated Press, "Study Claims Imaging Tests Show Larger Rubber Core," January 3, 2007, ESPN.go.com, http://sports.espn.go.com/mlb/news/story?id=2719191.

87 *The design is unique among all years:* University of Rhode Island, "Livelier Balls in Major League Baseball," *Newswise*, Oct. 27, 2000, http://www.newswise.com/articles/livelier-balls-in-major-league-baseball.

87 *As expected, the yarn from the 1963 ball dissolved completely:* Curtis Rist, "The Physics of Baseballs," *Discover Magazine*, May 2001, http://discovermagazine.com/2001/may/featphysics.

87 *In 1999, one year after Mark McGwire broke:* University Medical Systems, "Juiced Ball Generation: Bonds Hits Different Baseball Than Aaron, CT Scans Find," August 6, 2007, http://www.prnewswire.com/news-releases/juiced-ball-generation-bonds-hits-different-baseball-than-aaron-ct-scans-find-57881072.html.

88 *What he shows is that the* construction *of baseballs has changed:* Unpublished interview with Alan Nathan by Jay Jaffe, August 29, 2011.

89 *Although our principal finding is the lack of evidence:* Alan M. Nathan et al, "Corked Bats, Juiced Balls, and Humidors: The Physics of Cheating in Baseball," *American Journal of Physics* 79, no. 6 (June 2011).

90 *According to Hillerich & Bradsby Company:* "Facts About Louisville Slugger® Wood Bats," *Baseball: The Magazine* 1, 2009: 43.

90 *Willie Mays preferred a 34-ounce bat:* Jack McDonald, "The Flame in Willie's Bats," *Baseball Digest*, July 1966, 79, http://books.google.com/

books?id=XDIDAAAAMBAJ&pg=PA80&lpg=PA80&dq=al+simmons+38+
inches+heavy+ounce&source=bl&ots=BsQUKOPKLf&sig=smkT0yj
-mcNEI6CyC5yrEl_ol_k&hl=en&ei=PKJZTrCmNc-tgQe-lpyEDA&sa=X&
oi=book_result&ct=result&resnum=2&sqi=2&ved=0CCAQ6AEwAQ#v=
onepage&q&f=false.

90 *Mark McGwire's 35-ounce bats:* Elizabeth Parks, "Heavy Lumber," *Muscle
& Fitness* 69, no. 6, June 2008, 54, http://findarticles.com/p/articles/mi_
m0801/is_6_69/ai_n25469928/.

91 *According to the USDA Forest Products:* Roland Hernandez, "Wood Science
and How It Relates to Wooden Baseball Bats," http://www.woodbat.org.

91 *The split is about 50–50 between the two woods:* "Facts About Louisville
Slugger® Wood Bats," *Baseball: The Magazine* 1, 2009: 42.

91 *From elementary principles of mechanics:* Robert K. Adair, *The Physics of
Baseball*, 3rd ed. (New York: HarperCollins, 2002), 116.

92 *I am skeptical that there are any significant performance differences:* Dan
Fox, "Interview with a Physicist," August 2, 2007, http://www.baseball
prospectus.com/article.php?articleid=6539. Most of the published information regarding the differences between the two woods in a baseball
context comes from testing in the wake of a rash of broken maple bats in
2008, which prompted MLB to form an advisory committee of university-
based experts. From July through September of that year, 2,232 bats
broke during major league games, 756 of them into multiple pieces, with
maple bats accounting for 7.5 times as many multi-piece breakages as
ash (who knew they tracked such things?) As a wood, maple is "diffuse-
porous," in that its pores are evenly distributed throughout its annual
growth ring, making its grain structure relatively uniform. Ash is considered "ring-porous," in that its pores develop early in the annual growing
season, making for a greater contrast between its high-density bands,
which are similar to maple, and its low-density ones. When an ash bat
breaks from hitting a baseball, the wood flakes along those lines, while a
maple bat is more likely to disintegrate catastrophically, sending pieces
flying apart. As a result of these issues, one of the committee's key recommendations was to adopt strict specifications as to the slope of the
grain, which reduced the frequency of broken bats 30 percent in the first
year, and another 15 percent in the second. An ongoing issue toward further reduction is that maple's higher moisture content leads some bat
manufacturers to kiln dry the wood longer than ash, which reduces the
weight but also makes the bat more brittle.

93 *There is really no advantage in switching wood species:* Paul Basken, "University Scientists Go Extra Innings to Help Baseball Solve Breaking
Bats," *Chronicle*, November 1, 2010, http://chronicle.com/article/article
-content/125223/.

93 *Careful studies have shown:* Alan Nathan, "Comparing the Performance
of Baseball Bats," January 18, 2010, http://baseballanalysts.com/archives/
2010/01/comparing_the_p.php.

Chapter 1-2. How Should the Hall of Fame Respond to the Steroids Era?

98 *I used to look forward to the day:* Jayson Stark, "Mac Debate Sparks a Sad Start," ESPN.com, November 27, 2006, http://insider.espn.go.com/mlb/blog?name=stark_jayson&id=2677460.

99 *There's not a pill or an injection:* ESPN.com, January 12, 2010, http://sports.espn.go.com/mlb/news/story?id=4816607.

100 *Will keep everyone mired in the past:* George Mitchell, "Report to the Commissioner of Baseball of an Independent Investigation into the Illegal Use of Steroids and Other Performance Enhancing Substances by Players in Major League Baseball," December 13, 2007, Summary and Recommendations, SR-33.

101 *I'm not going to make a judgment on what the writers decide:* Jayson Stark, "The Commish Gives His State of the Game," ESPN.com, January 23, 2009, http://sports.espn.go.com/mlb/columns/story?columnist=stark_jayson&id=3853027.

101 *Voting shall be based upon the player's record:* BBWAA Election Rules, National Baseball Hall of Fame and Museum, http://baseballhall.org/hall-famers/rules-election/bbwaa.

101 *I'm not voting for any of those guys:* Tim Brown, "Pandora's Boxes," *Los Angeles Times*, July 31, 2006, http://articles.latimes.com/2006/jul/31/sports/sp-baseball31/2.

101 *If these traits didn't matter or shouldn't be considered:* Pedro Gomez, "Banned substances and the Hall of Fame," ESPN.com, May 9, 2009, http://espn.go.com/blog/sweetspot/post/_/id/182/banned-substances-and-the-hall-of-fame.

102 *No two teams in baseball had more PED connections:* Jeff Pearlman, "Jeff Bagwell and Why I Disagree with Joe Posnanski," jeffpearlman.com, December 30, 2010, http://www.jeffpearlman.com/jeff-bagwell-and-why-i-disagree-with-joe-posnanski.

105 *Distributes or possesses with the intent to distribute any anabolic steroid:* Charles Yesalis, *Anabolic Steroids in Sport and Exercise,* 2nd ed. (Champaign, IL: Human Kinetics, 2000), 343, http://bit.ly/nIetYC.

105 *The possession, sale or use of any illegal drug or controlled substance:* David Epstein, "The Rules, The Law, The Reality," quoting "Commissioner Fay Vincent's June 7, 1991 Memo," *Sports Illustrated*, February 16, 2009, http://sportsillustrated.cnn.com/vault/article/magazine/MAG1151761/index.htm.

000 *I could have done a better job of reporting:* Buster Olney, "An Outside-the-Park Investigation," *New York Times*, April 1, 2006, http://www.nytimes.com/2006/04/01/opinion/01olney.html.

106 *I have a hard time applying retroactive morality:* Don Amore, "Bagwell Gives Hall Voters Much to Consider," *Hartford Courant*, December 25, 2010, http://articles.courant.com/2010-12-25/sports/hc-bagwell-hall-of-fame-1226-20101225_1_jeff-bagwell-gain-induction-hall-of-fame-ballots/2.

106 *The clause is now causing real problems:* Joe Posnanski, "Hall of Fame Needs to Get Rid of Character Clause," SI.com, February 11, 2009, http://sportsillustrated.cnn.com/2009/writers/joe_posnanski/02/11/hall.steroids/.

107 *As good or better than the average enshrined player:* The positional standards are actually computed after eliminating the score of the lowest player at each position, and the four lowest among starting pitchers. Almost invariably, those dropped were elected by the Veterans Committee, though in the set used in this book, BBWAA honoree Catfish Hunter is among the four lowest starting pitchers.

108 *Bill James Hall of Fame Monitor:* All Bill James Hall of Fame Monitor scores cited are published on the individual player cards at the Baseball-Reference.com website, which has adapted the system James introduced in the *1983 Bill James Baseball Abstract* (Ballantine Books) and subsequently refined. A full list of rules for how the scores cited herein are calculated is published at http://www.baseball-reference.com/about/leader_glossary.shtml#hof_monitor.

112 *By the time he began using after the 1998 season:* "Barry Bonds Steroids Timeline," ESPN.com news services, December 7, 2007, http://sports.espn.go.com/mlb/news/story?id=3113127.

112 *More than $50 million in taxpayer money:* Patrick Hruby, "The Barry Bonds Trial: Was It Worth It?" *Atlantic*, April 14, 2011, http://www.theatlantic.com/entertainment/archive/2011/04/the-barry-bonds-trial-was-it-worth-it/237313.

114 *He was something of an enfant terrible:* Sheffield notoriously claimed to have intentionally made errors during his early years with the Brewers, who subjected him to non-random drug testing due to his relationship to Dwight Gooden, and once farmed him out for "indifferent fielding" only to discover once he reached the minors that he had been playing with a broken foot. Upon his retirement in February 2011, I took a detailed look at his statements and play-by-play accounts, and could find no incident that matched his description. See Jay Jaffe, "Never a Dull Moment with Gary Sheffield," baseballprospectus.com, February 18, 2011, http://www.baseballprospectus.com/article.php?articleid=12991.

114 *According to his grand jury testimony:* Lance Williams and Mark Fainaru-Wada, "What Bonds Told BALCO Grand Jury," SFgate.com, December 3, 2004, http://articles.sfgate.com/2004-12-03/news/17458729_1_clear-substance-balco-case-bonds-attorney-michael-rains/3.

114 *No different from the Neosporin you buy at Rite Aid:* Ben Shpigel, "Sheffield Makes Noise Again, This Time in a Book," *New York Times*, January 16, 2007, http://www.nytimes.com/2007/01/16/sports/baseball/16sheffield.html.

115 *Rick Reilly infamously went to the Cubs locker room:* Rick Reilly, "Excuse Me for Asking," *Sports Illustrated*, July 2, 2002, http://sportsillustrated.cnn.com/inside_game/magazine/life_of_reilly/news/2002/07/02/life_of_reilly/.

115 *His name was leaked to the* New York Times: Michael S. Schmidt, "Sosa

Is Said to Have Tested Positive," *New York Times*, June 16, 2009, http://www.nytimes.com/2009/06/17/sports/baseball/17doping.html.

116 *Piazza has said he briefly used androstenedione:* Rafael Hermoso and Tyler Kepner, "Steroid Use Becomes a Topic of Discussion in Clubhouses," *New York Times*, May 30, 2002, http://www.nytimes.com/2002/05/30/sports/baseball-steroid-use-becomes-a-topic-of-discussion-in-clubhouses.html.

117 *When the subject of performance enhancing was broached:* Jeff Pearlman, *The Rocket That Fell to Earth* (New York: Harper, 2009), 240.

Chapter 1-3. What Is the Next Stage in Athlete Enhancement?

121 *Opium derivatives were used:* M. Thevis, M*ass Spectrometry in Sports Drug Testing: Characterization of Prohibited Substances and Doping Control Analytical Assays* (Hoboken, NJ: Wiley, 2010).

121 *The abuse of anabolic steroids:* M. Janosfsky, "Coaches Concede That Steroids Fueled East Germany's Success in Swimming," *New York Times*, http://www.nytimes.com/1991/12/03/sports/olympics-coaches-concede-that-steroids-fueled-east-germany-s-success-in-swimming.html.

123 *Few studies have noted a positive effect:* Will Carroll, "Frickin' Laser Beams," www.baseballprospectus.com, http://www.baseballprospectus.com/article.php?articleid=9969.

124 *MSCs are present in everyone:* Stephen Faulkner, "The Use of Mesenchymal Stem Cells in Orthopedics," *Journal of American Physicians and Surgeons* 16, no. 2 (2011): 38–44.

125 *Two PRP injections spaced four to six weeks apart:* C. J. Nitkowski, "A First-Hand Experience with Stem Cell Treatment in Pitching Arm," *Sports Illustrated*, http://sportsillustrated.cnn.com/2011/writers/the_bonus/08/02/nitkowski/1.html.

126 *The idea of using genes to treat illnesses:* H. L. Sweeney, "Gene Doping," *Scientific American* 291, no. 1 (July 2004): 62–69.

126 *Gene doping involves changing the DNA structure:* A. J. Schneider and T. Friedmann, "Gene Doping in Sports: The Science and Ethics of Genetically Modified Athletes." *Advances in Genetics* 51 (2006): 1–110; G. R. Gaffney and R. Parisotto, "Doping: A Review of Performance-Enhancing Genetics," *Pediatric Clinics of North America* 54, no. 4 (August 2007): xii–xiii, 807–22.

127 *A 15 percent increase in muscle size:* P. McCrory, "Super Athletes or Gene Cheats?" *Journal of Sports Medicine* 37, no. 3 (June 2003): 192–93.

128 *Jay Howell wouldn't have been ejected:* http://sports.espn.go.com/espn/columns/story?columnist=wojciechowski_gene&id=2635618.

128 *Kenny Rogers's left hand:* http://articles.latimes.com/1988-10-09/sports/sp-5637_1_jay-howell. Oddly enough, both examples of pitcher cheating involve Tony La Russa.

128 *Artificial muscles that were over 100 times stronger:* "Scientists Demonstrate Nanotech Artificial Muscles Powered by Highly Energetic Fields,"

http://biosingularity.com/2006/03/20/scientists-demonstrate-artificial
-muscles-powered-by-nanotech-fuels/.

128 *While also able to produce 30 times more force:* Nanotechnology Now, "Carbon Nanotube Artificial Muscles for Extreme Temperatures Invented at UT Dallas," http://www.nanotech-now.com/news.cgi?story_id=32536.

Chapter 2-1. How Are Players Scouted, Acquired, and Developed?

Portions of this chapter are adapted from material originally published at www.baseballprospectus.com.

Chapter 2-2. How Does Age Affect the Amateur Draft?

156 *Bill James addressed this very point:* Bill James, *The Bill James Baseball Abstract 1987* (New York: Ballentine, 1987), 56.

158 *The expected value of a draft pick is highly dependent on when he was picked:* Rany Jazayerli, "The Draft," www.baseballprospectus.com, May 13, 2005, http://www.baseballprospectus.com/article.php?articleid=4026.

Chapter 2-4. How Can We Evaluate General Managers?

Portions of this chapter are adapted from material originally published at www.baseballprospectus.com.

204 *Theo Epstein in a Box:* Researched by Clark Goble and Ben Howard.

204 *He was in the strange position*: Christina Kahrl and Jonah Keri, "Shopping for Winners" in Steven Goldman, ed. *Mind Game* (New York: Workman, 2005), 21.

205 *Only four teams have ever exceeded the payroll threshold*: Maury Brown, "Yankees Surpass $200 Million in Total Luxury Tax Payments." *Bizof baseball.com.* http://bit.ly/u97ErN.

210 *Epstein's bravura performance*: *Mind Game*, 22–23; Jay Jaffe, "You Want Me to Hit Like a Little Bitch?" in Goldman, ed. *Mind Game*, 97–98.

216 *Ben Lindbergh recently argued:* Ben Lindbergh, "Keeping Up with the Friedmans," *Baseballprospectus.com*, December 20, 2011. http://www.baseballprospectus.com/article.php?articleid=15703.

Chapter 2-5. How Do Teams Like the Orioles, Pirates, and Royals Get Broken, and How Can They Be Fixed?

219 *A baseball continuum on which every team resides:* Jonah Keri, "The Success Cycle," *Baseball Prospectus*, http://www.baseballprospectus.com/article.php?articleid=1357.

220 *Where do you get, sticking along with the veterans?:* Steven Goldman, *Forging Genius* (Dulles, VA: Potomac Books, 2005), 191.

221 *Look at us, we build and win at the same time:* Goldman, *Forging Genius,* 262.

225 *No matter how much it might hurt his business:* Joe Posnanski, "The Cubs," *Sports Illustrated,* http://joeposnanski.si.com/2011/10/12/the-cubs/.

227 *And watch him continue to sink: Baseball Prospectus 2007* (New York: Plume, 2007), 398.

229 *Would have been overpaid at the major league minimum: Baseball Prospectus 2004* (New York: Workman, 2004), 392.

230 *The age of the great correctives to competitive failings: Baseball Prospectus 2010* (Hoboken, NJ: Wiley, 2010), 41.

Chapter 2-6. How Can We Evaluate Managers?

232 *He had never dreamed of managing a major league club:* Frank O'Rourke, "The Manager" in *The Heavenly World Series* (New York: Carroll & Graf, 2002).

233 *If I send Terry Crowley in:* Earl Weaver, *Weaver on Strategy* (Dulles, VA: Brassey's, 2002), 184–85.

236 *If [he had] got a hit:* Richard Bak, "Casey Stengel: A Splendid Baseball Life" (Dallas: Taylor, 1997), 105.

236 *The hardest part of managing:* John Thorn and John Holway, *The Pitcher* (New York: Prentice Hall Press, 1987), 117.

236 *It comes down to you make a move:* Anthony Castrovince, "La Russa's Moves Backfire, Benefit Texas," mlb.com, October 21, 2011, http://atmlb.com/oe3Wb8.

236 *In the end, we may be forced to concede:* James Click, "Is Joe Torre a Hall of Fame Manager?" in Keri, *Baseball Between the Numbers*, 153–54.

237 *Click performed a brief study:* Chris Jaffe, *Evaluating Baseball's Managers: A History and Analysis of Performance in the Major Leagues, 1876–2008* (Jefferson, NC: McFarland, 2010), 6–7.

238–239 *Modern managers make [their] strategic decisions:* James Click, "Is Joe Torre a Hall of Fame Manager?" in Keri, *Baseball Between the Numbers,* 141.

239 *Most managers have little effect:* Leonard Koppet, *The New Thinking Fan's Guide to Baseball* (New York: Simon & Schuster, 1991), 103.

240 *Ever occur to you tomorrow's another day?:* Willie Mays and Charles Einstein, *Willie Mays: My Life In and Out of Baseball* (New York: Dutton, 1966), 94–95.

240 *Durocher took Mays aside*: James S. Hirsch, *Willie Mays* (New York: Scribner, 2010), 244–45.

241 *By dissembling in the press in 1943:* Tom Meany, *The Incredible Giants* (New York: A. S. Barnes, 1955), 37.

241 *If nine of you fellows want to play: Sporting News,* July 15, 1943.

241 *The normally placid player preferred sudden retirement:* At Vaughan's Hall of Fame induction, his daughter insisted that although Vaughn "may not have liked the way [Durocher] did things," health and family concerns also played a part in his decision to retire, *Sporting News,* August 12, 1985, 10.

241 *When he stumbled Stengel quickly sent him packing*: Jaffe, *Evaluating Baseball's Managers,* 192.

241 *Shake my hand? He wasn't even there to say good-bye:* Goldman, *Forging Genius,* 83.

241 *You can't relax, . . . He did:* Dom Forker, *The Men of Autumn* (Dallas: Taylor, 1989), 3.

241 *After the Yankees had put Page on the trading block: Sporting News,* December 20, 1950, 9.

242 *Examples of the "what have you done for me lately" attitude*: Jaffe, *Evaluating Baseball's Managers,* 191.

242 *That little punk:* Fred McMane, *The Quotable Casey* (Nashville: Towle House, 2002), 93.

243 *An un-Yankee-like Yankee:* Maury Allen, *You Could Look It Up: The Life of Casey Stengel* (New York: Times Books, 1979), 184.

243 *I think Richardson can be a very good player: Sporting News,* June 26, 1957, 11; September 25, 1957, 3.

243 *The owners and Mr. Weiss didn't like that at all:* Casey Stengel, *My Turn at Bat* (New York: Random House, 1962), 204.

243 *What I thought wouldn't make a difference:* Maury Allen, *Damn Yankee: The Billy Martin Story* (New York: Times Books, 1980), 121.

243 *A sorrowful Stengel:* Robert Creamer, *Stengel: His Life and Times* (New York: Simon & Schuster, 1984, 270.

243 *I asked him, "Who else is in the trade?":* Peter Golenbock, *Wild, High, and Tight: The Life and Death of Billy Martin* (New York: St. Martin's Press, 1994), 121.

244 *Though McGraw produced a bountiful supply:* Jaffe, *Evaluating Baseball's Managers,* 105.

245 *Any time I was on the bench: Sporting News*, April 22, 1967, 36.

245 *You've been blaming other people:* Bob Broeg, *Superstars of Baseball* (South Bend, IN: Diamond, 1994), 464–65.

246 *A wonderful young man:* Whitey Herzog, *White Rat* (New York: Harper & Row, 1987), 105.

246 *Missed final game of playoffs with toothache:* Zander Hollander, ed., *The Complete Handbook of Baseball 1978* (New York: Signet, 1978), 131.

247 *If I knew a guy had a problem:* Whitey Herzog, *You're Missin' a Great Game* (New York: Simon & Schuster, 1999), 158. See also Bill James, *The Bill James Guide to Baseball Managers* (New York: Scribner, 1997), 270.

247 *No ballplayer should ever get into the habit:* Casey Stengel and Harry T. Paxton, *Casey at the Bat* (New York: Random House, 1961), 19.

247 *The Indian center fielder I inherited:* Bobby Bragan, *You Can't Hit the Ball with the Bat on Your Shoulder* (Fort Worth, TX: Summit Group, 1992), 224–25.

247 *Clashed with younger players John Olerud and Shawn Green:* Bob Elliot, "Shawn Green: Who Knew?," *Toronto Sun*, June 11, 2011, http://www.torontosun.com/2011/06/11/shawn-green-who-knew.

249 *Each new player delivered in the spring:* Hank Greenberg, "How We Got into the Series," *Life*, September 27, 1954, 148.

249 *Less than thrilled: New York Times*, December 13, 1995, B19.

249 *Jeter would only be given an "opportunity": New York Times*, February 21, 1996.

252 *To measure the ways teams under- or overachieve:* Jaffe, *Evaluating Baseball's Managers*, 7.

253 *I do not believe in limiting myself:* Jaffe, *Evaluating Baseball's Managers*, 11.

254 *The standing at present is 53 disputes:* Pete Williams, ed., *The Joe Williams Baseball Reader* (Chapel Hill, NC: Algonquin, 1989), 69.

254 *Huggins later argued: Sporting News*, July 29, 1978.

254 *That bastard in Baltimore wouldn't do it:* Hank Bauer, interview with Steven Goldman, 2006.

255 *Earl did have a strategy for that year:* Bobby Grich, interview with Steven Goldman. "MLB Roundtrip with Baseball Prospectus," MLB Network Radio, SiriusXM, December 9, 2011.

255 *There I was, my third year in the big leagues:* Alex Belth, "Mutiny on the Weaver," in Steven Goldman, ed., *It Ain't Over 'Til It's Over* (New York: Basic, 2007), 227.

255 *Was dictated or heavily influenced:* Ed Linn, *Steinbrenner's Yankees* (New York: Holt, 1982), 319.

255 *That sonofabitch:* Bill Madden, *Steinbrenner* (New York: Harper, 2010), 206.

Chapter 3-1. Why Is Building a Bullpen the Hardest Task a General Manager Can Undertake?

260 *According to research by Baseball Prospectus (BP) alum Eric Seidman:* Eric Seidman, "Relievers and the Value of Perfect Information," Baseball Prospectus, http://www.baseballprospectus.com/article.php?articleid=12622.

265 *According to research by BP's Derek Carty:* Derek Carty, "When Pitchers' Stats Stabilize," Baseball Prospectus, http://www.baseballprospectus.com/article.php?articleid=14293.

Chapter 3-2. Are Relievers Being Used Properly?

269 *Eckersley credited the movie with revitalizing his career:* Bob Ryan, "Saving the Eck: Dennis Eckersley's Move from Starter to Closer Extended

His Career," *Baseball Digest*, August 2003, http://findarticles.com/p/articles/mi_m0FCI/is_8_62/ai_104362913/.

270 *Long enough to squander a four-run lead:* Marc Carig, "Yankees Manager Joe Girardi and His Use of 'Our Eighth-Inning Guy,'" *New Jersey Star-Ledger*, April 6, 2011, http://www.nj.com/yankees/index.ssf/2011/04/yankees_manager_joe_girardi_an_2.html.

270 *Baseball Prospectus's Steven Goldman responded:* Steven Goldman, "Joe Girardi's Comfort Thing," Baseball Prospectus, July 19, 2011, http://www.baseballprospectus.com/article.php?articleid=14563.

277 *I'll let him explain:* Dave Studeman, "The One About Win Probability," *Hardball Times*, December 27, 2004, http://www.hardballtimes.com/main/article/the-one-about-win-probability/.

Chapter 3-3. Could Stephen Strasburg's Injury Have Been Predicted or Prevented?

283 *Strasburg's talent is historic:* Kevin Goldstein, "Nationals Top 11 Prospects," Baseball Prospectus, http://www.baseballprospectus.com/article.php?articleid=10121.

284 *The Shoulder and Its Miseries:* http://www.hss.edu/images/articles/shoulder_anatomy.jpg.

285 *During the windup and stride stages, especially:* Glenn Fleisig et al, "Kinetics of Baseball Pitching with Implications about Injury Mechanisms," *American Journal of Sports Medicine*, 23, no. 2 (1995): 233–39.

286 *At the end of the arm-cocking phase:* Glenn S. Fleisig et al, "Risk of Serious Injury for Young Baseball Pitchers: A 10-Year Prospective Study," *American Journal of Sports Medicine* 39 (2011): 253.

287 *According to medical studies, this late external rotation increases the load:* Rod Whiteley, "Baseball Throwing Mechanics as They Relate to Pathology and Performance: A Review," *Journal of Sports Science and Medicine* 6 (2007): 1–20.

287 *Strasburg's peculiar mechanics also had implications for his elbow:* Arnel L. Aguinaldo and Henry Chambers, "Correlation of Throwing Mechanics with Elbow Valgus Load in Adult Baseball Pitchers," *American Journal of Sports Medicine* 37, no. 10 (2009): 2043–48.

289 *A 2001 study noted a five-mile-per-hour drop:* Tricia A. Murray et al, "The Effects of Extended Play on Professional Baseball Pitchers," *American Journal of Sports Medicine* 29, no. 2 (March–April, 2001): 137–42.

289 *This relationship of increased hip extension:* Steve Scher et al, "Associations Among Hip and Shoulder Range of Motion and Shoulder Injury in Professional Baseball Players," *Journal of Athletic Training* 45, no. 2 (2010): 191–97.

289 *As a result, the upper extremity needs to generate more force:* Jeff Wright et al, "Influence of Pelvis Rotation Styles on Baseball Pitching Mechanics," *Sports Biomechanics* 3, no. 1 (2004): 67–83.

289 *Another study six years later:* Rafael F. Escamilla et al, "Pitching Biomechanics as a Pitcher Approaches Muscular Fatigue During a Simulated Baseball Game," *American Journal of Sports Medicine* 35, no. 1 (January 2007): 23–33.

289 *Proprioception suffered in the setting of muscle fatigue:* Michael Voight et al, "The Effects of Muscle Fatigue on and the Relationship of Arm Dominance to Shoulder Proprioception," *Journal of Orthopaedic and Sports Physical Therapy* 23, no. 6 (June 1996): 348–52.

290 *Anything prior to the 50-foot mark:* Mike Fast, "Pitcher Release Points," www.baseballprospectus.com, http://www.baseballprospectus.com/article.php?articleid=12432.

291 *Rany Jazayerli introduced the concept of "pitcher abuse points":* Rany Jazayerli, "Pitcher Abuse Points," www.baseballprospectus.com, http://www.baseballprospectus.com/article.php?articleid=148.

294 *By pushing through discomfort:* Stephen S. Burkhart et al, "The Disabled Throwing Shoulder: Spectrum of Pathology Part III: The SICK Scapula, Scapular Dyskinesis, the Kinetic Chain, and Rehabilitation," *Arthroscopy: The Journal of Arthroscopic and Related Surgery* 19 no. 6 (2003): 641–61.

294 *It is not until the pitcher is using maximum effort:* Glenn S. Flesig et al, "Biomechanical Comparison of Baseball Pitching and Long-Toss: Implications for Training and Rehabilitation," *Journal of Orthopaedic Sports and Physical Therapy* 41, no. 5 (May 2011): 296–303.

Chapter 3-4. What Has PITCHf/x Taught Us?

297 *Walter Johnson fastball hissed when it passed:* John Thorn and John Holway, "The Pitcher" (Prentice Hall Press, New York, 1988), 148.

297 *Sandy Koufax curveball dropped off a table:* Brian Endsley, "Bums No More" (McFarland, NC, 2009), 136.

297 *Hoyt Wilhelm knuckleball leapt and quivered:* Roger Angell, "Five Seasons" (Simon and Schuster, New York, 1977), 82.

297 *Adair researched and published a book:* Robert Adair, *The Physics of Baseball* (Harper-Collins, New York, 1990).

298 *Nathan has led the effort to learn about the aerodynamics:* Alan Nathan, "The Physics of Baseball," http://webusers.npl.illinois.edu/~a-nathan/pob/.

299 *Argued that a forkball was an off-speed pitch:* Bill James and Rob Neyer, *The Neyer/James Guide to Pitchers* (Fireside, New York, 2004), 50.

299 *Data on the forkballs thrown by three pitchers:* Mike Fast, "The Forkball," http://www.baseballprospectus.com/article.php?articleid=12558.

299 *They quoted veteran pitcher Tom Candiotti:* James and Neyer, *The Neyer/James Guide to Pitchers*, 13.

299 *Longtime pitching coach Bob Cluck:* James and Neyer, *The Neyer/James Guide to Pitchers*, 38.

300 *Shuuto appears to be a general description:* Mike Fast, "The Shuuto," http://www.hardballtimes.com/main/blog_article/the-shuuto/.

300 *Okajima's rainbow curve:* Matt Lentzner, "Okajima's Mystery Pitch," 2010 Sportvision PITCHf/x Summit.

301 *Taught us a lot about how pitchers use their pitches:* Harry Pavlidis, "Benchmarks for pitch types," http://www.hardballtimes.com/main/article/benchmarks-for-pitch-types/.

303 *Shedding light on its true nature:* Mike Fast, "The Real Strike Zone," http://www.baseballprospectus.com/article.php?articleid=12965.

304 *Catcher mechanics in receiving the pitch cleanly:* Mike Fast, "Removing the Mask," http://www.baseballprospectus.com/article.php?articleid=15093.

Chapter 3-5. Is Jack Morris a Hall of Famer?

311 *Each comparison starts with 1,000 points:* Per Baseball-Reference (http://www.baseball-reference.com/about/similarity.shtml), "Similarity scores are not my concept. Bill James introduced them nearly 15 years ago, and I lifted his methodology from his book *The Politics of Glory* (p. 86–106)." For pitchers, the method is to start with 1,000 points and subtract 1 point for each difference of one win, two losses, .002 in winning percentage (max 100 points), .02 in ERA (max 100 points), 10 games pitched, 20 starts, 20 complete games, 50 innings pitched, 50 hits allowed, 30 strikeouts, 10 walks, five shutouts, three saves. If a pitcher throws with a different hand and is a starter subtract 10, reliever subtract 25. For relievers, halve the winning percentage penalty, which can be up to 1.5 times the wins and losses penalty. Relievers are defined as more relief appearances than starts, and less than 4.0 innings per appearance.

314 *I know one of the huge knocks is my high E.R.A.:* Tyler Kepner, "Jack Morris Talks About His Place in History," *New York Times*, May 8, 2011, http://bats.blogs.nytimes.com/2011/05/08/jack-morris-talks-about-his-place-in-history/.

315 *The pitcher was four wins ahead of his projected record:* Greg Spira, "Pitching to the Score." Originally published at Stathead.com, date unknown, retrieved via the Internet Archive Wayback Machine (http://bit.ly/tX9bkc).

315 *Morris' team scored five runs in nearly half his career starts:* Joe Sheehan, "The Jack Morris Project," BaseballProspectus.com, April 24, 2003, http://www.baseballprospectus.com/article.php?articleid=1815. Previously published in the *Joe Sheehan Newsletter* 1, nos. 41–42.

Chapter 4-1. Is It Possible to Accurately Measure Fielding without Shoving a GPS Device up Derek Jeter's Ass?

325 *It's more than a little surprising:* Henry Chadwick, *The Game of Base Ball*, George Munro & Co., 1868, http://www.baseballchronology.com/Baseball/Books/Classic/Chadwick_Game_of_Baseball/Book-2.asp.

326 *Branch Rickey perfectly summarized the problems:* Branch Rickey, "Good-bye to Some Old Baseball Ideas," *Life*, 1954, http://www.baseballthink factory.org/btf/pages/essays/rickey/goodby_to_old_idea.htm.

327 *Bill James likened the problem:* Tom Tippett, "Evaluating Defense," *Diamond Mind Baseball*, December 5, 2002, http://web.archive.org/web/20100302043443/http://www.diamond-mind.com/articles/defeval.htm.

328 *Peter Jensen compared data:* Peter Jensen, "Is Seeing Believing?," *Hardball Times*, April 1, 2008, http://www.hardballtimes.com/main/article/is-seeing-believing/.

328 *Mitchel Lichtman compared:* Tom Tango, "UZR v PMR v UZR," *The Book*, December 9, 2008, http://www.insidethebook.com/ee/index.php/site/comments/uzr_v_pmr_v_uzr/.

328 *Comparing UZR based on two different data sources:* Tom Tango, "sUZR v bUZR," *The Book*, December 12, 2008, http://www.insidethebook.com/ee/index.php/site/comments/suzr_v_buzr/.

328 *Using stadium diagrams, photographs:* Colin Wyers, "When Is a Fly Ball a Line Drive?," *Hardball Times*, December 4, 2009, http://www.hardball times.com/main/article/when-is-a-fly-ball-a-line-drive/.

330 *Data provided by Lichtman suggests:* Tom Tango, "Our Lab: Bias in Batted Ball Data," *The Book*, December 2, 2010. http://www.insidethebook.com/ee/index.php/site/comments/our_lab_bias_in_batted_ball_data/.

330 *Data provided by Shane Jensen seems to indicate:* Shane T. Jensen et al, "Bayesball: A Bayesian Hierarchical Model for Evaluating Fielding in Major League Baseball," *Annals of Applied Statistics* 3, no. 2 (2009), http://www-stat.wharton.upenn.edu/~stjensen/papers/shanejensen.bayes ball09.pdf.

331 *A fundamental change to how we consider fielding stats:* Bill James, *The New Bill James Historical Baseball Abstract* (New York: Simon and Schuster, 2001), 354.

Chapter 4-2. How Do We Value Hitting vs. Fielding?

336 *Defense to me is the key to playing baseball:* Willie Mays, interview with the Academy of Achievement, February 19, 1996, http://www.achievement .org/autodoc/page/may0int-2.

337 *Some improvements since the formula's creation:* Bill James revised the fixed exponent from 2 to 1.83 in order to better match actual results. Clay Davenport and others determined that a floating exponent based on runs per game was a better approach for a wide variety of run scoring environments (see http://www.baseballprospectus.com/article.php? articleid=342). However, Davenport's Pythagenport formula still didn't account for extremely low run scoring environments (including the special case of one run per game). David Smyth and the saberist known as Patriot independently developed similar methods for calculating the proper exponent that provides the best fit for the variety of situations un-

der consideration (see http://gosu02.tripod.com/id69.html). The outcome, the Pythagenpat formula, is expressed as:

Win% = RS^X / (RS^X + RA^X) where X = ((RS + RA)/G) ^ .285

337 *What about teams that aren't as balanced?:* A 79-win team that adds 20 runs offensively will do approximately as well as one whose pitchers give up 20 runs fewer. Above 79 wins, adding runs is better. Below 79 wins, saving runs is more important.

337 *For good teams, reducing your overall runs:* Steven J. Miller, "A Derivation of the Pythagorean Won-Loss Formula in Baseball," *Chance Magazine*, 2007, http://arxiv.org/abs/math/0509698.

338 *A team's actual won-loss record:* Clay Davenport and Keith Woolner, "Revisiting the Pythagorean Theorem," Baseball Prospectus, June 30, 1999, http://www.baseballprospectus.com/article.php?articleid=342.

339 *A measure like WARP assumes we have equal certainty:* For more information about what goes into a win-based value calculation, check out the basis behind WARP (http://www.baseballprospectus.com/article.php?articleid=12377) as well as David Cameron's series on WAR (http://www.fangraphs.com/blogs/index.php/glossary/#winvalues).

339 *The rule of thumb:* Tom Tango, "Reliability of UZR," *The Book*, http://www.insidethebook.com/ee/index.php/site/comments/reliability_of_uzr/.

339 *By the time you get enough information*: Tom Tango, "Fielding Aging Curves," *Hardball Times*, http://www.hardballtimes.com/main/article/fielding-aging-curves/.

340 *Similar . . . forces are at play in the baseball talent market:* Baseball introduces many distortions into the classical microeconomic model. The guaranteed team control and arbitration process artificially lowers the cost of young players, while the relative scarcity of any given good (player) and the imbalance of available funds can over-inflate free agent salaries. Fixed roster sizes limit to some extent the ability of a team to leverage a wealth advantage, as does revenue sharing. Of course, market advantages granted by the cartel that is MLB create huge discrepancies in initial revenue distribution as well.

340 *The replacement level player is league average:* Jeff Sackman, "Another Look at Replacement Level," *Hardball Times*, August 12, 2010, http://www.hardballtimes.com/main/article/another-look-at-replacement-level/.

341 *Iron-gloved players like Pat Burrell:* Jayson Stark, "Rays Sign Burrell for 2 Years," January 6, 2010, http://sports.espn.go.com/mlb/news/story?id=3811501.

Chapter 5-1. How Did Jose Bautista Become a Star?

348 *I knew it was probably going to be my last chance:* Vinay Menon, "The Secret of Jose Bautista's Sweet Swing," *Toronto Star*, June 17, 2011.

350 *The explanation is simple enough:* Pat Borzi, "Bautista Shortens His

Swing and Sends More Balls a Longer Distance," *New York Times*, October 2, 2010.

351 *You've got to at least ask the question:* Damien Cox, *Toronto Star*, August 22, 2010, http://thestar.blogs.com/thespin/2010/08/gotta-at-least-ask-the -question.html.

352 *Bautista being heckled by White Sox relievers:* Amy K. Nelson and Peter Keating, "Signs of Trouble in Toronto," *ESPN: The Magazine*, August 10, 2011.

353 *We compare each player's production:* Colin Wyers, "A Walk in the Park," Baseball Prospectus, September 22, 2010, http://www.baseballprospectus .com/article.php?articleid=12047.

354 *Was it a good deal for Toronto?:* Keith Law, "Baseball Today," ESPN.com, March 2, 2011.

355 *Jason Whitlock offered the following:* Jason Whitlock, "Sports Closer to Art Than Science," Foxsports.com, http://msn.foxsports.com/mlb/story/ sabermetrics-moneyball-stat-geeks-are-ruining-sports-092211.

357 *Inexplicable changes in performance:* Nate Silver, "What Do Statistics Tell Us About Steroids?" in Keri, *Baseball Between the Numbers*, 340.

Chapter 5-2. When Does a Hot Start Become Real?

359 *Excellent leveraging of the bullpen:* Chris Jaffe, "No Mirage in Arizona," *Hardball Times*, http://www.hardballtimes.com/main/article/no-mirage -in-arizona/.

360 *Rany Jazayerli studied this very topic at our website*: Rany Jazayerli, Baseball Prospectus, http://www.baseballprospectus.com/article.php?article id=1818; http://www.baseballprospectus.com/article.php?articleid=1838; http://www.baseballprospectus.com/article.php?articleid=1866.

360 *And in the book* It Ain't Over 'Til It's Over: Rany Jazayerli, "The Break" in *It Ain't Over 'Til It's Over: The Baseball Prospectus Pennant Race Book* (Basic Books: New York, 1983).

360 *A phenomenon he dubbed the "whirlpool principle":* Bill James, *The Bill James Baseball Abstract 1983* (Ballantine Books: New York, 1983).

361 *How much of each to use is determined by the Pearson correlation:* What I've done is look at all teams in all years since 1962 (the year the 162 game schedule was adopted by both leagues), excluding the strike-shortened 1972, 1981, 1994, and 1995 seasons. I looked at each team's record in one-game increments—that is, after the first game of the season has been played, after the second game has been played, etc.—and run a Pearson correlation using each team's record to date as the first variable and its end-of-season record as the second variable. By finding the number of games at which R equals 0.50, we can figure out how much to weight performance and how much to weight league average when creating our expected end-of-season record. To do this, we use the formula $n/(n+x)$, where n is the number of games that the team has played and x

is the number of games at which R equals 0.50. So if R equals 0.50 once a team has played 50 games, if a team is playing .600 ball after 45 games, our formula is 45/(45+50) = 47 percent. That's the weight that the team's actual performance gets. The remaining 53 percent goes to league average. Therefore, our expected end-of-season winning percentage for that team would be 0.547 (.600*.47+.500*.53). And once we have our formula, we can do this no matter how many games have been played.

361 *See the endnotes for the specifics of how to do this:* Because we are always dealing with a limited amount of data, we're never going to be able to take a baseball player's performance at face value. If a batter hits .300 one year, are we going to say, "Okay, he hit .300 this year, so he's absolutely going to hit .300 next year, too"? Of course not. The batter hit .300 over just 600 at-bats, and it's very likely he could hit .250 or .280 or .320 next year; we've seen it happen thousands of times before. If we were able to give the batter one billion at-bats and he hit .300, then we might be able to say with more certainty that, yes, he is a true .300 hitter. But we can't do that. We have to work with what we're given, and we use regression to the mean to help us. Regression to the mean tells us that, absent other information, a batter or team that performs above or below league average in one season should be expected to perform closer to league average the next season. This may sound strange at first, but it is unequivocally true, and it really does make sense, when you think about it. If Albert Pujols hits .400 in 2012, what are you going to expect him to hit in 2013? Less than .400, I would think.

What regression to the mean does is look at the sample size we're dealing with and says, "Okay, the sample is big enough so that, in our projection, we can give the player's actual performance a weight of 60 percent. Because it's still a sample, though, and nowhere near the billion or so at-bats we would need to say that this performance is completely real, the player is bound to be drawn toward the center of that whirlpool to some extent, so we'll assign league average performance the remaining 40 percent of weight."

362 *A page from Bill James:* Bill James, *The Bill James Guide to Baseball Managers* (Scribner: New York, 1997).

363 *Jazayerli's studies . . . found the number to be closer to 48 games:* Rany Jazayerli, Baseball Prospectus, http://www.baseballprospectus.com/article.php?articleid=1866.

364 *Jazayerli took this second definition a step further:* If a team is expected to be good in February, it's going to be good in April and May more often than a team that was expected to be bad in February. Therefore, if you look at all teams that get off to a hot start in April and May, some of them would have been predicted to do so in the preseason. Others won't have been. Either way, that hot start is still going to be able to predict a team's final record reasonably well. What Jazayerli's method does is isolate the percentage of a hot start that would have been predictable before the season. It throws it in the trash and focuses only on the part that wasn't pre-

dicted, which reduces how well the hot start predicts the final record. Then he takes this and combines it with the preseason expectation to predict the final record. It's important for him to throw that part of the hot start away because, otherwise, you'd be counting part of the preseason expectation twice—once on its own and once where it overlaps with the hot start. If you're counting how many tacos you have, you don't want to count the same taco twice—you'll overestimate how many tacos you have.

Epilogue: Catching Up with Baseball's Hilbert Problems

379 *The progress of sabermetrics has always been:* Bastardization of a quote by Tsung-Dao Lee, "Weak Interactions and Nonconservation of Parity," Nobel lecture, December 11, 1957, in *Nobel Lectures: Physics 1942–1962* (1964), 417, http://www.todayinsci.com/QuotationsCategories/P_Cat/Progress-Quotations.htm.

380 *Keith Woolner . . . took a page from the great mathematician:* "Hilbert's Problems," Wikipedia, http://en.wikipedia.org/wiki/Hilbert%27s_problems; Keith Woolner, "Baseball's Hilbert Problems," Baseball Prospectus 2000, republished February 10, 2004, at http://www.baseballprospectus.com/article.php?articleid=2551.

380 *Pitchers had little variability in preventing hits on balls in play:* Voros McCracken, "How Much Control Do Hurlers Have?" Baseball Prospectus, January 23, 2001, http://www.baseballprospectus.com/article.php?articleid=878; although he stated the idea in multiple fora before this article. For a very interesting profile of McCracken, see Jeff Passan, "Sabermetrician in Exile," Yahoo! Sports: The Post Game, January 25, 2011, http://www.thepostgame.com/node/367.

Other contributions to this area are too numerous to list. Clay Dreslough, Tom Tippet, Chris Dial, J. C. Bradbury, David Gassko, and many others have greatly enhanced our understanding of the interaction of pitching and defense.

380 *Did playing next to quality third basemen:* Mike Emeigh explored this theory in a multi-part series of articles in 2002 and found a strange ball in play distribution for the Yankees that suggested that the third basemen took more balls in the hole than expected. Mike Emeigh, "And the Beat Goes On: Derek Jeter and the State of Fielding Analysis in Sabermetrics," Baseball Think Factory, November 21, 2002, http://www.baseballthinkfactory.org/files/primate_studies/discussion/emeigh_2002-11-21_0/.

380 *Did John Olerud make the 1999 Mets infield the best ever?:* Tom Verducci, "Glove Affair," *Sports Illustrated*, September 6, 1999, http://sportsillustrated.cnn.com/vault/article/magazine/MAG1016976/index.htm.

381 *You have to have a catcher:* Casey Stengel, http://www.caseystengel.com/quotes_by.htm.

381 *Woolner himself took the initial swing at solving this problem:* Keith Woolner, *Baseball Prospectus 1999* (Dulles, VA: Potomac Books, 1999) and Keith Woolner, *Baseball Prospectus 2004* (New York: Workman, 2004).

381 *Since that time, numerous researchers . . . have leveraged alternative approaches and technological data:* "With or Without You Approach:" Tom Tango, *The Hardball Times Annual 2008* (Skokie, IL: Acta Publications, 2008).

Blocking Pitches using PITCHf/x data: Dan Turkenkopf, "2010 Catcher Block Percentage," Beyond the Box Score, December 28, 2009, http://www.beyondtheboxscore.com/2009/12/28/1220699/2010-catcher -block-percentage;

Framing Pitches using PITCHf/x data: Dan Turkenkopf, "Framing the Debate," Beyond the Box Score, April 5, 2008, http://www.beyondthe boxscore.com/2008/4/5/389840/framing-the-debate;

Matthew Carruth, "Framing the Framing Debate," Lookout Landing, February 1, 2010, http://www.lookoutlanding.com/2010/2/1/1285412/ framing-the-framing-debate;

Bill Letson, "A First Pass at a Catcher Framing Metric," Beyond the Box Score, March 26, 2010, http://www.beyondtheboxscore.com/2010/3/ 26/1360581/a-first-pass-at-a-catcher-framing;

Mike Fast, "The Real Strike Zone," Baseball Prospectus, February 16, 2011, http://www.baseballprospectus.com/article.php?articleid=12965;

Max Marchi, "Evaluating Catchers: Quantifying the Framing Pitchers Skill Parts 1–3," *Hardball Times*, June 10, 2011, http://www.hardball times.com/main/article/evaluating-catchers-quantifying-the-framing -pitches-skill/;

Mike Fast, "Removing the Mask," Baseball Prospectus, September 24, 2011, http://www.baseballprospectus.com/article.php?articleid=15093.

381 *Fielding appears to peak right around age 27:* Jeff Zimmerman, "Determining a Player's True UZR," Beyond the Box Score, March 3, 2009, http:// www.beyondtheboxscore.com/2009/3/3/774477/determining-a-player-s -tru.

Other sources include Tom Tango, "Fielding Aging Curves," *Hardball Times*, February 7, 2008, http://www.hardballtimes.com/main/article/ fielding-aging-curves/, and Jon Shepherd, "Shortstop Aging Curve," Camden Depot, June 18, 2008, http://camdendepot.blogspot.com/2008/ 06/shortstop-aging-curve.html.

381–382 *Tom Tango, . . . used players who switched:* Tom Tango, "Fielding Differences in the Positions, Take 2," *The Book*, September 19, 2008, http:// www.insidethebook.com/ee/index.php/site/article/fielding_differences_in _the_positions_take_2/. Tango's prior looks at the topic are "Fielding Position Adjustments," *The Book*, June 6, 2006, http://www.insidethebook .com/ee/index.php/site/comments/fielding_position_adjustments/ and "Fielding Differences in the Positions," *The Book*, August 6, 2008, http://www.insidethebook.com/ee/index.php/S=7afe1d1006ab53a279d8 cfcfbb41cda87b442187/site/comments/fielding_differences_in_the_ positions/.

382 *Baseball Prospectus, on the other hand:* Colin Wyers, "Solving the Mays Problem," Baseball Prospectus, September 8, 2010, http://www.baseball prospectus.com/article.php?articleid=11934.

382 *Tango's method treats them as roughly the same value:* Colin Wyers, Twitter response to the author, September 9, 2011.

383 *Pat Venditte, best known as the switch-pitcher:* Sean Serritella, "Pat Venditte—Prospect Profile," Yankees Daily, March 16, 2010, http://www.yankeesdaily.com/post/13438.

384 *Is there anything at all to the "inverted W"?:* Dr. Mike Marshall (a former major league pitcher) claims to have discovered the secret to pitching mechanics (see http://www.drmikemarshall.com).

There's not a whole lot of evidence to suggest Marshall has any great insight in particular and a fair amount to suggest he's wrong. Chris O'Leary has assembled a very thorough response to the Inverted W movement: Chris O'Leary, "Death to the Inverted W," March 30, 2011, http://www.chrisoleary.com/projects/Baseball/Pitching/Rethinking Pitching/Essays/DeathToTheInvertedW.html.

384 *Brewers closer John Axford credits his success:* Albert Chen, "The long, Strange Journey of Brewers Closer John Axford," *Sports Illustrated*, August 25, 2011, http://sportsillustrated.cnn.com/2011/writers/albert_chen/08/25/john.axford.brewers/index.html.

384 *Carlos Gomez . . . was probably the first person*: Gomez, writing under the name ChadBradfordWannabe, analyzed pitchers and batters for both Baseball Think Factory (http://www.baseballthinkfactory.org/files/mechanics/archives/) and the *Hardball Times* (http://www.hardballtimes.com/main/authors/cgomez/2007/).

384 *His work has been carried on by Kyle Boddy:* Kyle Boddy, "The Science of Scouting: A Bio-Mechanical Look at Gerritt Cole," *Hardball Times*, August 11, 2011, http://www.hardballtimes.com/main/article/the-science-of-scouting-a-biomechanical-look-at-gerrit-cole/.

384 *J. C. Bradbury attempted to account for the effect:* J. C. Bradbury, "The Mazzone Effect Revisited," Baseball Analysts, March 17, 2005, http://baseballanalysts.com/archives/2005/03/the_mazzone_eff_1.php.

384 *Are the Rangers and Nolan Ryan on the right track:* Gary Thorne, "Nolan Ryan Stresses Conditioning Over Pitch Counts," *USA Today*, April 26, 2009, http://www.usatoday.com/sports/baseball/columnist/thorne/2009-04-26-thorne-column_N.htm.

386 *Based on an estimate of current and future value:* Sky Kalkman, "Saber-Friendly Blogging 101: Trade Value Calculator," Beyond the Box Score, July 15, 2009, http://www.beyondtheboxscore.com/2009/7/15/950094/saber-friendly-blogging-101-trade.

386 *Also appears to ignore the risk premium:* Risk premium represents the added return a risky asset must deliver in order to beat the return of a risk-free asset. In the case of baseball players, there's really no such thing as a risk-free asset, but a veteran who's a known quality might be close. By treating all players by the expected value of their future WARP, you're ignoring that some players are higher risk than others, which can definitely sway a trade one way or the other.

386 *Is Alex Anthopoulos a genius?* In November 2010, Anthopoulos traded for free-agent-to-be Miguel Olivo simply to decline his option and gain the compensatory draft pick based on Olivo's Type B status. Jordan Bastian, "Anthopoulos Gets Creative," Major League Bastian, November 5, 2010, http://mlbastian.mlblogs.com/2010/11/05/anthopoulos-gets-creative/.

387 *The value of which had been enumerated by Victor Wang:* Victor Wang, "Valuing the Draft (Part 1)," *Hardball Times*, January 13, 2009, http://www.hardballtimes.com/main/article/valuing-the-draft-part-one/.

   Wang references a number of studies on draft value including Nate Silver, "Valuing Draft Picks," Baseball Prospectus, August 25, 2005, http://www.baseballprospectus.com/article.php?articleid=4368, and Vince Gennaro, *Diamond Dollars: The Economics of Winning in Baseball* (Hanover, MA: Maple Street Press, 2007).

387 *How a team's success influences the bottom line*: Gennaro, *Diamond Dollars*.

389 *The quintessential expression of strategic analysis:* Andy Dolphin, Mitchel Lichtman, Tom Tango, "Chapter 9: To Sacrifice or Not," *The Book: Playing the Percentages in Baseball* (Dulles, VA: Potomac Books, 2007).

390 *As Ian Lefkowitz explained:* Ian Lefkowitz, email message to the author, July 2011.

390 *He investigated how pitchers ordered their various pitches:* Josh Kalk, "Pitch Sequencing," *Hardball Times*, February 10, 2009, http://www.hardballtimes.com/main/article/pitch-sequencing/.

About the Authors

Derek Carty joined Baseball Prospectus in 2011 as their fantasy manager after holding the post with the *Hardball Times* since 2007. He's also had his work published by ESPN Insider, SportsIllustrated.com, NBC's Rotoworld, FOX Sports.com, and *USA Today*, and maintains a personal website (DerekCarty .com) to aggregate his work. He's the COO of Fantasy Squared, a market-style game in which users "buy" and "sell" shares of events that transpire in an underlying fantasy league (either private or expert)—which team will win, who got the better end of a trade, etc. In 2009, he became the youngest champion in the history of LABR—the longest-running fantasy baseball expert league in existence—and graduated from the MLB Scouting Bureau's Scout Development Program (a.k.a. Scout School)—the only active fantasy writer to have graduated from the program.

Corey Dawkins is a certified, licensed athletic trainer who analyzes injuries and medical conditions in the Collateral Damage column for Baseball-Prospectus.com. He has worked with athletes of all ages and levels of experience throughout his professional career, including Division I and Division III collegiate sports as well as with internationally renowned orthopedic surgeons and sports medicine physicians. He adopted this career path after learning very early in his high school career that he would not play professional baseball—something about the slider still gives him nightmares. He lives just outside of Boston, Massachusetts, with his wife, Brenna, and their 14-year-old terrier mix dog, Scruffy, who runs the house.

Mike Fast has been a Kansas City Royals fan since 1986 and was introduced to his love of baseball analysis by Bill James through the *Baseball Abstract* series. He is recognized as a leader in pitching analysis using PITCHf/x data. Mike lives in Austin, Texas, with his wife, Lori, and their four children.

Rebecca Glass is a writer and assistant editor for Baseball Prospectus. A 2008 graduate of Syracuse University, she is one of the co-founders of the *You Can't Predict Baseball* blog, and has also worked for ESPN's Stats and Info Group. She lives in the Northeast and in her spare time, when not going to baseball games at all levels, enjoys collecting swords and all manner of medieval and Renaissance history.

Steven Goldman is the editor in chief of Baseball Prospectus. In addition to writing numerous columns for BP's website, including the current BP Broadside, he has contributed to and edited the BP-authored books *Mind Game* and *It Ain't Over 'Til It's Over* and contributed to *Baseball Between the Numbers*. Steven is also the author of the biography *Forging Genius: The Making of Casey Stengel*. He has contributed to the BP annual since 2005 and was editor or co-editor of the 2006 through 2011 editions. In 2011 he began co-hosting "MLB Roundtrip with Baseball Prospectus" on SiriusXM's MLB Network Radio. He is the creator of the long-running *Pinstriped Bible* (Pinstripedbible .com) for the YES Network, cited by *Sports Illustrated* as "an essential online baseball destination," and has appeared on several of the network's television programs. He was a baseball columnist for the *New York Sun* from 2004 to 2008, and his work has appeared in *Yankees Magazine*, the *Village Voice*, *Commentary*, *American Heritage*, and other publications. In his spare time, he publishes original songs at casualobservermusic.net. Steven lives in New Jersey with his wife and two children.

Kevin Goldstein is a national writer on scouting and player development for Baseball Prospectus. He speaks with people throughout the industry on a daily basis, talking, texting, and messaging with everyone from scouts to general managers, to find the next big thing and follow the trends in acquiring talent. When he's not writing, he's talking, be it for SiriusXM radio or one of the most popular sports podcasts, *Up and In*, which he hosts with fellow BP-mate Jason Parks. Kevin lives in DeKalb, Illinois, with his girlfriend, Margaret, minors Xander and Cameron, a pit bull named Otto, and three cats (Pickles, Underpants, and Neko-Chan). Because of this, many things in his house are covered with hair.

Jay Jaffe is the founder of the 11-year-old *Futility Infielder* website (www.futilityinfielder.com), one of the oldest baseball blogs. He's been a part of Baseball Prospectus since 2004, writing the Prospectus Hit and Run column, covering the annual Hall of Fame balloting, and contributing to seven BP annuals as well as *It Ain't Over 'Til It's Over* and *Mind Game*. Elsewhere, he has written regularly for *Fantasy Baseball Index* and the YES Network's *Pinstriped Bible*. He has placed third in the famous Milwaukee Brewers sausage race, dropped an f-bomb in the *Wall Street Journal*, and been voted into the Baseball Writers' Association of America.

Rany Jazayerli was a first-year medical student when he co-founded Baseball Prospectus in 1996. He's now a dermatologist in private practice in the western suburbs of Chicago, where he lives with his wife and three daughters. He writes regularly about the Kansas City Royals at ranyontheroyals.com, and hosts a weekly radio show on the Royals in Kansas City. He also writes regular baseball columns for Grantland.com. He still contributes to Baseball Prospectus when time allows. As you can guess from the rest of this paragraph, that isn't very often.

Christina Kahrl is one of the five founders of Baseball Prospectus. Like many of her colleagues, that led to an unexpected career in sports, sparing her from a life spent studying 19th-century Europe and trying to come up with witty jokes about *Junkers*. She has participated as a contributor or editor of every edition of the annual as well as *Mind Game* and *It Ain't Over 'Til It's Over*. She has contributed columns to *Playboy, Salon, Slate*, the *New York Sun*, Sports Illustrated.com, and ESPN.com, and is also an associate editor of *The ESPN Pro Football Encyclopedia*. She is now a member of BBWAA and an editor at ESPN.com, and lives in Chicago with her partner, dog, cat, fish, and an everlasting sense of curiosity.

Ben Lindbergh is an author and assistant editor of BaseballProspectus.com. He has contributed to three BP annuals and served as assistant editor of *BP 2011* and editor of the two-volume *Best of Baseball Prospectus* collection. He also works as a baseball analyst for Bloomberg Sports and has interned for multiple MLB teams. A recent graduate of Georgetown University, Ben makes his home on the western shore of his native Manhattan, where he fancies himself the first line of defense against New Jersey.

Jason Parks officially joined the Baseball Prospectus roster in 2011, having spent the previous three years covering the Texas Rangers minor league system for *Baseball Time in Arlington*, while also moonlighting as a pro scout in Mexico and the New York-Penn League. In addition to his regular writing duties, you can listen to Jason on the ever popular *Up and In: The Baseball Prospectus Podcast* that he co-hosts with Kevin Goldstein. A native Texan, Jason now calls Brooklyn his home, living in the Bushwick neighborhood with his lovely wife, Arden, their three cats, and his three personalities.

Dan Turkenkopf has devoted way too much of the past decade to studying baseball. When he doesn't have his head in a spreadsheet, he works as a sales engineer and product manager for a software startup in upstate New York. A lifetime Yankee fan, he's working on indoctrinating his children into the cult of baseball, to the amusement of his wife. Prior to working for Baseball Prospectus, Dan wrote for Beyond the Box Score and the *Hardball Times*.

Colin Wyers is the director of statistical operations for Baseball Prospectus, which means he does a fair amount of math and logical thinking. He also writes the Manufactured Runs column, which also entails a fair amount of math and logical thinking. When doing neither of these things he can frequently be found rooting for the Cubs, which requires him to ignore most of the math and logical thinking from the previous two items.

Acknowledgments

Derek Carty: Russell Carleton; Bryan Donovan.

Rebecca Glass: Dan Dilworth; Alison Glass, Irv Glass, Dan Glass; Andrew Kent, Audrey Kent, Eli Kent, Maya Kent; Doug Kern; Mackenzie Kraemer; Marc Normandin; Brent Nycz; Becca Priest; Mark Simon, Jordan Smedresman.

Steven Goldman: Andrew Baharlias; Steph Bee; Alex Belth; Cliff Corcoran; Clark Goble; Reuven and Eliane Goldman; Stefanie, Sarah, and Clemens Goldman; Jonah Keri; Dr. Richard Mohring; Marc Normandin; Daniel Rathman; Sam Tydings.

Jay Jaffe: Emma Span; Alex Belth; Nick Stone; Issa Clubb; Bryan Jaffe; special thanks to Alan M. Nathan.

Dan Turkenkopf: Thanks to my amazing wife, Elizabeth, and our two wonderful children, Ryan and Juliet; Ian Lefkowitz; Mike Fast; Rob McQuown; Ben Murphy; Tom Tango.

Colin Wyers: Jim and Astrid Wyers; Tessa Wyers; Samantha Trei.

Index